Beyond Science

Supernatural Solutions for Stress, Fear, Anxiety and Depression

Dr. Rodica Malos

Printed in the United States of America

First Printing, 2016

ISBN-13: 978-1534881204
ISBN-10: 1534881204

CreateSpace: A Division of Amazon

Endorsements

In *Beyond Science* Dr. Malos offers medical recommendations, as well as supernatural prescriptions that will never expire, to prevent or cure illnesses of physical or emotional nature or both. The book is not only informative, but also an inspiration to those who suffer, those who provide health care, and to educators. You will find it a valuable resource.

—Ligia Berci, MD

Child, Adolescent and Adult Psychiatry
Sacramento, California

As Rodica's daughter, I have seen her journey first hand and I can say with confidence that she practices the principles outlined in *Beyond Science* with excellence. Her passion to promote health through integrating mind, body, and spirit is apparent throughout the entire book. *Beyond Science* highlights non-pharmacologic solutions to prevent disease, and focuses on the Lord's supernatural prescriptions to overcome stress, anxiety, and fear. Rodica's words are practical and profound, supported by in-depth research. *Beyond Science* will strengthen your faith and inspire you to step into the freedom for which God destined you.

—Andreea (Malos) Steward, Doctor of Pharmacy

Portland, Oregon

Dr Rodica Malos miraculously merged the spiritual and scientific world in her book *Beyond Science*. After reading the book you are confident within the depth of your being that GOD is a reality of our world and ourselves, and that our faith in God has a scientific foundation which cannot be questioned or doubted any further.

She brings to the surface how much our spiritual heath can influence our physical health, and how nurturing our soul and mind is as important as nurturing our body.

Navigating through the message of *Beyond Science*, my faith in our eternal creator grew stronger, and my desire to live and give myself for others was deeper.

I value the effort Dr. Malos invested in her work. She is a spiritual giant and a scientist with great capacity to connect the two worlds.

—Emilia Arden, D.O., FACC
Cardiologist, GRH Cardiology Clinic, Oregon

Dr. Rodica Malos treats with realism, warmth and emotions a topical subject that generates concern. The 21st century is one of unprecedented technological advancement, providing solutions, comfort and support in all areas of life with the purpose of improving it. Even so, depression and other psychological problems, cardiac and cardiovascular diseases—along with cancer—bear on more and more people. The circumstances we live in, the events taking place around us, and the relationships we are involved in, influence our health, and the reasons behind the growth of such diseases are explained with scientific arguments in this book. We are also presented with ways in which these diseases, generally initiated by wrong choices and an unhealthy way of living, can be prevented.

This is a book worth reading by teenagers and older people alike. Man was created with body, soul and spirit, and should be treated as such. Medicine tries to treat the physical and psychological consequences of wrong choices that take place in our "heart". Dr Rodica is trying to make us aware of the real roots of the problems and to help us take action accordingly. *Beyond Science* is an honest, reasoned pleading for abundant Life.

God created us in an amazing way. Many scientists, in spite of sophisticated technological means, are slowly discovering the way we are created and the functional mechanism of the human body. They now acknowledge that the world was created by God and not by chance.

"The head controls the body. Everything the body does begins first in the structures of the brain…"

Albert Einstein: "The more I study science, the more I believe in God." Sir Derek Barton, awarded the Nobel prize in chemistry: "The observations and the scientific discoveries are so wonderful that the truth that they discover can certainly be accepted as another manifestation of God. God reveals Himself to us through the fact that He allows people to discover the truth."

God is Truth. There is no contradiction between true Science and true Religion. Both of them are in the quest of exploring the same truth. Man has departed from his Creator, who gave him clear instructions for living a fulfilled life both physically and spiritually. In *Beyond Science* we find an accurate description of modern man, quoted from the Bible: lover of self, lover of money, selfish, ungrateful, proud, lover of pleasure, living a lifestyle that brings stress, anxiety, fear and worry. The solution is "renewing of the mind", a return to God,and trusting completely in Him by knowing His character and His promises. "You keep him in perfect peace whose mind is stayed on you, because he trusts in you." (Isa. 26:3 ESV)

—Dr. Stefan Puscasu, MD, General Surgeon

Founder of Bethesda Hospital and Polyclinic
Suceava, Romania

Dr. Rodica's book *Beyond Science* brings spiritual food to a starving world. Her book highlights the keys to health as given to us in God's timeless Word. Science is finally catching up with God's plan for humankind, planted deep within our DNA. May this book open our eyes to see, and to know, the truth as we live out our destiny in these end times.

—Kay E. Metsger R.N., BSN

Former Nurse Manager, Cardiovascular Operating Room
Providence St. Vincent Hospital, Portland, Oregon
Star of Hope International Board Director

Dr. Malos gives an abundance of scientific research that confirms the timeless teachings of the Bible. She shows, through the latest medical discoveries, the clear link between stress, anxiety, negative thinking, and the most common diseases in our society. She also describes clearly the biblical solutions that can prevent and reverse these diseases and lead to optimal health. This brilliant and practical book has the power to transform lives. I highly recommend [it] to health care professionals, pastors, counselors, and any other person who wants to learn how to live the abundant, healthy life that God desires for all of us.

—Oliver Ghitea, MD
Anesthesiologist, Portland Oregon

In *Beyond Science* Dr. Rodica Malos reveals a remarkable correlation between medical science and biblical principles for our mental and physical health. We are created in the image of God, our Heavenly Father and we have all the potential of His DNA within us. "…I am fearfully and wonderfully made…" (Ps. 139:14).

My wife and I have had the distinct privilege of knowing Dr. Rodica for more than twenty years, working with us in our local church, as well as in missions. Dr. Rodica is a caring, compassionate soul—a visionary person of creativity and impeccable integrity. She has demonstrated extreme generosity with her personal time, resources and vast medical knowledge and expertise. This is evidenced in her personal, family, and church life and her private medical practice as a physician, as well as the ministry of adult senior care facilities, which she and her husband Stelica have operated for over 20 years.

Dr. Rodica's life has been marked by a spirit of excellence and enthusiasm. She is consumed with a passion to enrich and improve the life of everyone she comes in contact with. Hence, *Beyond Science* is a must read for invaluable information as well as personal inspiration and transformation.

—Pastors Ed & Cheryl Rebman
New Beginnings Church
Portland Satellite Campus

Dr. Rodica has been a member of our Church and a personal friend for many years. I have seen firsthand how she and her husband immigrated to the U.S. from Romania, not speaking English and having no formal education, skills or finances. They came here with nothing but hope, prayer and opportunities to build a new life for their family. Determined to make the most of their lives and future, they became avid students of the teachings, principles and promises in the Bible. They passionately pursued educations in medical, scientific, business and leadership principals and skills. Through years of hard work, perseverance, and a love for God, His Word and His people, they pressed through the limitations of their world and pressed into the unlimited promises of God's Word.

I vividly remember the church service when, like a lightning bolt, they realized that they were not meant to live their lives as victims of their past, current or future circumstances—but that their lives could change because, "With God, all things are possible!"

They chose to believe and act upon the understanding that, with God's help, there were no limits to their lives and futures. We have watched over the years as incredible results, influence and blessings have unfolded and evolved in them, for them and through them.

As Pastors for nearly 40 years, we have had the privilege and the challenge of teaching, counseling and praying for thousands of people from every nationality, background and walk of life. The greatest results we've seen for genuine long term positive change have come from combining the spiritual with the physical. In the spiritual realm, growth, understanding and obedience bring genuine hope and help from the Lord. In the physical realm the power of our thoughts, words and actions have the power to directly affect and alter our lives, circumstances and futures.

In this groundbreaking new book Dr. Rodica brings these truths to the next level. She has diligently researched for years to discover and link together the realms of the spiritual, physical and scientific. She teaches that the brain, human will, and the ability to choose are incredibly powerful forces. We can break free and overcome negative detrimental problems and patterns that have held us captive, perhaps for generations. She lays out a clear, easy to understand path to follow to step out of your past and step into your great future.

Dr. Rodica's teachings reveal that medical and scientific truths do not nullify God's biblical spiritual truths. They, in fact, prove God's biblical spiritual truths. Science doesn't disprove God's existence. It proves God's existence. Physical and spiritual realms do not contradict one another. They confirm and complete one another.

This breakthrough teaching is powerful, and so necessary for people today. She has woven together spiritual, scientific and medical facts that are cutting edge, powerful and life changing.

Through many years I've seen their passion and devotion evolve from creating a successful, blessed life for themselves to helping create the same for others.

At the heart of this groundbreaking book, is a deep, God inspired passion to:

- See people's lives change for the better.
- Rise above the circumstances of their lives.
- Experience the fullness of God's blessings and promises.
- Become and achieve all that God has destined for them.

The teachings in this book are groundbreaking, bold, brilliant, powerful, and will change your lives, circumstances and futures forever.

We are blessed to be a blessing! And Dr. Rodica is a living example of that.

—Pastors Larry and Tiz Huch

Senior Pastors, Founders and Directors
DFW New Beginnings Church, Dallas/Fort Worth
New Beginnings Stream Church, Portland, Oregon and Global Stream Ministries
Larry Huch Ministries Global TV and Media Outreach Network

A fascinating book in which Dr. Rodica masterfully uses the Word of God to explain the science and physiology of our brains. Dr. Rodica weaves together the Bible and biology in a way that brings validity to the Creator and lays out His step-by-step plan for our healing and wholeness.

—Pastor Brad and Lisa Makowski, Lead Pastors

Anthem Church, Portland, Oregon

Beyond Science is a revolutionary, life changing book, an essential training manual for the believer, and a must read for those who wish to walk in victory. Great practical and spiritual applications abound in this book. The extensive research this book brings will impact lives around the world.

I felt gripped throughout as the extraordinary scientific knowledge wrapped alongside the scriptures came together to highlight the genius of our Creator and the plan He has for us all. It is a book that you can read over and over again—an encyclopaedic revelation of the supernatural and a road map for the natural.

—Shaneen Clarke

Founder, Shaneen Clarke Ministries
Patron, Rhema Partnership
Founder, AWC Charity
Speaker, Author, Coach

x

Contents

Endorsements... *iii*
Foreword .... *xiii*
Preface.. *xv*
Acknowledgments.. *xix*
Introduction .... *xxi*

PART I

THE SCIENCE OF STRESS AND DISEASE

CHAPTER ONE
A World Full of Stressors 3
CHAPTER TWO
Brain Science and Stress... 13
CHAPTER THREE
Your DNA: Body, Mind and Soul............................... 29

PART II

ROOT CAUSES OF STRESS

CHAPTER FOUR
A World of Problems 37
CHAPTER FIVE
Pain 63

PART III

GOD'S SUPERNATURAL PRESCRIPTIONS

CHAPTER SIX
Creating Chemical Balance in Your Brain 87
CHAPTER SEVEN
Everything Starts in the Brain 101
CHAPTER EIGHT
Unexpired, Divine Prescriptions 109
CHAPTER NINE
Forgiveness Brings Joy 123
CHAPTER TEN
Identity 141
CHAPTER ELEVEN
Faith.. 145

CHAPTER TWELVE
Dreams.. 153

CHAPTER THIRTEEN
Supernatural Healing... 165

CHAPTER FOURTEEN
Enlarge My Territory... 171

CHAPTER FIFTEEN
Strategic Choices for a Healthy Lifestyle 173

CHAPTER SIXTEEN
Awakening Your Heart and Mind 177

CHAPTER SEVENTEEN
God's Word Reprograms Your Brain........................ 179

CHAPTER EIGHTEEN
Favors 189

CHAPTER NINETEEN
Keep a Biblical Attitude... 193

CHAPTER TWENTY
Thoughts.. 205

CHAPTER TWENTY-ONE
The Will of God 211

CHAPTER TWENTY-TWO
Gender Differences 217

CHAPTER TWENTY-THREE
Meditation and Anti-aging 227

CHAPTER TWENTY-FOUR
Helping Others.. 231

CHAPTER TWENTY-FIVE
Prayer Reduces Stress.. 245

CHAPTER TWENTY-SIX
Giving Thanks... 253

CHAPTER TWENTY-SEVEN
Lifestyle Change.. 261

CHAPTER TWENTY-EIGHT
Prayer and Fasting 273

CHAPTER TWENTY-NINE
Reassurance and Redirection 289

CHAPTER THIRTY
Relationships... 291

CHAPTER THIRTY-ONE
Our Hope Is in Heaven.. 295

Conclusion.. 315
Endnotes.. 317

Foreword

by Dr. Irene Stanciu

Rodica has been my best friend and sister-in-Christ for more than 30 years. What stands out to me much more than this is her wisdom, gentleness of spirit, tenacity, perseverance, and hard work. These have been incredibly inspirational examples for me throughout all our years shared together. Her deep love for the Lord and unwavering hope in the midst of numerous difficult circumstances has always been, for me, like a lighthouse in the middle of a raging ocean, proving that trusting the Lord in spite of our doubts, coupled with hard work and perseverance, will get you through no matter what the circumstances are.

"Beyond Science: Supernatural Solutions for Stress, Fear, Anxiety and Depression", is an excellent resource for any person that wants to live a healthy lifestyle and avoid disease. It is not only a fountain of up-to-date, well-researched scientific principles but also a river of life, bringing spiritual renewal of the mind.

From my personal experience of battling breast cancer at a young age, I remember being alarmed and surprised at the diagnosis. I had done, I thought, everything I could to protect myself in advance—I was a doctor after all. My family and I, like Rodica's, immigrated from Romania years ago in search of a better life free from communism and religious oppression. But even America's "freedom" can't solve the root issues that fester in the heart. Even with a better life, a good job, and many blessings, my soul was still dry and worn out from stress that is inescapable anywhere you may be physically located. What I did not realize until after my cancer diagnosis was that my thoughts poisoned my well being, my anger burned inside me, and the joy of the Lord that is available for all Christians was missing from my life. God used cancer to wake me up and reveal to me what I was missing. I then understood how only He could change me and heal me. I learned the principles to not only control and manage stress, but also take each thought captive, changing it from poisoning my soul and body, and using it to drive me to the Lord and strengthen my dependence and trust in Him. Naturally, this produced healing in the physical body as well. I was amazed at how interwoven the spiritual and physical realities are, but the Lord has created them both. All of this awakened me to the life-giving facts that Rodica is writing about in this book.

Rodica's book is very easy to read and understand, with or without a medical background. It brings new insights from the most recent scientific discoveries in regards to how stress affects our bodies and gives us "medication without side effects" from the Word of God, the Creator of our entire being, our Great Physician and Healer, Jehovah Rapha. With her extensive medical knowledge obtained during years of studying in the medical field culminating with her PhD thesis, coupled with her experience as a primary care doctor, filled with the Spirit of God, she reveals the life-giving principles applicable to us all. As an endocrinologist myself, I admire her wisdom and skill in putting together such a masterpiece, useful for every patient in my practice. It uncovers and explains many "hormonal imbalances" that a pill would not be able to completely resolve. Her book is a complementary treatment for anyone with any kind of medical diagnosis, and is also the much sought after "anti-stress pill" for anyone who wants to maintain or improve a healthy lifestyle.

I wholeheartedly recommend Rodica's book to all who want to live a long, healthy life, a life filled with inspirational purpose and meaning! Thank you Rodica for being a great example and a blessing for me and my family!

—**Dr. Irinel Stanciu** MD, FACE, ECNU, CCD,
Endocrinologist
Boise, Idaho

Preface

The purpose of this book is to demonstrate the powerful correlation between God's scriptural advice and promises (divine prescriptions) and modern scientific brain research related to stress management. My goal is to help you learn how to overcome the storms of life by adopting a healthier lifestyle, both physically and spiritually.

High levels of stress, fear, anxiety and depression can trigger catastrophic health problems, including mental, emotional and physical. The best tools for overcoming the stresses we all face involve a combination of spiritual awareness and faith—beyond science—and a healthier lifestyle.

Building a resiliency to high levels of stress, fear, anxiety and depression, and regulating your emotions is possible through meditation on the promises written in the Word of God. Meditation actually builds new, stronger neurons in your brain. This in turn will help prevent generational curses through the epigenetic mechanism—unaltered gene expression and protein synthesis. *Beyond Science* will show you how adopting positive lifestyle changes will give you efficient methods for stress management.

When you meditate on God's promises (bringing joy, peace, happiness and hope to calm your overactive brain), you create new neurons through neurogenesis. New dendrites will grow and rebuilt your hippocampus and anterior cingulate and repair your brain, which has been damaged by high levels of stress. Our brain is created by God to regulate itself and to be rewired for quick responses to high levels of stress and dangerous situations. It can actually change its structure based on its neuro-plasticity. Your brain structure can shrink or can grow, based on the quality of your thoughts and attitude.

The brain is programmed by our Super Intelligent Designer to release the right amount of necessary neurotransmitters and neurochemicals affecting our unconscious and conscious mind that influence our body to function normally. However, due to our human nature we are constantly disturbing the balance in our brain through unhealthy thoughts and unhealthy actions. Emotions from high levels of stress (perceived as threats) activate the Sympathetic Nervous System (SNS) to release norepinephrine at a high speed in response to stressors, causing rapid heart rate, increase in blood pressure, sweats, trembling and other frightening signs and symptoms. The SNS also activates the adrenal gland (medulla and cortex) to release large amounts of adrenalin and cortisol, creating more damage to the body, mind and spirit.

At normal stress levels cortisol is released for our benefit to increase glucose for energy, to increase the cardiac output, to decrease brain inflammation and to regulate our emotions through the Hypothalamic Pituitary Adrenal axis-pathway. Our uncontrolled emotion and unhealthy thoughts, however, increase stress levels, causing unhealthy amounts of neurochemicals, including cortisol. These will become toxic for the brain and will kill neurons in the hippocampus area (involved in memory consolidation). Excessive amounts of cortisol will compromise the immune system and circulatory system by damaging the arteries, increasing abdominal fat, increasing the risk for high glucose, diabetes, hypertension, metabolic syndrome, osteoporosis and others. High levels of stress cause decreased serotonin levels making people feel tired, decreasing their attention, and increasing the risk for heart attack, depression, and sleep disturbance, etc. Lack of sleep causes depression with all the consequences. Anxiety and depression will decrease the size of the brain. Fearful thoughts will enter through your cortex, but you can change those impulses based on the quality of your thoughts.

Throughout the Bible we find God's supernatural prescriptions and instructions, which will keep our thoughts healthy, thus implicitly regulating all the chemicals and neurotransmitters, releasing them in healthy amounts. Healthy thoughts through meditation and mindful thinking trigger electrical impulses to fire and to release neurotransmitters making dendrites to grow in minutes to connect and communicate strengthening neuronal connections. That is a miracle growth of the brain size through dendrites proliferation called neuro-plasticity. Mindful thinking and meditation help you pay attention to your thoughts and enable the release of acetylcholine— important in preventing Alzheimer's. The frontal lobe helps you change your thinking.

For good health, it is imperative that we grow healthy neurons by meditating on God's promises, memorizing and quoting Bible verses to consolidate memories in our unconscious mind and growing strong neurons. Healthy thoughts in our conscious mind are controlled by memories and unconscious activities. Our words and actions reflect the activity in our unconscious mind. Put the Word of God inside your heart and mind and invite the Holy Spirit to help you in any situation. It is the living Word of God, with supernatural power to transform your thinking process, enabling you to cope with the high levels of stress in your life.

Through joy, peace, happiness and an active healthy lifestyle (diet and exercise) our brain has the capacity to release neuro-protective proteins and to grow new neurons. Exercise is a big factor in decreasing anxiety and depression. So keep moving, exercise regularly, be active to stimulate the brain to release the brain-derived neurotrophic factor that is so important for a healthy body, soul and spirit. Scientists recommend managing stress through intellectual stimulation, enjoying God's creation, physical exercise, recreation, keeping active at work, helping others, and fasting and praying. Be grateful every day and count your blessings.

Stress management (through healthy habits, meditation, fasting, healthy diet and exercise) is truly an anti-aging therapy, preventing age-related memory loss. Medically speaking, stress management through exercise, meditation and healthy thinking are considered anti-aging treatments. Conversely, thoughts of fear lead to increased anxiety, shrinkage in the brain, impaired thinking, and neurocognitive disorders, and inhibit decision making, thus severely affecting one's quality of life.

With a mind renewed (one of the powerful supernatural prescriptions in the Word of God) through meditation on God's promises—prayer, fasting, compassion, gratitude, worshiping and rejoicing in the Lord—we embrace this supernatural solution—beyond science—to manage stress from fear, worry, anxiety and depression.

—Dr. Rodica Malos, DNP

Disclaimer

PLEASE NOTE: All information written in this book is for informational purposes only. It is not medical advice for any specific individual, neither is it applicable for specific medical problems of any individual. NO information presented in this book is written or intended to substitute for any medical professional intervention for diagnosing, treating, or for medical advice, and should not be construed as instruction or medical consultation for a specific person.

You should take no action solely on the basis of this book contents as treatment, diagnosis for your own health condition. Readers must talk to a health professional about any problem regarding their own physical or mental condition. The information found in this book is believed to be accurate based on the author's best judgment. Readers who fail to seek treatment from appropriate health professionals assume risk of any potential ill effects and expenses. Please note that this advice is not specific to any individual. It is generic, and before undertaking any medical or nutritional course of action you must consult with your doctor. Take your medications as prescribed by your medical providers, schedule follow up appointments, keep your appointments, and seek and follow medical advice for all your conditions.

—Rodica Malos, DNP

Acknowledgments

This book received support from the Creator of the Universe who gave the world supernatural prescriptions in His Living Word to overcome fear, and to manage high levels of stress, anxiety and depression every day.

The author thanks Jesus Christ, the LORD and Savior of the world, the Lamb of God, Who was slain before the foundation of the world, and Who delivers those who believe in Him from the stress of sin and from all their fears. Only He gives the joy of salvation, hope and peace that passes all understanding and guards their mind, spirit and body during stressful situations.

The author also acknowledges the Holy Spirit, the Great Comforter, Who literally transforms and renews our mind and guides every step, giving to those who ask Him inspiration, wisdom, knowledge, revelation, and discernment to cope with high levels of stress, fear, anxiety and depression.

The author gives millions of thanks to her beloved husband Stely and her precious daughter Andreea for their sacrifices, support, encouragement, and love. You both are a great team, overcoming fear and effectively managing stressful situations to reach your full potential and fulfill your destiny. Millions of thanks to my entire family, all friends, colleagues and all my patients who were in the author's sphere of influence, who provided support and inspiration throughout her entire life in Romania, in the USA, and everywhere on this planet.

Many thanks to all the writers and scientists cited in this book and all the teachers of truth in churches (the "spiritual clinics"). You sacrifice your time to make the information available, to inspire the author and the entire community. We benefit from your spiritual and scientific evidence. You change our thinking and motivate us to a better lifestyle, to live a quality life here on earth and for eternity.

Special thanks to Kay Metsger "Sora" who was by author's side (as the proofreader) during the author's education at OHSU, and special thanks to the editor of this book Laura Davis and her husband Jim, for helping the author to finish and publish this book.

Finally, many thanks to you who take the time to read the information in this book. It will strengthen your spirit, renew your mind and thoughts, improve your physical and spiritual health, and prevent physical and spiritual diseases resulting from high levels of stress, fear, anxiety and depression.

Introduction

S tress is an inescapable fact of life. According to Dr. Joseph Goldberg, MD, 75–90% of doctor visits are related to stress.[1] OSHA (the Occupational Safety and Health Administration) has also declared that stress is a hazard of the workplace. "Stress costs American industry more than $300 billion annually."[2] All over the world people are suffering from complications of high levels of stress from fear and worry, which cause anxiety and depression. Therefore it is imperative to assess and evaluate the root cause of this pervasive problem. Engrossed in our busy professional lives, we can easily become distracted and even dehumanized, ignoring the emotional and spiritual needs of our patients, friends, neighbors and co-residents on this planet. Despite all our advanced technology, our lives remain vulnerable to constant tragedies and high levels of stress. For this reason more and more health care providers are now discussing how to incorporate spiritual care into their medical practice. Let us not allow society to abandon spirituality, which is our best enduring hope for health.

American astronomer Carl Sagan said, "We live in a society exquisitely dependent on science and technology, in which hardly anyone knows anything about science and technology."[3] Because of this, in our postmodern era we cannot afford to ignore our spirituality. With more and more people living in fear, buried in worry, anxiety and depression, acute and chronic diseases continue to destroy people's overall wellbeing.

Scientists, experts and specialists in health care systems realize that medicine cannot rely only on randomized trials. We make everyday decisions based on our emotions and feelings, as reactions to everyday circumstances. Common sense is necessary when practicing medicine, and spiritual needs must be addressed. We are born with an innate need to seek the truth, to call upon God and His eternal presence in our life. The book of Ecclesiastes explains, "He has also set eternity in their heart" (Eccles. 3:11).

Despite health care professionals' constant efforts to educate, entice, advise, convince, indoctrinate, and persuade patients with smooth talk, bribes, guilt, and manipulation, to make people understand and follow medical advice, the results are often minimal. People continue to suffer from various diseases and chronic conditions. Many still die prematurely from high levels of stress caused by fear, worry, anxiety and depression.

Even with so much knowledge, the gaps in the way people manage stressors in their daily life need to be addressed. I hope this book will fill some gaps that we often ignore in our busy health professions, and in daily life. The insights you will discover in *Beyond Science* will transform your way of thinking, and give you the tools to change your life and even your eternity. You, in turn, will change the world around you. When people are transformed they can better cope with stress, and then help transform others. The world can be transformed, one person at a time.

If you experience high levels of stress, and are looking for ways beyond science to manage your fear, worry and anxiety, then keep reading. The following chapters will help you understand the scientific component of stressors and their harmful effects on our spirit, mind and body. Chronic worry produces high levels of stress, affecting our thoughts, our emotions, and our soul. Our environment is flooded with destructive events and behaviors that trigger unhealthy thoughts, yet we have the power inside us to change our perceptions about life and start thinking healthier thoughts. To protect both the soul and the body from consequences of unmanaged stress, our spirit needs a spiritual prescription. Our spirit and soul need spiritual treatments for spiritual maladies, just as our body needs treatment or therapy for a physical disease (see James 2:26). Despite scholars' many excellent ideas on how to manage stress, people continue to feel stressed out. It is a silent, worldwide pandemic.

Health care professionals who recognize peoples' need to overcome fear allow their patients to talk about their spiritual needs. According to Dr. Helming, nurses can help heal patients by allowing them to voice their fears, their mystical experiences, and their struggles with their own spirituality. Many people struggle to verbalize their fears, for fear of ridicule or because no one prompts them to explore these issues.[4] Fears of all kinds must be allowed expression if stress is to be dealt with.

Although stress causes real symptoms, the patient may have no conscious awareness of the connection. Physiological signs and symptoms, and panic attacks from fear and stress, lead to endless ER visits and multiple hospitalizations. Verbal clues of stress can include:

- "I'm too stressed"
- "I'm worn out"
- "I've hit the wall"

- "I can't take it anymore"
- "I can't cope"
- "I'm at the end of my rope"
- " I can't breathe"
- "My world is ending"
- "Life is not worth living"
- "My world is falling apart," and so on.

High levels of stress also lead to unhealthy decisions, behaviors and practices, with their subsequent degenerative diseases. The list of diseases caused by high levels of stress is long, including heart disease, lung disease, gastrointestinal disease, infections, degenerative and autoimmune diseases, cancer, musculoskeletal diseases, and even neurological deficits, psychological distress, or mental disorders. Researchers have demonstrated that reducing stress levels and bad behaviors can save many lives and trillions of dollars in health care costs. Rising health care costs create economic insecurity, more stress, and more diseases, threatening disaster on every level. It is a vicious cycle. We need to learn how to renew our mind with healthy thinking, resulting in healthy behaviors.

After my own experiences with stress, and observing other stressed-out people, I asked myself the question: Who will change the world? Who will fix these problems? In this book you will find God's supernatural prescriptions to prevent the physical and spiritual diseases caused by worry, fear, anxiety and depression. Scientists have suggested that "…chronic stress, in particular, may lead to structural changes in the brain that will persist even after the stressor ends. So for stress, as with many other health issues, an ounce of prevention may be worth a pound of cure—managing and reducing chronic stress may be an effective approach for preventing stress-induced changes in brain structure that may be very difficult to treat after they have emerged."[5]

PART I

THE SCIENCE of STRESS and DISEASE

CHAPTER ONE

A World Full of Stressors

"...you will hear of wars and rumors of wars...
nation will rise against nation, and kingdom against
kingdom. There will be famines and earthquakes in various
places. All of these are the beginning of birth pains."
(Matt. 24:6–9)

Stress is often defined as physiological and psychological responses to perceived threats. Today's world is rife with threats from chaos, instability, insecurity, violence, news of war, natural disasters, famine, economic crisis, terrorists, occupiers, and political confusion. Sexual immorality, incurable diseases, and unhealthy behaviors are increasing, and societies are in great turmoil. Billy Graham, world renowned evangelist who preached the Gospel in every continent, stated in his book *The Journey* that we live in a world of uncertainty. "The daily headlines don't give us much hope. War, famine, terrorism, racial and ethnic conflict, economic disruption, violence—the list is almost endless. Neither do our everyday experiences give us much hope: family and marital breakdown, sickness, addiction, accidents—again the list is almost endless. Uncertainty and insecurity seem to be the watchwords of our generation."[1]

Such events trigger fear, worry, anxiety and depression, increasing stress and bitterness in people's lives. Those feelings are like a cancer for the soul—a malignancy that spreads from the soul, to the body, and to entire families, friends, communities and nations. Listening to the news every day raises our stress levels. Uncertainty grows globally with economic and political instability. Violence threatens, bringing increasing corruption and immorality. Famous and wealthy people are dying from depression, committing suicide, and overdosing with prescription or illicit drugs. When fears of insecurity, anxiety, depression and worry grip your heart, your brain is flooded with unhealthy levels of neurotransmitters and neurochemicals, causing more damage to the body, mind and spirit.

Fear is a huge factor in increased stress levels. Fear paralyzes people, leading to panic attacks, anger, violence, hate, and murder. All these evils spread darkness and panic, propagating terror, worry, anxiety, panic attacks and depression. Nations are shaken from natural disasters and calamities, producing yet more pain and suffering. These are the culprits behind the majority of physical and spiritual diseases.

Despite all our efforts to manage stress from worry and anxiety at the individual and global level, high levels of stress continue to kill millions. My friend Shaneen Clarke from London, England, founder of A Woman's Call and an international speaker at conferences and churches, stated in her book *Dare To Be Great: Forget Your Past! Live Your Dream*:

> . . . in the words of author Lee Warren, "It should come as no surprise to anyone, especially medical science with all its technological innovations, that if our mind and souls are brimming with negative principles, our health, in general, will deteriorate and disease will be rampant in the world today. The streets, alleys, Skid Row, and mental institutions throughout the earth are crowded with those slain by the Goliath of hopelessness. Man-made philosophies, dogmas and religions stultified with ceremonies, rituals, and traditions have been unable to and have languished in dealing with this problem. They have failed to instill in the minds of the masses, knowledge of the principle of faith in the Creator within them."[2]

In my Masters and Doctorate studies at Oregon Health Sciences University in Portland, Oregon, I most enjoyed the courses on health promotion and disease prevention, particularly those on what science says about stress. I became a health care provider, and now I apply this scientific evidence in my practice, teaching others how to prevent and manage high levels of stress. Observing many people struggling with severe stress and its terrible consequences, I concluded there must be more answers than what we learned in school, and more than what science teaches us through the best evidence-based practice.

We share information and knowledge to impact the more vulnerable people in the world through education programs, international leadership conferences, mobile libraries, online discussion forums, and the media, but we must do more. Our view of the world is constantly evolving, especially when we see turmoil in developing countries or the clash of civilizations. I hear at international conferences that the "hope" of westernization is a mindset project for the entire world, but real hope and transformation come only through a renewed mind through healthy thinking.

The Effects of Stress, Fear and Worry

"I sought the LORD, and He answered me; He delivered me from all my fears. Those who look to Him are radiant; their faces are never covered with shame." (Ps. 34:4)

Did you ever experience uncomfortable feelings for no apparent reason? People experiencing high levels of stress from fear and worries—resulting in anxiety and depression—may manifest physical, cognitive and behavioral symptoms due to an abnormal level of neurochemicals, hormones, and neurotransmitters released in the body. As a biological response to stressors, people at some point in their life will experience one or more of these signs and symptoms: unexplained pain in the back and jaw, muscle tension, tension headache, aggressive body language, trembling of lips and hands, dizziness, lightheadedness, dry mouth, faintness, difficult swallowing, heartburn, enlarged pupils, nausea, stomach cramps, restlessness, trouble concentrating, increased perspiration, difficulty breathing, chest pain, heart condition, cold hands, sweaty extremities, constipation, frequent urination, night sweats, flatulence, diarrhea, fatigue, decreased appetite, decreased sexual desire, pounding heart, shortness of breath, insomnia, weight change and others.

Mental symptoms of great stress may include: anxiety, frustration, anger, trouble learning, depression, confusion, disorganized thoughts, discontentment, feeling overwhelmed, loneliness, negativity, defensiveness, low productivity, poor concentration, suspiciousness, spacing out, suicidal thoughts, etc. Other inappropriate behaviors may include nervous habits, rushing around, inattention to grooming, increased tardiness, increased alcohol and tobacco use, overspending, gambling, being accident-prone, overreacting, fast or mumbled speech, gritting of teeth, lying, making excuses, frustration, self-pity, social withdrawal, mood swings, strained communication, crying spells, excessive worrying, nervous laughter, discouragement, stuttering, procrastination, bad temper, nail biting, and others.[3]

High Stress Affects All Our Systems

"Can any one of you by worrying add a single hour to your life?" (Matt. 6:27)

Let's look at a few examples of how high levels of stress can affect the human body's systems.

Cardiovascular and Circulatory System: Increased stress on our cardiovascular system (due to increased epinephrine and norepinephrine) will increase blood pressure and heart rate, causing palpitations, shortness of breath, water retention, fatigue, weakness, dizziness, and chest discomfort (felt as pain, numbness, tightness, pressure, or fainting). People experiencing some of those symptoms may experience a panic attack and rush to the emergency room.

Respiratory System: High levels of stress cause vasoconstriction and poor perfusion with oxygen, increased respiratory rate, shortness of breath, and inflammation of the lung tissues, aggravating asthma, the common cold, and flu. Dyspnea will further decrease the amount of oxygenated blood in the lungs. All cells will have poor oxygenation, damaging cells throughout the body.

Neurological System: The neurological system under high levels of stress brings on tension headaches, forgetfulness, inability to concentrate, fatigue, sleep disturbances, anxiety, tremors, weakness, depression, syncope, and dizziness. The serotonin-melatonin balance in the brain is disturbed, affecting the quality of sleep. The serotonin level is affected when an overly stressed person ingests carbohydrates in higher amounts, leading to weight gain and obesity. Increased carbohydrate intake due to high levels of stress causes more sleep deprivation. Sleep deprivation and low levels of melatonin increase the risk for breast cancer in women, and prostate cancer in men, up to 50%. I will address this later.

Endocrine System: Stress causes increased levels of cortisol (the "stress hormone"). Cortisol kills neurons and damages regions in the hippocampus, reducing the secretion of acetylcholine, a neurotransmitter that helps us think. The hippocampus is involved in filing information in the brain, but when neurons are destroyed—causing forgetfulness—personality changes can lead to a neurocognitive syndrome. If stress is not managed appropriately, cognition impairment and neurocognitive disorders such as Alzheimer's and other types of dementia may result.[4]

Diabetes may develop if cortisol levels are increased for long periods of time due to prolonged high levels of stress. Bone mass may decrease, leading to osteoporosis. Thyroid function is affected, causing unpleasant symptoms of abnormal thermoregulation. Your thyroid gland regulates the metabolism and temperature in your body. This gland receives messages from the hypothalamus, your "body thermostat", and the pituitary gland, which releases the thyroid hormones T3 and T4 (regulating the heart rate, production of protein, calcium used in the bones by calcitonin, etc).

The thyroid gland senses insufficient or excessive amounts of these two hormones and lowers or raises the amount of thyroid-secreting hormone that keeps T3 and T4 balanced. High levels of stress will disrupt the normal functions of the thyroid gland.[5]

Integumentary System Under Stress: The integumentary system, when affected by stress, increases itching or irritation of the skin and the risk of developing eczema, psoriasis, lupus and other autoimmune disorders, due to decreased effectiveness of the immune system.

Musculoskeletal System: The musculoskeletal system is affected by stress through the inflammation process, which causes degenerative diseases and flare-ups of arthritis, lupus, and fibromyalgia with all its complications.

Gastrointestinal System: Stress on the gastrointestinal system causes nausea, vomiting, constipation, diarrhea, irritable bowel syndrome, bladder and bowel accidents, and an electrolytes imbalance.

Lymphatic System: The lymphatic system plays a central role in our defense against different types of infections, microorganisms, viruses and cancer. It contains lymphatic liquid, a web of lymphatic vessels, specialized cells called lymphocytes, and tissues and organic lymphoid (spleen as an example). The body is vulnerable to interior and exterior attacks such as traumas, disease, stress, aging, cell destruction and gene mutations, which develop into cancer.

Immune System: Although extremely vulnerable, the human body has an extraordinary power to protect itself with the immune system. The immune system has its own mind and the capacity to discern between what belongs to our body, versus foreign microorganisms and viruses. It attacks any strange particles or molecules to eliminate them. The fascinating part is how the whole defense process stops at the right time, to prevent it from self-destructing.

High levels of stress will cause high levels of cortisol, suppressing the immune system, and rendering your body more susceptible to infection and cancer. The immune system secretes natural chemicals to kill foreign microbes, forms lymphocytic nodules, promotes lymph circulation in the blood, and filters cancer cells, bacteria and other foreign elements. Cancer cells will alert the key cells from the immune system. New lymphocytes and macrophage can be mobilized in just a few minutes to fight these enemies. It is a miracle. In fact the entire body, mind and spirit are incomprehensible— an amazing, miraculous creation with visible and invisible functions. We are truly God's masterpiece.[6]

High levels of stress, causing an increased production of cortisol, will suppress our entire self-defense mechanism. Stress is the body's enemy—killing, stealing and destroying—working against our divinely designed immune system. The body's whole defense mechanism is damaged by high levels of stress from worry, fear, and anxiety.

Stress Is Environmental and Dangerous

"But mark this: There will be terrible times in the last days. People will be lovers of themselves, lovers of money, boastful, proud, abusive, disobedient to their parents, ungrateful, unholy, without love, unforgiving, slanderous, without self-control, brutal, not lovers of the good, treacherous, rash, conceited, lovers of pleasure rather than lovers of God—having a form of godliness but denying its power. Have nothing to do with such people." (2 Tim. 3:1–5)

People living in the environment described in 2 Timothy 3:1–5 will develop high levels of stress. This is extremely dangerous for the human body and may cause many diseases. As mentioned before, most visits to a medical office are due to symptoms caused by high levels of stress.

The whole body is affected by stress physically and spiritually, prompting people to seek medical attention and often requiring many unnecessary tests and procedures. Those will increase the costs for care and bring on more stress if people do not have health insurance, or if they lack finances to pay all the medical bills. Prolonged symptoms lead to acute diagnosis which, if not treated with the right interventions, will become chronic diseases. More complications and comorbidities may lead to early physical and mental disabilities, putting a burden on oneself, one's family, the community, and society.

All of these signs and symptoms can be minimized or avoided if we learn more about what triggers them. We can change our perception about life's problems and learn how to manage stress in our life by following God's supernatural prescriptions. We will benefit by simply taking to heart all the instructions and directions in the Word of God, plus the results of scientific knowledge that God has allowed us to develop in this postmodern era. More on this later.

The Brain—Gateway for Stress

"Banish emotional stress from your mind and put away pain from your body; for youth and the prime of life are fleeting." (Eccles. 11:10 NET)

There is a strong interdependence between the brain structure, the thinking process, and how thoughts are translated into actions in stressful situations. Advanced technology in the last 50 to 60 years has allowed scientists to discover more insights about the microscopic universe of our neurons. More and more we read the results of scientific research about mindfulness, and how the brain structures function, connect, grow, heal, restore, renew and learn.

Your brain is the gate that allows external and internal stressors to stimulate its structures, affecting the whole body. Billions of neurons can release different neurotransmitters in unhealthy toxic amounts to flow into the body as a biological response, causing physiological and psychological manifestations through unpleasant signs and symptoms. Sooner or later we all experience high stress levels (rooted in fear, uncertainty, disappointment, insecurity, unmet expectations), causing emotional distress and pain from multiple chronic conditions. The book of Ecclesiastes contains a strong prescription—beyond science—to prevent the pain in our body that emotional distress causes: "Banish emotional stress from your mind and put away pain from your body; for youth and the prime of life are fleeting" (Eccles. 11:10 NET). He is able to heal us physically and emotionally of any kind of disease.

Worry, Anxiety and Depression Hurt

"Why, my soul, are you downcast? Why so disturbed within me? Put
your hope in God, for I will yet praise Him,
my Savior and my God." (Ps. 42:5)

High levels of stress, anxiety, worry, fear, doubt and unbelief will cause depression. Depression causes physical pain, due to dysfunction of the serotonergic and noradrenergic neurons and pathways. Stephen Stahl and Mike Briley wrote:

> A dysfunction of the serotonergic and noradrenergic pathways is commonly accepted as playing a major role in the etiology of depression. Serotonergic cell bodies, located in the raphe nucleus, send projections to various parts of the brain where they are involved in the control of mood, movement, and emotions (such as anxiety) and regulate behaviors (such as eating, sexual activity and the feeling of pleasure). Similarly, the noradrenergic neurons located in the locus ceruleus project to the same regions where they regulate attention and cognition. A further projection to the cerebellum regulates motor control. A dysfunction at the level of the monoamine neurons thus results in the classical symptoms of depression.

In addition to these ascending pathways, however, the neurons in the raphe nucleus and the locus ceruleus also project to the spinal cord. These descending pathways serve to inhibit input from the intestines, the skeletal muscles and other sensory inputs. Under normal conditions, these inhibitory effects are modest, but in times of stress, in the interests of the survival of the individual, they can completely inhibit the input from painful stimuli. A dysfunction at the level of the serotonergic and noradrenergic neurons can thus affect both the ascending and descending pathways resulting in the psychological and somatic symptoms of depression but also in physical painful symptoms.[7]

To prevent dysfunction of the noradrenergic and serotonergic neurons and their pathways (the etiology of depression), we must follow God's powerful prescriptions given thousands of years ago. He admonishes us: do not worry, do not be anxious about anything, do not be afraid, but have faith in the King of Universe and in His promises. He is taking care of our needs so we can avoid depression and physical pain. Throughout the Bible we find spiritual prescriptions full of supernatural potency, which can protect our mind from the disastrous pain of physical, emotional and spiritual diseases caused by fear and worry. We just need to "banish emotional stress from our mind," as prescribed in the book of Ecclesiastes.

Fearful, worried and anxious thinking causes the brain to release unhealthy levels of neurochemicals from the hypothalamus, which receives messages from the thalamus (the center that processes information and directs it to different brain structures), and from the limbic system (associated with emotions and memories). When we perceive a threat, unhealthy amounts of neurotransmitters are released. Those unhealthy levels of neurochemicals will trigger diseases, as discussed above.

The brain was created with its own natural pharmacy. It produces natural chemicals that can heal and restore when the right amounts of neurochemicals are released. Or it can kill and destroy the body when these are released in unhealthy amounts. Our amazing brain has the ability to produce natural endogenous substances: antidepressants, natural antibiotics, natural tranquilizers for pain management and to heal itself.[8] For this to work, we need to have the right reactions to circumstances and wise actions to create the right atmosphere in our brain, even when stress is overwhelming.

So many people do not know where to turn for answers and security in tough times. Some will seek refuge in synthetic prescriptions, illicit drugs, alcohol, tobacco, and destructive behaviors. But all those are just Band-Aids for deep emotional infections, which later will result in spiritual septicemia and imminent physical and spiritual death.

CHAPTER TWO

Brain Science and Stress

"Then God said, 'Let Us make man in Our image, according to Our likeness; and let them rule over the fish of the sea and over the birds of the sky and over the cattle and over all the earth, and over every creeping thing that creeps on the earth.' God created man in His own image, in the image of God He created him; male and female He created them."
(Gen. 1:26–27)

God's first supernatural prescription was for human beings to be created in His image. Not just to "look like" God, but even to share a fraction of God's creative abilities, enabling man and woman to create visible things from invisible thoughts. Everything that was created in the beginning was God's invisible thought, and the visible world was created from invisible things at His command. Human beings were created in His image, thus we also are creative and can participate in the divine nature (2 Peter 1:4).

He gave mankind the gift of creativity through the power of thoughts. We are not only God's image bearer. We also carry God's breath in our lungs, and the seed of multiplication in every man and woman. The Holy Spirit is still hovering over the surface of this planet, waiting to get into the inner being of His creation—a population of over seven billion people who are predestined to be conformed to the image of His Son (Rom. 8:29). Through the "seed" planted in our brain we inherit the ability to transform our perceptions of things (thoughts). We have within, the power to create. So often we credit man for inventions and advanced technology, but we forget God's investment in the human brain. He is sharing invisible thoughts, through the power of His Spirit, every moment in every human being. It is written that everything exists not by might, or by power, but by His Spirit (Zach. 4:6).

God gives revelation, inspiration, discernment, determination, passion, perseverance and endurance to fulfill His plan for this planet. Thoughts are invisible until we put them into action. God continues to create through our thoughts in our brains. He drops ideas, inspiration, and revelation into our spirit and brain structures. Invisible thoughts create things that exist around us. "For by Him were all things created that are in Heaven, and that are in earth, visible and invisible, whether they be thrones, or dominions, or principalities, or powers: all things were created by Him, and for Him" (Col. 1:16 KJV).

Not surprisingly, everything that happens to you begins in your brain. Through your brain (thoughts), stress gets into your body. It is critical that we learn about physiology and psychology in order to understand the science of stress. We will consider the brain's structure and the body's systems, scratching only the surface of its anatomy, to see how high levels of stress affect the entire body, mind and spirit—and thus our future. It is well documented in scientific literature that chronic stress leads to excessive damage to the entire body (which is composed of about 60–100 trillion cells with complex interconnections throughout all the systems).

Our Brain: the Control Center

Trillions of highly specialized cells of different sizes are interconnected for different functions, making up our vital organs and all the systems of the human body. Billions of nerve cells with trillions of synapses compute all the information in our brain. The neurons help the body adjust to stimuli in any environment, and to inside stimuli when we are physically sick or in emotional pain.

Sensory receptors in our eyes, ears, nose, mouth, skin, muscles, and joints perceive impulses from different stimuli inside or outside the body, then adjust or make necessary changes. Neurons communicate among themselves through synapses and dendrites via neurochemicals and neurotransmitters. Messages are received from outside or inside stimuli through electrical impulses entering the neurons through dendrites. They travel through axons and across the synapses' thresholds as action potential.[1] Connections between neurons are performed through thousands of branches called dendrites, and trillions of synapses and axons. Axons facilitate messages from nerve cells to other neurons and can be almost as long as the height of a person. Messages are carried through synapses—bridges as I see them—which are extremely small.

About 100 neurochemicals are manufactured from amino acids by the neurons and glands throughout our body as a result of perceived external and internal stimuli.[2] They travel across synapses and some are synthesized and stored in neurons. Our thoughts, actions, attitudes, and habits will boost or inhibit many of the neurotransmitters. Neurotransmitters are stored at the ends of axons in vesicles, and then are released in the synapses when an electrical impulse (caused by outside or inside stimuli through our five senses) travels to the end of the axon.[3] Those impulses are our perceptions of things, our thoughts, our emotions and our memories, stored in our brain's structures. They are affected by our good or bad actions in the past or present, and by what we see, hear, feel, smell, and taste.

The Limbic System

Our feelings, thoughts and memories take place in our limbic system (situated beneath the cortex). This limbic system consists of the hypothalamus, the amygdalae, the hippocampus, the cingulate gyrus, the mammillary bodies and other brain structures.[4] The autonomic nervous system, with its parasympathetic and sympathetic branches and endocrine system, is influenced by the limbic system structure, which, in communication with other areas in the brain and other complex systems, contributes to learning, emotions, motivation, and memory.[5]

Just a small example: Dopamine is the neurotransmitter involved in motivation. Our motivation can be affected by drugs. For example, marijuana (one drug that is now legalized in many states) kills neurons and depletes the brain of dopamine, leading to anti-motivational syndrome in marijuana users (see neurotransmitters section). On the other hand, stress management (through healthy habits, meditation, fasting, healthy diet and exercise) acts as an anti-aging therapy, preventing shrinkage of the hippocampus and age-related memory loss.

How Stress Begins

The amygdala is associated with emotions, which in turn are attached to thoughts. Emotions from thoughts of fear create memories felt as worry, anxiety, anger, bitterness, irritation, or depression. Each time thoughts of worry and fear bombard our mind, we will feel signs and symptoms of anxiety.[6] The hippocampus is associated more with conscious memories.[7] The structures in the limbic system bring up good and bad memories in our daily activities in many ways. *We are in charge of our limbic system's functions when we decide what kind of emotions and thoughts to process, store and memorize.* Our response to stress from worry and anxiety begins in our mind and continues in our body. Everything the body does begins first in the structures of the brain and those billions of neurons, and trillions of synapses, axons, receptors and pathways.

Anatomy and physiology tell us that the brain has three levels: Neocortical—for rational thought processing; Limbic system—emotional thought processing and memories consolidation; Vegetative—with autonomic responses controlled by two branches (sympathetic and parasympathetic systems).[8]

The autonomic nervous system works automatically at the unconscious and subconscious levels. We are usually not even aware of what we are doing, how we breathe, how our heart is beating, how we fall asleep and wake up in the morning, and how we function during our daily routines. For example, the parasympathetic branch controls our breathing, blood pressure, peristalsis, sleeping, relaxing, and resting, while the sympathetic branch controls our "fight or flight" response to fear when we are in a dangerous situation.[9] The nervous system contains the central nervous system (brain and spinal cord) and the peripheral nervous system (neural pathways to the extremities).

Mysteries of the Subconscious and Unconscious

"A good man brings good things out of good stored up in his heart, and an evil man brings evil things out of the evil stored up in his heart. For the mouth speaks what the heart is full of." (Luke 6:45)

We know by now that inside every human being is an invisible world—our thoughts. Let's look briefly at the brain's subconscious functions. The brain receives information from inside and outside the body and computes it all automatically and subconsciously at such a speed, day and night, that you do not even notice what is going on. Dr. Caroline Leaf, in her book *Switch On Your Brain: The Key to Peak Happiness, Thinking, and Health*, mentioned that 90–99% of the activities in your mind happen at the unconscious level, where thoughts are built. The thinking process at night operates at four billion actions per second, including thought selection, dreams, and memory consolidation.[10]

Your thoughts and memories coordinate all the systems unconsciously, 24 hours a day, seven days a week. For example, the endocrine glands release hormones to regulate body temperature, energy, reproduction and growth. The nervous system regulates the circulatory, musculoskeletal, gastrointestinal and genitourinary systems. Think about your musculoskeletal system with all the bones, joints and muscles groups connected via tendons, cartilages, sockets, synovial fluids, nerves, fibers, receptors and pathways for neurotransmitters. All the sockets in each joint assist in mobility—sitting, standing, walking, turning, bending, extending—and all are coordinated by the brain at the unconscious level.

Think about the skin as an amazing organ representing our integumentary system. Its function is to cover and hold together all systems, tissues, and organs lying within the body. Our skin must prevent disconnection and protect us from exposure and from unseen environmental insults. It is fascinating how all our internal organs function with precision to keep our body alive, even renewing skin cells every three weeks. It is beyond our comprehension. Your body is doing an unimaginable job, continually receiving commands at the subconscious level.

Another small example is how the pancreas reacts within seconds after we have that yummy ice cream. Blood sugar rises in the bloodstream, ready to release the right amount of insulin to transport the sugar to every cell, providing us with energy to function. Your body is doing an incredible job, digesting and absorbing all the micronutrients and minerals in the gastrointestinal tract.

Then apoptosis (another amazing built-in feature in our DNA, with programmed instructions to constantly clean all debris from the body) removes all residuals from our dying cells in order to regenerate our body. Our body continually fights with residuals from cells, which can cause degenerative diseases, infections and cancer. Our entire body is constantly manufacturing natural chemicals in every system to promote homeostasis for a healthy body. Every cell is working hard every single moment, and we need time at night for rest and rejuvenation, another miracle of life.

God's "Glue" Particles Inside Us

The body has such intricate architecture, with orderly interconnections always working at the unconscious level. The anatomy and physiology of the human body is fascinating. Cells are programmed to protect us from invasions of neoplasm and cancer cells. Our cells are held together with laminin, a cell adhesion protein molecule called the "basement membrane" in all structures of the body. This "God's glue" as I call it holds the cells and organs together. Millions of laminin molecules are even in the shape of a cross! One study reported: "Rotary shadowing electron microscopy revealed a structure of human laminin which is essentially similar to the cruciform structure."[11] The Bible tells us that God holds all things together. "For in Him all things were created: things in Heaven and on earth, visible and invisible, whether thrones or powers or rulers or authorities; all things have been created through Him and for Him. He is before all things, and in Him all things hold together" (Col. 1:15–16). All things are held together at the subconscious and unconscious levels through Jesus Christ, who died on the cross. In Him, through Him and by Him we have our being. (Acts 17:28 NIV)

Another amazing function is that all receptors in all systems, including the bladder and intestines, communicate with the brain when to void or when to eliminate waste. This leaves room for new, fresh nutrients to enter the body. Inability to control the bowel and bladder would be a disaster.

Bone mineralization, preventing bone diseases and fractures, is an incredible art. For example, the manufacture of Vitamin D in the skin from sunlight exposure is fascinating. Sunlight passes the threshold of the skin, where it is absorbed, manufacturing Vitamin D and helping the body to absorb calcium. This strengthens the bones and helps them grow, keeping them healthy and preventing broken bones. If it was not in God's plan for the body to manufacture Vitamin D naturally from sunlight, everyone would be in a wheelchair or bedbound from bone fractures. Vitamin D also naturally boosts testosterone levels in men, assisting with reproduction, the immune system, and cognition (helping to regulate outbursts of anger). Thus, men need to spend time in the sun, about 15 minutes a day, for natural testosterone production.[12]

Symmetry in the human body is incredible. In medicine, symmetry is the key to assessing and diagnosing patients who seek medical attention. In fact, the existence of the entire universe depends on symmetry. Mathematicians and physicists often discuss the necessity of symmetry. Clearly there is a divine, Super Intelligent Being who designed our body, as well as the entire Universe. Evolution could not produce such mysteries.

Surviving Stressful Situations

"Have I not commanded you? Be strong and courageous. Do not be frightened, and do not be dismayed, for the Lord your God is with you wherever you go." (Josh. 1:9)

"Do not be afraid of those who kill the body but cannot kill the soul. Rather, be afraid of the One who can destroy both soul and body in hell." (Matt. 10:28)

Did you ever ask yourself how you've survived so many stressful events? Your brain and your body in general are doing amazing work, without you realizing it, at the subconscious and unconscious levels. The nervous, endocrine and immune systems are involved in responding to high levels of stress. The job of the autonomic nervous system with its sympathetic and parasympathetic branches is to regulate the homeostatic balance in the body for daily normal functions, during normal levels of stress as necessary. The autonomic nervous system is responsible for the vital organs and visceral activities' regulation, circulation, respiration, digestion and temperature regulation.[13]

The parasympathetic nervous system will respond to stimuli by releasing acetylcholine to help the thinking process and slow the heart rate. It also assists with digestion to eliminate residual substances from the body, preventing constipation and assisting with bladder function to eliminate unnecessary fluids, maintaining homeostasis in the body. It conserves energy and promotes relaxation.[14]

All these functions can be affected by our decisions to respond to God's prescriptions—or not. When our stress level is high, the sympathetic nervous system will respond to internal or external stimuli by releasing the catecholamine as epinephrine and norepinephrine in large amounts, as a "fight or flight" response. God built into our human body those features for self-preservation to protect us from a dangerous environment, but if they are supra-solicited with no godly thoughts and unhealthy behavior, those features can be destroyed. That is why it is so important to know that too much or too little of these neurotransmitters or neurochemicals released during stressful situations will compromise our entire wellbeing. I will explain this more in the next chapters.

The endocrine system plays an important role. It is composed of glands, circulation, and organs, and regulated by hormones released by the hormonal glands. This regulates the metabolic functions. The pituitary gland, the master gland of the endocrine system, and the thyroid and adrenal glands, are most involved in responding to the stressors mentioned earlier.

The nervous system and endocrine system are connected, forming the metabolic axis. These are the ACTH (adrenal-cortico-thropin-hormones) vasopressin and thyroxin axis.[15] The way we respond to stress from fear, worry and anxiety in our daily life will influence the functions of the nervous and endocrine systems. We will see in the following chapters how our behavior and attitude can affect the release of neurochemicals either healing and restoring our body, or leading to fatal diseases.

How Stressors Enter the Brain

Let's look at how stressors from the outside world get into our brain. Information from the outside world (your environment) enters your brain as electrical impulses originating from your five senses. These influence your thought-forming, decision-making capacity, emotions and actions. All electrical impulses get through the thalamus, a structure in the brain that connects all other structures of the brain and activates other thoughts that already exist in the neurons in the cerebral cortex. Those thoughts that already exist in the cerebral cortex are brought into our consciousness when triggered by the electrical impulses from our five senses.[16]

Dr. Caroline Leaf, a Communication Pathologist, Audiologist and Cognitive Neuroscientist, and a biblical and scientific expert of the mind, stated in her book *Who Switched Off My Brain?* that "this wonderfully complex transmission through the cerebral cortex or the 'breeze through the trees' alerts and activates attitude. Attitude is a state of mind (all the thoughts on the tree) that influences our choices and what we say and do as a result of our choice."[17]

The Five Senses: Information Gateway

Your five senses are the entryway for outside information. Electrical impulses trigger the thinking process by crossing the threshold from electrical impulses to thoughts in "the forest" of the neurons (in the cerebral cortex) with a "tree-like" configuration with dendrites as branches of those "trees". Thoughts activate other thoughts that already exist with emotions, and memories in other brain structures, and are sent to the hypothalamus (the fabric of natural chemicals), which is sending messages to the pituitary gland, the hormones' master gland. This in turn sends messages further to other glands to release excessive amounts of chemicals such as cortisol, epinephrine, aldosterone, norepinephrine, and decreased amount of serotonin, dopamine, acetylcholine and melatonin, and other neurochemicals according to the level of stress perceived.[18] The physical response to the stressors begins, and the whole body will experience the uncomfortable signs and symptoms presented in the beginning of this chapter. When the neurotransmitters or neurochemicals and hormones are released in the Central Nervous System (CNS) and the endocrine system as a cascade from all the glands in abnormal amounts—in response to unhealthy stressors from fears and worry—the human body experiences the signs, symptoms and diseases mentioned earlier in this book.

The Stress Response

The stress response consists of increased neural excitability, and increased cardiovascular activity (increased heart rate, stroke volume, cardiac output and high blood pressure).[19] Metabolic activity is increased through glycogenesis, turning glycogen into higher amounts of sugar for energy, mobilizing proteins, decreasing antibody production and increasing muscle waste. Fats are mobilized to breakdown into sugar, further elevating sugar to an unhealthy level. Salt is retained, irritating the nerves, and producing and increasing neurological sweating, confusion, and salivation. Gastro-intestinal system mobility and tonus are changed, resulting in dry mouth, nausea, vomiting, diarrhea or constipation, and frequent urination.[20] All those symptoms frighten the person experiencing them, causing yet more stress. The cycle will repeat, damaging the body more and leading to panic attacks, emergency room visits, and unnecessary hospitalization and higher costs. These raise the level of stress more, both for individuals, and for society as a whole.

Our only hope in stressful circumstances resides in the promises written in the Word of God, as supernatural prescriptions—beyond science. These can cause constructive thoughts to be born, with healthy restoration and manifestation then taking place. Such will be presented later in more detail.

According to brain research in the last two decades, using MRIs, PET and other procedures, scientists can measure when conscious thoughts increase the aging process of the brain by repeated exposure to high levels of cortisol, "the stress hormone". This damages and shrinks brain tissues irreversibly in the hippocampus area responsible for memory consolidation, and increases the size of the amygdala (through the inflammatory process), causing paranoid thoughts and impaired cognition.[21]

Neurotransmitters and Your Thoughts

"As a man thinks in his heart, so is he." (Prov. 23:7 KJV)

Scientists have shown interest in researching and investigating how chronic stress and the resulting stress hormones, neurotransmitters and neurochemicals induce DNA damage, thus impairing the immune response and often leading to cancer. They have found that the excess amounts of neurotransmitters released in stressful situations will impact cancer progression in the body through a process of transformation at the cellular level. Frank J. Jenkins stated in a study:

> …psychological stress, acting through increased levels of catecholamine and/or cortisol, can increase DNA damage and/or reduce repair mechanisms, resulting in increased risk of DNA mutations leading to carcinogenesis. A better understanding of molecular pathways by which psychological stress can increase the risk of cancer initiation would open new avenues of translational research, bringing together psychologists, neuroscientists, and molecular biologists, potentially resulting in the development of novel approaches for cancer risk reduction at the population level.[22]

How Nerves Send Messages

Neurotransmitters play a huge role in our daily functions. Throughout the day and night your brain's structures (thalamus, hippocampus, amygdala, hypothalamus, etc.) are communicating with all the other structures at the subconscious and unconscious levels. They store memories, thoughts and emotions that determine the amount and kind of natural chemicals the brain needs to manufacture, and send messages to different parts of the body to act accordingly. All the cells in our organs are interconnected and are affected by our thoughts, memories and emotions. This dictates the amounts of neurochemicals circulating in our body. About 100 billion cells in our brain (neurons) help us think, learn, remember and reason, and we behave accordingly. Neurons help the body adjust to stimuli, in any environment.[23] Our eyes, ears, mouth, nose, skin, muscles, and joints have sensory receptors and perceive the impulses from stimuli in our environment. This creates changes at the conscious and unconscious levels every moment, thus preserving our life so we can exist and function.

Recently when I got home one mid-afternoon, I parked my 2014 Lexus in the garage. But before I got the car in the right position the sensor started sending audible and visual signals that the car was too close to the wall on the right. I completely ignored all the signals and moved the car a little closer to the right, and I damaged the right side of the car. The wired equipment in my car had tried insistently to communicate the dangerous position and situation that I put my car in, trying to protect both me and the car from damage.

In a similar way, neurons are communicating messages among themselves through electrical impulses and neurochemicals to alert us and to keep us safe from threatening environments every single moment. Connections between neurons are performed through thousands of branches of dendrites, synapses and axons. Dendrites facilitate message transmission to the nerve cells, and axons allow messages to travel away from nerve cells to other neurons. The messages are carried through trillions of synapses—one millionth of an inch between the dendrites of one neuron and the axon of the next. It is known that the brain has one quadrillion connections (1 million billion) and a 100,000 mile transport system, including blood vessels and capillaries, according to the new statistics.[24]

It is also known that about 100 different neurochemicals made by your body travel across synapses. Neurons synthesize and store neurotransmitters based on our thoughts and actions, which boost or inhibit and influence the amount of these chemicals so necessary for our normal daily routine.

Neurotransmitters are stored at the end of axons in vesicles, and when an impulse or electrical current from our thoughts travels, the neurotransmitters are released from the vesicles in the synapses and travel to the end of the axon.[25] Each thought you allow in your brain will cause impulses that will cause neurochemicals to be released, in the amount according to the quality and kind of thoughts.

The autonomic nervous system and endocrine system are both influenced by the limbic system and the activities taking place in your life, which in communication with other areas in the brain and other complex systems contribute to learning, memory, motivation and emotions, every moment of your life. Your behavior and your thoughts will dictate your ability to learn, to memorize, and to control your emotions and motivation. For example, using marijuana kills millions of neurons, potentially causing a long-term, severe anti-motivational syndrome. People lose interest in studying, learning, or working. Other disturbing consequences are impaired cognition, memory loss, poor coordination, impaired driving skills (increasing fatalities), acute psychosis, panic attacks, paranoia, schizophrenia, lethargy, ataxia, dizziness, respiratory insufficiency, diarrhea, sedation, toxicity, and tachycardia. "Getting high" with synthetic cannabinoids in diverse products such as chocolate, candy or soft drinks, can also result in seizures and renal failure. Marijuana opens the door for more dangerous drugs, such as heroin, with all its consequences.[26]

On the other hand, it has been demonstrated that healthy habits prevent shrinkage of the hippocampus and prevent memory loss related to aging. Medically speaking, stress management through exercise, meditation and healthy thinking are considered anti-aging treatments. Conversely, thoughts of fear lead to increased anxiety, cause shrinkage in the brain, lead to impaired thinking and neurocognitive disorders, and inhibit decision making, thus severely affecting one's quality of life.

High Stress and Your Neurotransmitters

"Be careful what you think, because your thoughts run your life." (Prov. 4:23 KCV)

Your behavior and your life in general are shaped by your values and beliefs because they affect your thinking process. That dictates the kind and amount of neurotransmitters released in your body. Let's look at the best-known neurochemicals and their roles and actions in the body in our busy and stressful daily life. From those 100-plus neurochemicals, I will mention just a few. Acetylcholine, norepinephrine, dopamine, GABA, glutamate, serotonin, endorphin, and oxytocin are chemicals produced by neurons and glands, such as the pituitary, thyroid, adrenal and other glands. They facilitate the transmission of signals between neurons through synapses.[27] All these neurochemicals are released automatically, either excessively or deficiently, based on the quality of your thoughts and behaviors, subconsciously dictating your signs and symptoms from stress due to fear and worry. Sometimes these can be frightening.

Acetylcholine is the neurotransmitter that stimulates the muscles in the body, assists with the thinking process in neurons, and, in the autonomic nervous system, it assists in REM sleep. When acetylcholine is reduced, cognition is impaired; when reduced to 90% due to plaque formation it leads to Alzheimer's disease.[28] Epinephrine and norepinephrine are also involved in memory formation. During high levels of stress, abnormal levels of these neurochemicals will be released, depleting the storage of this neurotransmitter and affecting our cognition negatively.[29] Drugs like amphetamines also will deplete the body's norepinephrine, dopamine and serotonin.[30]

The neurotransmitter dopamine is a chemical with inhibitory action. It has an important role in the brain's reward mechanism. The brain is genetically programmed to search for food, drink, sex, sleep, comfort, and pleasure through thoughts and emotions (automatically generated inside of us) and activates the reward pathway (nucleus accumbens). Anticipation of rewards from eating, drinking, sleeping, sex, comfort and other pleasures activates neurons that release the dopamine neurotransmitter.[31] Overstressed, anxious and depressed people overstimulate the dopamine neurons with drugs, tobacco, alcohol, opioids, marijuana and other stimuli, causing excessive dopamine secretion and uncontrollable impulses.[32] People lose self-control, leading to pathological changes seeking "comfort food" like carbohydrates, causing excessive weight gain.

The dopamine amount will increase to an abnormal level and will cause very serious addiction if stimulated with wrong behaviors and abuse of heroin, nicotine, opium, cocaine, alcohol, gambling, unhealthy sex, etc. This causes lifelong physical and mental disability. When dopamine is very high, schizophrenia will develop with frightening hallucinations and delusions. Scientists have developed medications to help with these devastating mental conditions.

The GABA (gamma amino butyric acid) neurotransmitter has an inhibitory action and tells the body when to stop doing bad things and when to calm your brain down, if one is extremely anxious and angry from excessive worrying. When GABA is released in low amounts people will become more anxious, and at times epilepsy develops if people are lacking the GABA neurotransmitter. Glutamate is an excitatory neurotransmitter and it is involved in the memory process. In excess amounts it is toxic and kills neurons.

The neurotransmitter serotonin and its receptors exist throughout the body, with many functions. People with low levels of serotonin will become depressed, angry, obsessive and compulsive, and can be suicidal. They also will crave carbohydrates, and can develop a compulsive eating disorder, gaining weight, developing metabolic syndrome and increased blood pressure, even diabetes and increased cholesterol levels. Those diseases, left untreated, will lead further to heart disease, stroke, disability and premature death. Abnormal levels of serotonin will also cause migraines, sleep disorders, mood disorders and other emotional syndromes. Serotonin is affected also by illicit drugs that block transmission of serotonin in the right pathway, causing hallucinations, delusions and impaired cognition.[33]

Endorphin, the endogenous morphine, is naturally manufactured by the human brain. It possesses the same functions as synthetic morphine, helping to reduce pain and make people feel well. It slows the heart rate and respiration as needed, when stress from unhealthy thoughts increases. But when people abuse those synthetic drugs such as heroin and opioids that mimic endorphin, the natural endogenous morphine suppresses the respiratory center and lowers the heart rate to an abnormal level, until the heart stops.[34] That is why people die from drug overdoses.

The brain is programmed by our Super Intelligent Designer to release the right amount of those necessary neurotransmitters to be able to function normally. However, the human race is constantly disturbing the balance in the brain through unhealthy thoughts and disobedient actions. Throughout the Bible we find God's prescriptions and instructions, which will keep our thoughts healthy, thus implicitly regulating all the chemicals and neurotransmitters, releasing them in healthy amounts, if we follow the Divine prescriptions for a healthy physical and spiritual life.

We also have natural built-in nicotine and marijuana receptors, with calming effects on our brain and with beneficial effects when triggered by our right response to high levels of stress. When people use synthetic, manufactured nicotine and marijuana they become dependent on those counterfeit stimulants and their body and mind will be slowly destroyed.

The Role of Serotonin

We have many receptors throughout our body with different functions, built in by our Creator to help our body function in a proper, healthy way. These receptors attract neurochemicals or neurotransmitters that either inhibit or stimulate the natural neurochemical release, breaking down molecules to get in and out of cells through different pathways and processes.[35] Neurons make the necessary amount of neurotransmitters when receiving the messages and electrical impulses through our five senses and thought processes. We are indeed fearfully and wonderfully made, with all these complex chemicals and their functions to keep us alive and functioning normally. For example, when our serotonin level is low we experience depression or irritation. When our serotonin is too high it can cause anxiety. In this situation GABA needs to increase to inhibit brain activity in order to decrease anxiety. But if the GABA level is too high, and blocking too many serotonin receptors, it will increase our appetite, then increase our risk for metabolic syndrome with all its dangers.

As we know, drug companies develop drugs to increase or decrease the serotonin level. But they have many side effects and are very expensive. Scientists have discovered serotonin receptors in the brain, the gastrointestinal system, and in the blood.[36] Drugs affect not only the brain but many functions of the body. Everything that influences changes in the brain will influence changes in the entire body. For example, increased serotonin through drug ingestion may increase diarrhea and nausea. That is why people with high levels of stress and worry develop anxiety, panic attacks, and irritable bowel syndrome (spasms in the intestine). We have many supernatural prescriptions written by divine inspiration in the Word of God for natural serotonin to be released in the body to prevent those unwanted signs and symptoms. God also gave people inspiration to develop synthetic chemicals needed to treat many man-made mental conditions. As a Primary Care Provider I am not against medications. I prescribe them to treat my patients' acute and chronic conditions as necessary. But most of the time they don't experience full relief of the signs and symptoms, and they also report side effects.

We can prescribe many antidepressants and anti-anxiety medications to keep people happy, but we have a more potent Divine prescription, with no side effects. God gave all of us instructions 2,000 years ago: rejoice, and socialize with the right people who will encourage us. God wants us to know who we are created to be, to have confidence, to have hope, to feel good about ourselves and our divinely given identity. He tells us to believe the promises in the Word of God—that we are the sons and daughters of the King of the Universe, a special people with a Heavenly citizenship, and we do not need to live under high levels of stress from fears and worries. Those promises make you feel good about yourself and increase your self-esteem, even when you go through tough situations. Your serotonin level will naturally increase to a healthy level and will influence your habits, making you feel fulfilled (even helping you to make the right choices, such as to eat less and lose weight, influencing the satiety and appetite center in the hypothalamus, etc).

Serotonin helps you sleep and rest better by boosting melatonin, so you can function normally, as you were created to function. Sleeping normal hours will help your entire body rejuvenate, recover and be restored, by boosting your defense mechanism and immune system to fight diseases caused by high levels of stress. The Word of God gives us instructions to live at peace, to stay still in any situation, and to know that our Creator is our Father and He is God (see Ps. 46:10).

CHAPTER THREE

Your DNA: Body, Mind and Soul

"You have searched me, LORD...For you created my inmost being; you knit me together in my mother's womb. I praise you because I am fearfully and wonderfully made; Your works are wonderful, You know that fully well. My frame was not hidden from You when I was made in the secret place, when I was woven together in the depths of the earth. Your eyes saw my unformed body; all my days ordained for me were written in your book before one of them came to be. How precious to me are your thoughts, God. How vast is the sum of them!" (Ps. 139:1–17)

Science clearly shows that high levels of stress affect the DNA in every cell. The body contains thousands of incredibly complex systems. Highly specialized in their unique functions and interconnected and programmed to help the whole body grow, they produce energy for motion and reproduction. They also repair, restore, regenerate, refresh and respond to daily stress.[1] All those commands are embedded within the DNA. Deep within the cells' extreme complexity, stress affects every function. I like what Dr. Jeffrey Grant explains in his book *Creation: Remarkable Evidence of God's Design*. He describes the cell as functioning like a "modern city" possessing defense systems, chemical factories, energy-producing facilities, a heating system, transportation system, post office and communication system, administration office, information warehouse, library, and a waste disposal system.[2]

Trillions of "Modern Cities" Inside You

Let's take a look inside the cell to discover how its functional complexity can be affected by high levels of stress when your fearful, worried thoughts are uncontrollable. You do not need to memorize the cell description that follows. Here is a very short description of the complexity of a microscopic human cell, according to Martini in *The Fundamentals of Anatomy and Physiology.*

A molecular biologist probably will be able to aptly describe the function of the cells in our body. They have a complex structure of cell membrane, cytosol, non-membranous organelles with microtubules and microfilaments, microvilli, cilia, centrosome, with centriole, ribosomes, membranous organelles with mitochondria, endoplasmic reticulum with rough ER and smooth ER, golgi apparatus, lysosomes, peroxisomes and nucleus with nuclear pore, nuclear envelopes and nucleolus with complex compositions. The cell membrane is composed of a lipid bi-layer composed of phospholipids, steroids and proteins used for isolation, sensitivity, protection, support, and controlling the entrance and exit of materials into and out of the cell. The cytosol is composed of a fluid component of cytoplasm, which distributes material by diffusion. Cytoskeletons are composed of proteins organized in fine filaments used for strength and support and movement of cellular structure and material. Microvilli are a membrane extension containing microfilaments that help to increase surface area to facilitate absorption of extracellular materials. Centrosomes are the cytoplasm that contains two centrioles, each containing 9 microtubules triplets essential for movement of chromosomes during cell division and organization of microtubules in the cytoskeleton. Ribosomes containing RNA+ protein containing fixed ribosomes bound to endoplasmic reticulum and free ribosomes scattered in cytoplasm for protein synthesis. Mitochondria composed by double membrane, with inner membrane folds enclosing important metabolic enzymes which produces 95% of the ATP required by the cell. The endoplastic reticulum contains a network of membranous channels extending throughout the cytoplasm necessary for synthesis of secretory products, intracellular storage and transport. Rough endoplasmic reticulum has ribosomes bound to membrane used for modification and packaging of newly synthesized proteins. Smooth endoplasmic reticulum with attached ribosomes used for lipids and carbohydrate synthesis. Golgi apparatus contains saccules with cisternae for storage, alteration and packaging of secretory products and lysosomal enzymes. Lysosomes that are vesicles contain powerful digestive enzymes used for intracellular removal of damaged organelles or of pathogens. Peroxisomes are vesicles containing degradative enzymes used for neutralization of toxic compounds. Nuclei are nucleoplasm containing nucleotides, enzymes, nucleoproteins and chromatin, surrounded by a double membrane, a nuclear envelope to control metabolism, to store and process genetic information and to control protein synthesis. The nucleolus is a part of the nucleus structure that is a region dense in nucleoplasm, containing DNA and RNA as site of rRNA synthesis and assembly of ribosomal subunits.[3]

High levels of stress, thoughts of fear, anxiety and worry of all kinds are an outside insult, more like "a tsunami" affecting every cell in this "modern city" in your body, bringing devastating, irreversible damages. It is extremely important to follow God's prescriptions—presented later in this book—to obtain His promises in our life so that we can reduce our anxiety and stress levels.

Stress "Tsunamis" Affect Your DNA

"My soul is overwhelmed with sorrow to the
point of death." (Mark 14:34)

Our DNA tells our cells (where the DNA resides) what they need to produce in order to maintain life. The genetic code, our life's blueprint, is packed into the DNA. I believe this is God's language built into our human chromosomes, designing and developing every organ in our extremely complex body. Dr. Geffrey Grant wrote the following in his book *Creation: Remarkable Evidence of God's Design.*

> . . . to record the genetic instructions encoded in human DNA we would need more than five billion letters that would require up to three thousand volumes to print out. This enormous amount of information would fill a library shelf over one hundred yards long. Yet it is intricately encoded in a tiny double helix curled up in a microscopic cell. This degree of micro engineering is so far beyond the ability of humans that it fills the mind with wonder at the work of the Creator.[4]

If your stress level is very high and lasts for a long period of time, it can even modify your marvelous DNA through gene mutation, leading to abnormal, uncontrollable cell division. We call it cancer. DNA, the genetic blueprint, has encoded instructions for growing, reproducing, repairing, restoring and building life.[5] You were created in such an orderly, disciplined way that your DNA enables your organism to produce energy, to regenerate, repair, restore, heal, reorganize, and reproduce, expressing protein according to the quality of your thoughts and behaviors. All these functions of every cell, with help from the DNA, are affected by the high levels of stress, worry and anxiety you experience, along with the actions and behaviors you exhibit.[6]

The Unconscious Brain

"For God does speak—now one way, now another—though no one
perceives it. In a dream, in a vision, of the night, when deep sleep falls
on people as they slumber in their beds, he may speak in their ears and

terrify them with warnings to turn them from wrongdoing and keep
them from pride, to preserve them from the pit, their lives from perishing
by the sword." (Job 33:14–18)

Studies have shown that past emotional memories from stressful events affect our future at the unconscious level, as well as the way we react to future situations. Suvrathan, Aparna, et al, affirmed:

> Explicit memories of facts or events, encoded by a brain structure called the hippocampus, tend to fade away with time. In contrast, unconscious emotional memories of stressful experiences, formed in a brain structure called the amygdala, appear to leave an indelible mark that may last for a lifetime. The rapid and efficient encoding of fearful memories by the amygdala helps us cope with threatening stimuli in the future, but it also comes at a high price. These emotional memories etched into the amygdala circuitry can also become maladaptive. For example, high anxiety and mood lability are cardinal symptoms of many stress disorders. Here we review recent findings that provide insights into the cellular and synaptic mechanisms underlying the cognitive and emotional effects of stress.[7]

The brain has built-in features of incredible computation power at the unconscious and conscious levels. The unconscious mind (in areas such as the amygdala and nucleus accumbens) assesses threats and sends signals to the physical body through the neurochemicals and neurotransmitters, released in the body automatically as a response to your thoughts of fear, worry and anxiety. They direct your behavior, desires, actions, and attitudes, affecting the cellular functions including gene expression and protein synthesis, and all your systems. Just a quick calculation of the power of your brain, based on what is known at this time, shows that at a synapse the circuit can fire 100 times per second when the electrical impulse arrives to pass the synapses' threshold.[8] Each neuron has about 10,000 to 100,000 synapses. Our brain has about 1000 trillion synapses to process our thoughts, communications and actions every moment.[9]

It is beyond our comprehension how the body has been created by the Super Intelligent Designer, the Creator of the Universe. Indeed we are an amazing, complex creature, and wonderfully made, as the king and psalmist David stated thousands of years ago—before modern, scientific evidence flooded our libraries. He stated, "I will praise You, for I am fearfully and wonderfully made; marvelous are Your works, and that my soul knows very well" (Ps. 139:14, NKJ). Deep in his inner being David knew (approximately 3,500 years ago) about these complex functions of the human body, mind, soul and spirit, having been shown by the Spirit of God. It is extremely important to select quality thoughts that trigger healthy neurotransmitters, and not to destroy neurons and synapses, with their great impact on our cognition.

Stress Affects Your Neurochemical Balance

"The human spirit can endure in sickness, but a crushed spirit who can bear?" (Prov. 18:14)

"You will keep in perfect peace those whose minds are steadfast, because they trust in you. Trust in the LORD forever, for the LORD, the LORD Himself, is the Rock eternal." (Isa. 26:3–4)

Studies show that those who have suffered from chronic depression can develop metabolic syndrome (glucose intolerance, diabetes, hypertension, dyslipidemia, and obesity) and vice versa.[10] Those who suffer from metabolic syndrome can likewise develop depression with its complications. The cycle repeats itself. Diabetes is increasing so much that in America over 50% of the population will suffer from this disease by 2020. The cost of these diseases will be $3.35 trillion.[11] This can be reduced if people will understand that depression and diabetes can be prevented by changing their lifestyle, ways of thinking, and attitudes, when fear, worry and anxiety hit. We need to react appropriately to avoid bad habits. Diseases and high costs will cause stress levels to go up even more. This becomes a national and global problem affecting everyone in the world, now and for future generations.

Stress and unwise behaviors cause more damage, making people more dependent on others. If the world ignores God's prescriptions for managing stress, there will be more and more dependent people and even fewer able to provide care to all those affected by the diseases and consequences of bad behavior and unhealthy thinking. Changing the world's thinking is urgent if we want to prevent the disaster of a stress pandemic. God's prescriptions, which function beyond the scope of science, will lead us in the right direction. They can heal emotionally broken people for all eternity. With God's healing, people are stronger at that place of brokenness, just as in a human body a broken bone is stronger after it heals. He heals the brokenhearted and binds up their wounds (Ps. 147:3). When God heals us, we are stronger in the place of brokenness and able to comfort the world around us with the same comfort. We can help heal people's brokenness with a Godly approach. We can grow healthier and stronger by knowing God and His prescriptions for stress management.

PART II

ROOT CAUSES of STRESS

CHAPTER FOUR

A World of Problems

"Therefore, I urge you, brothers and sisters, in view of God's mercy, to offer your bodies as a living sacrifice, holy and pleasing to God—this is your true and proper worship. Do not conform to the pattern of this world, but be transformed by the renewing of your mind. Then you will be able to test and approve what God's will is—His good, pleasing and perfect will." (Rom. 12:1, 2)

Hearing or reading the daily news, we know the entire world is suffering from unsolved problems. Fear, worry and anxiety are everywhere, and stress rises exponentially. People fear the future. They worry about being rejected, or not forgiven, or unable to forgive. About their lack of finances, poor health, or lack of friends. Loneliness further affects the thinking process. People fear losing their job, losing a loved one, being rejected, not being able to succeed, chronic health conditions—it can seem like your situation is getting worse despite all your efforts to overcome.

You may have the same question I often had: who will fix the world's problems? Who will change this world? Many think advanced technology, or armies, or corporations, or talented people, or new scientific discoveries will save us. Even in this postmodern era so many problems remained unsolved, and people live under constant pressure. When we are under a lot of stress, dangerous levels of neurochemicals and neurotransmitters are released as cortisol, the "the stress hormone". High levels of cortisol released in the hippocampus area kill millions of neurons.[1] Unfortunately, most people do not understand these disease processes and how high levels of stress, fear, worry and anxiety can damage their brain—indeed their entire body.

Since the dawn of creation, mankind has made great progress in many directions, yet in many areas humanity is experiencing drastic deterioration. When people experience fear and worry from uncertainty, financial insecurity, separation, divorce, drug abuse, abortion, violence, murder, guilt, adultery, immorality, suicide, homicide, discouragement, bitterness, dishonesty, corruption, greed, laziness, ignorance, etc., the stress level keeps going up, further damaging the whole body. The supernatural prescription for preventing physical and spiritual damages resonates in my mind: *"Do not conform to the pattern of this world, but be transformed by the renewing of your mind" (Rom. 12:1, 2).*

Unhealthy Individuals, Unhealthy Society

The world's culture is deteriorating, marred by widespread drug use, alcoholism, violence, anger, divorce, abortion, immorality, pornography, and prostitution, human trafficking—all leading to fear, worry, and anxiety, resulting in multiple chronic diseases and death. If not properly addressed, all the unhealthy behavior displayed in this generation will lead to physical and spiritual diseases—and physical and spiritual death. We hear the cliché that it takes a village to raise a child. In order to have a healthy child, that village must itself be healthy.

We must change our thinking about family life, the foundation of any society. A society cannot remain healthy if individuals, families, and the educational system are unhealthy and the politicians are untrustworthy. Schoolteachers know that nothing can be fixed at school before the family is fixed at home. Too many children do not have their biological father in their life as a role model, and they often become rebellious at home, at school, and in their community. They may have a stepfather who is trying hard to provide care to his stepchildren, but this is not the same as having their biological father. Children can become bitter, feeling rejected by their biological father and accumulating bitterness in their souls that can express itself in outbursts and angry episodes. All too often we see teens committing murder, and even suicide.

When the biological father is not in a child's life—not available to share feelings, needs, joys and sorrows—then all the bad feelings accumulate in the area of the brain associated with memories and emotions (the limbic system's hippocampus and amygdala), causing anger and leading to violent, destructive behaviors. They do not know what it means to honor their father, to be encouraged, to show respect, and to feel their father's love. Divorced and dysfunctional families are epidemic. All the distress, depression, anxiety, dissatisfaction, and other unhealthy emotions and stress are transmitted from a single mother to her children. Children without both parents are suffering and cannot concentrate to perform well at school, thus they tend to suffer more from low self-esteem. On the other hand passive, permissive, inconsistent and poor parenting creates more problems in society. We live in a painful world, and we need to have clear expectations for children in order to avoid chronic problems in the future.

Stress Starts in Childhood

"Jesus said, 'Let the little children come to me, and do not hinder them, for the kingdom of Heaven belongs to such as these.'" (Matt. 19:14)

"He took a little child whom he placed among them. Taking the child in His arms, He said to them, 'Whoever welcomes one of these little children in My name welcomes Me; and whoever welcomes Me does not welcome Me but the One who sent Me.'" (Mark 9:36–37)

It is well documented in scientific literature that the brain structure is altered in children facing family adversity during their childhood.

Accumulating evidence suggests a role of FKBP5, a co-chaperone regulating the glucocorticoid receptor sensitivity, in the etiology of depression and anxiety disorders. Based on recent findings of altered amygdala activity following childhood adversity, the present study aimed at clarifying the impact of genetic variation in FKBP5 on threat-related neural activity and coupling as well as morphometric alterations in stress-sensitive brain systems.

Functional magnetic resonance imaging during an emotional face-matching task was performed in 153 healthy young adults (66 males) from a high-risk community sample followed since birth. Voxel-based morphometry was applied to study structural alterations and DNA was genotyped for FKBP5 rs1360780. Childhood adversity was measured using a retrospective self-report (Childhood Trauma Questionnaire) and by a standardized parent interview assessing childhood family adversity. Depression was assessed by the Beck Depression Inventory. There was a main effect of FKBP5 on the left amygdala, with T homozygotes showing the highest activity, largest volume and increased coupling with the left hippocampus and the orbitofrontal cortex (OFC). Moreover, amygdala-OFC coupling proved to be associated with depression in this genotype. In addition, our results support previous evidence of a gene-environment interaction on right amygdala activity with respect to retrospective assessment of childhood adversity, but clarify that this does not generalize to the prospective assessment. These findings indicated that activity in T homozygotes increased with the level of adversity, whereas the opposite pattern emerged in C homozygotes, with CT individuals being intermediate. The present results point to a functional involvement of FKBP5 in intermediate phenotypes associated with emotional processing, suggesting a possible mechanism for this gene in conferring susceptibility to stress-related disorders.[2]

We now know that stressors in childhood form memories of traumatic events, which can affect us as adults, as well as our offspring, from generation to generation.[3] Everything parents go through reflects on their children, due to the mirror neurons in the brain.[4] As a child I lived in a big family of eight children, and my father worked prolonged hours to provide for our needs. One day my mother was very sick, and my father arrived home and rushed her to the hospital. My mother had been falling on the floor, because she had very weak legs from acute thrombophlebitis and other complications. There was no telephone to call an ambulance for my Mom in a timely manner.

When I saw her falling, something broke in my heart and my mind. I was so distressed, and started to cry—almost paralyzed by my own thoughts of discouragement when I saw my mother collapsing on the floor and unable to walk. I was only 11 years old when I experienced those feelings of hopelessness and helplessness. But those painful memories are still so fresh in my mind stirring my emotions each time I "visit the storage of old memories and emotions" (in my unconscious mind, even after 45 years).

Even now when I see disabled people who are suffering, those memories stored long ago in my brain structures are activated. They produce emotional pain if I do not suppress them with the promises of God, that He is our constant Healer and our Great Physician. Children feel the stress of their parents' problems, and that stress remains with them for a long time if not addressed properly. The mirror neurons built into our brain structures are involved in this process. But for children it is more intense, because their brain is not completely developed until their 20s.[5]

It is also well known that children will mirror their parents' behavior. What children learn at home on a daily basis remains with them when they grow up. If they see parents loving each other they will imitate them later in their life. If they see parents fighting, hating, divorcing, committing adultery, drinking, consuming drugs and alcohol, and smoking, the children will do the same. Thus the cliché: "Like father like son." Children mirror their parents' behavior by consolidating those memories, influencing their behavior in the future.

Looking through some drawers, seeking information for the business demands of the day, my eyes were caught by a folder with pictures of my best friend Mary, who died of cancer long ago. All the memories were so fresh in my mind, as if it had just happened. She was divorced, with three small children who were emotionally devastated by seeing their mother die of cancer at such a young age. I already knew their struggles, and I understood why they did not have a father like a normal family. Their mother needed to fill that gap left by her husband, who had abandoned his family for another woman. Even now, those children continue to struggle emotionally, although their parents were intellectuals with advanced degrees in education, and even though their mother left a house for the children to live in and money for food, clothing and other expenses.

Despite good advice and committed help from very good friends, who were available for those children after their mother passed away, they used up all their resources and have had a very difficult time succeeding. You could easily read the distress in their heart on their faces, and their struggles to cope with life's challenges. Children with no family structure suffer, and they struggle to make it in life.

Mirror neurons in childhood actively mirror those around them, helping with mental development and growth. Science has discovered that mirror neurons are active in a child's brain when health care professionals are doing therapy. Children are forming a mirror image of the behavior they see repeatedly, and will behave later in the same way, mirroring those behaviors.[6] For example, children living with depressed parents or siblings, or with divorced parents, or drug addicts, or alcoholics, will suffer later because of the mirror neurons. Our Creator built mirror neurons into our body for nurturing, healthy growth, self-actualization and great achievements in life. We must create a healthy environment for children so they will do the same for their future family, in order to have a healthy society.

In today's society the level of stress is high, and children feel it too. We know that high levels of stress will reduce the serotonin level in the brain, causing more depression. Statistics tell us that millions of people are on antidepressants.[7] Demands in this postmodern era make everybody feel stressed out, and the use of antidepressants is on the rise. When stress is high, our brain registers stimuli that influence our thinking process in unhealthy ways. The atmosphere is created for more cortisol to be released in the brain, killing neurons responsible to produce serotonin, and then more depression is seen in the children. Families often put stress on children, expecting high performance and perfection in everything at a very young age. Children also experience high levels of stress and anxiety from dysfunctional families— no love, rejection, low self-esteem—and in a short time they can become depressed. But here is hope in the supernatural prescription: "Jesus said, 'Let the little children come to me, and do not hinder them, for the kingdom of Heaven belongs to such as these'" (Matt. 19:14).

Stress in Adolescence

"Start children off on the way they should go, and even when they are old they will not turn from it." (Prov. 22:6)

"...from infancy you have known the Holy scriptures, which are able to make you wise for salvation through faith in Christ Jesus. All scripture is God-breathed and is useful for teaching, rebuking, correcting and training in righteousness, so that the servant of God may be thoroughly equipped for every good work." (2 Tim. 3:15–17)

Now let us look into what is happening in the brain of a child or an adolescent who becomes addicted to illicit or prescription drugs, which invariably will lead to unhealthy behaviors. The prefrontal cortex, the conscious part of the brain used to evaluate situations and to make decisions, is the last area to finish developing in children—not until they are in their 20s.[8] Young children, then, cannot be expected to make consistently good decisions. Adolescents are impacted by memories of their childhood, and also by peer pressure, activities, school attendance and performance, friends, sleep disturbances, medical issues, and family dynamics, any of which can cause physical and psychological pain.

Poor parental modeling, as well as psychological stress (fear, anxiety, and depression) will cause abnormal nervous system activities. This will lead to withdrawal from society, missing school, and poor socialization with peers. Pain will cause more stress and emotional thoughts. Fear itself can cause a child to avoid healthy behavior. Fear can also cause more pain, leading the young person to be overly worried and sensitive to pain, which then can bring on further anxiety and depression. Chronic illness is potentially a sad result.

Parents usually restrict children from some otherwise healthy activities when they are ill, but allow them to stay home and play games on the internet—an immediate reward system for illness through the dopamine neurotransmitter. We already mentioned that high dopamine levels can lead to substance abuse such as alcohol, stimulants, opioids, sedatives, marijuana and tobacco. Healthy family life and wise parental decisions play a major part in a child's recovery. The more attention you pay to the pain, the more the pain will grow, causing you to seek pain killers with increased risk for addiction in the future. Positive confrontation is needed to recover from pain. Parents must interact with children positively and provide a healthy home environment. In a family under constant stress, the children will develop psychological pain. Culture, beliefs, behavior during illness, social interaction, and emotional support play a huge role in an adolescent's recovery from pain.

Some will seek narcotics when they're experiencing stress, anxiety or worry. Fear and anxiety increase the adolescent's risk for substance abuse, including alcohol, cigarettes, and or medication. They crave something to relieve the pressure and tension built up from psychological distress. The results can be low self-esteem, trouble with their peers, poor grades in school, poor socialization, weak coping mechanisms, and feelings of rejection, etc.

Parents' behavior directly affects their children's behavior. Parents need to know that pain "loves" an audience. Overly coddling children to reinforce bad behavior is never good, but reasonable expectations are vital. Do not allow children to avoid healthy activities. Escaping activities shouldn't be the solution to avoid consequences from pain. Good relaxation techniques, such as deep breathing, will decrease anxiety and loosen tight muscles—a mindfulness approach to relieving stress.

Increased pain will increase stress. So we need to teach children to use positive coping strategies that provide a distraction. Reducing the focus on pain will reduce physiological arousal, and that produces physiological changes that will reduce pain.

We can suppress an existing habit by understanding the source of that habit and redirecting to a better source. Rewards for participation in activities are contingent reinforcement to pain-control strategies. If a child fails to meet specific goals, it helps to ensure there will be consequences. For example, let the child know that he or she has normal privileges when attending school, and no privileges if they miss school.

Parents need to help their children learn how to deal with pain. It takes good, family-based problem-solving management to guide children toward success, and prevent school failure, addictions, and other tragedies. Help children manage the associated stress if they have a medical condition. Help them reengage in life and manage their pain when they have a crisis. Allowing a child to withdraw from physical activities will only increase their anxiety. "Start children off on the way they should go, and even when they are old they will not turn from it" (Prov. 22:6).

Volunteering in the community is a wonderful, positive activity. Our brain likes to be active all the time. Neurons require constant stimulation to stay alive. An inactive cell is a dying cell. My daughter was in 7th or 8th grade when she started volunteering with the elderly in foster homes. Later she volunteered at Portland Adventist Community Service Health Clinic, where I was volunteering as a Primary Care Provider, and then at Emanuel Hospital, working with children suffering from cancer. She also volunteered in the church, working with small children. Volunteer experience gave her the drive to study more and helped her choose a profession with a great future. She never touched drugs or any other unhealthy behavior and enjoyed a healthy adolescence.

Constructive thoughts, facing our fears, and moderating our pain language will improve our mood, help us be more active, decrease our anxiety, and increase our whole quality of life.

Too many young people live with feelings of anxiety and depression, lack of self-esteem, and rejection. They start looking for affection, love, and acceptance in the wrong groups, leading to unhealthy behaviors and bad habits—drugs, gangs, adultery developing AIDs, and STDs (sexual transmitted disease). They become emotionally disabled at a very young age as a consequence of behaviors that were triggered by an unstable environment, creating psychosocial distress in their life. Some become so overwhelmed that they resort to violence or suicide.

When very young children consume drugs, they develop delusions and cannot think clearly. Thoughts are distorted and they develop an anti-motivational syndrome that will eventually ruin their future. They are not motivated to study to finish high school, not able to get and keep a job, not able to get married and have a family. Their future is destroyed. As we learned earlier, marijuana kills neurons in the brain, with long term consequences. As the gateway to more dangerous drugs like heroin, it is the road to disaster for individuals and for society.

It is obvious to most of us that the world is going in the wrong direction. To change the world we must fix things that are not right. We must influence our community, including the politicians, to find the root cause of all the problems that adversely affect our society, and start from there to correct the defects.

Frequently I have young patients coming into the clinic asking for a prescription, for example for a "marijuana card" for different kinds of "pain". When I check their health records and ask them about their disease history, there is nothing indicating they need that drug! We need to change our approach in the health care system, and educate our adolescents to think productive, healthy thoughts by bringing spirituality back into medicine, because "All scripture is God-breathed and is useful for teaching, rebuking, correcting and training in righteousness, so that the servant of God may be thoroughly equipped for every good work" (2 Tim. 3:15–17).

The Burden of Hidden Stress

"Come unto me, all ye that labor and are heavy laden, and I will give you rest. Take my yoke upon you, and learn of me; for I am meek and

lowly in heart: and ye shall find rest unto your souls. For my yoke is easy, and my burden is light." (Matt. 11:28–30)

People suffering from hidden stress often have unexplained signs and symptoms, making a doctor's heart "sink". In my practice I see these patients presenting with the same signs and symptoms over and over again, but no physiological causes. Patients become more worried about their sickness and are restless if their provider cannot find a diagnosis for their symptoms. Physiological diseases get much more attention than psychological problems. Yet doctors need a psychological framework to achieve better outcomes when dealing with hidden stress. People with hidden stress may experience many of the signs and symptoms listed in the first chapters. They visit Emergency Rooms frequently and consult with specialists for tests, with no physiological explanation. Even psychiatrists cannot diagnose them. It is costly and very frustrating, due to all the workups and false positive results. Serious illnesses are ruled out, but patients remain ill. People are reluctant to accept "hidden stress" as a cause of illness. It may not be mental illness, or delusional, but they have "hit the wall" and are deficient in self-care skills.

Childhood stress can carry over, making people sick in adulthood. From long term stress the intestines develop permeability, and nutrients "leak out" and are not absorbed into the bloodstream. Then the cell can't get the right nutrients for health, resulting in unpleasant physical symptoms.[9] From childhood emotions stuffed in the back of their mind (physical, psychological and sexual abuse, substance abuse, domestic violence), chronic stress diminishes self-esteem, and later on those children are involved in drug use, suicidal attempts, alcohol abuse, anxiety, panic attacks and depression.

Often specialists have those patients journal their feelings and address them directly toward the person who abused them in their childhood. It is shown that writing down feelings, addressing them to the person who caused trauma to their soul, and forgiveness, will bring much-needed relief and healing. Writing about stress and worry is more helpful than people realize. We need to reflect, think of solutions, and learn self-care skills. Finding activities we enjoy, and finding time to focus on our spiritual needs is important. Become aware of bad habits and reinforce positive habits. Patients with massive stress in their life are not always consciously aware of it.

Anger is transferable. Mothers with displaced anger will then transfer that to their children. For example, if after a divorce the mother needs to overwork to take care of everything, and then uses words that are verbally and emotionally abusive, her children will suffer emotional damage. Stress from childhood can be hidden for a long time, even a lifetime, whether we are consciously aware of it or not. But similar thoughts will trigger memories and emotions later, with unpleasant feelings and disastrous illnesses if not properly addressed. You can find rest for the burden of hidden stress when you follow Jesus' instruction, "Come unto me, all ye that labor and are heavy laden, and I will give you rest" (Matt. 11:28–30)

Stress Leads to Unhealthy Lifestyles

"Be very careful, then, how you live—not as unwise but as wise, making the most of every opportunity, because the days are evil. Therefore do not be foolish, but understand what the Lord's will is." (Eph. 5:15–17)

Due to thoughts of hopelessness and disorientation in life, many people are prone to unhealthy lifestyles. Overeating, lack of exercise, and inactivity will develop into metabolic syndrome—a cluster of diseases (hypertension, diabetes, dyslipidemia, obesity) which damage the body, mind and spirit. It is a vicious cycle with no hope. Hope is complete when we are connected with God, as we read in Romans chapter five: "…since we have been justified through faith, we have peace with God through our LORD Jesus Christ, through whom we have gained access by faith into His grace in which we now stand. And we boast in the hope of the glory of God (Rom. 5:1–2).

Hope in the Word of God does not disappoint. God is speaking to people through dreams, visions, and signs, but most of the time through His Word. We have access to His grace by faith in the LORD Jesus, and faith in His Word helps to prevent unhealthy lifestyles. The brain, through communication between the prefrontal cortex and basal ganglia, has the ability to learn new habits and modify bad habits.[10] Meditation on the promises of God will help the brain focus on positive thoughts and healthy coping mechanisms to deal with stress, and overcome it to prevent an unhealthy lifestyle.

Risky Technology Addiction

"There are three things that are never satisfied, four that never say 'Enough!': the grave, the barren womb, land, which is never satisfied with water, and fire, which never says, 'Enough!'" (Prov. 30:15–16)

Addiction in the body is triggered by a high level of dopamine (through the immediate reward mechanism), a neurochemical that, when released, produces "feel good" emotions. Scientists have found that in order to overcome addiction people need to strengthen their anterior cingulate circuits, found in the frontal lobe, in order to control the neurochemical dopamine involved in addiction.[11] Dopamine in unhealthy levels "clouds" the brain and reduces one's judgment capacity—which can be lethal. To strengthen the neurochemical fabric in our brain we must control our thought process and change our thinking. Only the Word of God has the power to transform our mind and our way of thinking.

People often get addicted to video games, gambling, internet pornography, web shopping, overeating (junk food causes you to gain weight, leading to metabolic syndrome and all its signs and symptoms), drinking, drugs, and internet dating—anticipating the immediate gratification of feeling good. These bad habits will boost the dopamine level in the brain. High levels of dopamine can cause immediate gratification, but in the long run the storage runs out, creating emptiness in people's hearts and terrible lifelong consequences.

Preserve your ability to store dopamine by staying away from compulsive, unhealthy behaviors so you can preserve your good judgment and enjoy a better quality of life in the future. You are in control of your life and your thinking process. You have the ability to reconstruct your neurons, your brain, and your judgment. When you feel euphoria, it comes from a high dopamine level, which is responsible for motivation and rewards. We want more and more of those feelings, described thousands of years ago in Proverbs 30:15,16: "There are three things that are never satisfied, four that never say 'Enough!': the grave, the barren womb, land, which is never satisfied with water, and fire, which never says, 'Enough!'" When people develop compulsive, unhealthy behaviors that cause addiction, there will never be "enough".

All addictive activities (eating unhealthy food, gambling, unhealthy shopping, drugs, internet, pornography, alcohol, etc.) activate the neurons in the frontal lobe controlling short term memories and decisions.[12] This releases more dopamine (responsible for pleasure) and leads to dependency with bad consequences.

Worry Increases Stress

"…therefore do not worry about tomorrow, for tomorrow will worry about itself. Each day has enough trouble of its own." (Matt. 6:34)

The root causes for stress are many, but the biggest one is worry about tomorrow. We know that worry causes increased anxiety and depression. But the Bible gives us the prescriptions for worry about tomorrow. In Matthew 6:34 we read, "Therefore do not worry about tomorrow, for tomorrow will worry about itself. Each day has enough trouble of its own." Every single day God gives strength to those who are burdened by worry. I was worried and anxious many times in my life, and I couldn't seem to do anything to get out of my hopeless situations.

I had to trust God every day and believe in His divine intervention to bring supernatural solutions for my problems. I had to meditate on the promises of God and repeat them throughout the day and night, through the worst and best times of my life. Many Bible verses are written for our benefit, to prevent us from worrying about tomorrow. The Word of God teaches us how to cope and manage stress, to prevent the brain from responding to high levels of stress by releasing toxic chemicals and neurotransmitters that would destroy our health. The threats of worry about tomorrow—the stressors—will send signals through the pathways that the Creator wired inside the body to fight threats. But if we ignore God's instruction and allow our mind to wander with thoughts of worry and high anxiety, the brain will be flooded with many neurochemicals in abnormal quantities—toxins poisoning and affecting the whole body.

Excessive Worry

Excessive worry causes an acute stress disorder, with uncomfortable signs and symptoms and toxic amounts of neurotransmitters. People endure endless tests, with negative results, yet uncomfortable and unexplained medical signs and symptoms remain. Normal life includes a normal amount of anxiety for success, but excessive anxiety causes unhealthy amounts of neurochemicals to be released, which will cloud your mind. If you feel irritation building inside, or tension, sleep disturbance and fatigue, or if your cognition is affected, or you have other signs and symptoms discussed in this book, then your anxiety is growing and your mind is "clouded" from too many neurochemicals.

I remember the nuclear accident in Chernobyl, USSR in the spring of 1986. The resulting nuclear cloud reached all over northwestern Europe. Millions of people were affected, and even today many diseases and disabilities, especially of the thyroid gland, remain in the adults who were children at that time. Using that analogy, the "clouds" of neurochemicals released in your brain and body from unhealthy thoughts can modify your DNA through epigenetics. The gene's expression is altered, increasing the risk for diseases in future generations. Just remember that meditation on the promises of God, written in His powerful Word, pushes away the "clouds" of unhealthy neurochemicals and neurotransmitters from your mind and builds new neurons through neurogenesis, divinely strengthening your mind and body.

No matter your age, you can still benefit from making changes. All mental and physical conditions start with anxiety, cognition impairment, increased short-term memory loss, depression, etc. MRI tests have shown that mild cognitive impairment can precede Alzheimer's disease.[13] People with excessive worry, who do not sleep enough hours, develop early signs of neurocognitive disorders. The best way to prevent cognitive impairment is to start right now by reducing your excessive worry, anxiety and depression and focusing on positive attitudes and faith in God's prescriptions.

Use relaxation techniques and deep breathing whenever you feel stressed. Take your mind off those things that cause your anxiety and emotional distress, and redirect your thoughts to past positive experiences that brought you success and victory. Take a quick walk, even 5–10 minutes, when you feel overwhelmed with worry and fear. Physical exercise, even walking, is equivalent to pharmacotherapy, and just 1.5 miles a day will be a benefit. More than that is even better. The faster you can walk, the less likely you are to die. Speed correlates with longevity. Evaluate the increased level of stress in your life by verifying your feelings at the end of the day. Are you emotionally drained? Do you feel tired when you get up to face another day of work? How is your relationship with those around you? Do you feel burned out, frustrated, hardened emotionally, uncaring, or victimized?

Fear and Worry

"My life is consumed by anguish and my years by groaning; my strength fails because of my affliction, and my bones grow weak." (Ps. 31:10)

"...corrupts the whole body, sets the whole course of one's life on fire and is itself set on fire by hell." (James 3:6)

Fear comes from doubt and unbelief. Healthy faith comes from meditating and hearing positive promises for your life from God's Word. "The One who is in you is greater than the one who is in the world" (1 John 4:4). "If God is for us, who can be against us?" (Rom. 8:31). Neuroscientists have discovered that meditation affects the Alpha brainwaves, enabling the brain to filter unnecessary information and focus on the most important ones, to improve cognition for basic operations in our daily life.[14] Meditate on this promise and do not let people speak fear into your life, causing doubt and unbelief. Doubts and unbelief are unhealthy faith. It is called fear.

Both faith and unbelief come by hearing. If you hear discouraging words, your faith decreases and fear increases. That produces stress, with all its physiological and psychological manifestations. The brain perceives fearful thoughts as a threat. When you speak encouraging words, your faith will be increased and your fear will disappear. Faith brings hope, peace and joy. Our words hold the power of life and death.

2,000 years ago James wrote about our tongue that "…corrupts the whole body, sets the whole course of one's life on fire and is itself set on fire by hell" (James 3:6). That statement is still true. We see all over the world today that the tongue "…is a restless evil, full of deadly poison." The human tongue causes damage when one speaks words against the promises of God, then the spoken words enter someone else's brain, and the spoken words are transformed into electrical signals that travel through synapses and axons to neurons, forming fearful or threatening thoughts. These trigger poisonous amounts of neurochemicals to be released from those neurons that affect the emotions, mind, spirit and body.

Use your tongue to declare encouraging words from the life-giving promises of God. It is very important to pray God's promises over your life. Your prayer will be full of healthy words, and hearing those words will build your faith. God loves people with great faith, who believe the promises written in His word. Without faith you cannot please God. "Without faith it is impossible to please God, because anyone who comes to Him must believe that He exists and that He rewards those who earnestly seek Him" (Heb. 11:6). The reward for your faith will be a healthy, happy life—here on earth and in eternity.

People live with fear every day, refusing to believe God's promises. For many years I feared losing everything. The communists threatened us because of our values and beliefs. Christians had to live on the margins during Ceausescu's communist regime—a harsh dictatorship—or take the exile route. We suffered brutality, ruthless repression, harassment and death threats. Communists in Romania were suffocating our individual freedom and human rights with Marxist-Leninist atheistic doctrine. Ordinary Christians were arrested, brainwashed, and threatened with losing their privileges for education and jobs. All aspects of a Christian's life were controlled by the communists. But for me the fear of God was stronger than the fear of men. I reminded myself constantly that "The One who is in you is greater than the one who is in the world" (1 John 4:4), and "If God is for us, who can be against us?" (Rom. 8:31).

Fear of Failure Brings Stress

"…being confident of this, that he who began a good work in you will carry it on to completion until the day of Christ Jesus." (Phil. 1:6)

"But the Lord is faithful, and he will strengthen you and protect you from the evil one." (2 Thess. 3:3)

Insecurity and fear of failure bring anxiety and depression. Fear of failure is not uncommon. We are afraid of not being excellent, not being perfect. I often experienced anxiety from the fear of failure, especially in Romania's communist regime. I needed to avoid the persecution of the communists, whose mocking attitude never ended until they were overthrown. Then when I moved to the US, I was even more anxious. I did not speak the language, and I was unable to express myself and make my needs known. To illustrate, one time somebody told me to bring something from an area from the right side of the building. I said, "OK," and then to that person's amazement I turned to the left and started to walk away. I did not have a clue what she wanted me to do. I was so embarrassed; it felt like the earth was sinking under my feet.

In college, all the exams were very difficult, and I had such a fear of failure. I had to work harder, spending prolonged hours to meet all my school requirements, while at the same time operating my business responsibly. I learned many times from my own mistakes, even though I was afraid. I worried that I would fail to manage the business and I might lose it. You must give yourself permission to learn from mistakes. U.S. Army General Omar Bradley stated, "I learned that good judgment comes from experience and that experience grows out of mistakes."[15]

Fear and Anxiety Paralyze

"A thousand may fall at your side, ten thousand at your right hand, but it will not come near you. You will only observe with your eyes and see the punishment of the wicked." (Ps. 91:7)

The devil wants to mutilate us and reduce us to silence. The power to do what is right is built in us. Maybe that is why the Creator designed our system with neurotransmitters to inhibit abnormal actions and calm the brain down when we are overwhelmed by anxiety, and agitated by fear and worry. GABA, the inhibitory neurotransmitters, bring calmness, but must be activated through the power of the Holy Spirit, with the promises of God and His instructions for life: "Do not be afraid."

The Holy Spirit is our helper and brings the Word to our memory. The Holy Spirit created order in the Universe when it was all just chaos, according to Genesis 1:2. The same Spirit is hovering over us, ready to intervene, according to God's promises in the Word of God. The Comforter will bring order into our brain when we are under excessive pressure from worry and stress—but only when we give Him permission to do so. Through prayer we enter into the spiritual realm, activating the promises of God.

Many times fear has gripped my heart about uncertain things, but whenever I was afraid, I prayed.

Nothing will harm you when you pray and do the right thing, "for the eyes of the LORD are on the righteous and his ears are attentive to their prayer, but the face of the LORD is against those who do evil" (1 Peter 3:12). God fights for you. He reduces the wicked to silence. "He will guard the feet of His faithful servants, but the wicked will be silenced in the place of darkness" (1 Sam. 2:9). I believed the promises of God, which say that man can do nothing to me when I trust in the promises of God, through all my fears and struggles.

I believed nothing would touch me, according to Psalm 91:7. "A thousand may fall at your side, ten thousand at your right hand, but it will not come near you. You will only observe with your eyes and see the punishment of the wicked." I experimented with this truth in my life even as a youth in Bucharest, without parents or any support nearby. I had no one to protect me at that early age. When I was not even 15 years old, I arrived in Bucharest, the capital city, knowing nobody. Growing up in my small village, where I knew each family, then going to a completely strange environment, was a shocking experience. No family and no friends! It was dangerous to live in a big, corrupt city with a communist population of three million people, who at that time had no fear of God. But I put my trust in Him, and He protected me always and watched my steps. He will keep you from evil when you trust Him. "But the Lord is faithful, and he will strengthen you and protect you from the evil one" (2 Thess. 3:3).

Fear will disappear when you focus on God's promises. He will keep you from falling when things go wrong and there is no hope. "To Him who is able to keep you from stumbling and to present you before his glorious presence without fault and with great joy—to the only God our Savior be glory, majesty, power and authority, through Jesus Christ our Lord, before all ages, now and forevermore! Amen" (Jude 1:24, 25). The enemy will be blocked by the Spirit of the Lord when you shift your focus from the things that bring worry and fear, to the fear of the Lord. God is faithful to His people who obey Him. He will punish your enemy that causes fear in your life. "According to what they have done, so will He repay wrath to his enemies and retribution to his foes; he will repay the islands their due" (Isa. 59:19). You are in the Father's hands (John 10:27–29).

Do not let your thoughts be controlled by your enemies: worry, fear and anxiety. God is in control over your life. He will perform the good work He began in you, as we read in Philippians: "...being confident of this, that he who began a good work in you will carry it on to completion until the day of Christ Jesus" (Phil 1:6).

Low Self-Esteem and Distress

"But the LORD said unto Samuel, 'Look not on his countenance, or on the height of his stature; because I have refused him: for [the LORD seeth] not as man seeth; for man looketh on the outward appearance, but the LORD looketh on the heart.'" (1 Sam. 16:7 KJV)

Low self-esteem makes people anxious. It can even cause depression. Stop everything you are doing right now and look at yourself in a mirror. See how perfectly everything has been made and programmed by the Super Intelligent Designer. Think about all your vital organs and your extremities that keep you moving all day. You are "...wonderfully and fearfully made" (Ps. 139:14).

Many men and women pay a lot of money for their beauty, fashion, makeup and jewelry, but your beauty comes from the Lord. I always saw myself as less physically attractive, but I was confident that what I had inside me was more precious than my looks. Many times since my childhood people have told me, "I'd like to have your brain." I am glad they did not ask for my nose, because I do have a big nose and I could feel offended by that! They wished for my brain, because in my brain I had the beauty of the Lord, which meant God's Word in it came out through my thoughts, my vocabulary, and my behavior. No one could miss that. I didn't hear anybody say, "I'd like to have your face, either.

When I was two years old my older sisters were cooking corn at the farm, and reaching for the pot with boiling water, I burned my face. I got a severe burn on my right chin that stayed with me all my life. So you can see why a lack of self-esteem could have destroyed my future, if I had not held on to the promises of God. Instead, I value how He created me, and what He poured into me through the baptism of the Holy Spirit at a very young age. All my beauty was internal, from the power of God's Word at work in my mind through the Holy Spirit.

Rejection Leads to Destruction

"As you come to him, a living stone rejected by men, but in the sight of God chosen and precious..." (1 Peter 2:4 ESV)

"In Him we have redemption through His blood, the forgiveness of our sins, in accordance with the riches of God's grace that He lavished on us." (Eph. 1:7–8)

Some people have a strong fear of rejection, even from childhood. They work hard to be accepted, but when they feel like everything is falling apart they make bad decisions and end up in the wrong crowd. As a result there are many teens committing suicide, many families going through separation and divorce, many children with one or no parents, and they also experience feelings of rejection or abandonment. They keep looking for a group that will accept them. This leaves them vulnerable to the wrong groups that, while accepting them, also draw them into all kinds of destructive addictions.

The Bible teaches that we are accepted through Jesus Christ. "In Him we have redemption through His blood, the forgiveness of our sins, in accordance with the riches of God's grace that He lavished on us" (Eph. 1:7–8). People everywhere are hungry for love, affection, acceptance and a sense of belonging. God is love. Run into His arms and you will feel the love of our eternal Father in Heaven, who saved us through the blood of His own Son Jesus. In Him you will find divine acceptance and protection.

Avoiding Responsibilities

People often choose to disregard the Word of God and run from their responsibilities. In every city I visit I look for homeless people, because I think they are the most vulnerable population. This group just moves my heart. I asked a security person one time how we can help the homeless besides giving them money for food and clothes. The security person said there are shelters and housing available for them, but they refuse them because they do not like to follow rules or take responsibility for their own behavior. They choose to live in misery, even with unmet basic needs. The same thing happens with people who run away from the Word of God. Their spiritual needs remain unmet and their spiritual life is miserable. But spiritual irresponsibility and unbelief do not change who God is, or the truth of His Word.

Bitterness, Discouragement and Your Limbic System

"The LORD is close to the brokenhearted and saves those who are crushed in spirit." (Ps. 34:18)

"He heals the brokenhearted and binds up their wounds." (Ps. 147:3)

What goes on in your brain affects your whole body and your wellbeing. That is why it is essential to feed your brain with healthy thoughts that bring joy and peace. The devil's goal is to steal, kill, and destroy, and he knows that if your brain is fed with healthy thoughts he cannot destroy your body. Satan tries to bring bitter and unhealthy thoughts to destroy you emotionally and physically. Harmful emotions like fear, anger, and bitterness are processed in the limbic system. This causes a cascade of unhealthy amounts of neurochemicals to be released, poisoning every cell in your body—enough to alter your gene expression, damage your DNA, and change your personality.

All those negative feelings and their consequences can be prevented by healthy thoughts and healthy emotions, through prayer and meditating on the Word of God. Prayer and meditation prevent fear and worry, increase peace, calm your brain, keep you healthy, increase your mental function, help you solve conflicts, improve your relationships, and help with forgiveness, so you can be more optimistic and live a happier, healthier, longer life. Prayer and meditation alleviate anxiety and bitterness, dissipate anger, dissolve feelings of depression, reduce blood pressure and blood sugar, reduce pain, improve your immunity, and increase your positive outlook on life.

Discouragement and bitterness will go away if you pray. Our Lord Jesus Christ, in the Garden of Gethsemane, was brokenhearted and filled with sorrow. He prayed to the Father, and after He prayed He accepted the will of God in His life to die on the cross for the sins of the world, to save humanity from eternal punishment. His inner fleshly man was bitter and discouraged that He had to endure the cross, but His spiritual man wanted to die for the sins of the world, to save us as His heritage for eternity. The Father strengthened Him to accomplish that.

Run to God when you are discouraged. Find rest in God. God is involved in your life when you are discouraged. His love for you is the same everywhere, and in every situation He loves you. Tell Him about your situation, your fear and worry, talk to Him, and stay in His presence. He is the only One who can help you when you are in distress, because only "The Lord is close to the brokenhearted and saves those who are crushed in spirit" (Ps. 34:18). I am writing from my own experience. I felt the healing power of God during my brokenness, bitterness and discouragement in the most difficult time of my life.

Wrong Conclusions Bring Discouragement

"My clan is the weakest in Manasseh, and I am the least in my family."
(Judg. 6:15)

"I am the only one left, and now they are trying to kill me too."
(1 Kings 19:11)

The devil brings wrong thinking, wrong accusations, wrong conclusions, and wrong comparisons, which are activated when you are discouraged.

Inactivity brings even more discouragement and destruction. Brain cells die from inactivity. When you are discouraged and worried, get busy and get involved in constructive activities. That will build you up. You need to go to work and be active. Distract yourself from thoughts of bitterness and discouragement with healthy activities, and God will give you new ways to overcome your difficulties. You are in the center of His attention. God is interested in each one of us.

In the Old Testament when Gideon was approached by an angel of the Lord with a divine plan, he complained, "My clan is the weakest in Manasseh, and I am the least in my family" (Judg. 6:15). Gideon was the least in his own eyes, very discouraged and bitter in his soul, but the Angel of the Lord came to reveal to Gideon who he was in God's eyes, and what God could do through Him. God lifted Gideon from insignificance and gave him courage and hope for his future. He can do that with you, too. You have more value in God's eyes than in your own eyes. Gideon was comparing himself with people around him. He thought, I am not better than my parents. Do not compare yourself with others. Competition has consequences. Be who God made you to be with purpose in life. The one true God is calling us to leave behind discouragement and bitterness and move forward to a life of prayer, to repent, and to desire to know Him more and reach new spiritual dimensions.

Another example is Elijah, who was very discouraged. He lamented, "I am the only one left, and now they are trying to kill me, too" (1 Kings 19:11). He was wrong. He felt so lonely, afraid, anxious and depressed, but God told Elijah that He had reserved seven thousand in Israel, and that Elisha would take his place. God does not want you to isolate yourself. Loneliness can lead to bitterness and destruction. You must pray like Jesus did when he was left alone in Gethsemane and all His disciples had left Him in the hands of the enemy. The Bible tells us that God sends His angels to keep company with lonely people and strengthen them. He sends His angels for you, too, even as you are reading right now.

When you feel alone, remember that an angel is beside you at all times to strengthen you. One of my friends said, "God is always with me, and He keeps me company every moment to comfort me when I am discouraged." Find rest in God, like Elijah under the juniper, and talk to God when you are alone. When you talk to God your faith will increase, creating a shift from discouragement to hope and encouragement. Healthy thinking will release the right neurotransmitters, preventing illness in your body. We were created to talk. Talk with God, and the right persons around, you who will know how to encourage you. God will send an angel to strengthen you, like He did for

Jesus after His 40 days of fasting. He will encourage you, just like He sent angels for Gideon and Elijah when they were at their lowest moments.

I was extremely discouraged and at a very low point in my life while waiting for my daughter and my husband to get visas and come to the US, after a few years of struggles. The Lord knew my brokenness and sent an angel in my dream, showing me that my family would come soon. My discouragement and bitter thoughts scattered immediately. In a few months my husband and my daughter received visas from the embassy to travel to the US. God knows the details and feelings of brokenness deep in your heart, and He will replace them when you stay firm in your faith and trust in His promises.

Sin Creates Stress

"...for our struggle is not against flesh and blood, but against the rulers, against the authorities, against the powers of this dark world and against the spiritual forces of evil in the Heavenly realms." (Eph. 6:12)

Sin destroys your soul, your emotions, your life, and those around you. It will bring fruits of its own kind. "They sow the wind and reap the whirlwind" (Hosea 8:7). Yes, sin activates a destructive cascade of unhealthy neurochemicals in the brain, ultimately weakening us. But repentance cleans our brain's structures from bad memories, which result from the emotional distress of all the garbage from years of unbelief and sin.

Sin Brings Discouragement

"The heart is deceitful above all things and beyond cure. Who can understand it?" (Jer. 17:9)

When we focus on harmful thoughts rather than the power of God, we end up discouraged and depressed. You can read discouragement on people's faces. They know deep in their heart when they have done something wrong. The voice in our spirit will whisper to our mind. It is the Spirit of God's role in our brain to make us vigilant when an evil thought crosses our mind, and to help us inhibit bad actions. If we have sinned, we can cry out in prayer and ask forgiveness, and God will answer and provide a pathway to our restoration. His forgiveness brings us joy, peace and hope, and welcomes us back to God's kingdom.

Sin originates in the hearts of people. "The heart is deceitful above all things and beyond cure. Who can understand it?" (Jer. 17:9). We can see proof all around us that the heart is deceitful. Only through the love of Jesus can the heart be changed.

Follow God's prescriptions and maintain a good relationship with God Almighty, who is Love. Love always makes a difference, and is a key ingredient in our relationship with Jesus. Being born again, you love the Lord and you cannot get enough of Him. Spend time in His presence and He will saturate your soul. Be ready to answer God's call in your life, cheerfully obey Him, and have faith that you are created to do good work, activated and multiplied by the Spirit of God. You are saved by grace.

Guilt and Shame

"The wages of sin is death." (Rom. 6:23)

Sin makes people feel ashamed, withdraw from social activities, and become lonely and depressed in a vicious cycle. The Super Intelligent Designer of the Universe did not create us to bear emotional distress from guilt and shame (originating from sin in our soul and/or our body). Identify the sin in your life, confess it in your prayers to God, and let your requests be known to Him. Run from sin, because "The wages of sin is death" (Rom. 6:23).

People always ask why bad things happen to good people. It is a cause and effect. The cause is sin, and the effect is that bad things happen. The effect of sin continues from generation to generation. Our Father God's desire is that all people will come to repentance, so none will perish, but have eternal life (John 3:16). Sin is forgiven, but the consequences of original sin still remain. Humans must die because of the sin committed in the Garden of Eden by the first human beings, Adam and Eve. They disobeyed God's prescriptions and did what was specifically forbidden. Through the sin of disobedience, death entered into God's creation. Sin results in death, but the antidote for sin is the blood of Jesus. It is very important for every human being to confess their sin and be cleansed by the blood of Jesus. Search your heart, turn from evil, and let your spirit, soul and body be healed.

The sin virus enters the spirit just as viruses enter computers, or our human body, causing signs and symptoms in the spirit that can be recognized in our life as bad emotions, unhappiness, depression, bitterness, ungratefulness, ignorance, negligence, loneliness, anxiety, agitation, anger, resentment, chronic fatigue, and weakness. Strengthen your spiritual immunity and prevent the "sin virus" from contaminating your soul. Do not allow anything from the world to contaminate you or keep you from reaching your full potential. God gave you a glorious destiny. He pours out

His "blessings that we cannot contain," as written in His Word, when you follow His prescription for repentance and live in obedience to His Word. By knowing the Word of God and living accordingly, you become a new person with a changed mind and a new way of thinking (Rom. 12:2). You will discover God's will, and His perfect plan for your life, when you meditate on His Word.

When you sin against God, you sin against people too. Be careful—your gestures and words can hurt. Distance between us and the Word of God also creates distance in families, between spouses and between parents and children. When you get closer to the Word of God, you get closer to your family and your loved ones. We must turn away from sin through repentance. "Repent and be baptized, every one of you, in the name of Jesus Christ for the forgiveness of your sins" (Acts 2:38).

Desire for the Supernatural

" Then Manoah intreated the LORD, and said, O my Lord, let the man
of God which thou didst send come again unto us, and teach us what
we shall do unto the child that shall be born. And God hearkened to the
voice of Manoah; and the angel of God came again unto the woman as
she sat in the field: but Manoah her husband was not with her."
(Judg. 13:8–9)

God put the desire for the supernatural in humans at creation. For that reason we are not satisfied with who we are, what we are, and what we have. Our desire for the supernatural was hijacked in the Garden of Eden by satan, who put evil thoughts in the mind of man, to pervert that desire for a Supernatural God into a desire for worldly satisfactions. That is why God gave us His Word to teach us, direct us and keep us focused on Him. Only God can fulfill our heart's desires.

God puts eternal thoughts and a desire for the supernatural in our minds (Eccles. 3:16). My friend Lea (a doctor I will call Lea for privacy) decided to receive Jesus. She was born again, and the Word of God began to work in her heart, giving her eternal hope on her dying bed. The Word of God was speaking to her soul, giving her confidence, reassurance, and hope for eternal life. She was a scientist, but when the news came about her deadly disease she needed an answer from God, and she was comforted by His supernatural prescriptions, beyond science.

She knew she could not lean on her own understanding, but the Bible answers the mysteries of life. Her spiritual eyes were opened. She started to follow God's prescriptions for eternal life when all the medical prescriptions failed her. She started to see the world around her in a totally different way. She felt so sorry for people who didn't know Christ and the Word of God, and regretted wasting so many years ignoring God and living an atheistic, worldly life with no meaning. The Word of God had the power to change her story and her spiritual resumé after she accepted Jesus as her own Savior. Her passing was peaceful, with new hope in God, who saved her soul. She passed away with confidence in her eternity.

Spiritual Needs

In my profession I care for dying people and I witness their last d able to breath esire to hear the Word of God. It speaks to the soul even during the dying process. My friend Dr. Lea wanted to have a Bible study in her home every day before her death. I saw people coming night after night to her house, and I thought it was too tiring for her. I intended to stop them to protect her from being too tired in her last days. When I asked her how she felt about cancelling the meetings, to my surprise she said, "This Bible study is the only thing that sustains me every day."

She had been an atheist, and didn't believe in God or own a Bible until she was 43 years old. When she was diagnosed with an incurable disease, she started looking for spiritual reassurance, knowing her life on earth would soon end, and not knowing where she would go from this planet. She was a physician—a specialist caring for many patients—and she knew what was happening in her physical body, now invaded with cancerous cells. Her whole being was shaken and she started to think seriously about the purpose of life on earth, and her destiny. She knew that there is life after death, and her spiritual needs were so obvious. As a medical professional she knew that physiologically her cells had started an abnormal proliferation process, dividing uncontrollably and metastasizing in her vital organs, shutting them down and causing multiple organ failures. Science was helpless, and she was hopeless during her dying process. She knew her life was coming to an end, but her soul was eternal, and she needed to feed her soul with spiritual food.

Broken Heart Syndrome

"The human spirit can endure in sickness, but a crushed spirit who can bear?" (Prov. 18:14)

Psychological trauma including death of a loved one, divorce, children on drugs, abuse, catastrophic loss, and unbearable stress cause excess catecholamine (adrenaline) to be released in the muscles of the apex of the heart, causing a heart attack in many cases.[16] In medicine it is called the "broken heart syndrome" and is similar to emotional brokenness. God may allow you to enter a place of brokenness so you will have compassion for others who have a broken heart, but it is not His will to crush your spirit.

All kinds of physical and emotional diseases are caused by brokenness. A crushed spirit is harder to bear than a physical sickness, as was written over 3,500 years ago. "The human spirit can endure in sickness, but a crushed spirit who can bear?" (Prov. 18:14). Medicine has no cure or answer for a crushed spirit. Educate your soul to let go of everything you cannot control and keep praising God even in hard times. He will bring healing and hope to your soul supernaturally.

Educate yourself with the promises of God, through His powerful Word. Know that the Word has healing power to penetrate your heart, to transform you and to bring deliverance from all "the noise and bondage" of the world. Quiet your soul by shutting down secular music, the internet, Facebook, Instagram, Twitter, TV, iPod, iPhone, etc. There is no healing in those atmospheres full of distressing news and distracting information. Comfort your spirit by trusting in the Lord, who can bring healing, salvation and deliverance. Hope in God's promises, for His Word is the anchor of your soul. You cannot be shaken when you put all your worry, fear, anxiety, and depression in His hands and rest in Him.

God restores your soul. He knows your situation, and He knows you by name. He shows up to give you victory. He is the Creator of Heaven and earth, and nothing is too hard for Him. "I am the LORD, the God of all mankind. Is anything too hard for me?" (Jer. 32:27). Through the Word, God can perform spiritual surgery in our brain and heart and bring back to life what was poisoned (Heb. 4:12). The Word continues to transform lives, even today. For spiritual health and fruits of the Spirit we need spiritual surgery by the Word of God, and "neuroplasticity of the brain" from a transformed mind.

CHAPTER FIVE

Pain

"The night racks my bones, and the pain that gnaws me takes no rest." (Job 30:17 ESV)

"Why is my pain unceasing, my wound incurable, refusing to be healed? Will you be to me like a deceitful brook, like waters that fail?" (Jer. 15:18 ESV)

"Man is also rebuked with pain on his bed and with continual strife in his bones..." (Job 33:19 ESV)

Pain in any form increases our stress level. Science has advanced so much and developed myriads of pain medications, methods and techniques that are used for acute and chronic pain management, especially at the end of life. I know this for a fact since I have taken care of dying people with multiple chronic conditions since 1990. I joke sometimes with people and tell them that I could have a "mega church" by now, with how many people passed in my years of caring at the bedsides of dying people.

But with all the pain killers developed lately, we still do not know how much physical and emotional or spiritual pain a person has when he or she is passing on from this life, even with all our interventions and advanced technologies. In the US alone, over 4,000,000,000 prescriptions were written in 2015 for pain.[1] Seeking relief, people crave more and more pain medication, while ignoring the side effects, and mortality is rising. Young children and teens are especially vulnerable to addiction to narcotics. Even prescription drugs cause addiction, opening the door for illicit drug addictions in huge proportions. Their immature systems metabolize codeine and morphine more quickly, and they easily become over sedated.

Our Creator designed pain modulators in our nervous system, and receptors for natural chemicals, including endorphins to decrease pain—the same effect on pain as synthetic morphine. Fear of pain causes yet more stress. The pain threshold then decreases and even a little pain is felt and perceived as "lots" of pain, leading to overuse of medication.

Scientists do research, trying to discover how much pain a person can endure and what kind of medication will be needed to control that pain to provide maximum comfort, but usually conclude that "more research is needed." People continue to be afraid of pain and stress themselves, thinking nobody will be able to control their pain. In America it is estimated that about 100 million suffer from chronic pain, costing Americans about 600 billion dollars each year.[2] Pain results in so much suffering, including fear, anger, guilt, loneliness, helplessness, catastrophizing, limited coping skills, passive thinking, negative emotions, suffering, and more.

In children, perception of pain is a combination of genetic predisposition with environmental influence such as poor parental support, stress, sexual abuse and early substance abuse. All of these lead to opioid seeking and craving. This gives euphoria and anhedonia as a reward, but also results in dependency, withdrawal symptoms and depression when drugs are not available—repeating the vicious cycle. Both illicit and chronically used prescription drugs destroy neurons in the brain, disabling them in time. [3]

From Panic to Joy

"He will wipe away every tear from their eyes, and death shall be
no more, neither shall there be mourning, nor crying, nor pain anymore,
for the former things have passed away." (Rev. 21:4 ESV)

Children suffer complex changes with development, as changing hormones play a huge role in their temperament. If they experience fear they react with fear, which can become chronic, causing chronic post-puberty pain. This can lead to depression and constant doctor shopping. One young girl came to my office after many doctors and multiple visits to Emergency Rooms. She had been treated with many medications for different symptoms and was still afraid and unable to stay in her classroom at school. She was not able to function normally at home or in society, due to her signs and symptoms of severe panic attacks. After a close examination I advised her to join a group of young teens at her parents' church. But she was afraid that she would "not be able to breathe" and other people would notice and she would be embarrassed. After many attempts and long discussions, she was able to attend that group and made some very good friends. Now she enjoys a normal adolescent life, involved in her church activities and even an athletic club. I meet her in the community at the gym and other events, and she is a completely different person—happy, joyful, and full of energy and motivation.

Chronic pain in adolescents is often due to stress and anxiety. A. from fear and stress is debilitating for the younger generation. M adolescents present to the clinic reporting debilitating headaches, abdominal pain, excessive worry about their health, and imagining that they have a horrible illness such as cancer. Or sometimes they worry about not performing well in school, about their parents' financial situation, frequent sleep disturbances, or lack of ability to succeed, etc. I believe that God is still in the business of managing people's pain, helping them manage their stress effectively, and comforting those who believe His Word and its supernatural prescriptions.

The Natural Analgesic

Emotional pain from stress causes people to experience more physical pain in their body. Anxiety from fear, anger, and bitterness, and frustration from every day worry will cause one's brain to release chemicals that tighten the muscles, creating more pain through an inflammatory process. In response, the brain will release a natural chemical from its own natural pharmacy—endorphin, the endogenous morphine—a natural human analgesic, built into our body by the Super Intelligent Designer to control the stimuli of pain. God built sensory neurons into our brain structures, in peripheral pathways, to protect us from damage when accidents occur.

Even professionals will often say that the pain "is in your mind." That is a valid comment, in a sense, because the brain interprets the severity of the pain and governs the response to those feelings of pain in our body. People can use medications for pain (acetaminophen, ibuprofen, Aleve, Advil and other over-the-counter medications, or prescribed narcotics), but using these for more than two weeks at a time and not carefully following the physician's instructions and the indications on the packages can cause more damage to the body. Hepatotoxicity, kidney failure, and dependency and addiction can cause severe consequences.

Supernatural Pain Modulator

Scientists have discovered that Anandamide is a natural, marijuana-like lipid derivative produced in the human body that provides pain relief. As an endocannabinoid, it binds and activates G protein–coupled cannabinoid receptors (CB) as well as several other targets, both within the plasma membrane and intracellularly"[4] It was also discovered that

> Endorphins are natural pain killing substances found in the human brain. The name comes from endogenous (meaning within) and

morphine (morphine being a pain killer). Endorphins are one of the neurotransmitters in the brain that is released to calm an overacting brain and to help people 'feel good" healing emotional pain. Levels of endorphins in the brain may be changed by taking a number of drugs including alcohol, anabolic steroids and heroin and other opiates."[5]

As science has proven, our Super Intelligent Designer built pain modulators, natural analgesics, into our system, while giving us instructions to pray and meditate on His laws, plus instructions for coping with pain. It is well documented in literature that meditation alters the neural circuits in the brain and reduces chronic pain.[6] Meditating, by focusing on God's promises, will improve our mood, bringing hope, joy, peace and happiness. The natural analgesics, such as endorphins, and other natural chemicals released by the brain's "natural organic factory" also help with healing.

The biggest promise we have is that "by His stripes we were healed." The reassurance from God's supernatural promises brings us so much hope. This hope causes more joy, creating the atmosphere in the brain to release more natural analgesics, endorphin and norepinephrine, regulating the pain. It also will change the atmosphere in the amygdala and other structures in the limbic system associated with memories, emotional pain and mood.

Besides all these natural processes there is a supernatural resource that can be activated by our faith in Jesus' healing power by the Holy Spirit. He is the same yesterday, today and forever. He supernaturally healed in the past and will do it again in the present and in the future. Our hope is in Him, and we do not lose hope in His Supernatural power to heal the sick.

Pain as God's Instrument

"No discipline seems pleasant at the time, but painful. Later on, however, it produces a harvest of righteousness and peace for those who have been trained by it." (Heb. 12:11)

Beth Moore, in her book *Jesus: the One and Only* wrote,

Eternal purpose is the central issue involved in whether or not God heals a believing (see Matt. 9:28) and requesting (see James 4:2) Christian's physical illness. Although I don't pretend to understand how and why, some illnesses may serve a more eternal purpose than healing, while other healings serve more purpose than illness. I cannot imagine what purpose some illness and premature deaths serve, but, after years of loving and seeking my God, I trust who He is even when I have no idea what He is doing. Above all things, I believe God always has a purpose in every decision He makes...developing the mind-set of one who is continually taking up his cross and following Christ is the heart of having "in mind the things of God" (Matt. 16:23) rather than man.[7]

That is the prescription to live daily a victorious life. People who put their mind on understanding God's heart soon realize that God's love is endless, and His last Word is for our benefit.

Do Not Lose Heart in Pain

"...after Job had prayed for his friends, the LORD restored his fortunes and gave him twice as much as he had before." (Job 42:10)

Your pain can be used to glorify God. Do not look back when life hurts the most, but set your eyes on Jesus and eternal life. Jesus' heart was touched by people with diseases, disabilities, infirmities, hunger and loneliness. He went to the cross to endure extraordinary pain, in order to free the human race from all of them. Jesus, as a human on earth, had perfect mirror neurons when with supernatural compassion He felt the weight of a sinful world. It drove Him to the cross to be crucified, and to deliver us from our iniquities.

We read in the Old Testament that after Job lost everything in his troubled time, God restored everything he had lost by double. We read, "...after Job had prayed for his friends, the LORD restored his fortunes and gave him twice as much as he had before." (Job 42:10). He blessed the LORD even in the most painful situation. Pain is God's instrument to shape us into a shining diamond, because He loves us. Do not lose heart when you go through extreme pain or trials. When God is disciplining you He pours out His great love, and you become stronger.

There is a point when you turn your heart to God, when the pain causes a cry from the bottom of your heart. We read in the book of Mark, chapter 10 verse 47, that Bartimaeus was crying out loud, "Jesus, Son of David, have mercy on me" (Mark 10:46). If Bartimaeus wasn't blind, or his blindness did not matter to him, or did not bother him enough, he would not have cried out so loudly for mercy. God used Bartimaeus' blindness for His glory. Millions, even billions of people can read his story today and cry out for their own physical needs, and for their spiritual blindness to be healed.

Getting Our Attention for Heaven

You might think you can have great thoughts and be transformed in your thinking, finding contentment, peace, joy, and happiness only during good times. People ask: If God is so good, why does He not spare His children from suffering? Disaster, trouble, disease and suffering are common to all people on earth. God allows those conditions to get our attention to prepare us for eternal life. During suffering He makes you feel His love. His peace will come into your heart and open your spiritual eyes. Your positive attitude and reaction to suffering will bring you victory and spiritual health.

Any parent with a disabled child has for that child a unique, extraordinary love and compassion. Any discipline is very difficult, but God has a divine plan to shape you. Your final spiritual shape implies physical and emotional suffering. Physical and emotional discipline is painful. Any person on earth knows about pain. Pain is universal. This is a mystery and God uses suffering and pain to grab our attention for Heaven. He wants us for eternity. We are here only temporarily. No one living on earth now will be here 120 years from now. Eternity matters.

Grace to Endure Pain

"A woman in that town who lived a sinful life learned that Jesus was eating at the Pharisee's house, so she came there with an alabaster jar of perfume. As she stood behind Him at His feet weeping, she began to wet His feet with her tears. Then she wiped them with her hair, kissed them and poured perfume on them." (Luke 7:37–38)

God's grace blesses everyone who comes into His presence with their broken heart, to worship. Worshiping will bring you into the presence of the Almighty and bring healing to your soul. Many fell at His feet and worshiped and were delivered from their inner pain. Brokenness brings you on your knees to a place of worship. The book of Luke depicts the story of Mary Magdalene, who needed to break her alabaster jar before the perfume could flow on Jesus' feet. We read:

> A woman in that town who lived a sinful life learned that Jesus was eating at the Pharisee's house, so she came there with an alabaster jar of perfume. As she stood behind Him at His feet weeping, she began to wet His feet with her tears. Then she wiped them with her hair, kissed them and poured perfume on them. (Luke 7:37–38)

Mary Magdalena's heart was heavy from the weight of her sins, but her broken heart brought her to a place of weeping (the "good cry" that brings healing), worshiping, and breaking the jar of perfume.[8] Brokenness is needed before the fragrance of anointing for worship flows. In 2 Samuel, chapter six, David's heart grieved when the Ark of the Covenant was gone. When he saw that the Ark of the Covenant was coming back he started to worship with all the assembly and was dancing with his whole his heart, rejoicing in knowing that the anointing of God was coming back. He knew what it meant to be in God's Presence, and he also knew the anguish and pain from being away from God. God's Presence brings healing.

Worshiping brings you intimacy with God, and by His grace you can endure the pain. People who worship will prevail, because the anointing heals our pain during our worship time. Paul declared that the anointing is sufficient, because grace was sufficient in his life and gave him the power to endure pain. Jesus took all our pain and suffering because the anointing of the Spirit of God was upon Him. He was wounded for our transgressions (Isa. 53). On the cross He conquered our sickness, disease and pain because He was anointed by God's Spirit. Jesus experienced the "broken heart syndrome" with all its signs and symptoms, in order to heal our broken hearts. By His stripes we were healed. This is the anointing to take the pain away and to heal the sick. The anointing of the Holy Spirit still heals. The spirit of anointing and passion enables us to do our ministry work and ignites a fire inside us to endure the pain (Matt. 3:11; 12:49).

The Holy Spirit gave the disciples boldness, power, zeal and passion to speak in the name of Jesus and to heal the sick in His name. The Holy Spirit is working miracles in your life today to heal your brokenness and pain. The Spirit of the Lord makes the difference in your life. You need a holy fire to impassion you to do the services of God. There is a fresh outpouring of the anointing oil in you, and in people around you, when the holy fire comes upon you. The fragrance in the perfume comes from crushed, bruised leaves. You must bring the fragrance of the anointing to other people's lives after your own soul experiences healing. This is how you help others find peace and grace to endure their pain.

In our facility I have often heard from patients' families and health care professionals who visit our patients, saying, "This is such a peaceful place. We feel something different that quiets the soul." Now in our facility we have 30 residents (patients) with Alzheimer's and dementia. Their severely challenging behaviors are difficult to manage. Many facilities in our city and state will not accept them because of their frequent behavioral disturbances. It is the anointing and the grace of God that takes the feeling of pain, anxiety and depression away, and people feel the peace of God.

This is beyond science. The miraculous anointing, that quiets the soul of these precious people we care for in their most difficult time, is rejected by many. Specialists have tried many potent treatments with minimal results. Our staff and caregivers notice the changes within a few days after the patients move in. Others from the outside, including health care professionals, often throw their hands in the air, feeling helpless and running out of solutions for these people suffering from aggressiveness and neurocognitive disorders. But in our facility they find the peace and grace to endure their pain, because of God's anointing.

"We are to God the pleasing aroma of Christ among those who are being saved and those who are perishing." (2 Cor. 2:15)

You must have the right response and right attitude to surrender to God for the anointing to work. The anointed ones, the followers of Christ, must respond in the right way and radiate the anointing to be the fragrance of Christ.

The more the apostles were persecuted, the more they spread the fragrance of Christ and the churches multiplied, because of the fragrance of the anointing after their brokenness. When I was threatened by communist persecution in Romania I shared the gospel more with my friends and people around me, and I was continually seeking God's presence in prayer and fasting. In the midst of your pain you must spread the fragrance. Through pain God creates your destiny. Sometimes through your pain your destiny is born, as Shaneen Clarke, author of *Dare to be Great*, states in her speeches around the world. You must show the world the appropriate way to serve God, even in painful situations. The world needs what you have—the hand of God in your life. The world is in terrible pain and turmoil and needs solutions, because medication alone cannot cure the world's pain. The Holy Spirit is alive in you, and you are anointed to endure the pain, and to serve by comforting and helping others in their painful time. You fulfill your destiny when you serve others, and by grace you endure a temporary pain.

Spiritually, pain and fear of death will make you pray more establishing your relationship with God, the highest power in Universe. You are not the only one to benefit from praying more but all around you and the society as a whole. You must activate the gift you have inside you to be willing to choose to look for meaning in troubles and pain and use those troubling situations for healthy, positive and constructive ways.

Dependent on God

"…who comforts us in all our troubles, so that we can comfort those in any trouble with the comfort we ourselves receive from God." (2 Cor. 1:4)

Fear of failure comes from a lack of confidence, due to our weaknesses. Our weaknesses help us develop a dependence on God and a humility before Him. We read in the book of Isaiah chapter 14 that Lucifer chose to be independent because of a lack of humility, and because of his pride he forever lost his place in Heaven. Billy Graham, in his book *The Journey— How to Live by Faith in an Uncertain World* stated, "Isaiah's portrait of Lucifer describes satan's arrogance and rebellion: "How you have fallen from Heaven, O morning star, son of the dawn!...You said in your heart, 'I will ascend to Heaven; I will raise my throne above the stars of God...I will make myself like the Most High'" (Isa. 14:12–14).[9] From this passage we know that satan in his pride will do anything to destroy God's people on earth. God gives grace to humble people in their weakness. In weakness we choose humility and obedience over pride, and we find victory over fear of failure.

All the characters in the Bible teach us dependency on the power of God and increase our faith. We just need to be hungry for knowledge and revelation from the Word of God, from stories of people who lived on earth before us and experienced God's supernatural power in their journey to Heaven. Life is a journey and we must keep notes of the events in our personal journey. God is moving through our weaknesses and is working in our heart, perfecting His power. Fear is not from God, because He did not give us a spirit of fear. The power of God is made perfect in weakness. He is a God of compassion and of all comfort, and He is the One "...who comforts us in all our troubles, so that we can comfort those in any trouble with the comfort we ourselves receive from God" (2 Cor. 1:4). The confidence we get when we are comforted in our trouble will increase confidence and faith in God in those around us.

Burnout

When you feel burned out and extremely weak, accept your imperfection and proactively face your uncertainties, limitations and mistakes. Stay current, build your skills and learn something new. Focus on the positive aspects of life, be flexible, and set professional boundaries. Consider what is essential. What are your talents, and what are you passionate about? Eliminate old activities before adding new ones, and decide what you would sacrifice for a new opportunity. Strengthen key relationships, prioritize your family and friends who are important, clear your calendar, and make a Do Not Do List. In your profession and business you must focus on positive relationships and rewards. And always remember that you have values.

Redirect your mind with meditation and spirituality, reflecting on good results, setting boundaries, and promoting a work balance. Pastor Larry Huch, in his book *Free at Last—Removing the Past from Your Future*, states that "Jesus has anointed us with the burden-removing, yoke-destroying power of God to heal the brokenhearted. Why the brokenhearted? Because

God desires for His people to live in joy. When we are filled with joy, we have the strength to fight the good fight of faith."[10] Your life has meaning, and you can live a life free of anger, insecurity, abuse, addiction and depression through Jesus Christ. Fill your heart with joy, because the joy of the Lord is your strength (Neh. 8:10). Joy is the opposite of depression, with all its signs and symptoms caused by unhealthy neurochemicals. All our physical and emotional damage is repaired through joy, which further prevents the stress level from increasing, causing less of the "stress hormone" cortisol in the body, and thus fewer neurons die in your brain.

Life Without Dreams

People often live without a dream, focusing more on harmful things than on the power of God. You can read discouragement on the faces of people who have no vision for the future. This is how medical professionals assess the pain level in those with neurocognitive disorders and dementia. We use a chart with sad faces, because those patients cannot express themselves verbally. The idea is to read the severity of pain, discomfort, distress and discouragement on people's faces, and to prescribe the right treatment. Discouragement leads to depression.

Discouragement brings bitterness, sadness, and discontent. After times of great success, when your excitement slows down, when you are facing the enemy of your soul and the scene changes, discouragement appears. In the book of First Kings, chapter 18, we read about Elijah on Mount Carmel. After his great success, when his life was threatened by his enemies, discouragement overcame him.

In his discouragement, Elijah did not call upon on the name of the Lord. While filled with wrong thoughts and discouragement, he desired to die. It is hard to believe that the great man of God, Elijah—one of the boldest prophets, who was anointed to perform staggering and stupendous miracles through the power of the Holy Spirit—became suicidally discouraged. He was the one whose prayers (1 Kings 17:1; James 5:17) brought drought and no rain on the earth for three and a half years! Another time, oil and meal were multiplied in the widow's house (1 Kings 17:14), and a widow's child was raised from the dead and restored back to life (1 Kings 17:22)! Even more astounding, through Elijah's prayers, sacrifices in a huge trench were consumed by fire on Mt. Carmel (1 Kings 18:38); men and captains were slain by fire at his word (2 Kings 1:10); clouds and rain came after three and a half years (1 Kings 18:41); and his mantle divided the waters of the Jordan River (2 Kings 2:8).

Elijah thought and "dreamed" that his enemy Ahab would be changed after the victory on Mt. Carmel, but he needed to change his thinking. A wrong dream will bring discouragement and bitterness. To avoid the emotional pain of disappointment and bitterness you must change your perspective and get visions and dreams from God's promises. Changes come when you humble yourself, seek the Lord's face, and call upon His name. The Lord is in control. God knows your heart, your feelings, your thoughts, your emotions, and your struggles. The One who gives dreams and visions is looking for a heart that is completely loyal to Him. He is the Potter, and we are the clay—not the other way around.

Finances and Stress

"Remember this: whoever sows sparingly will also reap sparingly, and whoever sows generously will also reap generously." (2 Cor. 9:6–8)

"Ship your grain across the sea; after many days you may receive a return." (Eccles. 11:1)

People facing serious financial stress suffer worry, fear and anxiety, with adverse physical and emotional effects. Medication will not always work for those conditions, because psychosocial and emotional distress disrupts neurotransmitters. Your finances will improve when you follow God's prescription (supernatural law) of sowing and reaping. You reap what you sow. (See Luke 6:38). God is generous and good, according to Matthew 6:25–33. God loves and also rewards you when you give cheerfully. "Remember this: whoever sows sparingly will also reap sparingly, and whoever sows generously will also reap generously" (2 Cor. 9:6–8).

Be a cheerful, generous giver and invest in charity. Charity yields high returns in God's economy. "Ship your grain across the sea; after many days you may receive a return" (Eccles. 11:1). When you give with joy, your brain cells are restored, repaired, renewed, and healed. You are able to produce more with a healthy body and mind. True wealth in your internal soul is eternal through God's grace. "For it is by grace you have been saved, through faith—and this is not from yourselves; it is the gift of God" (Eph. 2: 8). When you are tired, you are vulnerable and make bad decisions and mistakes in business or family life, affecting your relationships and your finances. Lack of finances will bring more stress, anxiety, worry, bitterness and anger in your soul, provoking you to think and speak inappropriate words.

You must watch your language during times of financial stress, so as not to bring more curses over your financial resources. We know that abundant life and lack of resources (death) are in the power of your tongue. "The tongue has the power of life and death, and those who love it will eat its fruit" (Prov. 18: 21). What you say is important, because words have the creative power to activate invisible thoughts in your brain. Words represent things. They put an image in your mind that will become visible when you act upon it. Words define your future.

Do not ignore the promises of God about finances and health. When the Word of God abides in you, then you know what to ask according to the will of God and He will give you everything for His glory (John 15:7). When you receive answers to your prayers, you will be full of joy and glorify God more (John 16:23). Just believe when you ask (Matt. 21:22).

God's prescription is "...take delight in the LORD and He will give you the desires of your heart" (Ps. 37:4). Do what is pleasing in His sight, then everything you ask according to His will, you will receive (1 John 3:22). The devil is the culprit of all the evil things happening in the world financially. He puts the seed of fear, worry and discouragement into people's minds. We do not see thoughts, but they control our life. If we had no thoughts, life would be aimless and purposeless. God's love gives us power to control our thoughts about our finances. Align your thoughts and actions about finances with God's Word and let the peace of God flood your mind and heart.

Stress from Lack of Finances

"...for the love of money is the root of all kinds of evil. Some people, eager for money, have wandered from the faith and pierced themselves with many griefs." (1 Tim. 6:10)

"Whoever loves money never has enough; whoever loves wealth is never satisfied with their income." (Eccles. 5:10)

Wealth does not always make people happy. Many people think that wealth will bring true happiness, but many wealthy people are emotionally broken. "Whoever loves money never has enough; whoever loves wealth is never satisfied with their income" (Eccles. 5:10). Those who have lots of money will never have enough, and will never be satisfied. "For the love of money is the root of all kinds of evil. Some people, eager for money, have wandered from the faith and pierced themselves with many griefs" (1 Tim. 6:10). Money cannot fill an empty heart.

Financial insufficiency does cause a big burden, but there are ways to approach this most unwanted stress. Consider the root cause of financial stress. God's economy is the best economy in the universe. He is the CEO of the Universe and He established the laws of sowing and reaping. You get what you give, you reap what you sow; whatever you do, you are rewarded according to your deeds on earth and in eternity. It makes sense that if you give using your skills, talent, and knowledge with effort and passion, you will receive a reward. To receive you must give. We must be good stewards of our God-given abilities.

Many times we spend our finances on things that are not strictly necessary, and they will not satisfy our soul. There are financial guidelines in the Word of God. Enjoy the work of your hands. Do not forget that God gives you power to gain wealth—meaning your finances. God has always cared about our finances. More than 3,500 years ago Moses wrote the book of Deuteronomy. "For it is He who gives you the ability to produce wealth" (Deut. 8:18). The ingredients for maximum potency are contained in His prescriptions for you to prosper financially, physically and spiritually.

Decisions

"Now fear the LORD and serve Him with all faithfulness...
But as for me and my household, we will LORD." (Josh. 24:14–15)

Difficulty making the right decisions can add to your emotional distress. The anterior cingulate in the frontal lobe is associated with making rational decisions.[11] If you decide to spend time in the Word of God you will have immediate gratification. Rejoicing in the Lord, you can develop a *good addiction* to joy and peace. The healthy amounts of dopamine, serotonin and endorphins will give you strength and increase your ability to make the right decisions.

When you saturate your brain with the Word of God, all the decisions made in your anterior cingulate will be according to the will of God, and you will not be afraid of making the wrong decisions. The "inner voice" in your anterior cingulate will slow down dopamine release, restraining any addictive behavior, even to your own epinephrine from fear and anxiety. The battle is between the dopamine (the perceptions of immediate reward of "feeling good" during addictive behavior) and the anterior cingulate in the frontal lobe (rational reasoning and good decision making).[12]

Life is the sum of our decisions. The world is where it is today due to the sum of decisions made in the past—at the individual level, and at the national level. Blessed is the man who fears the Lord and follows His instruction when making decisions in life (Ps. 128:1). Do not jump to a personal decision without asking God for wisdom. Do not let others make decisions for you on what to eat, where and how long to sleep, how to use your time, how to use your body, how to dress, or how to behave, as that will lead to destruction.

Your decisions determine your quality of life. Choices you make affect your health, finances, family life—your future and your eternity. Make decisions with eternity in mind. Every moment you make decisions that can affect you and those around you in a healthy way. Physically and spiritually, you have two choices. Choose between good and bad, life and death. "Now fear the Lord and serve Him with all faithfulness…But as for me and my household, we will serve the LORD" (Josh. 24:14–15). Joshua's decision can be yours, too—an unexpired prescription for all of us, even today.

My life now is the result of decisions I made in the past. Like everyone else, I had to make decisions about school, marriage, career, family, business, finances, faith, prayer, and spending my time on useful things. My blessed present is the result of my well-informed decisions in the past, even since childhood, and my future will be determined by all decisions I make today. If you choose to serve the Lord, you choose life here on earth, leading to eternity. Follow the Lord with more passion and courage and trust in the Lord.

What is written *will happen*, as the Lord promised in His Word. Decide to serve the Lord continually, in all situations. He will reward your obedience. Life is full of unexpected events and deceptions. They might look good on the surface, but deeper inside they are full of "thorns". That can increase your stress and affect your health. You need help to make good decisions, and only God knows your tomorrow. Ask Him to help you make the right decisions today and He will. Making wise decisions is a gift, and to have to make a choice is a privilege (Gen 2:16–19). Many people are not able to make decisions or choices for their life.

Recently I had the privilege of speaking at a Women's Conference for mothers of children with disabilities, and to visit a few centers sponsored by Star of Hope in Romania. A few hundred children are brought by their parents for therapy to those centers. It is hard not to weep when you see how those children struggle to live without the ability to make decisions or choices for their life. You have the ability to choose what kind of stimuli from your five senses will trigger and dictate your thoughts, what kind of thoughts will enter and take residence in your brain, what kind of actions to take and how to behave. Do not abuse this gift with destructive choices that lead to death. Choices about your relationship with God, your career, whom you should marry, what friends and groups to hang out with, where to live, and how to spend your time can have an enormous impact on your life.

I had to decide whether to follow God's Word instead of the communist, atheistic teaching in Romania. They taught that there is no God—from first grade until I graduated from the Academy of Economic Studies in Bucharest. Communism led to the destruction of the whole country. Even now, 25 years after the revolution of 1989, I still see the results of that communist education when I visit Romania. People are still oppressed and living under the curse from when they denied God's existence. Their anger, anxiety, bitterness, and discontent have been transferred to the younger generation, through epigenetics (bad genes expression), as a generational curse. People are still affected by the teaching that "there is no God." The Word of God stated more than 3,500 years ago: "The fool says in his heart, 'There is no God.' They are corrupt, their deeds are vile" (Ps. 14:1).

I had to be careful about whom I would marry, so that we could live together to the end of our lives in obedience to the will of God, follow the Word of God, be blessed, and avoid stress from unwise decisions. Now 30 years later, we enjoy life together more than ever before, serving the Lord. We are so grateful for all the blessings we have received, beyond what we could ask or think from our Heavenly Father, according to His riches in glory. And together we are able to bless many others in our community and abroad. For me, it was very important to know that I was in the will of God, no matter the circumstances. You may wonder how to know the will of God for your life. Fear God, and desire His will for you with your whole heart. Then He will put an impression in your spirit, and you will know confidently, deep in your heart, what is the will of God for you. God's will and plan for your life is in His Word.

Where do your passions, skills and abilities converge? Ask God about everything you want to do, or where you want to go. Cling to Him and come close to Him. Transformation starts when you renew your mind and continue making wise decisions. It doesn't happen overnight, or automatically. The grace of God works according to our growth. Feed yourself with right information. Read the Bible every day, memorize and recite the Word. During high school I had to memorize and quote scriptures, especially from the New Testament, to keep my faith alive in difficult and challenging situations.

We must pray according to the will of God. Jesus prayed in Gethsemane, "Father if you are willing, take this cup from me; yet not my will, but yours be done" (Luke 22:42). In the Lord's Prayer we are taught to pray, "…Your will be done, on earth as it is in Heaven" (Matt. 6:10). God has the last word in your decisions. How you invest your resources and gifts affects what you receive in the future. Make the right choices for your life, serve selflessly, and ask Jesus to live in you.

People reflect their culture, but if you choose to embrace Christ's culture, having the same thinking as Christ, you will be blessed. Your faith in God should influence your daily decisions for all your problems. Jesus has your solutions. God shows favors to those who walk in obedience. Enjoy the favors of God as a result of wise decisions. I chose to serve the Lord Jesus, even when the communists were against me. For many years they humiliated and mocked me, putting pressure on me to give up my faith and threatening to revoke all my privileges for an education and a job. I did not give up, even though it was painful and hard. Now I reap a great harvest from those decisions. Your attitude toward God must be right at all times. He is watching over you every moment. Pay attention to who guides your decisions, and what kind of decision you make, to prevent unnecessary stress and unwanted consequences.

Depression from Compromise

Don't let society rob you of what is most important in life. Say no to compromise and say yes to the principles of God. Ignoring God's Word led Solomon to a compromised life, and he became depressed. Against God's advice he married a woman from a nation that worshipped many false gods. He knew he was compromising, and he paid for his mistakes with his life. He had many wives, worshiping many gods. He was flirting with compromise. At the end of Ecclesiastes 12 he says, "Remember your Creator." At the end, Solomon regrets all he has done. He said God will bring all deeds before the Judgment. Solomon started well, but departed from God and ended up with regrets and depression.

David also compromised when he committed adultery, inviting depression as a generational curse. David's sin multiplied and ended up cursing his children's lives. Four of them were at war their entire life and died prematurely, breaking David's heart. Sin brings curses that break hearts and stay in the family "to the fourth generation" if not detected and dealt with. Do your own assessment about sin in your life and take action to repent and obey the Word. God wants to give you supernatural rest when you are stressed and depressed. Start meditating on the Word of God to be healed from your depression.

When I hear people say, "My life is falling apart," "I am resigning from the human race," or, "I am at my wit's end," I know that depression is settling in. People get discouraged when dark uncertainty overwhelms them. They become disoriented and cannot think clearly. Disappointed, they lose their direction. They feel miserably distressed by all their troubles and feel lonely and lost (Lam. 3:19). Depression overtakes them, bringing more disease in body and spirit. Jesus promised rest for those who follow His prescriptions and refuse to compromise with sin (Matt. 11:28–30).

If you feel depressed, come to Jesus. He is the light, and you will be able to see where you are going (Ps. 119:105). He will lead you and guide you through your darkness and into light. If you follow Jesus you will never walk in the dark. Encourage yourself like David did when was depressed and surrounded by his enemies, and his life was falling apart. (Read 1 Samuel 30.) Know the Word of God and His promises, and you will be able to unload your burden. When you lose all your hope, the Lord is near you (Ps. 34:18). I challenge you to encourage yourself to prevent depression.

In my desperation and dark uncertainty I had to unload my burden at the feet of Jesus, calling out for His provisions for my life. When you trust the Lord He preserves you (Ps. 138:7). God's potent prescription to prevent physical and spiritual disorder is, "Do not let your heart be troubled and do not be afraid" (John 14:27). He is able to deliver you from all your fears, anxiety and depression when you bring your worry to His feet, at the cross, where He took your burden. "I sought the LORD, and he answered me; he delivered me from all my fears" (Ps. 34:4).

Emotional Pain

People sometimes minimize or disregard emotions when talking about our Creator. But God grieves with us. Allow your heart to be broken, because Jesus' heart was broken. Jesus Christ has emotions about our pain. It is the fellowship of Jesus' suffering for our sins, so we suffer in many situations. Jesus in Gethsemane entered the fellowship of His sufferings because of the joy that was before Him, to give us eternal salvation from eternal punishment.

Sometimes we reach a point of desperation, like when I was a teenager in Bucharest, without my family, and then again when I left Romania and arrived here in the US with nothing. Even though I entered the US legally, I had to wait six years to get my documents ready, so I could travel back to Romania to see the rest of my dear family. During this time one of my sisters died at a very young age, and I was not able to attend her funeral service. My heart was so broken that I developed the "broken heart syndrome" and felt bitterness deep in my soul. "My bones were drying" from the bitterness and emotional pain. I was depressed and unable to eat or to enjoy food. Then later, my father and my brother died within a six-month period. The events of life can crush your soul. Your hope can disappear when you are devastated by such losses. Emptiness and despair can seem to last forever. But they last for a season. The Lord is able to lift you out of despair and renew your hope and joy, bringing life back to your "drying bones," as we find in Ezekiel chapter 37.

A passage in Ezekiel 37 tells of scattered dry bones, but the Lord gave instructions to the prophet to speak life over those dry bones. The prophet spoke life as the Lord instructed, the bones started to gather together, flesh began to grow on them, the breath of life entered those bodies, and they received life. That was a prophecy for our life, to be inspirational speakers. Speak life to yourself and to others, and declare the work of the Lord. You are called to speak life. To receive supernatural power, we must cultivate a sensitive spirit. The Holy Spirit is in rhythm with the hand of God. When the hand of God comes upon you, you can do what other people fail to do. When the hand of the Lord is on you, you function at a higher level and your emotional pain is healed. In the Bible are many stories written as examples for us to follow in our daily life, to help us overcome emotional pain and bitterness.

Bitterness

*"...get rid of all bitterness, rage and anger, brawling and slander,
along with every form of malice. Be kind and compassionate to one
another, forgiving each other just as in Christ God you."*
(Eph. 4:31, 32 NIV)

I remember how our parents described their bitterness in Romania. They lost everything when the communists came to power. Elena Rascol Rady's husband Vasile was imprisoned two years for his Christian faith, and for supplying Romanians with Bibles. In her book *Flight to Freedom: God's Faithfulness in Communist Romania*, she stated:

> ...everything people had earned up until then, after a lifetime of hard, honest work, was swallowed by that dragon in the name of the Party. People were stripped of their lands, houses, lives, freedom, conscience, joy and peace. Nobody owned anything anymore. The only owner was the State, the fierce dragon embodied by the Communist Party.[13]

Many unjust situations on earth can leave your soul bitter and empty. But that is only for a season when you trust God with your life.

The Bible tells us that after Naomi lost both her sons and her husband after many years in Moab, she returned to Bethlehem and told her friends to call her Mara, which means "bitterness." Naomi's situation made her feel empty and bitter (Ruth 1:20–21). But God caused Ruth's heart to be broken for Naomi, and she cared for her when she was in great need. Naomi's bitterness started to disappear when she watched how God provided for Ruth and brought Boaz into Ruth's life as a "redeemer". God turned her despair to hope and joy. Her season of despair and bitterness was changed. Naomi became the great-grandmother of King David when Ruth married and bore a son. That was God's greatest blessing, being placed in the lineage of the Messiah. When Naomi and Ruth left Moab, bitterness filled their souls, but God ordained their steps and planned a joyful future for them in Bethlehem. Ruth provided unconditional care for Naomi with gentleness and love, so all the city knew that Ruth cared for Naomi. God compensated Naomi's years of bitterness.

A godly, committed family and good, godly friends play an important role in turning our despair into joy, but above all, our hope, joy and strength come from the Lord. Our transformation and renewal will likely take time, as with Naomi, but change will begin as soon as we ask God to renew our hearts. Whatever kind of hurt or hopelessness you might be feeling, turn to God and ask him to heal your bitterness and restore your joy. God's heart is broken for you.

God does not want you to isolate yourself in your bitterness. He is the One who healed and transformed the poisonous, bitter waters into sweet, drinkable water at Marah, when the Israelites were thirsty in the wilderness (Ex. 15: 25-26). *Jehovah-Rapha*, our Healer, can heal all your emotional pain and transform your bitterness into sweet joy, peace and hope.

Loneliness

"But one thing I do: Forgetting what is behind and straining toward what is ahead." (Phil. 3:13)

Loneliness can lead to more bitterness and destruction. Run to God when you are discouraged and lonely. Do not isolate yourself when life is hard and hurtful. Pray like Jesus prayed when He was in the Garden of Gethsemane, when all His disciples left Him by Himself in the hands of the enemy. God's love is the same for everyone in every situation; you have value in God's eyes. Remember Gideon isolated himself when felt inadequate, saying, "I am nobody." But God sent His angel and lifted him from obscurity.

Confess your situation, and talk to the Lord throughout the day. Stay connected with your Heavenly Father. He can be your closest friend and comfort you. Elijah was lonely in the cave, but the Presence of God came to him there. God's Presence will come to you where you are. He is involved in your life, even when you are discouraged.

Inactivity brings loneliness and discouragement. When I arrived in the US in 1990, I was so discouraged. I started to criticize myself for leaving my family, my profession, my friends, and my home church and coming halfway around the globe (almost 10,000 miles) to a completely unknown situation. But I decided neither to isolate myself nor to let bitterness take residence in my mind. I decided to work two jobs and also not to miss church. I even helped friends paint their houses, then I took care of the elderly, even though I had no clue about caring for disabled people. As an economist I had very little knowledge of anatomy and physiology. Working reduces your discouragement, because it redirects your brain activity.

God reveals Himself layer by layer when you seek Him in your loneliness (Ex. 33:1–6). Moses asked God not to forsake the nation of Israel. He did not want to move on without God. When God is present all things become alive. Even the dry bones came to life (Ezek. 37). In your loneliness, always keep on praying. Prayer will bring people who are far away closer to your heart, to prevent loneliness.

God will send people to help you in time of need. You cannot be lonely (1 Kings 20). You must speak out of your anguish of loneliness like Job did (7:11). There are crises in life, and we all will experience emotional wounds and times of loneliness that need to be addressed and discussed in order to be healed. King David mentioned many times that he had unhealed wounds in his heart. He was desperate for his Healer. David lived a busy life surrounded by people, but still had emotional pain from loneliness in his spirit (Ps. 109: 22). He was running to God constantly for healing in his mind and soul. For emotional and physical healing you must run to God constantly. That is God's prescription for emotional healing. Love those around you and do not let loneliness ruin your happiness.

Christ accepted you as you are, and you must accept others as they are. Do not run away from people to isolate yourself (Rom. 15:7). Believe that God receives and accepts you the way you are as His son or daughter. You do not need to be overcome with fear. Just forgive people who offend you and ask for forgiveness if you offended them, and your burden will be removed. You will be free in Christ Jesus, saved by grace. Even though we do not understand everything, we must throw away our fears and worries and run to Jesus. We know that blind Bartimaeus lived in bitterness and loneliness due to his disability. He did not understand it, but when he heard Jesus passing by, he threw off his clothes and ran to Him (Mark 10:46–52). You have your "clothing" of fear, blindness, insecurity, bitterness and loneliness in your darkest moments. Run to Jesus, and ask Him to take them off one by one, even if you do not understand the process. He came to Earth just for this. God is giving you new "clothes", a new mind, new thoughts, and a new vision.

Start where you are. Throw away those blankets of fear and insecurity that create bitterness, isolation and loneliness. Exchange them for the love of Jesus, and you will never be lonely again. The love of Jesus will enable you to love others. Through Jesus' love you can lead other people to Jesus, now that you have met Him yourself. Christ's love will help you pray for their needs, their diseases, and their addictions and lead them to Christ. John Hagee, in his book *In Defense of Israel: The Bible Mandate For Supporting the Jewish State*, explained:

> The Christian doctrine of love was first taught by a Jewish Rabbi from Nazareth, who said: "Love your neighbor as yourself" (Matt. 19:19 NIV). "Love one another as I have loved you" (John 15:12). "By this all will know that you are my disciples, if you have love for one another" (John 13:35). "Love your enemies" (Matt. 5:44).[14]

God is constantly restoring our loneliness, and those around us, through love.

Even in the most lonely time of his life John the Baptist recognized that Jesus brings the Holy Spirit fire. In prison, lonely and isolated from the world, John received a revelation of Jesus. John looked for the Lamb of God even in his lowest moments, and his soul was protected from bitterness in prison. Redirect your focus to what Jesus is doing in other Christians' lives. He is willing to do the same for you.

When you defer hope, you postpone healing of your emotional wounds, and your heart will continue in loneliness, hurt and isolation. Everyone faces disappointments and losses, but God gives us hope for every day. The challenge we have is to know who God is, and *who we are in God*. Know your identity in Christ. Explore the fullness of God to hear His heartbeat. He takes delight in His children and expresses His heart to them in their loneliness.

Many people choose to live in bitterness when things do not go their way. The world all around us is in pain. We can get distracted by the things of life and miss the essential one, Jesus (Luke 10). We must be carriers of Christ, living a life of sacrifice, love, and freedom from bitterness and loneliness.

Leave behind your mistakes and wrong choices. It is never too late. Get a vision for accomplishments and manifestations of the power of God in you. Choose what is important. Do not use your energy on things that will perish or negatively affect your life. Do not miss the best that God has for you. Forget the past and look forward, as the Apostle Paul said. "But one thing I do: Forgetting what is behind and straining toward what is ahead"

(Phil. 3:13). You need the power of the Holy Spirit to move forward in God's dimension, because "with God nothing is impossible." Despise the shame and anchor your faith in the invisible power of God. With Jesus in your heart, you will never be lonely again.

PART III

GOD'S SUPERNATURAL PRESCRIPTIONS

CHAPTER SIX

Creating Chemical Balance in Your Brain

"Rejoice in the Lord. I will say it again: Rejoice!"
(Phil. 4:4–6)

" . . . the peace of God, which transcends all understanding,
will guard your heart and your minds in Christ Jesus."
(Phil. 4:7)

"May these words of my mouth and this meditation of my
heart be pleasing in your sight, LORD,
my Rock and my Redeemer."
(Ps. 19:14)

To create the best atmosphere for a healthy chemical balance in your brain, you must prevent anxiety, avoid worry, and change the way you perceive life. King David said in Psalm 19:14, "May these words of my mouth and this meditation of my heart be pleasing in your sight, LORD, my Rock and my Redeemer." Meditation that pleases the Lord must be increased to preserve our neurons and promote neurogenesis. We want new neurons to be developed to prevent neurocognitive disorders like dementia and Alzheimer's. Dementia presents with morphological changes in the brain structure, impairing cognition and executive functions.[1]

That is why the Bible teaches us to maintain a joyful attitude. Meditating day and night on the promises of God brings more hope, healthy thoughts and stronger neurons in our brain. We need to actively rejoice in the Lord of our salvation. The New Testament states God's prescription for neurogenesis—the creation of new neurons—instructing us, "Rejoice in the Lord. I will say it again: Rejoice!" (Phil. 4:4–6). This amazing prescription was written around 2,000 years ago, with no expiration date. Gladness and joy will assist the brain structures to create new neurons, calm an overactive brain and clear the mind, enabling us to filter out all unhealthy thoughts that would lead to a chemical imbalance in the brain. When you rejoice or feel happy, a healthy atmosphere is created in your brain. Your neurotransmitters (oxytocin, endorphin, dopamine, serotonin, etc) are released in healthy amounts, promoting the healing process.

When you bring all your worry to God in prayer, " . . . the peace of God, which transcends all understanding, will guard your heart and your minds in Christ Jesus" (Phil. 4:7). You can see why it is very important to have your heart and your mind guarded in Christ Jesus, bringing health to your mind, spirit and body. Continuous joy, love, peace, trusting God in all things, and not worrying are all on God's prescription pad for you. They will reduce anxiety and its symptoms and destructive complications. Do not allow those conditions to prevent you from fulfilling your God-given destiny.

God lovingly wrote another clear prescription approximately 3,500 years ago, advising us to neither worry nor struggle: "Be still and know that I am God" (Ps. 46:10). It is not only good to flood your mind (your brain's structures including your cerebral cortex, amygdala and hippocampus) with the Word of God—it is essential. Rest in Him and wait upon Him when you are depressed or anxious. His prescription for renewing our strength is written in Isaiah 40:31: " . . . they that wait upon the LORD will renew their strength." Anxiety and depression from excessive worry can kill you by stealing your strength, but when you are waiting on God and allowing the love of God to flow over you, your strength will be renewed through new neurons! This powerful prescription for neurogenesis was detailed for us in the Word of God—which reaches far beyond science—thousands of years ago. When you meditate on God's promises, new neurons will be created, your strength will be renewed, and you will grow stronger neurons, healthier thoughts, slowing the aging process. Meditation on God's word is an anti-aging therapy and a priceless treatment.

All people on earth should live with this hope. Look in the Word of God, the Bible. Reaching beyond science, it teaches that we must be filled with faith, peace, compassion and joy, which will drive out fear and all its consequences. By following God's prescription you will not lose heart.

I was in distress about who would change this world, so full of worry, problems and stress. Finally I realized that the power that can change the world is a mind renewed through the Word of God, which contains God's supernatural prescriptions, beyond science. Romans 12:1, 2 says:

> Therefore, I urge you, brothers and sisters, in view of God's mercy, to offer your bodies as living sacrifice, holy and pleasing to God—this is your true and proper worship. Do not conform to the pattern of this world, but be transformed by the renewing of your mind. Then you will be able to test and approve what God's will is—His good, pleasing and perfect will.

The perfect will of God is for each person on planet earth to be healthy and to prosper. God wants us to be healthy, so He gave us prescriptions, far above the scope of science, to stay healthy and to prevent diseases at any given time and age. In 3 John 1:2 we read, "Dear friend, I pray that you may enjoy good health and that all may go well with you, even as your soul is getting along well."

The fear of the Lord, which is the beginning of wisdom, can change you. People who fear the Lord have a treasure—the wisdom to apply God's prescriptions and instructions from His Word in their daily personal life. The world will change if each person's mind is renewed by exercising that wisdom. Each person can be transformed through wisdom received from God—His prescriptions in His Word.

Restoring Right Attitudes

" . . . one generation commends your work to another; they tell of your mighty acts. They speak of the glorious splendor of your majesty—and I will meditate on your wonderful work. They will tell of the power of your awesome works—and I will proclaim your great deeds. They celebrate your abundant goodness and joyfully sing of your righteousness."
(Ps. 145:4–7)

This generation, the next generation, and the generations after them will be changed if we change our thinking about teenagers' attitudes at home, in school, in the community and in the world. They are the leaders of tomorrow. Students should be eager to learn with discipline, to gain wisdom, knowledge and revelation, and to change their attitude in the classroom. This will even improve their exam scores!

What we teach our children at home and in our schools is very important. They need to learn healthy values and beliefs that promote health and prevent disease. What they learn in school, at home, at church and in their community will remain in their brain (prefrontal cortex, hippocampus, amygdala, nucleus accumbens, and other brain structures), regulating their emotions and memories and dictating their behavior for life. If society allows the education standards to deteriorate, the future will be ruined for our next generation.

I experienced the tremendous earthquake in Bucharest, Romania on March 4, 1977. Three million people felt the violent tremors, measured at 7.2 on the Richter scale. Thousands died under collapsed buildings, leaving the city devastated and in great turmoil. That fault line transverses Bucharest. Thousands of smaller seismic aftershocks continued all night long and the next day, such that people thought it was the end of the world. Just as a fissure—a fault line deep in the Earth—will bring disaster to a city or a nation, so a fault in the education system can ruin the entire future generation.

Misunderstanding true freedom, and lowering moral and educational standards, will degrade a society. Unhealthy behavior, even exposure to movies whose actors live unhealthy lifestyles, should not be promoted in schools. Kids are not supposed to engage in premarital sex. They should not be exposed to teaching that promotes adulterous relationships, drugs, alcohol, pornography, violence, and all the destructive habits currently popular in the media.

Vaccination is not the answer to destructive sexual behavior. When taking a patient's past history to decide on the right diagnosis, interventions and treatment, I see patients that do not even know how many partners they have had. Our schools are preoccupied with providing condoms to boys in the sixth grade, and encouraging their use, instead of promoting abstinence and discipline. There is no such thing as safe sex. Scientifically, only abstinence from unhealthy behavior is 100% risk free from sexually transmitted disease, yet it is seldom taught.

Sex is more than sleeping with another person to satisfy the flesh's momentary desire. Sexuality is not meant for fleeting pleasure. Sex outside of marriage involves emotional pain, intense psychological distress, and sadness, causing a "broken heart syndrome". During episodes of great emotional distress due to broken relationships, toxic levels of neurochemicals are released in both ventricles of the heart, weakening them until they are unable to contract properly. This impairs circulation in the body, with long-time, unhealthy consequences. Then we wonder why so many young people are unhealthy. Sex will create a physical and emotional bond which, when broken, creates deep "emotional wounds" and high levels of stress, with its complications.

We need serious teaching on this important subject that affects the body, mind and spirit of the future generation. Current instruction in our schools on adultery, premarital sex, chemical abuse, pornography, and other unhealthy behaviors is woefully superficial. Students are not taught how to seriously analyze the consequences. So many lives are destroyed, costing society a fortune. Our broken human nature was the very reason God gave us His divine instructions and prescriptions. He wants to show us how to prevent those diseases through abstinence and self-control.

Billions of dollars are spent on our military to fight overseas to protect our freedom and preserve our lives. At the same time we slowly destroy our future generations at home by avoiding teaching abstinence in schools, promoting destructive behaviors, and exposing them to a culture of filth. Children are our future, who in turn will influence the next generation coming after them.

Victory in a Changed Attitude

". . . be made new in the attitude of your minds;" (Eph. 4:22 NIV)

Attitude is one key for a stress free life. Changing your attitude will help you reduce your stress level. Nick, an Australian boy with no limbs (no legs and no arms), decided to change his attitude despite his unfortunate condition. Instead of being bitter and angry at God, Nick decided, "God knows what He is doing." Even though he has neither legs nor arms, as a grown man now he is involved in more activities than many perfect human beings, because everything changed in his attitude. He looks not at his disabilities, but at all his opportunities and possibilities. He is even married and has a normal, beautiful wife and a normal, precious child.

When you go through the fire, through trials and discouraging situations, remember that God is in the middle of your trial to reveal His glory. His eyes are watching over you day and night, ready to fulfill His plan in your life when you renew your attitude. We do not see beyond the trial, but a supernatural intervention is available, as we learn from so many Bible characters' lives. The barriers that hinder God's interventions include our old mental attitudes of unforgiveness, bitterness, laziness, narcissism, greediness, fear, doubt and hopelessness. All these degrade our health and leave us unable to function.

You can change things inside you and deal with your circumstances better if you grow in the knowledge of God. Only He will enable you to be the best person, mother, father, sister, brother, friend, colleague, and neighbor possible, despite all your unfavorable circumstances. With that attitude you can move forward. Just open your brain to better visions and dreams. Change your attitude and find victory in every area.

Epigenetics in the Bible

" . . . for I, the LORD your God , am a jealous God, punishing the children for the sin of the parents to the third and fourth generation of those who hate Me, but showing love a thousand generations of those who love Me and keep my commandments." (Ex. 20:5)

Daily environmental stresses, combined with an unhealthy lifestyle, will alter and influence our gene expression through an epigenetic mechanism.

Genetic changes (epigenetics) can be passed down through gene expression, affecting the next generation.[2] Everything parents experience in their everyday life, including memories and associated thoughts related to their emotions, will be transmitted to the next generation through epigenetics, even in utero, through the genes.[3]

Children are the most vulnerable population. As they are exposed to information through the media and the internet, the changes occurring in society now will be carried further to become either a burden or a blessing for the next generation. T.D. Jakes, pastor of a 30,000 member Church whose TV show reaches over 67 million, says in his best-selling book *Reposition Yourself: Living Life Without Limits*: "Repositioning your children and acclimating them to a new financial environment may be the hardest thing to do. As we change not only financially, but morally, and socially, don't forget that the children carry the weight of the change we make."[4] Studies show that the epigenome is influenced by physical and emotional stress, altering the gene expression in the human body. Those changes can be passed down through at least three or four generations.[5]

The study of " . . . epigenetics has led to new findings about a host of disorders, including cancer, mental retardation, immune disorders, neuropsychiatric disorders and pediatric disorders."[6] This discovery confirms what the Bible mentioned more than 3,500 years ago, regarding the curse that lasts to the third and fourth generation. " . . . for I, the LORD your God, am a jealous God, punishing the children for the sin of the parents to the third and fourth generation of those who hate Me, but showing love to a thousand generations of those who love Me and keep my commandments" (Ex. 20:5). God's pure love can reprogram genetic mutations for thousands of generations, for those who follow God's supernatural prescriptions. Scientists have also discovered that the epigenetic mechanism is reversible with healthy lifestyle changes. Using our conscious mind, the prefrontal cortex, we can modify bad habits.[7] (More about lifestyle changes later.)

As parents, our lifestyle affects our children. Children from divorced families suffer from poor social development. Poor emotional support and inconsistent role modeling can lead to depression and early-onset personality problems. Seeking relief from worry, anxiety and depression, children engage in risky behaviors. Statistics show that in 2013, over 19.8 million in the US alone were addicted to alcohol and illicit and prescription drugs.[8]

Low self-esteem and early peer pressures escalate, abstinence is rare, and life becomes complicated by social, medical, and legal expenses for teens and young adults. Some of them inherit that burden from their parents through (epigenetic) gene expression. They go out to have a good time, engaging in multiple sexual relationships, abusing alcohol and drugs for immediate gratification, while this wreaks silent havoc on the dopamine storage at the cellular level. Many times they mirror their parents' behavior, socializing with drinkers, and thus develop a high risk for mortality. Feelings of hopelessness only worsen the situation.

We as parents need to tell our children and their generation about God's miracle-working power to transform minds, thoughts and lives. Psalm 145 exhorts us:

> . . . one generation commends your work to another; they tell of your mighty acts. They speak of the glorious splendor of your majesty—and I will meditate on your wonderful work. They will tell of the power of your awesome works—and I will proclaim your great deeds. They celebrate your abundant goodness and joyfully sing of your righteousness. (Ps. 145:4–7)

These positive habits are learned by reinforcement, and internally, dopamine is released throughout our system. What a healing power is hidden in God's prescriptions for joy and His abundant goodness—with no expiration date!

May the Word of God be known to the next generation, and may His promises permeate their brain structures. Addictions have a neurobiological origin in the limbic system (hippocampus and amygdala). This plays a huge role in the storage of emotions and memories.[9]

Bad habits need to be replaced with healthy habits. Anxiety, and all the emotions and memories from a dysfunctional family life, can be replaced with the powerful promises in God's Word. His restoration power brings glorious hope, casting out fear and worry and reducing anxiety and depression from feelings of neglect, rejection, isolation, exploitation, humiliation and terror. Children in an abusive, chaotic environment often overreact. They adopt unhealthy, risky behaviors, and develop diseases, disabilities, even early death. Kids under stress will eat more for comfort to sooth their emotions. This causes weight gain, then diabetes, hypertension, high cholesterol, metabolic syndrome, sleep disturbance, sleep apnea, and nightmares in early childhood.

Following a healthy lifestyle will activate healthy epigenetics. Your lifestyle can either optimize your health or contribute to disease development, which will carry on into future generations. It is your choice.

Intrinsic Motivation

"For I know the plans I have for you," declares the LORD, *"plans to prosper you and not to harm you, plans to give you hope and a future."*
(Jer. 29:11)

Building intrinsic motivation and regulation in our brain is crucial to the restoration of relationships in families with children, in schools, and in society. Children need healthy challenges, realistic expectations and encouragement. Memories of appropriate rewards and punishments will empower children to develop useful skills. We have already seen that the neurotransmitter dopamine in the brain is associated with the reward, gratification and expectation of reinforcement. In the brain, the limbic system (including the amygdala, associated with emotional and behavior responses to memories stored in the hippocampus, interconnected with other brain structures) will store those memories of reward or punishment.

Raising our children in a healthy emotional environment will bring the future generation to higher standards of behavior. This is one way to prepare them for a promising future. "For I know the plans I have for you," declares the LORD, "plans to prosper you and not to harm you, *plans to give you hope and a future*" (Jer. 29:11). God has set high standards for us. These are meant to protect us and ensure a higher quality of life. His standards also demand immediate obedience. God's supernatural prescriptions (laws and promises) protect us from the adverse effects of disobedience. Those who follow neither Biblical guidelines, nor the Lord's superior standards, will suffer harmful consequences. Thankfully, the Holy Spirit works in the believer's conscience, motivating us to fulfill God's superior standards. *God's Spirit in us* becomes our intrinsic motivation. Then we make better choices that will set us on the right path for a meaningful life—if we are willing to listen and obey.

Considering where the future generation will arrive, and laying the foundations for our own children, what principles do we promote? Our whole culture today is globalized and countless cultures intermingle. Furthermore, cultures and technologies change continually. The question is: whose culture do we follow and what are the immediate and eternal consequences? Pursuing a Biblical culture will build a strong foundation for the future. That is the antidote to disaster for the future generation.

Our body is a gift from God and the Temple of the Holy Spirit. The Holy Spirit within us helps us develop an intrinsic motivation to honor God with our lifestyle. We honor Him through prayer, fasting, reading the Word of God regularly, exercising, eating healthy, helping others, and making good decisions to protect our future from dangerous diseases. Positive attitudes increase healthy dopamine activity. Do not use substances or foods that poison your body and brain. Elevate the way you manage your body, your heart and your mind, by following the world's most powerful wisdom—the Word of God—through the power of the Holy Spirit. That gives us hope for the future.

Honor God from Generation to Generation

"Know therefore that the LORD your God is God; he is the faithful God,
keeping His covenant of love to a thousand generations of those
who love Him and keep His commandments." (Deut. 7:9)

He lifts the poor from the dust and raises the needy from their misery. I grew up under communism, but I felt God's invisible grace. I remained in awe of God because of the passion of my parents to keep us true to the knowledge of God and His miracles. When you teach your children God's Word to set their hope in God, He will put you in a place of honor. I recently learned that my paternal grandfather was a very rich Jew. He owned farms and forests, but the communists took everything away and left the family in poverty, even though we were working hard. Many days we had only polenta or simple crackers to eat for breakfast, lunch and dinner. We girls had only one dress and one pair of worn-out shoes, but our hearts were filled with joy because we had God on our side.

With God's help I finished my secondary education in Bucharest, Romania. Then He brought me to the US, where many doors opened for me to learn English and find jobs. I had jobs even before I could speak English! I worked extra hard so people would let me keep the job. Then I started taking care of elderly people. I went back to school and got my associate's, bachelor's, master's, and then my doctorate degree. God gave me favor everywhere I went. He put me in a place of honor, as His Word says: " . . . puts them in a place of honor" (1 Sam 2:8). God did that for me. He literally moved me from the dust and poverty of a small village in northern Romania, oppressed under a brutal communist regime, to freedom and a high position, and riches in the city of Portland, Oregon, USA. That is a place of honor, where only God could position me. Since my childhood I have followed God's prescriptions for living—long before I was a medical provider— because I believed obedience would bring great rewards here on earth, and for eternity. Everything I have gained came only through prayer, obedience to the Word of God and His prescriptions, and the Lord's grace. He is able to do it for you, too, and for your children, and your children's children.

Why would anyone choose disobedience, with its dreadful consequences of chronic stress and physical and spiritual damage?

The Most Powerful Force on Earth

"These are the things God has revealed to us by his Spirit. The Spirit searches all things, even the deep things of God." (1 Cor. 2:10)

The Spirit searches all things visible and invisible. He is searching your heart, mind, and thoughts, and His thoughts about you are overwhelming. God has been thinking about you forever. He has dreams for your life that you can see only with your spiritual eyes. To see what He sees, you must recognize God's presence in your life. He is speaking directly to you. You can recognize the voice of God, speaking directly to you through the power of the Holy Spirit, through your conscious mind.

The Spirit who resurrected Jesus Christ from death lives in you, if you believe in Jesus and have received His forgiveness of sins. Jesus is the Lord of all creation. Pray through the Holy Spirit for transformation to reach a new level. Revelation will come through obedience and prayer. God expects us to act responsibly and obey His Word. Wisdom from the Holy Spirit, and a revelation of Jesus, will bring transformation and breakthrough in your thinking process.

Don't let unhealthy thoughts invade your brain. Tune in to His spiritual realm to discern the truth and reach wise decisions. The human mind in tune with the Holy Spirit is a powerful engine, through which God accomplishes His work on earth and fulfills His plan in our life. The Holy Spirit-renewed mind has indescribable power to transform your brain's structures, creating new neurons for better health and blessings in your life.

Guard God's prescriptions for decision making, and His instruction, deep in your heart. Understanding the mystery of the work of the Holy Spirit in people's lives can empower educational reforms to change the next generation. The concept of an eternal soul must be understood in our society, so people can make wiser decisions. Lack of wisdom brings destruction.

Our education system is failing to teach children the truth about the human spirit, soul, and body. We must filter our thoughts, discard negative thoughts, and focus on what is necessary to accomplish our daily tasks. If we are honest, we recognize that we are eternal, spiritual beings living in temporary physical bodies. Our physical body is only the temporary home of our eternal spirit, the temple of the Holy Spirit. God's spirit of wisdom and revelation is waiting to be released in our mind, but lack of knowledge brings destruction. Hosea tells us, "My people are destroyed from lack of knowledge" (Hosea 4:6). Let your soul and spirit be hungry for more knowledge, revelation and understanding to live a healthy life, physically and spiritually, on earth.

Parameters of our Prescriptions

"Fear not, for I am with you; be not dismayed, for I am your God; I will strengthen you, I will help you, I will uphold you with my righteous right hand." (Isa. 41:10)

God gave people clear parameters in His written prescriptions in the Word in order to function and live a healthy life. In medicine, if you do not follow the parameters for your treatment you do not obtain the desired therapeutic, expected outcomes. People can die if they ignore medical advice and do not take what their doctor prescribes.

Here is a very simple example of parameters for an over-the-counter pain medication: Acetaminophen (Tylenol). The prescription is "Acetaminophen 325 mg tab, 1–2 tablets every 4 to 6 hours for pain, as needed, for two weeks. Do not use more than 3000 mg of acetaminophen in 24 hours." Taking more than 3000 mg in 24 hours for several days can cause liver toxicity, even without a history of liver disease. For some patients Acetaminophen is not enough to control pain, and they need to talk to their health care professional for further interventions. They must seek advice from their medical provider to prevent liver damage. Some who already have liver disease or allergies cannot use this medication at all.

Another parameter for a common non-steroidal, anti-inflammatory medication is "Ibuprofen 200 mg tablets; use 1–2 tablets by mouth every 4 to 6 hours as needed for pain for two weeks. Do not use more than 1,800 mg in 24 hours." Using more than 1,800 mg in 24 hours for more than two weeks can cause water retention, kidney damage and heart disease. Some people cannot use this medication at all. Always check for adverse reactions, side effects, and allergies—for any kind of medication you take. Always communicate with your primary care provider for clear instructions for any medical advice and intervention.

Clear Parameters for a Renewed Life

Spiritually, you need to seek knowledge from the Word of God. In the Bible we find prescriptions with clear instructions and parameters for spiritual therapy that benefit our body, soul and spirit for eternity. The Bible is a book full of written prescriptions that need to be followed correctly to bring spiritual health and prevent spiritual diseases, because our body benefits from spiritual decisions here on earth. God's revelations are a vast resource. They are available to everyone, but must be respected and obeyed to fulfill their potential, which is divinely imprinted in each individual's DNA.

Through the supernatural power of the Holy Spirit, we access God's knowledge by faith—beyond science, beyond natural circumstances, beyond the world's understanding. There is a realm of revelation through divine inspiration for medical professionals, business people, politicians, educators, ministers—everyone. Revelation is given by Divine grace for us to accomplish the will of God on earth, for His purpose and His glory. The Word and its clear parameters will transform and modify your thinking process, transforming your unhealthy thinking into healthy, productive thinking according to the promises of God. Healthy, normal levels of neurotransmitters and chemical messengers will prevent toxicity in your soul and body. Allow godly thinking to trigger the right emotions in your brain. This is the blessing of a transformed mind.

Fasting and prayer have incredible power to help us transform our mind. When we pray and fast, we humble ourselves before God, meditating on what is good and bad. Redirecting our thoughts, we can then make well-informed decisions.

Good Seed, Good Harvest

With the seed of the Word deep in your heart and mind, new neurons develop and your life is transformed. There is a supernatural law about sowing and reaping. The unhealed areas of your life do not allow the Word of God to penetrate the callous, hidden places of your soul. First a cleaning process, a healing of your emotions and your memories, must take place. The soil must be fertile and well prepared—a healthy mind and body and a new life—for the seed to bring forth a good harvest. The brain's amygdala can protect your emotions from stress, but you must allow the Word of God (the Seed) to penetrate the deepest place of your mind to clean out old, hidden thoughts of rejection, bitterness, unforgiveness, anger, anxiety, depression, and low self-esteem.

The Word of God is powerful beyond imagination. The universe was created through God's Word, and this same Word of God has the power to align your thoughts with the Father's divine purpose. Many people think evil is stronger than the power of God, but we have power over evil through the Word of God, when it fills our mind through the Spirit of God.

Shift Your Priorities

"Create in me a pure heart, O God, and renew a steadfast spirit within me." (Ps. 51:10)

Renewing our mind means a shift of all our values and our belief system, starting inside. Do not set your mind on earthly things that influence you in an unhealthy way. Change your values. Shift your priorities. The Word of God, changing hearts one by one, will reshape history. Lives are transformed because of God's grace, freely given, and He will raise you up. Live your divine destiny by deciding every day to transform your thinking and obey the Word of God.

Obedience brings miracles. God will bless not only you, but your children and your children's children—even those not yet born. The epigenetic process through gene expression in the next generations will continue to work both physically and spiritually until His coming. King David asked God for a transformed heart and a spirit of wisdom. "Create in me a pure heart, O God, and renew a steadfast spirit within me." (Ps. 51:10). David shifted his priorities because he learned how much destruction and disaster a selfish, sinful heart could bring, even to an innocent soul. He also realized that the heart without the spirit cannot change.

Desperate for God's Presence

"Now show me your glory." (Ex. 33:18)

Where there is sin and unbelief there is no presence of God. There is emptiness, loneliness, depression, fear, worry of uncertainty, anxiety, depression—and the stress level rises. This is a serious situation. We must be desperate for God's presence. Moses, in heartfelt desperation, cried, "Now show me your glory" (Ex. 33:18). God's presence brings His goodness (Ex. 33:19). You will be a different person when the Holy Spirit comes to live in you. It dispels fear, worry and anxiety from your body, and restores your soul and spirit. In God's presence you experience His Supernatural power—joy in sadness, peace in crisis, and strength in weaknesses. God is full of compassion. He is angry for a moment when we are disobedient, but He is merciful always. God's heart is moved because of your situation. God feels the effect of our sins, and He wants us to feel His goodness. God is a covenant keeper, without boundaries, infinite. Let His presence invade your mind and change your destiny.

CHAPTER SEVEN

Everything Starts in the Brain

"People perish because of the lack of knowledge." (Hosea 4:6)

Your physical and emotional health begin in your brain, which receives information from the outside world and interprets those messages. Drawing on your prior knowledge, experiences, emotions and memories stored in your brain's structures, your thoughts form instantly. The more knowledge you have, the better you can interpret the threats you receive and formulate better responses. As mentioned before, the Bible explained the consequences of a lack of knowledge, thousands of years before Christ (BC), stating that "People perish because of the lack of knowledge" (Hosea 4:6).

Clearly, in order to thrive you need to understand what happens in your brain. Information processed there can prevent the destruction of your body, mind and spirit. The brain is like a muscle that needs the right food (good thoughts and healthy emotions) to stay healthy and avoid mental decline, neurocognitive disorders, and other physical and spiritual illnesses. Positive affirmations found in the promises of God throughout the Bible create healthy thoughts and positive attitudes that strengthen your neurons and brain structures.

As your knowledge grows, your faith will increase. Faith creates confidence in God's promises and affects your mental and physical being in a healthy way. Fearfulness and worry are destructive thoughts, causing anxiety from a wrong thinking process. This affects your whole being. It decreases your quality of life, leading to physical and spiritual damage to your body, mind and spirit. To be healthy, your body, mind, and spirit must be in harmony. (Read Ex. 23, 24, 25.)

Detoxify your emotions and thoughts by renewing your mind through a healthy thinking process. A clear mind and clean thoughts will bring health to your entire being. Submission to the Word of God will bring life, healing and deliverance from the strongholds of fear, worry, anxiety and depression. Be desperate for a visitation from God and the manifestation of His power in your life. When you have a visitation from God, your life is changed and your spirit comes alive. He will breathe from His spirit into your spirit so you can worship Him in spirit and truth. Worship is a great weapon in your daily battle with the worries of the world. Adoring God and worshiping Jesus restores your heart, your emotions, and your spirit and calms your overacting brain. What God is doing in your heart and mind is supernatural. (Read Isa. 40:29–31).

God's Healing Presence

In our postmodern era, pressure is increasing in all areas of life. Get smart and protect your body, mind and spirit through healthy thoughts. God holds the answer to your fear and worry. He wants your heart to be entirely His. Get closer to Him, because in His presence is fullness of joy. He wants to draw you into His presence to be fully transformed. Many times I have felt the joy of His presence in my life, even in the midst of struggles. He wants to fill your heart with joy, too. Love and joy will sustain you in a broken world by reprogramming your brain with healthy neurotransmitters. Reprogram your brain by praising God, drawing near to His presence, and joy will overtake you and elevate your thinking process. Believe in His Mighty power. God moves supernaturally on behalf of His people.

You can find refuge in the Word of God with *prescriptions beyond science* to manage your fear, worry and stress. Keep reading, and you will realize that Jesus Christ, the Son of God, is the answer to all the problems people have around the world in countless terrible, uncontrollable, unpredictable and disastrous situations. Knowing that here on this planet we live as visitors with "a temporary visa" will reduce your stress. You cannot control everything, but you can control your decisions and your attitude. What you believe, and whose prescriptions and instructions you follow, will determine your quality of life here on earth and your eternal home in Heaven.

Managing Pressure

Worry, fear and anxiety overwhelm so many people. God created us to be able to manage the pressure from worry, stress and anxiety only one day at time. You cannot correct the past, but by faith you can look to the future with joy, hope and love. David prayed to be cleansed from problems inside him. There are things inside your subconscious, stored deep inside your memory, that create inside pressures when triggered by unhealthy thoughts. God, however, has access to your subconscious areas and He can heal them right now. Release every unhealthy, threatening thought and concentrate on

God's instructions. Embracing godly thoughts and obeying God is renewing and creates a healthy lifestyle.

Low self-esteem can make peer pressure feel even worse. When your peers in school try to humiliate you, declare the word of God. You are truly a unique creature on earth, "…wonderfully and fearfully made" (Ps. 139:14). God knew exactly who He wanted you to be—your hair, your skin and your eyes, your nose and your ears, short or tall. You were created for His purpose, to glorify His name. Everything was deliberately placed in your DNA and your genes.

Peer pressure can isolate us in loneliness. Some young people, trying to escape peer pressure, loneliness, anxiety, depression, boredom, stress, or relationship problems, become addicted to the internet. To cope with loneliness they seek refuge in games, social media, or chat rooms, to the point of addiction. Statistics shows that before age 18, 93% of boys and 62% of girls have seen internet pornography.[1]

Renew Your Joy

We have the ability in our conscious mind, through the prefrontal cortex and other brain structures, to reason with our thoughts, and decide how to act.[2] For example, maybe you used to be active in church, and enjoyed group activities, but you have lost your interest in going out and sharing your thoughts with others. Maybe you feel depressed, not even wanting to leave your house. Use your frontal lobe, and think about what made you so devoted and passionate in the past for the Word of God, and what changed. Reflect on your positive experience with God in the past and revive your passion. Find joy with God and His Word in your life again. Even specialists and psychologists will tell you to count your blessings to prevent pressure caused by depressive thinking.

The Word of God that we hear, meditate on, and memorize is converted in our brain into electrical impulses. These trigger neurons to release neurochemicals, according to the intensity and quality of those impulses. When we meditate on the Word of God we receive wisdom and clarity to interpret information received from our environment through the five senses. When we encounter problems and temptations, we can then reject unhealthy thoughts, reflect on God's prescriptions for the situation, and focus on the promises of God to bring us hope, joy and happiness. The Bible has an answer for every situation, but we must train our brain to reason according to what God says about those situations.

Bring any problem to the Lord, let your request be known to God, and you will find peace. God's strongest prescription for worry, with a maximum potency, is far beyond the scope of science. According to Philippians 4:6, 7:
. . .

> "Do not be anxious about anything, but in every situation, by prayer and petition, with thanksgiving, present your requests to God."

Follow that instruction in the Bible and you will find that,

> "...the peace of God, which transcends all understanding, will guard your hearts and your minds in Christ Jesus."

It is well documented that peace decreases anxiety, calms an overactive brain, helps us relax, and allows our brain to release healthy neurotransmitters into our body, starting the healing process and preventing illness.

Divine Prescriptions in the Bible

> "Do not fear, for I redeemed you: I have summoned you by name; you are mine. When you pass through the waters, I will be with you; when you pass through the rivers, they will not sweep over you. When you walk through the fire, you will not be burned; the flames will not set you ablaze." (Isa. 43:1–3)

Fear, worry, anxiety and stress can kill. It is impossible to overcome all the stressors in the world without following the principles of God and His prescriptions for supernatural solutions. Only the Bible has the right prescriptions to treat this paralyzing pandemic. The Bible is a book of God's prescriptions, directions, instructions, and recommendations, and its effectiveness reaches far beyond science. Instead of pills to cover worry and pain, God's divine prescriptions prevent spiritual and physical diseases and promote spiritual and physical health. God exhorts and instructs us repeatedly in His Word, as in Isaiah: "Do not fear, for I redeemed you: I have summoned you by name; you are mine. When you pass through the waters, I will be with you; when you pass through the rivers, they will not sweep over you. When you walk through the fire, you will not be burned; the flames will not set you ablaze" (Isa. 43:1–3).

Prevent Worry and Anxiety

> "Do not be anxious about anything, but in every situation, by prayer and petition, with thanksgiving, present your requests to God. And the peace of God, which transcends all understanding, will guard your hearts and your minds in Christ Jesus." (Phil. 4:6–7)

Worrying about the future triggers thoughts of fear and anxiety, which affect the thinking process. This impairs your cognition and interferes with your ability to make decisions. Even scientists agree that lack of knowledge, feelings of rejection, unforgiveness, financial problems, sickness, and loneliness will trigger more worry and increase your level of stress, affecting your entire wellbeing.

Recognize what kind of worry is triggering the stress in your life. Is it fear of losing your job, losing your loved one, being rejected, a lack of money, or poor health? The Word of God gives you God's remedies and His prescriptions and antidotes for worry of all kinds.

When you are worried about being rejected, you need to know that you are accepted! God predestined you for adoption. You can be adopted into God's family at any time. You only need to say yes to Jesus Christ as your Lord and Savior. (Read Eph. 1:5.) "He predestined us for adoption to sonship through Jesus Christ, in accordance with His pleasure and will." It is God's will for you to be His son or daughter through Jesus Christ. My heart is always touched and I am always moved in my spirit by adopted children, even when they are very old. I have known many patients in my practice who were adopted, and automatically they receive a special place in my heart and I go extra miles for them. I realize how their adoption changed their destiny. Our own worldly and eternal destiny is changed by our Lord Jesus Christ, through whom we are adopted by God. We receive special attention from Heaven as adopted sons and daughters for eternity.

Pastor Larry Huch, in his book *Free at Last: Removing the Past from Your Future*, stated:

> Our finances, marriages, homes, emotions, and minds have been kidnapped by the devil. But Jesus came and paid the ransom for every area of our lives in full and has brought us back to the way we are supposed to be ... there is a transformation that takes place by the renewing of our minds. It is a spiritual metamorphosis. When we think right, our words are right; when our words are right, our actions are right. Our potential is multiplied hundreds of times beyond anything we can think, but it happens through a metamorphosis of God's Spirit changing us by the renewing of our minds.[3]

Due to the changes in your brain structures, and the healthy amounts of neurochemicals released, you regain power to live with real hope, joy, peace, healed relationships, restored health, and a prosperous spirit, mind and body.

Discover Your Destiny

The power of the Holy Spirit can help change your image of yourself, your attitude and your destiny. The book of Acts (Chapter 2) describes how the Holy Spirit came as a mighty rushing wind and touched everybody who was there, both before and after Peter's preaching. Their thinking changed instantly and their lives were transformed forever. Their worries and fears were gone, because they discovered their destiny. Likewise, when the Holy Spirit comes upon you, your spiritual eyes will be opened and you will be convinced that you need to repent and be baptized. You will become a new creature, with new thoughts and a new view of yourself. Your low self-esteem will be gone forever. But you need to collaborate with the Spirit of God.

Even if you feel no motivation, or do not see any reason to change your thinking and attitude, do it anyway and you will be the one to benefit the most. When God put the thoughts in my mind, and desire in my heart, to leave Romania, it did not make sense to me at all. Better circumstances were in my favor in Romania after the revolution in December, 1989. I knew how to live a simple life. I had my family, many friends, a house, my education, a job, a good church, spoke my native language, and practiced the profession I had studied for so many years. But I followed my God-given instinct and His instructions step by step, until I finally became what I am today, even though it was an extremely difficult process.

Now I know why I needed to be here in this country. I am glad that I listened to the small voice inside of me and obeyed the Holy Spirit, who has guided and instructed me all these years. The small voice inside me reassured me all the time that all was right with my soul, even though I often felt like I was walking in the valley of the shadow of death. It was tough, but everything that I perceived as impossible in the beginning, with God, became possible in every way.

Change your attitude and start to work even though you feel like you are in the "desert with no water" or in the "valley of the shadow of death," like I felt when I arrived in the US—knowing no English, having no plans, and not knowing what to do next. For months I did not know where I would sleep or where I would eat my next meal. Honestly speaking, I was homeless. God prepared "angels"—good friends who took care of me. I will mention their names so you will know they were real people: Arina, Nely, Maria, Marcela and many others. Through them God was working out my destiny.

I knew the Word of God and His promises, and I believed He had a destiny for me and my family, but that was a difficult time. People were giving me instructions to go to the left, and I was going to the right, because

I did not understand a word in English. I make fun of this now, but at that time it wasn't fun at all. Going to work and not being able to communicate with those around me was like going to a "funeral service" with sadness in my heart. I was afraid of failure and couldn't see myself succeeding in my own power and abilities. But I trusted God always.

See yourself through God's eyes to increase your self-esteem, and your dreams will become true when you start to work, continue to serve others, and pray and fast even though you do not feel like it. Your work may be hard, but be faithful in small things, even though they seem unimportant—even if bitterness floods your soul. Remember that God's eyes are always watching over you to fulfill your destiny.

God's Global Health Prescription

"...if My people who are called by My Name, will humble themselves and pray and seek My face and turn from their wicked ways, then I will hear from Heaven, and I will forgive their sin and will heal their land."
(2 Chron. 7:14)

God is in the business of healing and He wants the human race to be healthy. From creation God has shared divine, unexpired prescriptions in His Word for all His creation. His provision is made clear in this verse: "If My people who are called by My Name, will humble themselves and pray and seek My face and turn from their wicked ways, then I will hear from Heaven, and I will forgive their sin and will heal their land" (2 Chron. 7:14).

What I want to convey in this book is that God gave us instructions from the beginning on how to behave, how to stay healthy, and how to regain our health if we become ill. In the Ten Commandments God gave clear directions on Mount Sinai about right attitudes toward God, toward our neighbors, and toward ourselves. He set forth rules on what to eat, how to dress and how to behave in any situation. The Word of God taught us from the beginning how to react in stressful and uncontrollable circumstances. We cannot control death, but we can control the way we react when facing death. The Word of God ultimately is written to prevent spiritual diseases and the eternal death of our spirit.

There are still opportunities to return to God's instructions and restore healthy thoughts by renewing our mind and heart to follow a healthy lifestyle physically and spiritually. Many times we complicate things by trying to solve problems in our own strength. We don't want to follow God's instructions. God who created us knows our capacity to cope with situations. But many deceptions in the world blind people's eyes, so they cannot see God's plan or His desire for them to follow His divine prescriptions to stay healthy and prosperous.

The devil used evolutionists and atheistic communists to distract millions of people with lies about the non-existence of God, insulting the Creator of the Universe. This dogma confused the people, who gave up believing in the Word of God for physical and spiritual healing. I experienced this when living in a country victimized for several decades by the lies of a communist regime. It tortured me to hear the communist lies all the time.

People turning their back on a Sovereign God think they can control everything. I remember as a student in high school, and at the university in Bucharest, how we were taught by atheists that there is no God. The entire country was hopelessly deceived under the brutal, ruthless, false teaching for over 40 years.

I was disturbed by their false teaching, because I experienced God's Supernatural power and treasured His Word that transformed my life from a very young age. Many times in class, hearing the atheistic affirmation about an orphan planet with no Creator, I had to quote scriptures and write verses from the Bible on my notebook right in front of me to keep up my hope, stay strong, and preserve my faith in God. The communist teachers negated the existence of God and the power of His Word for decades. The false doctrine and the lies in the educational system continued in Romania until the revolution of December, 1989, but lots of confusion still remains today. Communist education had put the whole nation under the curse of a lie, denying God's existence in the Universe, and leaving the whole nation in terrible, hopeless distress.

Each time I visit Romania I see the consequences of those curses from the communist generations that reverberate even today in the lives of many people, both in Romania and abroad. The generational curse continues. The country that was so prosperous and blessed before communism has remained under a curse of physical and spiritual poverty for generations.

God's ways are the best plan for managing stress on a global scale. Stress is the root cause of all disease and turmoil in the world. Stress levels will decrease when you refuse to let your heart be troubled by bad thoughts and bad circumstances. Our thoughts and actions will shape our future and our eternity. Do you know God's prescriptions for your life? How carefully do you follow His instructions for a future that is safe and secure in His hand?

CHAPTER EIGHT

Unexpired, Divine Prescriptions

*"A cheerful heart is good medicine, but a crushed spirit
dries up the bones." (Prov. 17:22)*

*"I rejoice in following your statutes as one rejoices in great
riches, I meditate on your precepts and consider your ways,
I delight in your decrees." (Ps. 119:14)*

A Merry Heart

*T*he Book of Proverbs indicates that "A cheerful heart is good medicine, but a crushed spirit dries up the bones" (Prov. 17: 22). Yes, there is a medicine that makes a merry heart—the joy that fills our spirit. Healthy thoughts and the fruits of the spirit are able to reprogram our brain to release healthy amounts of neurochemicals and neurotransmitters throughout our system, to heal our body, mind and spirit. Scientists are now studying this ancient prescription from the Word of God. The best medicine of all—a merry heart—has the highest potency, and no expiration date.[1]

Divine Guard

*"And the peace of God, which transcends all understanding, will guard
your hearts and your minds in Christ Jesus." (Phil. 4:7)*

Our heart and mind are protected only when we follow God's prescriptions. "And the peace of God, which transcends all understanding, will guard your hearts and your minds in Christ Jesus" (Phil. 4:7). The Creator knew that only the peace of God could guard our mind, calm an overactive brain from stressful thoughts, and relieve our heart from emotional distress. About 3,500 years ago, after years of war, turmoil and depression, King David realized that only God's principles and prescriptions for a cheerful heart could heal his body and restore his crushed spirit. He valued God's prescriptions more than great riches, exclaiming, "I rejoice in following your statutes as one rejoices in great riches; I meditate on your precepts and consider your ways, I delight in your decrees" (Ps. 119:14).

God's decrees are His prescriptions for us. Prophetically David knew the blessing of being physically healthy. The health of our body, mind and soul depends on meditating on God's instructions.

Meditation, mentioned many times thousands of years ago, is a helpful treatment for high levels of stress from fear, worry, anxiety and depression. David, the strongest man of war against God's enemies, often meditated on God's precepts to receive peace and divine protection for the wars in his mind. It was the tool God recommended in the Old Testament for people to use to win physical and spiritual wars.

Around the end of the 20th century scientists discovered that meditation can reduce stress and promote neurogenesis. [2] New neurons created during meditation strengthen our thinking, providing a "divine guard" for the mind and releasing healing neurotransmitters. The Word of God that effectively healed people in ancient times works the same today. It also helps us discover who and what we are, who we can become, and how we can fulfill our destiny.

We are created with unimaginable power and built-in features to be creative. Our skills to cope with high levels of stress are amazing. Inspired by the Holy Spirit, King David exclaimed, "I am fearfully and wonderfully made; your works are wonderful" (Ps. 139:14). God included in our DNA everything we need to reach our full potential. When we follow God's divine prescriptions, through the power of the Holy Spirit we experience the peace that guards our heart and spirit in Christ Jesus.

Our DNA is the creative fingerprint of God in us. It is the language of the Super Intelligent Designer in each person, with all the characteristics God encoded in our genes. We just need to let the Holy Spirit transform our thinking and renew our spiritual DNA through His supernatural power.

DNA gives instructions to the cells, in order to maintain life. In the same nucleus where the DNA resides, there is a smaller *nucleus* called the nucleolus that contains RNA (Ribonucleic acid), with a genetic message to create proteins specified by messenger RNA for gene expression. Its thousands of amino acids are arranged in complex, precise sequences. This genetic life blueprint packed into the DNA carries genetic information which I believe is God's language in our human chromosomes. It gives instructions for life to each cell in the body. How can a human being's character be transformed and modified when our physical DNA intertwines with new spiritual DNA? Let's see how that can be possible.

New Spiritual DNA

"You must be born again. The wind blows wherever it pleases. You hear
its sound, but you cannot tell where it comes from or where it is going.
So it is with everyone born of the Spirit." (John 3:5–8)

"I will put My laws in their minds and write them on their heart. I will
be their God and they will be my people." (Heb. 8:10)

That brings to mind the Bible story of Nicodemus, a member of the Jewish ruling council in John, Chapter Three. Nicodemus came to Jesus to ask how to get into the Kingdom of God. The Lord Jesus replied, giving him (beyond science) a spiritual prescription almost 2,000 years ago.

> "Very truly I tell you, no one can enter the Kingdom of God unless they are born of water and the Spirit. Flesh gives birth to flesh, but the Spirit gives birth to spirit. You must not be surprised at my saying, You must be born again. The wind blows wherever it pleases. You hear its sound, but you cannot tell where it comes from or where it is going. So it is with everyone born of the Spirit." (John 3:5–8)

In my opinion, the "breeze" of the Spirit of God "blows" through our brain's cortex with "the forest" of our neurons—the "tree" configuration—to renew our thoughts and change our attitude, personality and identity As a born-again believer you become a godly, spiritual person with new thoughts, new attitudes, a new character, and new life in the Spirit.

When you are born again by the blood of Jesus, your personality will be changed completely. When Jesus Christ lives in you, your "spiritual DNA" is reborn, affecting your personality by activating Jesus's DNA in you. You are prone to righteousness, because the nature of Christ, who knew no sin, is righteous. Your personality is changed through His new covenant in His blood, shed on the cross. Even when Jesus was living on earth as a Man, He possessed God's "spiritual DNA".

I like to imagine that He enters from His spiritual realm, crossing (as the Spirit of the Lord did when Jesus was conceived in the body of Virgin Mary) into your physical body through the "buffering zone" of the subatomic quantum world (as described by Phil Manson in his book *Quantum Glory*).[3] You do not want to live in sin anymore because the Lord Jesus said, "I will put My laws in their minds and write them on their heart. I will be their God and they will be my people" (Heb. 8:10). The Word of God in our mind, and His prescription in our life, will change our thinking and behavior, and the new spiritual life will become part of our personality. The ability to obey the Lord and follow His law is built into our spiritual-biological DNA.

We just need to activate what He wrote on our heart and mind by the power of the Holy Spirit and the new covenant through the blood of Jesus. Only God knows your heart. No one else can know your thoughts and heart. Through advanced imaging technology scientists can observe the electrical impulses and the gene expression through the proteins that are created in our brain, but they cannot know our thoughts. Through God's grace humanity gained new "spiritual DNA" for a new destiny when Jesus died on the cross. He will extend His grace to anyone.

Desperate Inner Cry for Spiritual Health

"O Lord my God, I cried to you for help, and you healed me."
(Ps. 30:2 ESV)

"Sir, give me this water so that I won't get thirsty and have to keep coming here to draw water." (John 4:15)

Besides your physical health, it is very important for you to be aware of your need for spiritual health. God built the need for spiritual health into our unconscious mind, but in our consciousness we do not always want to listen to the Master. If we quiet our soul and listen to the small inner voice that seeks our attention, we realize that we need a healthy spirit to have a healthy body. There are no exceptions. There has always been a cry deep inside me for integrity, purity, honesty, emotional health, and problem-solving abilities. I always wanted to know who I was created to be, what God wanted me to be, and what I needed to learn from the experiences in my life. Many times I have literally cried out to God for a healthy spiritual life. That "good cry" always brought healing to my life. This has been my experience.

The Holy Spirit knows our inner cry for a restoration of our relationship with the Divine, and this will come when we turn our hearts and minds toward God. God will restore your relationship with the Father, the Creator of Heaven and earth, and with your Savior, Jesus, the Son of God, who died on the cross for the sins of the entire world. Through daily repentance, you receive the power to restore your relationships with God and everyone around you, through the power of forgiveness and divine love.

Even on the cross Jesus prayed for His enemies. They mocked Him, spit on Him, perforated His hands and feet with sharp nails, and His forehead with sharp thorns, and beat Him with heavy whips. Then they pierced His ribs and heart with a sharp spear and made Him suffer and hang on the cross in indescribable pain. Dying in agony, He prayed for them, "Father forgive them because they do not know what they do." He restored our relationship with the Father through the power of His crucifixion. Jesus took the weight of your sins on Himself, dying on the cross to bring deliverance of sin, and to give spiritual DNA to the entire world. You receive forgiveness for all your sins when you invite Jesus in to take control of your life, and return to the Father who deeply loves you.

Getting in line with the Word of God and His prescriptions for your life will deliver you from the stress of sin. Jesus died to restore you to what God planned for your life. You are the unique creation of God. God was thinking about you, even before the foundation of the world. The Father is looking for people to love Him back, who are sold out for Him, and thirsty for the "living water".

Prescription for Living Water

"...repent and be baptized, every one of you, in the name of Jesus Christ, for the forgiveness of your sins. And you will receive the gift of the Holy Spirit. The promise is for you and your children and for all who are far off—for all whom the LORD our God will call." (Acts 2:38–39)

Are you thirsty for the "living water" deep in your soul? In the Gospel of John, Chapter 4, the Samaritan woman was thirsty for more in her life. She wanted the "living water" to quench her spiritual thirst. In her conversation with Jesus at the well, she stated, "Sir, give me this water so that I won't get thirsty and have to keep coming here to draw water." Her deep inner needs made her thirsty for the living water. Nothing she had done in her life, including having five husbands, had satisfied her, but when she met the Lord Jesus, who gave her the "living water" her life changed. That "living water" began bubbling inside her instantly. She had to tell others that she had found Jesus, and people followed her because they saw the change in her. You need to meet Jesus, who can change your thoughts, attitudes and character. When your life is completely changed, people around you will see Jesus' work in you, and they will want to meet Jesus too.

People want to see an honest business person, a loving husband, a submissive wife, obedient children, and a young couple living in purity, a life of redemption, beauty and humility with no contamination from the secular world. You must develop an identity that will draw people to Jesus. Sinners are attracted to people who are living an uncompromised life, where there is uncontaminated "living water". The Word of God is the uncontaminated "living water" that will restore individuals, families, communities, societies and nations. This is God's vision for global health.

The book of Acts describes how, on the day of Pentecost, 120 people were drinking the uncontaminated "living water" from the Holy Spirit, and

3,000 sinners cried out the "good cry" for restoration of their spiritual health. After being touched by the power of the Holy Spirit, they cried, "What should we do?" and were immediately saved through the "living water". The same answer is available today for anyone who cries out for spiritual transformation. "Repent and be baptized, every one of you, in the name of Jesus Christ for the forgiveness of your sins. And you will receive the gift of the Holy Spirit. The promise is for you and your children and for all who are far off—for all whom the LORD our God will call" (Acts 2:38–39).

God's prescription for you, and for the whole world, has no expiration date. You are called to be forgiven of your sins and to receive eternal life. Follow God's prescription that transforms lives through the power of the Word, "the living water" and the anointing of the Holy Spirit. He intercedes for you even in this moment because of His covenant of relationship through the blood of Jesus. He will redeem your spiritual health for the sake of His love for you and He will not abandon the work of His hands (Ps. 138:8).

Learn to Hear God's Voice

"Although the Lord gives you the bread of adversity and the water of affliction, your teachers will be hidden no more; with your own eyes you will see them. Whether you turn to the right or to the left, your ears will hear a voice behind you, saying, "This is the way; walk in it."
(Isa. 30:20–21)

The promises of God will transform you, even when you are in despair, and without hope. Search the scriptures to find Jesus. Jesus has transformed billions of lives and hearts, and He can transform yours, too. [4] You must train your eyes to see the things of God and train your ears to hear His voice. Early in my career I was listening carefully with my stethoscope to an 83 year-old woman's heart. It sounded normal but there was a mild regurgitation from a mild stenosis in her aorta (i/vi on i-vi murmur scale), a very quiet murmur that I couldn't hear even with my stethoscope in my ears. I asked the cardiologist why I couldn't hear the murmur, and she explained that my ears were not trained to hear such a quiet murmur in a healthy heart. I later learned that only a cardiologist can hear that heart murmur, because of their specialty and experience. Their ears are trained.

When you study the Word of God every day, you will begin to recognize His voice every day in your life. It is important to get the Word of God into your mind and heart and to train your "spiritual ear" to hear His voice. Nobody can take away things hidden in your heart. During the communist regime we couldn't carry a Bible with us in our purse or take one to work. For the inner voice to be easily activated, we had to learn the Word, memorize verses, and recite those verses in hidden places so as not to forget them. Many Christians, when found reading the Bible or talking about God's goodness with others, lost their jobs. They relied on Christian friends to feed them and their family secretly. Communists did not provide social services or food stamp coupons. They did not encourage charity work at all. It was a difficult time, but I was able to train my ears to hear Jesus' call through His Word. Everything changes when you hear Jesus' voice in your heart. In the toughest circumstances His voice will bring you joy, love, peace, faith and hope that will last forever.

The Word of God transforms lives. If you meditate on the Word of God your thinking process will be changed, and your brain will be reprogrammed to think differently. Hope originates in the Word of God, which must become part of our daily life. You must invest time in the Word of God and pray for revelation and knowledge to be able to hear His voice. The Word gives you clear directions for eternal life. When the world around you falls apart, hope comes from the Word of God. Man lives by every Word that comes from the mouth of God. Continue to train your ears to hear the voice of the Lord through the Word.

The Small Voice

"And after the earthquake a fire; [but] the LORD [was] not in the fire: and after the fire a still small voice." (1 Kings 19:12 KJV)

There is a still, small voice inside your spirit. How amazing that the Creator placed in our brain the capacity to physiologically release GABA neurotransmitters into our physical body, as a biological response, to protect us from harm.[5] In the same way spiritually, the small voice is built into our spirit to protect us from physical and spiritual harm. A few years ago, close to midnight, one of my friends called me to consult about a new client who had just been admitted to her foster home. She asked me to assess this new patient tomorrow and make the necessary recommendations. I was in bed, in my pajamas, ready to fall asleep!

But after I hung up, the small voice inside me spoke to my heart that something was not right. My mirror neurons were activated in that moment to respond to someone's needs. I got up from my comfortable bed (after a very long day of taking care of many patients), changed my clothes, jumped into my car and drove to my friend's house. We resumed our conversation, and just when I got ready to leave her house the small voice came back again. I knew I had to go back to the patient's room, even though I was assured by the business owner that the patient was sleeping quietly in her room and that I could see her tomorrow during my normal visit.

Once in the doorway, I scanned the room and the bed where the patient was lying. The old woman's skin was so pale, and when I got closer and touched her skin it was cool and clammy. The linens were soaking wet. Immediately I began interventions to wake her up, and got the stat order to check her blood sugar level, which was a very low 37 mg/dl. She was semi-comatose, but aroused upon our verbal and tactile stimuli, and I gave her the right treatment. I observed her until she had fully recovered from her symptoms of hypoglycemia, and then I went home. My friend was shocked. She had never seen someone in this condition before. But she was even more shocked when she saw me show up at her door at midnight!

The small voice led me to save the life of the old woman, who could have died that night from a hypoglycemic reaction. Health care professionals are often in the position to rely on the inner, small voice, when interventions are needed to save lives. Everyone on earth has an inner voice and the mirror neurons, but they need to be activated by the Spirit of God.

God's Spirit Envelops Our Spirit

"For the Lord is the Spirit, and wherever the Spirit of the Lord is, there is freedom." (2 Cor. 3:17 NLT)

"...nothing in all creation is hidden from God's sight. Everything is uncovered and laid bare before the eyes of Him to whom we must give account." (Heb. 4:13)

In our genes, God designed everything we need to help us reach our full potential and fulfill our divine assignment. We must let the Spirit of God envelop our spirit to activate our God-given ability. We have God's Spirit in us and we must live in obedience to the will of God to fulfill our destiny. Imagine if the seven billion people on earth at this moment carried with them the Spirit of God. "What then shall we say in response to these things? If God is for us who can be against us?" (Rom. 8:31). Recite this verse when uncertainty and fear flood your heart, mind and soul. Your future will explode with blessings when He pours out His promises in your life.

God is *Jehovah El Roi*, Who sees everything in the Universe. We must give account to Him because "...nothing in all creation is hidden from God's sight. Everything is uncovered and laid bare before the eyes of Him to whom we must give account" (Heb. 4:13). He gave us His own breath and life, and we must be responsible before Him. He gave us His Spirit to envelop our spirit, to carry out God's plan for our life in spiritual health.

Manage Stress Through Repentance

"Surely the arm of the LORD is not too short to save, nor His ear too dull to hear. But your iniquities have separated you from your God; your sins have hidden His face from you." (Isa. 59:1–2)

Sin consumes people. Sin, and feelings of guilt, have consumed people since creation. And sin ultimately leads to death. God felt the pain of our sin, and He longed for man to reconcile with Him. Jesus came to earth to bring us back into relationship with our Creator and to bring us the joy of salvation. We need Jesus' continuous presence. He promised that He would be with us every day (Matt. 28:5–20). Trials will come, but through them He is in us, and with us always.

Life is empty without Jesus. Without Jesus, even the wealthiest person's life is empty. Sin and guilt make us feel separated from our Creator. "Surely the arm of the LORD is not too short to save, nor His ear too dull to hear. But your iniquities have separated you from your God; your sins have hidden His face from you" (Isa. 59:1–2). Yet that which separates us from God is invisible. "…for our struggle is not against flesh and blood, but against the rulers, against the authorities, against the powers of this dark world and against the spiritual forces of evil in the Heavenly realms" (Eph. 6:12). The invisible spiritual forces of evil tempt people to sin, including unhealthy thoughts and actions, bad habits, and unhealthy levels of stress.

Sin can creep into our life slowly and bring so much harm. Satan with his hideous strategies wants to separate us from God completely. Yet God, who is holy, does not tolerate sin. It is easy to become hardened by sin and stray far away from our Creator. We need to be rescued, but only through repentance and obedience to God's Word can we find our way back to God's plan for our life. God is fighting for us to fulfill our destiny, by providing a way to bring us back to Him when we repent of our sins. Obey, walk in the spirit, trust God and believe His Word, and you will overcome stress from sin. Obedience leads to intimacy with God.

Biblical Evidence

"Now these things happened to them as an example, and they were written for our instruction, upon whom the ends of the ages have come." (Cor. 10:11)

"…for whatever was written in earlier times was written for our instruction." (Rom. 15:4)

Apply the Word of God, with total repentance, fervent prayer and disciplined fasting to prevent the contamination of sin, paying careful attention to any destructive behaviors. Use the Word like a shield against sin, which can radiate through your entire body with "harmful chemicals" leading to incurable spiritual "cancer".

All things become new when you return to the Word of God, obey the Lord, hunger to know Him more, and follow God's prescriptions. King Solomon had great wisdom, but chose to live outside godly boundaries, consumed by materialism. A good man separates himself from the world, does not associate with sinners, nor listens to ungodly advice, nor does he sit in the seat of mockers. He is like a tree planted by the water; his works prosper when he "drinks" from the Word of God (Ps. 1).

The Word of God is valid. There are over five billion copies of the Bible worldwide. The Bible's 66 books were written by 40 different authors with different backgrounds over the span of about 1,500 years. What a miracle book.[6]

The Old Testament looks forward to the cross, and the New Testament looks back at the cross, representing God's truth. You shall know the truth, and the truth will set you free of all unhealthy, contaminated behavior. When people engage in destructive behavior, it is usually due to the lack of knowledge of God's Word and His Supernatural prescriptions. The choice you make about the Word of God is the prognosis of your destiny, on earth and for eternity. Through the Word of God you have the best prognosis ever known to mankind. Your prognosis for life is that you will live forever, when you follow God's unexpired, Supernatural prescriptions.

I used to study Bible characters' testimonies, hoping to learn how to cope with my own issues. "Now these things happened to them as an example, and they were written for our instruction, upon whom the ends of the ages have come" (Cor. 10:11). "For whatever was written in earlier times were written for our instruction" (Rom. 15:4).

God speaks to us every day through His Word. When I was lonely, with no family or friends around me, I was extremely worried. What if something happened to my husband and my daughter back in Romania? Many times I read, memorized and recited Jacob's story in Genesis. I learned that Jacob, in his loneliness, cried to the Lord, and the Lord revealed Himself to him. What a spectacular scene—he was lonely in a desert place, and God sent angels to ascend and descend on a ladder in his dream. Jacob was surrounded by angels! Sleeping with his head resting on a stone, "He had a dream in which he saw a stairway resting on the earth, with its top reaching to Heaven, and the angels of God were ascending and descending on it. There above it stood the Lord, and said: "I am the LORD" (Gen. 28:12,13). That gave me so much hope, knowing that God sends His angels to surround me, also. Each time I felt lonely and depressed I knelt before the Lord. I often read the Psalms King David wrote, inspired by the Holy Spirit, when he was depressed, discouraged, lonely, and crying out to God. And God fulfilled His promises and answered my prayers.

Holy "Macrophage"...for Spiritual Diseases

In the Bible, God's heart was moved when a nation repented, and He spared them. The people of Nineveh changed the way they were thinking, from the King on down to the least citizen, and when they repented before God the whole city was saved from destruction. The Jewish people renewed their mind, changed their thinking, and cleansed their hearts through repentance and fasting for three days and nights. Nineveh was in a moral crisis, and the King spoke to his nation to repent in order for God to have mercy on them and to spare them from wrath (Jonah chapter 3). Do not take a neutral position about a moral crisis in your personal life, your community, or your nation. John F. Kennedy, the 35th US President, stated: "Dante once said that the hottest places in hell are reserved for those who in a period of moral crisis maintain their neutrality."[7]

People need deliverance from all kinds of bondages. Put your deliverance in God's hands. In a moral crisis the battle is fought by the thoughts in your brain structures, with the "forest" of neurons. You must renew your thoughts to be transformed completely (Rom. 12:1–2). When you change your mind and become a new creation, you are a different person in your attitudes and your thoughts.

You have what I call "holy macrophages" in your spirit, given by the Holy Spirit when you renew your mind and become a new creation in Christ. In microbiology, macrophages are known as phagocytes that engulf and destroy cells that are enemies of the body, as apoptotic cells (programmed to die after their job is finished) and pathogens. These large white blood cells, called macrophages (part of the human immune system), locate the foreign bodies, engulf their microscopic particles through the process of phagocytosis, and destroy them.[8] In the invisible spiritual world, synonymous actions are done by "spiritual macrophages" that will engulf and dissolve your thoughts of anger, depression, bitterness, ungratefulness, ungodliness, unforgiveness, and the thoughts of doubt and unbelief that create so much stress and damage your spirit and your body. Continual repentance will amplify your "spiritual phagocytosis" and allow you to experience victory in your life. Do not remain bound by the past. If you are bound and spiritually debilitated, that will destroy your relationship with your Father. Do not wait until you go to Heaven. Repentance will guarantee your salvation, and you will be free of the stress of unforgiven sins.

Jesus is our Redeemer from any kind of sin. He became sin for us, so we could become righteous. Jesus was cursed for us, so we could be blessed.

Repentance Brings Forgiveness

"If we confess our sins, He is faithful and just and will forgive us our sins and purify us from all unrighteousness." (1 John 1:9)

Sincerely forgive everyone who has sinned against you. "Necrosis" happens in your soul when you cannot forgive. Physically, necrosis means dead tissues, devoid of life or circulation, which create more damage and disease.[9] Your brain, affected by unforgiveness, gets damaged. Unforgiveness causes feelings of anger, increasing your cortisol level, shrinking the dendrites of your nerve cells in your hippocampus, and killing neurons. Unhealthy levels of neurochemicals and neurotransmitters are released in the body, causing physical disease. You are not even able to make right decisions because your thinking process is further affected, creating imbalances in the chemical messengers and damaging your body, mind and spirit.

The Holy Spirit in you works to regenerate your soul. Get rid of the sin of unforgiveness. When you pray for forgiveness of sin, you must forgive others, too.

David changed his attitude through repentance, by weeping in prayer and fasting. Sin had brought disaster to his and Bathsheba's life when they lost their son. He needed deliverance from the bondage of sin to be able to move on in life and accomplish his assignment as King. He needed God to help him change. These examples are in the Bible to get our attention. Bible characters had to follow God's prescriptions for healing, and we have to do the same.

Recent scientific discoveries show that the human heart has nerve cells (neurons) that control the electrical impulses in the heart.[10] In order for you to turn your heart toward God, so your thoughts become actions, you must obey Christ's commandments with both your mind and heart and follow His Word (prescriptions) through fasting and praying. Let the power of the Holy Spirit change your mind and your heart.

Repentance Brings Peace

"I am the LORD *your God, who teaches you what is the best for you, who directs you in the way you should go. If you only had paid attention to my commands, your peace would have been like a river, your well-being like the waves of the sea." (Isa. 48:17)*

"...if it is possible, as far as it depends on you, live at peace with everyone." (Rom. 12:18)

You are called to turn to God, repent and be baptized (Acts 2:38). When you get baptized, all your sins that tormented you day and night, even sins in your unconscious mind, are forgiven. Then you receive the gift of the Holy Spirit to empower you with supernatural power to follow God's prescriptions for your life, as written in His Word.

You are not alone in fighting your battle with sin. You will receive a peace that passes all understanding. It will bring healing and restore your spirit, soul and body. That is the promise we have if we bring all our worries and problems to God in prayer. "Do not be anxious about anything, but in every situation, by prayer and petition, with thanksgiving, present your requests to God. And the peace of God which transcends all understanding will guard your hearts and your minds in Christ Jesus" (Phil. 4:6). His Word gives us His prescription for our emotional state: "Do not be afraid." The Lord remembers your prayers, and you will be the only one to see the supernatural power of God working in your life. Others will not see the same thing you see. Behind the veil, supernatural things happen. You are chosen the see the glory of God. Pursue God with a renewed heart for a successful life, and know that only God exercises kindness, justice and righteousness on earth (Jer. 9:23–24).

Trust in Jesus

"In Him we have redemption through His blood, the forgiveness of sins, in accordance with the riches of God's grace that He lavished on us." (Eph. 1:7)

You must find fulfillment in God and His Son Jesus Christ. Jesus' thoughts were 100% about you and me, and He chose to love us so much that He took our sins to the cross. He chose us before the foundation of the world. He eliminated sin by asking from the cross, "Father, forgive them, for they do not know what they are doing" (Luke 23: 34). He finished paying for our sins when, on the cross, He cried out to Heaven, "It is finished" (John 19:30).

There is no more separation between us and the Father, but many still live in doubt and unbelief and separate themselves from God, the source of life.

People are looking for reassurance and approval, but fail to find them outside of the Word of God. Yet true confirmation and approval come from the Lord. You are not perfect, so surrender and trust completely in the Lord Jesus. If you do not trust the One who died for you, whom do you trust? He is the only refuge for lost sinners. Only God can bring revival in your spirit and soul. Only Jesus can reveal Himself to you, relieve your stress, and reveal God's calling for you. Your expectations are in Jesus.

CHAPTER NINE

Forgiveness Brings Joy

"The joy of the LORD is your strength." (Neh. 8:10)

God's design is perfect. His prescription is: Trust in the Lord and in His power to receive His joy. If you accept His Word, it goes into your mind (brain), which will also affect your heart's "brain".[1] Our Maker built joy, and the power to love and trust, into our spiritual DNA. Sin hardens our heart, and robs us of joy, but peace and joy are ours when we confess our sins and ask to be forgiven.

Every day we must embrace God's forgiveness. Only joy can help soften the calluses in our heart. Do not give power to things that steal your joy. A joyful heart should be our goal, for that is exactly what God desires for us. Only through joy can we achieve strength physically and spiritually, for "...the joy of the LORD is your strength" (Neh. 8:10). Jesus' death and resurrection brought us the New Covenant, and the joy of salvation is for every heart whose sins are forgiven. Through Christ the whole world has access to the joy of the Lord and God's kingdom. Take a megadose of joy daily, because your sins are forgiven!

All Your Sin Debts Are Paid

"You forgave the iniquity of your people and covered all their sins."
(Ps. 85:)

Did you ever receive bills that were more than you could pay that month? Do you remember the butterfly feelings in your stomach (from increased, unhealthy amounts of neurotransmitters) when your anxiety level rose? You were reading the bad news that your balance was due before you got your paycheck! In response to your worry, fear and anxiety, your neurotransmitters were released in unhealthy amounts. Thinking of how you could pay your bills, anxiety rushed through your nerve cells, synapses and axons, and into your body tissues, slowly intoxicating all your cells. You created that atmosphere in your brain with your worried, fearful thoughts and anger. Spiritually, our Father paid the bills for our sins in full with His

Son's blood and sacrifice. We must listen to His voice, obey Him, trust His promises to take care of our needs, and receive His joy.

Declaring God's promises out loud with your voice will embed positive thoughts in your brain, affecting your physical body, because "...life and death is in your tongue" (Prov. 18:21). The promises of God are the seeds for your thoughts. His Word produces and develops thoughts that give life. Healthy levels of neurochemicals in your brain promote restoration and healing in your spirit, soul and body.

Receive Forgiveness

"...as far as the east is from the west, so far has He removed our transgressions from us." (Ps. 103:12)

Change your thinking and receive forgiveness for your sins through the power of the blood of Jesus who died on the cross. You need a relationship with the Father through Him. Your life no longer belongs to you. Reading the Word of God daily can wash you clean every day, refreshing your soul, just like taking a shower every day makes you feel and smell good and fresh. You can develop a sweet aroma with your Christ-like attitude and become more like Jesus, when you are washed in the Word of God daily and follow His prescriptions for supernatural solutions.

The stress from the weight of sin will dissipate when you are cleansed in the Blood of the Lamb of God, who took the sins of the world and is willing to give you forgiveness. Receive the gift of forgiveness by the unmerited grace of God: "In Him we have redemption through His blood, the forgiveness of sins, in accordance with the riches of God's grace that He lavished on us" (Eph. 1:7). The psalmist said, "You forgave the iniquity of your people and covered all their sins" (Ps. 85:2).

Sins are removed. "As far as the east is from the west, so far has He removed our transgressions from us" (Ps. 103:12). To reduce stress and eliminate its consequences you must not live in sin. First John 2:1 describes how we can be free from sins and their punishment. "I write this to you so that you will not sin, but if anybody does sin, we have an advocate with the Father—Jesus Christ, the Righteous One..." who died on the cross for the sins of the whole world. Confess your sin and you will receive forgiveness. "If we confess our sins, He is faithful and just and will forgive us our sins and purify us from all unrighteousness" (1 John 1:9). Your sin will not be remembered any more. By being purified from all your sins and unrighteousness, your spiritual health is completely restored through His unfailing love.

Train Your Mind for Change

"Dear friends, I pray that you may enjoy good health and that all may go well with you, even as your soul is getting along well." (3 John 1:2)

We must train our mind and change our thinking habits by meditating day and night on the Word of God and His promises. This develops new neurons, so we can think clearly and make the right decisions in crises. When you meditate on the Word of God, intrusive thoughts dissipate. Our Lord Jesus Christ wants us to be healthy. "Dear friends, I pray that you may enjoy good health and that all may go well with you, even as your soul is getting along well." (3 John 1:2). God wants us to be stress free. God allows problems in our life so we can learn patience, perseverance, and complete dependence on Him. He delays for a season, but His promises will be fulfilled. Just be patient.

Do not miss the opportunities in your trials. One of my friends, a divorced single mom, prayed for more time after being diagnosed with cancer. Her children were young, and there was no one else to provide for them. God answered her prayer by prolonging her life with 3.5 more years, not 4–6 months. So her children got a little older, could make decisions for themselves, get an education and find jobs. They were surrounded by godly advisers who helped them until they were able to work and make their own living. (You ask why God did not heal her completely. That I do not know. That is beyond our comprehension. Many things in life are a mystery.)

Trust God in Any Situation

"Be still and know that I am God." (Ps. 46:10)

Trust God even though it seems that He delays in answering your prayers. Many times we are in the shadow of thick, gray clouds and it is hard to believe the sun is shining somewhere else. Even in your seasons of doubt and unbelief, you must know that God's love shines on you continuously and He has a plan and a purpose for your life. His light is shining even in the darkest hour of your life. I cannot emphasize enough the importance to stay still and know that God loves you. He has a great interest in your life. God tells us, "Be still and know that I am God" (Ps. 46:10). Let hope arise inside you. The Son is shining for you, even though the "clouds are thick and dark" and you cannot see light on the horizon. In God there is no limit. Do not limit God's options. God has a purpose, so wait for His timing, and He will fulfill His plan and His purpose in your life.

He has given me victory many times, in the darkest moments of my life, and brought me out of many wilderness trials with great victory, beyond whatever I asked or imagined. He did it for me and my family and He will do it for you. Trust Him and be still.

Repentance Brings Restoration

"Blessed is the one whose transgressions are forgiven,
whose sins are covered." (Ps. 32:1)

Physiological and psychological crises are born from fear and worry. Fear of punishment and of the unknown can be major factors in creating high levels of stress, resulting in emotional and physical conditions. That is the time to seek God. We read in Jonah 3:7–9 that the whole city of Nineveh, in their crisis, feared punishment for their sins, and the unknown gripped their hearts. They all sought God and turned away from their evils, from the King's house to the animals, humbling themselves through fasting and repentance. Fasting bring solutions in your spiritual and physical being, promoting spiritual and physical restoration and health and preventing spiritual and physical disaster.

Through crisis, God creates a necessity so you will seek Him. In times of crisis run to God, because He promised that when you seek Him you will find Him, and when you ask of Him He will answer your requests, and when you knock He will open the doors for you. Sin brings fear of punishment and spiritual and physical illnesses. We need prescriptions and treatments for both spiritual and physical illnesses. The breath in our lungs and the heartbeats of our heart are from God, to sustain this body that carries the eternal soul and spirit. When we are touched by the power of God and by His Holy Spirit; and when the Holy Spirit collides with our spirit threshold, we instantly get His spiritual DNA intertwining with our physical DNA, restoring our inner being.

Repentance restores and regenerates your entire wellbeing. Physically we carry our parents' DNA in our body, and our children carry our DNA. Spiritually, when we become God's children, we receive His spirit, and we carry our Heavenly Father's DNA intertwined with our DNA. God is love. Our hearts are filled with supernatural love. Being born of God through His supernatural power, being full of unspeakable joy that reprograms activities in our brain for healthy amounts of neurotransmitters to be released, we enjoy physical and spiritual healing and restoration.

When people repent, God takes action. He revokes the punishment of their sins and shows mercy and compassion toward them and saves their lives. God's compassion for people is tremendous. He is a Holy God, waiting for people to follow His instructions for consecration and repentance.

Scientists and psychologists talk about the importance of forgiveness in our physical health.[2] It is human nature, that when somebody is doing something wrong to us we wish they would get what they deserve, but then we accumulate destructive thoughts of anger and bitterness in our mind and soul. As a result the stress hormone cortisol increases to unhealthy levels, shrinking the hippocampus area. Its activities with other structures of the brain are impaired. The hypothalamus (the pleasure center) deprives our whole being of joy and happiness, leading to depression.

To prevent this process we must follow Jesus' example of forgiveness. At the worst times, when life hurts the most, you must pray for the power to forgive. When you forgive, deliverance comes. You will feel relief and peace, and love will replace your bitterness and anger. The people you forgave will change. God's prescription is, "…if it is possible, as far as it depends on you, live at peace with everyone" (Rom. 12:18). Peace is an extremely important part of restoring your emotional and physical health.

Confession Brings Health

"…bones wasted away through my groaning all day long." (Ps. 32:3)

The psalmist stated, "…bones wasted away through my groaning all day long" (Ps. 32:3). As long as he did not confess his sins, even his bones were affected. When you confess your sins before God and are forgiven, your soul is restored and your health improves! Healthy means a healthy heart, with no high blood pressure, no palpitations, no cardiovascular diseases, no diabetes, no high cholesterol, no anxiety, no depression and no other diseases related to high levels of stress. All those can be avoided when we are free from internal sins, unrighteous thoughts, unnecessary worry, fear, and high stress.

Spiritually Redeemed DNA

"…very truly I tell you, no one can see the kingdom of God
unless they are born again. (John 3:3)

"…though your sins are like scarlet, they shall be as white as snow;
though they are red as crimson, they shall be like wool." (Isa. 1:18)

Only being born again can renew your mind. In John 3:3 Jesus said, "…very truly I tell you, no one can see the kingdom of God unless they are born again." To be born again means you become spiritually a new creation, your thinking is transformed, and your lifestyle is changed completely. Your spiritual DNA is renewed. Your personality and character will be changed. This happens only when you accept Jesus Christ as your Lord and Savior, and His spirit takes residency in you. You let the Holy Spirit take control over your mind and spirit, which further controls your entire being.

Supernaturally, He will give you a new beginning, and unspeakable joy will fill your heart and soul. The burden and stress from past sins will fall away. Your life will be led by the Spirit, and you will be careful not to grieve the Holy Spirit with worldly thinking, actions and unhealthy choices. Now you will focus on things above, where Christ is seated at the right hand of the Father. You will think more about your purpose in life. Now your desire will be to do good deeds, and you will have great rewards, on earth and in Heaven.

Jesus was born in a humble place—a manger—to show the world that He did not need a fancy birthplace, even though He came from the glories of Heaven. He wanted to show mankind that He could be born in anyone's heart—even the most miserable heart, full of sin and oppression—through His Holy Spirit. "Though your sins are like scarlet, they shall be as white as snow; though they are red as crimson, they shall be like wool" (Isa. 1:18). Even though Jesus was the Son of God, He died on the cross among thieves and murderers, demonstrating that any person, with any kind of sin, can receive salvation through His precious holy blood shed on that cross over 2,000 years ago. No sin is too big for Him to forgive, or too dirty to wash it clean.

A Supernatural Event

"…you will receive power." (Acts 1:8)

When you become a child of God, your entire mind and soul are instantly and supernaturally transformed. I myself experienced this incredible process of forgiveness of sins and getting born again by the power of the Holy Spirit. Up until then, I was aware of the emptiness in my heart even at that very early age. When I was 13 years old God touched my heart during prayer time one evening with a small group of teenagers. They were on their knees praying, in a small house where we met regularly as a church. I joined them, but I did not know how to pray. I had only heard my parents and my older sisters and brothers praying. At that particular prayer meeting my uncle George, a devoted Christian, asked me to pray with a loud voice. Never had I prayed with a loud voice! I was very shy due to low self-esteem. When I heard my name called to pray I began to shake with fear, not knowing what to say. All the other children were on their knees, quietly waiting to hear my voice rise in prayer. To their surprise I opened my mouth, and the words started to flow. So my mouth was filled with words that evening as I opened my mouth to pray with a loud and passionate voice. It was a sincere, fervent prayer from the bottom of my heart, because I wanted to know God for myself. From then on my heart started to change. I wanted to pray more. I became hungry and thirsty for more of Jesus in my life.

Through that prayer my heart was touched by God. Each time I heard there was a prayer meeting I just wanted to be there, even though it was dangerous to attend a prayer group during the communist regime at that time in Romania. The prayer meetings usually met secretly in different houses, because it was against the law to meet for prayer groups or even to talk about prayer or about God. We often had to walk two or three kilometers to secret prayer meetings. We didn't have cars or public transportation at that time.

A New Year's Eve to Remember

I remember New Year's Eve of 1974, a few years after my first encounter with God. We met in a widow's house in another village to pray. I walked in the snow about three kilometers for that night of prayer. The widow's house had pillows stuffed in the windows, and the doors were blocked with wood for secrecy and protection from the communist authorities. She was a very poor widow woman with five children, and we had to kneel on that dirt floor. There was no modern flooring, but you could feel the warmth of their hearts. When they started to pray, it was like the house was "on fire". I was filled with the power of the Holy Spirit during the prayer time that night.

I will never forget the power of God as it filled my whole being. I was overwhelmed and enveloped in the power of the Holy Spirit. It was a supernatural experience. I felt His presence when the power of the Lord fell on me and the Holy Spirit joined my spirit. God made me consciously aware of His presence. I was immersed in the power of the Holy Spirit and a shift happened in my whole being. The power of God was intense. It overwhelmed my soul and spirit as exceeding joy flooded my soul. At that moment the Holy Spirit crossed the threshold into my physical being from the spiritual realm. The Spirit of God collided with my spirit and I was born again and changed into a different person. Something supernatural happened in my soul. My thinking was changed instantly and completely. I was born again with new spiritual DNA.

Invasion of the Supernatural

"You must be born again. The wind blows wherever it pleases. You hear its sound, but you cannot tell where it comes from or where it is going. So it is with everyone born of the Spirit." (John 3:5–8)

Phil Manson, Author, Christian Theologian and Pastor from Australia, describes in his book *The Quantum Glory*, how the relationship between electricity and natural light parallel the glory and power of God. He stated,

> Individual quanta of natural light travel as a wave of electromagnetic radiation. A photon leaves the sun as a particle; it travels through space as a wave but arrives at its destination as a particle. The wave-particle duality of photons is a property of all quanta, including electrons.... photons actually carry electrical charges so that when a photon collides with a metallic surface such as in a solar panel the energy of the photon is absorbed by the electrons and an electrical current is created as electrons break away from atoms. That is why solar panel can convert photons into electrical power. In a similar manner the supernatural light of God energizes those who are radiated by the glory of God. God's glory is extremely powerful. It is not an inert substance; it actually imparts spiritual power or energy.[3]

I love the science of quantum physics because it explains what happens in the subatomic, invisible world—the building blocks for the physical, visible world. Using our imagination and intuition we can imagine and understand how it is possible for the invisible supernatural world to invade our physical world.

Divine Touch

The spirit of the Lord came to dwell in my spirit, crossing from the invisible spiritual world to my physical being. How can that be? One example is the threshold crossed when ice becomes water. Zero degrees Celsius is the freezing threshold of ice. Above that the ice molecules become water (liquid), and water molecules become steam at 100 degrees Celsius.[4] Using our gift of intuition, we can imagine a threshold in the spiritual realm. The power of the Holy Spirit breaks out from the invisible world and crosses into the threshold of our physical world with a speed faster than the speed of light. Invading our soul, the Holy Spirit transforms our old person into a new, spiritually redeemed creation.[5]

Our Universe has many invisible waves—electromagnetic radiation, microwaves, X-rays, radio waves, gamma waves, infrared light, and ultraviolet light. All the seen and unseen elements of the universe interact in complete harmony. Why not invisible spiritual waves too, that are often felt as an "electrical" force when Christians experience the power of the Holy Spirit. Our physical world interacts constantly with the Spiritual world. The Spirit of God sustains all things in perfect harmony in the Universe. He is communicating to us when He pours out His Spirit, crossing our physical threshold and allowing us to feel His divine touch through a deep joy, peace and happiness.

Transformation Through Spiritual "Electrocution"

It is hard to describe the feelings and emotions that rushed through my body, like an electrical current sending warmth from the top of my head to the tip of my toes. I sensed a divine transformation through the supernatural power of God. It was like the ceiling disappeared and Heaven opened wide over me, and my soul was immersed in a Heavenly realm. I had never felt that sensation of the power of God touching me. I just felt connected to the supernatural power of God. I was crying out loud that, "I was touched by God." I felt the harmony of Heaven. I started to glorify God like never before. Nobody could stop me. All the sisters around me felt the same touch, and all of them were crying for joy. Suddenly my thoughts and emotions were different under the Holy Spirit's control. The chemistry of my thinking changed the moment I felt the power of the Holy Spirit coming over me. Inside me every cell received a "transplant" of my spiritual DNA. Everything in me became new, and I was a new person with new thoughts, a new character and a new personality. I was born of the Spirit. It was a *supernatural* event. I received unspeakable joy. It was exactly how Jesus told Nicodemus in John 3:5–8:

> "Very truly I tell you, no one can enter the kingdom of God unless they are born of water and the Spirit. Flesh gives birth to flesh, but the Spirit gives birth to spirit. You should not be surprised at my saying, 'you must be born again.' The wind blows wherever it pleases. You hear its sound, but you cannot tell where it comes from or where it is going. So it is with everyone born of the Spirit" (John 3:5–8).

That was exactly what I experienced. God's spirit gave birth to my spirit through the "wind" of the Holy Spirit.

Benny Hinn, founder of the World Healing Center in Dallas, Texas and "This Is Your Day" TV program, in his book *Good Morning Holy Spirit*, describes his feeling when he met the Holy Spirit:

> "...like a jolt of electricity, my body began to vibrate all over—exactly as it had through the two hours I waited to get into the church. It was the same shaking I had felt for another hour once inside...vibrating from

my head to my toes…I was shaking, but at the same time I again felt that warm blanket of God's power wrapped all around me. I felt as if I had been translated to Heaven."[6]

It was amazing to find out later, from reading *Good Morning Holy Spirit*, that the same feelings and symptoms felt by Benny Hinn at the age of 21 in December, 1973 in Pittsburgh, Pennsylvania, were the same that I felt on New Year's Eve that same year and the same month (December 31, 1973—January 1, 1974), about 4,870 miles away in that poor village in northern Romania. I was profoundly moved, realizing this was no coincidence. It was the manifestation of God's presence. Perhaps it is a kind of spiritual electrical discharge from the invisible spiritual realm into billions of neurons in our brain cortex. Firing through trillions of synapses, they release an optimal amount of healthy neurotransmitters, making us feel incredible joy, peace and happiness in that moment when Heaven is open and the Holy Spirit is poured out. We who are touched by Him experience a divine, indescribable phenomenon. It is both a mystery and a reality.

At that time I did not know anything about Christians elsewhere in the world. In Romania we were not allowed to read Christian literature, and our TV programs only featured communist personalities. We had no international TV shows, and I did not speak English at all. I had never heard any talk about other Christians receiving the power of the Holy Spirit. Now, when I hear about other Christians' encounters with the Holy Spirit, I connect the dots. The Jesus Movement was during the 1970s. Christians all over the world felt the Holy Spirit's power and the revival, even in the spiritually dark, far corners of communist countries.

Holy Spirit Thinking

What Jesus explained to Nicodemus so long ago happened to me 2,000 years later. While I was fervently praying on my knees I felt the sudden power, the electricity, the unusual warmth, and a great joy flooded my soul with feelings that words cannot describe. I felt like a fire was burning in my body. The Spirit gave birth to me spiritually. Before that happened my heart was so cold, and my brain was filled with unclean thoughts of doubt and unbelief. But when Jesus was born in my heart, the miracle took place suddenly through the power of the Holy Spirit. My life has been changed completely. From that moment on I did not want to grieve the Holy Spirit through my thinking or behavior. My mind has been reprogrammed with the desire to learn the Word of God, to saturate my soul with His presence, His instructions, His prescriptions—beyond science—and His promises for life. I now desire to be filled with the fruits of the spirit: joy, love, happiness, kindness, patience, gentleness, and self-control. I want to do good deeds all the time to those around me.

Now I understand how all the clean thoughts started to flow through the billions of dendrites of my brain cells with a "tree" configuration and brought forth the fruits of spiritual thinking, as joy, love and peace flooded my soul. I became more patient with everybody around me. My friends, colleagues and everyone noticed a radical change in my character and personality. They started to see more kindness, gentleness, faithfulness, goodness and self-control in my behavior. I was a different person, born in the spirit, just like Jesus told Nicodemus. All things became new. I had to say "No" to all intrusive thoughts and distractions. Immediately I started to focus on what the Word of God says about living a new life in Christ.

I know that with God, all things are possible. I lived that experience. I know that millions of Christians have experienced the power of God in their life, but only a few are actively sharing it. The supernatural power of the Holy Spirit is working in people's lives today. He is the same yesterday, today and forever. The Holy Spirit is real.

Access to Jesus

You can consciously experience—literally, beyond science—the power of God through the Holy Spirit's power. If you draw near to Him, He will draw near to you. The Holy Spirit interferes with our conscious mind in the prefrontal cortex and makes us conscious of His presence.[7] Our spiritual eyes are opened so we can see ourselves and the world around us through the eyes of Jesus, changing our thoughts through His divine power when we access Him.

Holy Spirit—Beyond Science

"If you then, though you are evil, know how to give good gifts to your children, how much more will your Father in Heaven give the Holy Spirit to those who ask Him." (Luke 11:13)

Though we live in a visible world, we can communicate with the invisible spiritual world when there is a true burning desire in our heart. I have heard neuroscientists lecture on how the mind's conscious and unconscious states are completely hidden, and we are strangers to ourselves.[8] Scientists have no direct access to a conscious human mind or to unconscious experiences. But the Holy Spirit has *always* been giving humans life-changing, amazing, divine experiences.

The Holy Spirit, God's supernatural power working on earth today, can come and change your thinking completely if you ask God the Father. The Holy Spirit will not come if you do not ask in prayer. See the Book of Luke. "If you then, though you are evil, know how to give good gifts to your children, how much more will your Father in Heaven give the Holy Spirit to those who ask Him!" (Luke 11:13).

It is God's pleasure to give the Holy Spirit to those who ask Him, just like earthly fathers like to give good gifts to their children. We have one daughter, Andreea. I don't remember one time when she asked us for something she wanted that was useful to her, that we as her parents said no. Many times we did express our rules, like be a good student, do what is right, be home no later than 10 p.m. and be obedient. But everything we asked her to do was for her benefit as a teenager. She willingly followed the rules and we, as her parents, gave her the things she asked for with so much pleasure, even more then she could ask or think. This is exactly the same thing Jesus taught us in Luke. Jesus knew how we were created. God put that desire in our DNA and our mirror neurons to bless our children, and meet their needs and their heart's desires.

The same way, our Father in Heaven will give good gifts, including the Holy Spirit, to those who ask and follow His directions and live in obedience. The relationship between parents and children illustrates the relationship of our Father in Heaven with us, His children, who are desperately in need of the power of the Holy Spirit to change our thoughts and to restore and heal our emotional and physical needs.

Supernatural Prescription Inside Us

Even when we eat there is a physical prescription inside us in our satiety center that enables us to ingest what is necessary.[9] There is also a *spiritual prescription* inside us to make us hungry for spiritual food, so our soul can be satisfied and we can function spiritually. With all our advanced technology and scientific information about the human body and DNA, it takes more faith to believe the world happened by accident than to believe we were created by the Creator, whose love for us put inside us a hunger to seek Him. He does not force His ways on us. We must choose to follow Him. Everything that exists in nature has a mirror in the spiritual realm. That is why we have unsatisfied spiritual needs, just as we have physical needs waiting for His power to satisfy them.

Obey the Holy Spirit

"If you love Me, keep My commands. And I will ask the Father, and He will give you another Advocate to help you and be with you forever—the Spirit of truth. The world cannot accept Him, because it neither sees Him nor knows Him. But you know Him, for He lives with you and will be in you." (John 14:15-17)

The Holy Spirit is talking to you all the time. He is talking about your future; you just need to listen. The promise of God to give us the Holy Spirit has been fulfilled. Jesus promised that the Father would give another Comforter. "If you love Me, keep My commands. And I will ask the Father, and He will give you another Advocate to help you and be with you forever—the Spirit of truth. The world cannot accept Him, because it neither sees Him nor knows Him. But you know Him, for He lives with you and will be in you" (John 14:15-17). The Holy Spirit is given to those who ask for Him to be their Counselor, Helper, Intercessor, Advocate, and Strength.

The Holy Spirit activated thoughts of eternity in me. Without the Holy Spirit I could never have coped with all the stressful situations in Bucharest under communism, much less when I immigrated to a strange country, not speaking the language. All our success came about through the power of the Holy Spirit who guided us, helped us, advocated for us, and strengthened us. I challenge you to invite the Holy Spirit into your heart. You will have a supernatural adventure, experiencing the presence of God as never before. He will help you more than you can imagine.

Connect with God's Supernatural Power

"Not by might nor by power, but by my Spirit, says the LORD Almighty." (Zech. 4:6)

In a moment, with one touch, you can be connected with the supernatural power of God and be transformed. His supernatural power is like a magnet attracting people. His heart is filled with compassion for a broken world. He can open your spiritual and physical eyes. God will never withhold things from us. He gave His One and Only Son to save the world. He did not send an angel or some special mortal. He gave us His Son, who stepped onto Earth from eternity, and He promised to give us the Holy Spirit. God's power breaks all the chains—addictions of any kind: drugs, alcohol, adultery—as well as cancer, depression, poverty, deception, doubt, unbelief, fear and anxiety.

People are transformed through the power of God's Word, the power of the Name of Jesus, and the power of the Holy Spirit. Just wait for God to show up in your life, giving you power to face temptations when you are connected with His supernatural power. Many human traditions lead to destruction. You can overcome those human traditions only through the power of God from above. It is a spiritual battle that you can win only through the power of the Holy Spirit. "But you will receive power when the Holy Spirit comes on you; and you will be My witnesses in Jerusalem, and in all Judea and Samaria, and to the ends of the earth" (Acts 1:8).

The power you receive will help you do great things. But you cannot do it alone. Ask God to fill you with His Spirit. His promise connects you with His supernatural spiritual realm. God is with you! "By this I will know that God is for me" (Ps. 56: 9). And, "If God is for us who can be against us?" (Rom. 8:31). Your stress level will decrease, your brain will calm down from worry, fear and anxiety through the power of God's Spirit, as it is written: "Not by might nor by power, but by my Spirit,' says the LORD Almighty" (Zech. 4:6).

The Word Changes Behavior

"For this reason I kneel before the Father, from whom every family in Heaven and on earth derives its name. I pray that out of his glorious riches he may strengthen you with power through his Spirit in your inner being, so that Christ may dwell in your hearts through faith. And I pray that you, being rooted and established in love, may have power, together with all the Lord's holy people, to grasp how wide and long and deep is the love of Christ, and to know this love that surpasses knowledge—that you may be filled to the measure of all the fullness of God. Now to Him who is able to do immeasurably more than all we ask or imagine, according to his power that is within us." (Eph. 3:14–20)

Even behavioral scientists use biblical principles to change peoples' behavior when they are desperate and uncertain of their future. The principles from the Bible work to change our behavior, and they give us assurance. Scientists feel limited and powerless to change people's behavior, but the Bible is the foundation for hope. Even though there is no hope here on earth, there is hope for eternity for suffering people, and for everyone when it is our time to leave this planet. I have worked with patients with serious behavior problems, mental conditions and neurocognitive disorders for about 26 years, and I use non-pharmacological and pharmacological interventions to manage their behavior. Specialists recognize that medications alone have limited results.[10] Many mental conditions are developed as a result of bad behaviors earlier in life, such as drugs, alcohol, adultery, etc. Science is often powerless to help these people with mental diseases.[11] Even with medications, in many cases we see little improvements or none at all. I advise you to visit a few memory care units, psychiatric units in geriatric and state hospitals, and even nursing homes to get some insights and reevaluate your belief systems and values.

The most often used non-pharmacological methods are love, prayer and the promises in the Word of God. I was impressed with one scientist's method to treat the symptoms from fear, anxiety and depression that one of his patients had experienced for years. After extensive treatments, therapy sessions, multiple ER visits, and hospitalizations, with the same signs and symptoms but no physiological diseases, the specialist decided to have the patient reflect on his past relationship with his parents. That was what seemed to trigger the patient's symptoms.

This highly specialized physician asked the patient to forgive his parents for abusing him as a child, and to ask his parents for forgiveness. He was reluctant—afraid of worsening the relationship, and his symptoms as well. For many years he had suppressed his harmful feelings, being afraid to expose them. The physician asked his patient to write his issues on paper and read it to him over the phone, but the patient declined that too. The physician insisted that he write all his feelings on the paper, and then next, write out the conversation he would wish to have with his mother. Finally, he agreed to follow his doctor's recommendation. After he wrote the letter, pouring out his heart and mind to his parents, his symptoms disappeared.

When the Psalmist David was in great distress he wrote psalms, pouring out his heart to God, His Creator. This gave him peace and joy, healing his broken heart and restoring his soul. If you are in psychological distress, causing physical symptoms, write down your feelings and pour out your heart. Ask God for forgiveness, and then forgive whomever you need to forgive. (Read all of David's 150 Psalms. It will do so much good to your body, mind and soul.) This supernatural prescription also applies to future unborn generations. "This will be written for the generation to come, that a people yet to be created may praise the LORD" (Ps. 102:18).

Remember, joy is also transferable. Empty your brain of those hidden, harmful emotional triggers and memories, and renew your thoughts with the Word of God. Exchange anger and fear with joy. Recognize that you have been offended in the past, write a letter to that offending person, and read it out loud as you imagine having that person in front of you. A better way is to address that letter to God and read it to Him in prayer. He will hear from Heaven and will heal your emotions.

It is well documented that when people write a letter to the person who offended them, and read out it loud (even if that person is dead), there is a huge therapeutic effect, which prevents further physical and psychological damage. Harmful emotions and thoughts are replaced with peaceful thoughts that bring joy and hope.

Confidence Comes from God

"Let us then approach God's throne of grace with confidence, so that we may receive mercy and find grace to help us in our time of need."
(Heb. 4:16)

Because of worry, pessimism, depression and anxiety our confidence and vision is stolen and our mind is "clouded", further increasing our stress level. As we continue to struggle with our emotions our inner being is further harmed. God has the answers to all the puzzles in His almighty hand. If you look at your circumstances your spirit will suffocate. Jesus is ready to rebuke the "wind" of worry and calm the "storms" in your life if you trust Him, obey Him, wait for Him to intervene, and rest confidently in Him.

Confidence is a very important element in reducing stress and accomplishing our daily tasks. We need confidence to have a clear vision for our future. Joyce Meyer, a number one New York Times bestselling author, in her book *Power Thoughts: 12 Strategies to Win the Battle of the Mind*, says one way to defeat fear is to be confident, even if you do not feel that way. She states,

> "I have decided that I am confident, whether I happen to feel confident or not. Sometimes I feel more confident than I do at other times, but I go out confident that God is with me, and because of that I can do whatever I need to do and enjoy the process. I choose to be confident instead of fearful, even when potentially fearful situations arise."[12]

That confidence comes from God alone, as we read in Hebrews: "Let us then approach God's throne of grace with confidence, so that we may receive mercy and find grace to help us in our time of need" (Heb. 4:16). You must know God, open your heart, and talk to Him. Rest in Him and have confidence that He is ready to help you in small and big things. Each time you have a victory, write it down. When you feel worried and anxious about your future, look at those notes and regain your confidence.

On December 18, 2008 we opened our 30-bed health care facility for the first time in the US. That was such a great accomplishment for my husband and me. Looking back, we had come into this country with empty hands, speaking no English. We had no money and were basically homeless, sleeping in different friends' houses, and not knowing where we would eat our next meal. So when we opened our facility we literally put a stone of remembrance right on our desks with a verse from 1 Samuel 7:12: "Thus far the Lord has helped us." That gave us confidence, knowing He had helped us so far, and He would help us the rest of our lives. What an encouragement for us.

Each time a thought of discouragement crosses our minds and worry tries to "cloud" our vision for future projects, we are reminded that God helped us so far, and He will do it again. Our confidence in God's power increases, and His promises strengthen us every day. We cannot do anything without God. We must trust Him in every situation. He can bring restoration of your visions and dreams miraculously when you have confidence in His unfailing love and mighty power to do everything above what you can ask or think. When you trust in the Lord He will fight for you and bring you peace. God is faithful to fulfill, for you, all the promises written in His Word, like He did for me and my family. Supernatural power can touch your life when your hope is in Him. You must forget what is behind you and move on with confidence, motivation and perseverance. You must persist and ask God to touch you again with His power. He will do it if you hunger to know Him and His mighty power with all your heart.

Not Your Own Understanding

"Trust in the LORD with all your heart and lean not on your own understanding; in all your ways submit to Him, and He will make your paths straight. Do not be wise in your own eyes; fear the LORD and shun evil. This will bring health to your body and nourishment to your bones." (Prov. 3:5–8)

People who lean on their own understanding are more stressed. The world will blind our spiritual eyes, limiting our ability to cope with stress. Facing unknown situations is stressful. For many, just hearing about a crisis situation makes their heart pound and race. Neurochemicals are released in uncontrollable amounts at the first thought of it, knowing that there is no logical solution for the problem. People crave reassurance to cope with high levels of stress from the unknown.

We need to trust in the Creator of the Universe, the omniscient *Jehovah El Roi*, who knows the solutions for all our problems. We cannot trust in our own understanding, intelligence and accomplishments, because it is written: "Trust in the LORD with all your heart and lean not on your own understanding; in all your ways submit to Him, and He will make your paths straight. Do not be wise in your own eyes; fear the LORD and shun evil. This will bring health to your body and nourishment to your bones" (Prov. 3:5–8).

I learned to trust God through faith and follow God's prescriptions for supernatural solutions, and I received health in my body and overflowing blessings. This is how it works. In any given situation you trust that He is in control. The fear is gone, the neurotransmitter level is normalized, and the parasympathetic system will help your body to maintain a homeostatic balance. You relax and return to a normal blood pressure, normal heart rate, normal breathing, and normal digestive function. We have God's prescriptions inside us to maintain our health, because He knows how we are created, and what state of mind and what kind of thoughts we need for homeostasis (balance). He knows what happens in our body, even our bones, when there is an imbalance. All our hairs are numbered by Him. "Indeed, the very hairs of your head are all numbered. Don't be afraid; you are worth more than many sparrows" (Luke 12:7). You are precious in His eyes. This will bring you hope and unspeakable joy if you believe.

CHAPTER TEN

Identity

*"Behold, what manner of love the Father hath bestowed
upon us, that we should be called the sons of God: therefore
the world knoweth us not, because it knew him not."*
(1 John 3:1–3 KJV)

God Changes Your Identity

Weaknesses and failures in our life develop our dependence on God and change our identity, allowing us "…to be called the sons and daughters of God." People who choose to be independent of God will fail continuously. Those who humble themselves and obey God's instruction will have victory, even in their weakness. God's strength changes brain structures, hearts, and identities. He will use our weakness for His purpose. Bible characters and their stories are in the Word of God to increase our faith and teach us to depend on God, just as they did. We must be hungry for His Word and learn to follow His prescriptions and directions in our everyday life. God is working in our heart when we read His book. God is changing your identity and giving you the right to be called the son or daughter of God for your own benefit, just as He changed those believers who lived before us.

When we hear the Word of God, it is transformed into electrical impulses in our neurons, passes the threshold through the cochlear nerve in our brain cortex, and becomes powerful thoughts that will change our behavior, habits and identity for eternity. Without the Word, people are heading for destruction. The Word of God will encourage you and give you strength and boldness. Get into the Word and let it change your identity and lead you in the way you should go. Sin leads to destruction and death, but the Word of God gives life. It is the very power of God to change our destiny.

With God It Is Impossible to Fail

*"And the LORD God formed man [of] the dust of the ground, and
breathed into his nostrils the breath of life; and man
became a living soul." (Gen. 2:7 KJV)*

Fear of failure can cocoon you when you feel weak, preventing you from moving ahead. When your heart is gripped by fear, do not forget that in God's eyes you are strong. You carry the breath of life from Him. Your weakness can be an opportunity to experience God's hand and His power in your life. I experienced God's hand so many times in my weakness. When I thought my life was ruined, God showed His power and lifted me up far more than I could ask or imagine.

Your weakness can be the key to open up Heaven for you. God can show Himself strong on your behalf when your heart is entirely His. Fear of failure is not from God. With God it is impossible to fail. He did not give us a spirit of fear. Jesus Christ walked in courage to the cross, to finish His call on earth for the world's salvation from sin, including yours and mine. Walk in confidence to fulfill your calling and purpose, because His victory on the cross outlines your destiny and your victory.

God Gives You Strength

Recognize who is giving you strength and power. It is all from the hands of God. Genesis 31:1–32 tells us that Jacob returned strong with huge riches, even though he had left his homeland weak and empty-handed. But God gave him strength all that time he was away from his parents' home. He learned on the job, and matured in his walk with God. I often think about how I came to the US with empty hands. When I was at work, I knew 100 percent that it was God who gave me strength every single day, in every area of my life.

When I first arrived in the US, I felt like a failure in every way. I didn't know the language; I worried about leaving my young husband by himself (I was the first one in my family to get a visa to come to the US); I was a young woman in a foreign land; I worried about leaving behind my two year-old, fragile child in a very poor village; I regretted leaving the profession I had worked so hard for in Bucharest; I had no house; no friends; I missed my church, etc. I had nothing but God. I just trusted Him totally. I recognized His supernatural power every day. Recognize who God is in your life. Do not lose heart.

Discouragement will make you afraid of losing everything, increasing your stress even more. But remember the LORD your God, who is willing to bless you. Only God can give you power in everything you do. Do not listen to deceitful thoughts that everything is a failure. It is written in the book of Jeremiah that "The heart is deceitful above all things and beyond cure; who can understand it? It is the LORD who searches the heart and examines the mind" (Jer. 17:9). Our thoughts and our mind are examined by God every moment. He knows the inclination of the human heart, so He gave us spiritual prescriptions with supernatural solutions to strengthen us.

Insecurity is quite common, but God's strength is perfect in our weaknesses. God can change our heart and our mind, even in our weakness. He uses our weaknesses for this purpose. God changed Gideon's identity when he identified with "the least" and He can change yours in your humble state. Weakness is the key to unlocking God's strength! Weakness can be a gift from God, unleashing an unprecedented experiment in your life.

CHAPTER ELEVEN

Faith

"Truly I tell you, if you have faith as small as a mustard seed, you can say to this mountain, 'Move from here to there,' and it will move. Nothing will be impossible for you."
(Matt. 17:20)

Faith Transforms Thinking

When Christ gives you a renewed mind, your thinking is transformed. Having faith to follow God's prescriptions and instructions will transform your life. Faith in Jesus transformed my life, and now I look at life through Heaven's eyes, not from the world's point of view. Looking at life from the world's point of view, we tend to forget God's purpose for our life. Looking from a human point of view, we set ourselves up for failure, and destruction, missing opportunities to accomplish our God-given assignment.

From Heaven's point of view, we have the promise in Jesus Christ that we will inherit eternal life after this short life on earth is gone. We do not need to worry about houses or properties, because we do have real estate in Heaven through Jesus Christ. We are heirs with Christ, on earth and in Heaven.

Faith that "moves mountains" and makes the impossible possible is required if we want to enjoy God's promises. This requires a radical change in our point of view, and we must adopt God's viewpoint and adapt to Heaven's culture. This is our assurance: "Truly I tell you, if you have faith as small as a mustard seed, you can say to this mountain, 'Move from here to there,' and it will move. Nothing will be impossible for you." (Matt. 17:20). Throughout my life I have had to face many figurative "mountains" that required great faith to move them out of my way. I had to exercise unconditional faith. Even though things did not always go the way I wanted, I believed that God would work in my favor behind the scene, even though I didn't know how.

God had an algorithm for all the difficult situations I had to go through to bring me to this point in life, and to take me where He wants me to be.

In every situation I believed that God would guide my steps according to His promises, and that the Holy Spirit would guide me in all truth. You will need the supernatural power of the Holy Spirit (beyond science) to be able to follow God's prescriptions and to be in God's will. Have the faith that can move all the "mountains" and don't let worldly obstacles keep you from accomplishing your heart desires. Persevere through your trials and pursue your God-given vision.

When you exercise your faith, there is a reward here on earth, and later in Heaven. I believe that in Heaven there is a crown waiting for you and me, and for all who believe and live according to the Word of God. Do not let circumstances and "mountains" of this earth steal your crown. The crown is promised to those who persevere in their faith, as we read in the book of James: "Blessed is the one who perseveres under trial because, having stood the test, that person will receive the crown of life that the LORD has promised to those who love Him" (James 1:12).

You have inherited faith, because God put the seed of faith in your DNA. Faith was built into your genetic make-up to enable you to "stand the test". That is why faith is required in difficult situations. In the natural, you cannot take a single step without faith. God gave everyone free will, and it is your choice whether or not to believe in God. Let your faith arise and continue to grow. "Your faith is growing more and more and the love all of you have for one another is increasing" (2 Thess. 1:3). Impossible situations will become possible, because everything is possible for those who believe when they allow their faith to increase. Faith will always remain with love and hope. "... and now these three remain: faith, hope, and love" (1 Cor. 13:13).

Believe in the power of the Holy Spirit, your Helper, Who is hovering over us continuously. Expect miracles when the Spirit of God touches your life. The Spirit convinces you about your sinful nature, and convinces you about salvation and righteousness through Jesus Christ and His resurrection power, when you let Him merge with your spirit through faith.

Genesis tells us that in the beginning the Spirit of God was moving over the water. He is moving over us continually—we just don't see Him. The "wind" blows where it wants, but nobody knows where it is coming from. It is the energy of God. People are hungry for that energy, but many are blinded by their unbelief. And without faith we cannot perceive the Holy Spirit. Before our character and personality can be transformed, before we can cope effectively with problems and crises, real faith must fill our mind, consciously and unconsciously.

With the Holy Spirit in us, we have a closer relationship with our Heavenly Father, through His power, the breath of God. "But when He, the Spirit of truth, comes, He will guide you into all the truth" (John 16:13). Many people treat the Holy Spirit superficially. But take care not to grieve the Holy Spirit. "Do not grieve the Holy Spirit of God, with whom you were sealed for the day of redemption. Get rid of all bitterness, rage and anger, brawling and slander, along with every form of malice. Be kind and compassionate to one another, forgiving each other, just as Christ forgave us" (Eph. 4:30–32). This amazing supernatural prescription can transform our thinking and bring physical and spiritual health through faith.

Through faith you must trust that He will protect you always. He will never forsake you or leave you, no matter what your circumstances. He is your King, reigning in your life. He is the King of kings, everlasting. Nobody can save you from your sin but Christ. Go to the cross for forgiveness, where Christ regenerates your soul with new spiritual DNA, a new personality, new faith and new life. Your past is erased by the blood of Jesus. "In Him we have redemption through His blood, the forgiveness of sins, in accordance with the riches of God's grace that He lavished on us" (Eph. 1:7).

Believe that God knows your past, present, and future, and He has a wonderful plan for your life. We are God's handiwork. He is the Super Intelligent Designer, the beginning and the end. He knows all things, even from before creation. He knows the end of any situation, right from the beginning. God is never surprised by events in your life, but He is always there to guide you. He *creates* events for you. He is YAHWEH. He is. He is self-existing. He gives you confidence, even when you are not sure about your circumstances.

When you try to run from God to ignore Him, He sees you. You cannot run from Him. He is not surprised by your ignorance, but He does have a plan for your life. He sees everything and knows everything—beyond any science. Just believe God and His Word. Remember the story of the Apostle Peter. He ran when Jesus was on trial, and he denied Jesus right before the crucifixion, but Jesus was not surprised by Peter's denial (John 18:15–27). Our conscience is used by the Spirit of God to remind us about our wrongdoing, whether we face our mountains or try to avoid them.

Have faith that God is the source of all blessings in life. All Heavenly and earthly gifts come from the God of light. He prepares gifts before we ask for them to build our faith. Our very life is a gift from God. We were chosen before the foundation of the world, and all our days are written in the Book of life. David exclaimed, "Your eyes saw my unformed body; all the days ordained for me were written in your book before one of them came to be" (Ps. 139:16).

Modern embryology classes now teach what was written in the Bible more than 3,500 years ago—beyond science—about how our life begins in our mother's womb. It is a mystery how a baby girl can have over six million eggs in her ovaries, when she is not even born yet.[1] God works in miraculous ways, creating new life. Each baby begins when a microscopic half-cell from a female and another half-cell from a male combine, joining their invisible thoughts and desires together to conceive a new human being. Just embrace God's mysterious hand at work and believe that everybody's days are numbered since before their life began. In the same amazing way, mountains of impossibilities in your life will be moved according to God's plan, when we obey His Word and believe. Nothing is impossible with God, and nothing is too hard for Him.

Believe that His plan is better than your plan. His agenda is better than your agenda. He said, "I am the LORD your God, who teaches you what is the best for you, who directs you in the way you should go. If you only had paid attention to my commands, your peace would have been like a river, your well-being like the waves of the sea" (Isa. 48:17). When you have God's peace, your health will flourish. Your brain relaxes, your stress decreases and homeostasis in your brain and body systems will prevent sickness and disease. God is teaching you the way you should go for your well-being. He is showing you your path, and if you follow His instructions you need not worry. Your peace will be "like a river".

Nothing to Fear

"So if the Son sets you free, you will be free indeed." (John 8:36).

To overcome fear, remember that you are His son or daughter and you belong to God. You are His creation, and you are forgiven from your sins. There is nothing to be afraid of. The old life is gone. "Therefore, if anyone is in Christ, the new creation has come; the old is gone, the new is here" (2 Cor. 5:17). You have new spiritual DNA, reprogrammed by the Lord. Your healthy level of neurochemicals in your nervous system is maximized, and the balance is shifting in your favor because the Son sets you free.

You are now Heavenly minded, because this life is short. Thinking about your future with the Lord in Heaven takes away all your fears. Looking at life from Heaven's perspective, your direction changes and you walk on a new path. Be careful not to fall into temptation. You are still responsible for your conduct, and you carry your own responsibilities. "Each one should

148

test their own actions. Then they can take pride in themselves alone, without comparing themselves to someone else, for each one should carry their own load" (Gal. 6:4–5).

Do not deceive yourselves with unhealthy thoughts. "Do not be deceived: God cannot be mocked. A man reaps what he sows. Whoever sows to please their flesh, from the flesh will reap destruction; whoever sows to please the Spirit, from the Spirit will reap eternal life" (Gal. 6:7–8). You are now freed from your old fleshly desires. "So if the Son sets you free, you will be free indeed" (John 8:36). When your mind is renewed you have new spiritual DNA. You are free of the old bondage and fear of the past.

Faith for Supernatural Restoration

"The fear of the Lord adds length to life." (Prov. 10:27)

All things are possible when you believe. Restoration is coming, and even in tough times your health can be restored. Amazingly, it was written more than 3,500 years ago in the Word of God—beyond science—that "The fear of the Lord adds length to life" (Prov. 10:27). God gives you instructions for your life through the Word of God. His words of hope bring restoration, healing and a prolonged life when you overcome fear, worry and anxiety, by fearing the Lord and following His commandments. The Word of God has the power to "detoxify" your soul from spiritual contamination and diseases—the power to clean, transform, change and add years to it.

Faith gives you hope for supernatural restoration. When you said "Yes" to Jesus Christ as your personal Savior, you got a "spiritual DNA transplant" as I like to call it. This helps you to function according to His will. He will add length to your life. Otherwise, under extreme physical stress the structure of your DNA can be altered. The cell can divide uncontrollably, leading to cancerous tumors and shortening your life.

When you pray, asking God to come into your life and change your thinking, read His Word and memorize scriptures and quote and declare the promises of God, your thinking is reprogrammed. There is a spiritual change in your mind and your DNA. You become what the Word says. You start to think like Christ. Every thought becomes captive to Him and your mind is renewed (Rom. 12:1–2). You can change the world around you, because you are a new creature. You act, talk, and walk differently. You now represent another Kingdom here on Earth, your Heavenly Father's Kingdom.

Faith Like a Little Child

"He called a little child to him, and placed the child among them.
And he said: 'Truly I tell you, unless you change and become like
little children, you will never enter the kingdom of Heaven. Therefore,
whoever takes the lowly position of this child is the greatest in the
kingdom of Heaven.'" (Matt. 18:2–4 NIV)

Children believe everything you tell them. Their brain is not contaminated until they are exposed to ugly things on TV, books, magazines, the internet, or bad influences from peers or dysfunctional family behavior. We must protect our innocent children from frightening news and evil influences. God wants us to be like children in our faith, to believe God's Word and receive the Kingdom of God like a little child. God expects honor and reverence from His children, who live by faith.

When you worship Him with a sincere heart like a child and give Him honor, the veil is pushed away. You start to express your heartfelt praises and recognize His role in your life. He is pleased when you praise Him, and when you have faith like a child. When I spend more time in prayer on my knees worshiping God, I feel closer to Him. It is like the roof of the house disappears, Heaven opens up above me, and I am soaked in His Presence. I had that kind of experience in my childhood. I was refreshed, renewed, and restored. I received revelation, inspiration and discernment for my daily assignments.

If you want to see God more clearly you must read and study His Book, the Bible. The more you read the Word of God the clearer picture you will get of the spiritual world. More wisdom, knowledge and understanding will benefit your body, mind and soul, and worry, fear and discouragement will disappear. You will feel the love of your Heavenly Father in your heart. "He will be the sure foundation for your times, a rich store of salvation and wisdom and knowledge; the fear of the Lord is the key to this treasure" (Isa. 33:6).

People who do not fear the LORD carry fears around in their heart and mind, allowing sin to bring disaster. God has a plan to destroy those who refuse His directions, commandments, instructions and prescriptions, as stated in the book of Jeremiah. "This is what the Lord says: 'Look! I am preparing a disaster for you and devising a plan against you. So turn from your evil ways, each one of you, and reform your ways and your actions'" (Jer. 18:11 NIV). The divine prescription is to turn from your evil way to prevent disaster. God wants you to have faith like child and be a part of His kingdom. "Whoever takes the lowly position of this child is the greatest in the kingdom of Heaven" (Matt. 18:2–4 NIV).

CHAPTER TWELVE

Dreams

"...we also glory in our suffering, because we know that suffering produces perseverance; perseverance character; and character hope." (Rom. 5:3–4)

You were born with God-given dreams in your DNA—yes, in your thoughts. Nothing can get in the way of your dreams and visions. You were born with healthy dreams. God gives good ideas, to be implemented at the right times, with the right people in the right places. Jentezen Franklin, Pastor of Free Chapel in Gainesville, Georgia (teacher, musician, author, and founder of TV's "Kingdom Connection"), in his book *Right People, Right Place, Right Plan: Discerning the Voice of God*, stated:

> There is a right plan for you. One idea from God can change your life. Thomas Edison had one idea, and today we have the electric light bulb. The Wright brothers had one idea, and now we have aviation. Bill Gates had one idea, and today we have personal computers. There are "good ideas", and there are "God ideas." The Holy Spirit wants you to discern the difference between the two.[1]

God allows you to discern His voice and gives you favor in your life to fulfill your dreams. Do not be afraid, do not be discouraged, and do not lose heart. Step into the things God wants you to do according to His plan and purpose for you. Do not waste time where God does not want you to waste time. Quit things that do not please God. Be involved in things that bring pleasure to the Lord, because things you are going through will work together for your good when you love God and do what pleases Him.

God allows difficult things in your life so you can learn from them. He delays for a season, but He will fulfill His promises if you follow His instructions. Do not miss the opportunity to pray when trials come. Trust God even if He delays working on your dreams. Even through seasons of doubt, even though your heart is broken and you are discouraged, God sees your trouble. Stay still and know that God loves you and He will accomplish the dream inside you. Let hope arise, for in God there is no limit. At the right time He will intervene on your behalf to finish what He started in you.

The Apostle Paul said, "…we also glory in our suffering, because we know that suffering produces perseverance; perseverance character; and character hope" (Rom. 5:3–4). God is always working in your life, building your character to become what God wants you to be, in order to fulfill your dream and visions. Hope working in your brain structures builds healthy thoughts. Gifts and skills are important, but character with healthy thinking is vital. The Holy Spirit helps you change your attitude. "Hope does not put us ashamed, because God's love has been poured out into our hearts through the Holy Spirit, who has been given to us" (Rom. 5:5).

With help from the Holy Spirit, the potential in your DNA is activated and you make progress toward your destiny. The supernatural power of God will activate your DNA, the fingerprint of God, and your genetic code will enable your true character. You become the person God predestined you to be from the foundation of the world, to participate in building His Kingdom. This is amazing. God, through the power of the Holy Spirit, decodes your genes to display who you were created to be through your changed attitude for His glory.

Invisible Imagination

"For as he thinks in his heart, so is he." (Prov. 23:7)

God does speak to us through dreams, visions, and signs, but most of the time through His Word. When God speaks to you, your thoughts are aligned with His vision for your life. Your thoughts are the recipe for your personality. Proverbs clearly explains that your thoughts dictate who you are. "For as he thinks in his heart, so is he" (Prov. 23:7). Your thinking is assisted by your imagination. You first see things in the "imaging center" in your brain, then your thoughts develop the person that you will be. God created you in His image. He used imagination when He created the Universe, and man, after His own image.

Use your imagination about the promises of God, and who God wants you to be through the power of His Word. Everything man has created, and all our advanced technology, comes from a God-given ability to think, imagine and create. When you meditate on the promises of God—in His Word—you create new neurons, which enable healthier thinking and create an atmosphere in your brain for God's promises. You empty your unconscious mind of all unhealthy thoughts, bad memories and negative emotions and replace them with joy, peace, happiness and hope for your future. Anointing for breakthrough and solutions for your dreams happen through prayer, fasting, giving, and believing God's Word for your life.

Dreams from the Foundation of the World

Dreams always amazed me. I could have remained in my small village, farming and owning a few cows, and sheep, and some chickens, as my parents used to. (There is nothing wrong with farming, but at that time in Romania you had to work the ground manually with your hands to feed your animals, as we had no machinery at all). I could have kept working the ground with my hands and living a primitive life, if God had not worked on my mind and given me the desire for more education and a different future. I simply had to follow a desire for higher achievements that God put in my imagination, to fulfill the dream God had for me from the foundation of the world. So I went to the capital city for vocational school when I was not yet 15 years old, then finished high school and University in Bucharest. In God's timing, I decided I must do something more, to be able to help others.

One day God brought a Christian lady to find me in that big city of about 3,000,000 people. She obeyed the voice of God to come back to Bucharest from the US, after 10 years of living in exile. She called me to talk about an invitation to come to the US. I'd forgotten that she even existed. When I heard her voice on the phone, the Holy Spirit reminded me who she was. In just a few minutes we reconnected, refreshing our memories and making new plans for the future. God orchestrates things in ways we cannot even imagine. He does more than we can ask or think, while making plans totally different from ours. We must keep our mind open and be receptive to His call.

The most powerful engine in the world is our brain—our unconscious and conscious mind, influenced by our senses. We must guard the quality of the thoughts we allow to take residence in our brain's image center. You have the power to be the gatekeeper of your eyes, ears, taste, smell, and touch. Use them well when you need to make decisions and do not contaminate the "image center". Job knew that we have the power to control what gets in our brain through our senses, and the ability to exercise self control. He stated, "I made a covenant with my eyes not to look lustfully at a young woman" (Job 31:1), because he knew that through his eyes his brain could get a message to develop lustful thoughts for a woman, contaminating his image center and bringing spiritual disaster.

Be discerning about the thoughts you allow into your mind from movies, books, magazines, TV shows, ads, and events in your community.

Make a covenant with your eyes and ears to avoid those things that promote unhealthy thoughts. God honors our attitude to promote healthy thinking. There are no limitations in creating healthy and useful things. God gives desires, dreams and visions, and only God can breathe life on your dreams to bring them alive for His glory.

Keep your dreams alive. There is pain in death. I see people dying all the time, and their dreams die with them. But Heaven's supernatural hope is superior to earthly hope. Through faith, God can do anything through your dreams. God will do greater things, because Jesus changes everything, bringing you life. The gift of the Holy Spirit can breathe life into your dreams. Live up to the Biblical standards and your God-given dreams will be fulfilled.

Your Dream Can Be Restored

"When I heard these things, I sat down and wept. For some days I mourned and fasted and prayed before the God of Heaven." (Neh 1:4)

In the Old Testament we read about Nehemiah's dream. He had a dream and a vision to rebuild the walls of his city, the old Jerusalem, so he fasted and prayed day and night to fulfill this desire (Neh. 1:5–11). Circumstances were against his dream, but God gave him supernatural favor with the king where he was living in exile, and the governor provided materials and resources to build the walls and an army to protect him. God even changed the law for Nehemiah to fulfill his heart's desire, according to God's purpose for his life.

God works the same today to fulfill your dreams. He worked in my dreams in Romania, and beyond. To get an education and a job during the communist regime, to marry the right husband, to have a child, to come to the US, to have my business, continue my education, finish my degrees, operate and own a business, help needy people, serve the Lord, write a book, and to speak at professional and spiritual conferences, and more. All of these were my dreams at one point in time, and yes, they became reality by God's grace.

He can change laws and people's hearts for you to fulfill your vision, your dream, your destiny here on earth, according to His will. God's will is to bless you, and when God's hand is with you He will protect you, and give you victory. There will be challenges, but have patience for the right timing and persevere in your prayer and fasting. Do not give up in the hard moments. God will send the right person for the right plan, as He did for so many people in the Bible, and as He has done for me and for countless other Christians.

God gave victory to Gideon even though he was so afraid of the enemy and hid himself; to Esther, an orphan who became a queen and was the instrument to save the entire Jewish nation; to Nehemiah who rebuilt Jerusalem's ruins; to Joseph in Egypt—rejected and sold by his brothers and falsely accused by his boss—who was used to save the life of his own nation, and to enable the Egyptian nation to survive a severe famine; to Jacob, threatened by his brother and deceived by his father-in-law, but used by God as founder of a great nation. The Bible is full of stories of dreams becoming reality, and God is still working for us, in our time, for His glory. In times of distress I like to recite Habakkuk's prayer. Habakkuk reminded the Lord of His fame for working in people's lives in the past. He pleaded, "LORD, I have heard of your fame; I stand in awe of your deeds, LORD. Repeat them in our days, in our time make them known; in wrath remember mercy" (Hab. 3:2).

All these persons mentioned above had to face fear, worry and distress in their particular unfavorable circumstances, but they stayed strong in their faith, and fear vanished through God's supernatural power and miraculous work. Do not give up the dream God put in your heart because of fear. All fearful circumstances are temporary. Jacob's dream was to be blessed. He started to manipulate things around him to fulfill his dream, and it took 20 years of serving his father-in-law to get all the blessings prepared by God for him. God gave him many favors, and when he was really blessed, his brother wanted to kill him. But Jacob's only choice was to fight in prayer and his dream was restored in one night while he was wrestling with an angel (Gen. 32:22–32). In one night prayer changed everything, and Jacob was blessed indeed and became the nation Israel.

Jabez, another biblical example, was afraid of suffering because he was born in pain. But his dream was to be blessed and free of pain. He prayed a bold prayer to be blessed, for God to enlarge his territory, and for God's hands to be upon him to protect him from evil and to prevent disaster in his life (1 Chron. 4:10). So many examples in the Bible record situations when natural fear, worry and anxiety were overcome with supernatural interventions and brought purposeful victory when people believed, prayed, and obeyed. Many people in the Bible went through terrible circumstances that caused excessive fear in their life, but through prayer they became strong and overcame fear under the powerful hand of Almighty God.

When you face big challenges in your life, you must pray as Hezekiah did to surrender his future to the Lord when the enemy sent him a threatening message to destroy the people of Israel (2 Kings 19:14). Take your "letter from the enemy" with bad news that tries to bring you fear, worry, and anxiety, and spread it out before the Lord. Tell Him why you are afraid.

When fear paralyzes you, you must seek God as Hezekiah did when the enemy threatened his life and the life of his nation. Bring your situation before the Lord in prayer. He hears your prayer and intervenes on your behalf, as He did in all the above examples.

The Promises of God Are Your Dreams Fulfilled

To fulfill your dream, start your day with the promises of God. Tiz Huch, in her book *No Limits No Boundaries: Praying Dynamic Change into your Life, Family, & Finances*, wrote:

> Always try to make your first and last appointment of the day with the Lord. As soon as you wake up in the morning, allow His Spirit to instill in you a sense of expectancy and a faith for the plans He has in store for you that day. Let Him pour into your mind and spirit His joy, confidence, strength, wisdom, and insight to equip you to serve Him and others. Then, at the end of the day, just before you go to sleep, let His Spirit fill you with peace, calm, hope, and rest.[2]

Cast out fear and increase your faith. Let the promises of God frame your life and your world. Let your brain's structures (with the "forest of neurons" and the limbic system, involved in your thinking, emotions, mood and memories) be filled with the Word of God and His promises for any situation. I wake up every morning and start my day by declaring God's promises over my life and over those around me and far away, even for the entire world.

I start with the Lord's Prayer and acknowledge who God is for me. I tell Him in my prayer, "Father God, You are *Jehovah-Elohim*, the Creator of Heaven and earth. You made us in Your image and I carry your breath in my lungs every single moment. You are *Jehovah-Tsidkenu*, God my Righteousness, through the power of Jesus Christ your Only Son, who shed His blood on the cross when He died for my sins. I acknowledge that all my sins are forgiven and I am not stressed anymore by the weight of my past sins. You are *Jehovah-M'Kadesh*, God who sanctifies me and gives me power over temptations and sins every single moment. By the authority of Christ's sacrifice on the cross I have the authority over all evil thoughts today, and over any bad habits and attitudes.

You are *Jehovah-Shalom*, God who gives me peace that passes all understanding in a world of uncertainty, worry, and fear. My thoughts are submitted to Jesus. I declare that I am covered with the blood of Jesus by faith, and I have authority over all the wicked spirits. You are *Jehovah-Shammah*, God who is present, Self-Existent. You are always there when I need You. You are from eternity to eternity the Everlasting Father, The Great "I AM". In Your Presence is peace, joy and happiness. In Your Presence all demonic spirits faint. What You speak will be created. Nothing is impossible for You. You have solutions for all my problems today. You are *Jehovah-Rapha*, God my Healer, Who heals all my diseases. I declare that by your Son Jesus' stripes I am healed completely. Jesus' body was broken so there will be no diseases, no pain, no brokenness, no bruises, no infirmity, no disability, no abnormality in my body.

Each cell in my body will function perfectly according to Your divine programming. Father God, I declare that in my body there are no abnormal genetic mutations or uncontrolled cell divisions. I declare divine health and complete healing in Jesus' Mighty Name.

I proclaim that You are *Jehovah-Jireh*, God my Provider, Who provides all my needs. You have blessed and You continue to bless me and my family so much more than I could ask or think. You enlarged my territories in every area, Your divine hands are upon me to protect me from evil, and nothing will harm me. You bless me at home and in society, when I go out and when I come in. Everything I put my hands to, You will cause to prosper. You give me favor with all whom I speak with and come in contact with today.

You are *Jehovah-Nissi*, God Who is my victory and my protection from my enemy. You send your angel ahead of me, and your angels surround me and fight for me. All the demonic strategies are in vain. I declare that You, Lord, fight for me. Your plans and Your will are done in my life to fulfill my dreams, visions and destiny, and to help me reach my full potential. I declare that no weapon formed against me shall prosper, and any language against me is condemned according to Isaiah 54:17.

My Heavenly Father, You are *Jehovah-Rohi*, God my Shepherd, my guide. I shall not want. You cover my head with oil and my cup is overflowing. You give me inspiration, revelation, clear thoughts and discernment and I do not make any decision without You. You give me wisdom from Heaven and the Holy Spirit takes control over my life, my emotions, my feelings, my thoughts, my entire being. You fill me with the Holy Spirit, take possession of all my being, and I surrender to you.

You are *Jehovah-El Roi*, God who sees me when I stand up and when I sit down. You know all my deep thoughts. Nothing is hidden from you.

My Heavenly Father, You are *Jehovah El-Elyon*, the most High God, and in the shadow of your wing I find divine protection. I rest because you put my enemies under my feet."

Those are my declarations in my morning prayers, and my soul and spirit are flooded with unspeakable joy. Then I worship Him, bringing my petitions one by one. Then the Holy Spirit starts to intercede through me for my family, friends, business, city, nation, and the world with prayers and intercessions. God will work with you to stay in His way, when you declare His promises. He desires that none of His creation should perish, but have eternal life.

Purpose of Visions and Dreams

"I keep asking that the God of our LORD Jesus Christ, the glorious Father, may give you the Spirit of wisdom and revelation, so that you may know Him better. I pray that the eyes of your heart may be enlightened in order that you may know the hope to which He has called you, to riches of His glorious inheritance in His holy people." (Eph. 1:17–18)

Your fear starts to dissolve when you believe in the promises of God and trust in Him. Keep declaring His promises over your life and the fear will evaporate. When you laugh at fear you have a breakthrough. God honors your faith and raises you up to a new level to fulfill your dreams. You are on the path that will take you to your godly destiny. The enemy will fight your visions and dreams with fear of failure. But stay connected to Jesus and stay focused, and your vision and dream will be accomplished. God orders your steps. Be determined to trust God to get where God wants you to be. God is giving you wisdom, revelation, and understanding to know the hope of His glory. "I keep asking that the God of our LORD Jesus Christ, the glorious Father, may give you the Spirit of wisdom and revelation, so that you may know Him better. I pray that the eyes of your heart may be enlightened in order that you may know the hope to which He has called you, to riches of His glorious inheritance in His holy people" (Eph. 1:17–18).

God's dream is to use you to bring hope to a broken and dying world. Everything in your life can change in one day at God's command. Just be faithful. Genesis 28:10–22 records Jacob's dream, and in Genesis 37–50 we read about Joseph's dream from God, confirming His will for Jacob and Joseph each to fulfill their personal destiny. Both men had an eternal impact on the nation of Israel and the entire world. When your dream is from God you will know it. It lifts you up and preserves lives either physically, emotionally, or spiritually. My dream was to be successful and to help needy families and poor people left behind in Romania. Here in the US I dreamed of helping God's Kingdom expand. He has fulfilled my dream, and continues to do so.

No Harmful Thinking, No Discouragements

Renew your mind with new thoughts, and believe that God will bring solutions to your problems. "Do not conform to the pattern of this world, but be transformed by the renewing of your mind. Then you will be able to test and approve what God's will is—his good, pleasing and perfect will" (Rom. 12:2). Jesus wants you to be like Him. God sees us as his children. Open your spiritual eyes to see the invisible spiritual realm and start thinking differently. Pursue God. When you make that determination in your heart, things start to change in your life. Learn how to see God with your mind's eye. When you have that desire, you will picture things differently, with no harmful thinking or discouragements.

When we hear something, it often triggers our vivid imagination. We start to see things in our mind, based on our imagination and our past experiences. If bad news arrives, you start to picture those bad things and fear invades your brain. Bad memories and emotions stored in your brain structures conjure up more fear associated with the bad news in your conscious mind. God can open your spiritual eyes to see Him working in your life; this can replace those bad memories and emotions with good memories and good thoughts of love, joy, peace, goodness, kindness, and happiness and dissipate harmful thoughts.

When bad news comes, confront it with the promises of God, and healthy thoughts will form based on His promises. God is always with us, but our natural eyes are limited. God can open your spiritual eyes to see what you were not able to see before. The spiritual eyes will give you hope, courage, confidence, contentment and healing. God wants to work miracles in your life.

Many times the eyes of our mind are clouded by anger, unforgiveness, envy, jealousy, immorality, or pride (when the cortisol level is very high). All our flesh that triggers unhealthy levels of neurochemicals makes those clouds even thicker, causing more discouragement. Cleanse your heart, and honor God in your daily life. In order to see with your spiritual eyes you need a close relationship with God the Father and Jesus Christ His Son. We are broken people due to the sin we were born in. You start the repair process when you confess your sins and begin to live in purity and be honest with yourself. That will give you a clearer vision to see God working in your life. "Blessed are the pure in heart, for they will see God" (Matt. 5:8). Your discouragement will be replaced with hope.

From Nobody to the King's Table

"Since you are precious and honored in my sight, and because I love you,
I will give people in exchange for you, nations
in exchange for your life." (Isa. 43:4)

God made us in His own image, and this means *you carry God's image.* You are descended from a royal family. You are His child. Your Heavenly Father cares about you more than you care about yourself. When our daughter was living with us, even from her birth, we as parents were more worried for her and loved her more than she knew. Your Heavenly Father's heart is touched by your problems. Jesus wept for the city of Jerusalem (Luke 19:41), and He weeps for you, too. Your soul is precious to God, more than all the wealth of the world.

God wants to raise you up, as He did for Jonathan's son, Mephibosheth. "Jonathan, son of Saul, had a son who was lame in both feet. He was five years old when the news about Saul and Jonathan came from Jezreel. His nurse picked him up and fled, but as she hurried to leave, he fell and became disabled. His name was Mephibosheth" (2 Sam. 4:4). Mephibosheth was brought by King David from disaster to the King's table for the rest of his life. You and I are victims of another kind of fall—a spiritual fall. The prescription for your spiritual fall is, "Go and sin no more." Once you are forgiven you can follow God's prescription for a new life. You have the Holy Spirit to lead you, guide you, and give you directions. God wants to wash your sins away with the blood of Jesus and to put "holy oil" on your emotional wounds to heal them. God wants to lift you up from your failure and bring you into fellowship with the King at His divine table.

"My son pay attention to what I say; turn your ear to My words. Do not
let them out of your sight; keep them within your heart; for they are life
to those who find them and health to one's whole body. Above all else,
guard your heart, for everything you do flows from it." (Prov. 4:20–23)

Physically, our body cannot function without the heart. Amazingly, the heart is situated upside down, with the base of the heart up and the apex down, and twisted to the left in order to function well. This position regulates and oxygenates the blood flow to the lungs before it is pumped throughout the body. To cope with stress God's way and be healthy, so blessings will overflow in your life, you must follow God's prescriptions for a clean heart in a right position spiritually. Be humble, joyful, thankful, kind, trusting, open, forgiving, confident, pure, wise, sincere, sensitive and happy. You can have that kind of heart through consistent time in the Word, prayer and fasting.

"My son, pay attention to what I say; turn your ear to My words. Do not let them out of your sight; keep them within your heart; for they are life to those who find them and health to one's whole body. Above all else, guard your heart, for everything you do flows from it" (Prov. 4:20–23). The heart is deceitful. Pay attention to God's Rx for a healthy spiritual heart and guard it from evil, so you can feast at the King's table forever.

CHAPTER THIRTEEN

Supernatural Healing

God Wants to Heal You

*I*t is better to stay healthy than to seek healing. We were designed by God to walk and function in health. Sickness, then, can be devastating. Chronic medical conditions create not only emotional pain, anxiety and depression, but impaired physical abilities. One of the most prevalent diseases today is metabolic syndrome (a cluster of related diseases: hypertension, diabetes, dyslipidemia—high lipid levels—and obesity), which leads to cardiovascular disease, heart attack and stroke. The best way to prevent complications from these diseases is a change in thinking and a healthier daily lifestyle. The power for physical and spiritual healing comes from God through His powerful Word.

Sickness can make life miserable. If you feel miserable in your sickness and bondage, Jesus is there to lift you up. It is His will to heal you. Take it to Him in prayer with childlike faith. Jesus was God in a human body, but fully anointed by the Holy Spirit. He completely understands your situation now. You can go to Him in prayer and ask for His mercy and healing.

The Lord also gave us instructions to go into the entire world to spread the good news and heal the sick. All the mirror neurons and compassion cells in our brain were created by God to help us feel others' pain. We were created to serve with the same passion and compassion as Jesus, whose passion and compassion for lost souls drove Him to the cross. He suffered and paid with His holy blood for each person on earth, because He cares for each one of us more than we do for ourselves. He forgives our sins and heals our diseases. Forgiveness and worship come first, then healing. Jesus always addressed the sinful nature of the soul, and then the healing of the body. He is interested first in our eternal soul, and then in our temporary body. The biggest miracle is the transformed human mind through renewed thinking. Scientifically, as I described before, many diseases are caused by emotional pain in our soul: fear, worry, anxiety, depression and high levels of stress due to unhealthy and corrupted thinking. It is extremely important in medicine to address the spiritual sickness first, then the physical condition.

Jesus Heals Physically and Spiritually

Jesus "...laid His hands on sick people and healed them." (Mark 6:5)

"He sent out His Word and healed them;
He rescued them from the grave." (Ps. 107:20)

The body's healing process is astonishing. Surgeons are amazed by the healing process that takes place in the body after surgery. The programming and built-in features in our DNA repair damaged cells and heal them, as described by Michael Mercandetti and Joseph A Molnar, who stated:

> Within these broad phases are a complex and coordinated series of events that includes chemotaxis, phagocytosis, neocollagenesis, collagen degradation, and collagen remodeling. In addition, angiogenesis, epithelization, and the production of new glycosaminoglycans (GAGs) and proteoglycans are vital to the wound healing milieu. The culmination of these biological processes results in the replacement of normal skin structures with fibroblastic mediated scar tissue.[1]

This is just a short description of what scientists have discovered about the healing process at the cell level, without mankind's intervention. That natural healing process after surgery is God's programming in our DNA.

Jesus' desire to heal was so strong that even after His death and resurrection, He gave instructions to His disciples to go into all the world to heal the sick in His Name. This has never changed. Jesus wants to heal the sick today, too, through believers. He spent about two thirds of His ministry on earth healing people. People's faith made them whole. The blind were able to see, the mute were able to speak, the deaf were able to hear, the lame were able to walk, leprosy was cleansed, and the demon possessed were delivered. You need to believe that Jesus is willing and able when you need a miracle. He heals through believers by laying on hands. He said in the book of Mark that "...they will place their hands on sick people, and they will get well" (Mark 16:18). Jesus "...laid His hands on sick people and healed them" (Mark 6:5).

Laying on of hands is in the Scriptures. When we practice laying on of hands there is nothing magic about it. It is a way of activating the faith that is in one's mind and heart, as we focus on Jesus' Word that brings healing miracles. People were healed by His Word. We are reassured of Jesus' will to heal, because through His Word people were healed and rescued from the grave. "He sent out His Word and healed them; He rescued them from the grave" (Ps. 107:20). You need a point of contact that will release faith. Jesus had authority and He had the power of the Holy Spirit. People who were healed had faith. (See Matt. 8; Mark 2; Mark 10; Luke 6). Anointing with oil is God's stamp (Read James 5). and the symbol of the Holy Spirit (Read Mark 6). The New Testament speaks of people using handkerchiefs touched by the disciples, as a sign of their faith in God's healing power. All are biblical and useful when people have faith in God for signs, miracles and wonders through the power of the Holy Spirit (Read Acts 19.)

This command is for all those born-again Christians who believe in the gifts of the Holy Spirit to heal the sick. You can do greater works as Jesus said, "Very truly I tell you, whoever believes in Me will do the works I have been doing, and they will do even greater things than these" (John 14:12). You are the instrument to bring healing through your hands and faith. You just need to lay your hands on the person and pray in Jesus' Name. Nothing is impossible with God.

Scientists know there is power in touching someone, and when praying for the sick. Physical touch increases endorphins, and oxytocin is released.[2] This neurochemical in the brain is a natural chemical from the "brain's natural pharmacy" with power to restore and heal the body. God knows the chemistry of our body, how our body functions, and what touching does to the physical body. His invisible supernatural touch from the spiritual realm will collide with our physical natural touch, causing faith to increase and healing to occur.

Passion and compassion are important ingredients in God's healing power. Humans have spindle neurons, special cells residing in the anterior cingulate in the brain, which are activated through prayer and meditation to increase compassion for sick and needy people.[3] When we are afraid, have no faith, and are anxious and stressed out, some cells in the anterior cingulate responsible for compassion will be deactivated. Passion changes the brain's function and the heart's condition. Watch out for demonic spirits that come to steal, kill and destroy by distorting your perceptions about external and internal stimuli. They are driven out by the supernatural power of God when you use God's "lenses" through faith. Stay in the Word, and the supernatural power of the Holy Spirit will be at work for you.

Prescription with No Expiration

"...the grass withers and the flowers fall,
but the Word of our God endures forever." (Isa. 40:8)

You need to know God, have a relationship Him, and go deeper than ever before in order to receive emotional and physical healing. Be courageous and be optimistic in all circumstances. Take courage, not only in your daily routine but in your challenging situations. Do not be discouraged in times of terrible sickness or severe emotional distress, for the Lord is with you. Even in ancient times God's prescription was to be brave in tough situations. "Have I not commanded you? Be strong and courageous. Do not be afraid; do not be discouraged, for the Lord your God will be with you wherever you go" (Josh. 1:9). This prescription has never expired, and the same prescription is available for your soul today. The Word of God remains forever.

There is no expiration date on God's directions, instructions and prescriptions. We can be strong, live in victory, and be filled with joy and gladness, because God's love endures forever. Feed your mind with God's prescriptions for supernatural power from supernatural ingredients every day, to live a victorious life and enjoy divine interventions when you need them the most. God wants His Word and His promises with no expiration date to be fulfilled in His creation, including you. Be sensitive to the Holy Spirit and agree with His treatment and supernatural therapy for your emotional, spiritual and physical diseases, preventing complications and promoting spiritual and physical health.

In my clinical practice many patients remain sick despite the best treatment, because of their noncompliance with instructions. Noncompliance is detrimental in any intervention. Nothing is too hard for God when you comply. You can rely on God in any situation when you follow His instructions. Do not give up in prayer, meditating on God's instructions and promises as long as it takes until you see God moving. Prayer will cause a shift in your heart and mind, and your perceptions of things around you, so God will take all the glory. You will recognize that truly this is the hand of God. God will fulfill His promises so we can give Him glory through Jesus Christ, His Son.

God fights for you, and Jesus, your Advocate in Heaven, intercedes for you. The Holy Spirit intercedes for us also, so keep praying, fasting, giving, working, helping, loving, and believing. God is a miracle worker and you will see His miracles in your life. God is doing a new thing in your heart right now. He makes a way in "the desert" of your life, and your "dry places" will flourish when you trust in Him completely. His promises will last forever.

The United States became a great country by following God's prescriptions for success. President Abraham Lincoln realized the great spiritual and emotional needs of the whole country when he proclaimed a day of prayer and fasting on March 30, 1863:

> "And whereas it is the duty of nations as well as of men, to own their dependence upon the overruling power of God, to confess their sins and transgressions, in humble sorrow, yet with assured hope that genuine repentance will lead to mercy and pardon; and to recognize the sublime truth, announced in the Holy Scriptures and proven by all history, that those nations only are blessed whose God is the Lord. And, insomuch as we know that, by His divine law, nations like individuals are subjected to punishments and chastisements in this world, may we not justly fear that the awful calamity of civil war, which now desolates the land, may be but a punishment, inflicted upon us, for our presumptuous sins, to the needful end of our national reformation as a whole People? We have been the recipients of the choicest bounties of Heaven. We have been preserved, these many years, in peace and prosperity. We have grown in numbers, wealth and power, as no other nation has ever grown. But we have forgotten God. We have forgotten the gracious hand which preserved us in peace, and multiplied and enriched and strengthened us; and we have vainly imagined, in the deceitfulness of our hearts, that all these blessings were produced by some superior wisdom and virtue of our own. Intoxicated with unbroken success, we have become too self-sufficient to feel the necessity of redeeming and preserving grace, too proud to pray to the God that made us! It behooves us then, to humble ourselves before the offended Power, to confess our national sins, and to pray for clemency and forgiveness. Now, therefore, in compliance with the request, and fully concurring in the views of the Senate, I do, by this my proclamation, designate and set apart Thursday, the 30th. day of April, 1863, as a day of national humiliation, fasting and prayer. And I do hereby request all the People to abstain, on that day, from their ordinary secular pursuits, and to unite, at their several places of public worship and their respective homes, in keeping the day holy to the Lord, and devoted to the humble discharge of the religious duties proper to that solemn occasion. All this being done, in sincerity and truth, let us then rest humbly in the hope authorized by the Divine teachings, that the united cry of the Nation will be heard on high, and answered with blessings, no less than the pardon of our national sins, and the restoration of our now divided and suffering Country, to its former happy condition of unity and peace"[4]

The Holy Spirit Sets Us Free

In order to truly repent, and seek forgiveness through prayer and fasting, we need the Holy Spirit's supernatural anointing. God tells us to pay very close attention to specific ingredients of His prescription for anointing (Read Exodus 30). God's Word and the anointing never change. The Word of God and the Holy Spirit always remain the same. In the New Testament, the acts of the apostles were accomplished through the Holy Spirit. God anointed Jesus and the apostles, and the same anointing is still available. Jesus told His disciples, "Do not depart from Jerusalem…" (Acts 1: 4) until they received the anointing of the Holy Spirit. God wants perfection for the Holy Spirit to work in our life. He gives us the clear instruction, "Do not depart from the Word." The Holy Spirit wants to flow freely as a divine invasion in people's hearts. Be open to the Holy Spirit to have His way. (See Isaiah 61:1–2; Luke 4:11.) The anointing breaks bondages and chains. One touch from God destroys the work of the enemy in your life, and changes the chemistry in your brain.

When I was child I had the opportunity to spend time at my grandfather's house. He was a strong believer and very strict in teaching us the Word. He had zero tolerance for sin. He had so much passion for God that people in the village would pass his house from a distance and sense that the presence of God was there. He would point out things in the Bible that still remain with me after 50 years. We did not like his discipline for our bad behavior as children, but I still treasure his life-giving teaching about the anointing that set me free.

CHAPTER FOURTEEN

Enlarge My Territory

"Jabez was more honorable than his brothers. His mother had named him Jabez, saying, 'I gave birth to him in pain.' Jabez cried out to the God of Israel, 'Oh that you would bless me and enlarge my territory! Let your hand be with me, and keep me from harm so that I will be free from pain.' And God granted his request."
(2 Chron. 4:9,10)

God is willing to enlarge your territory. Everything that happens in our life is the result of our attitudes and actions. Sometimes we move around in circles, but nothing is moving. Yet God is always working more than we could think or ask. Pray without ceasing and expect supernatural results. Prayer through the Holy Spirit brings supernatural results. The Holy Spirit knows the answers to our prayers and intercedes for our needs. For years I prayed, "Lord, enlarge my territory," because I knew the story of Jabez.

> Jabez was more honorable than his brothers. His mother had named him Jabez, saying, "I gave birth to him in pain." Jabez cried out to the God of Israel, "Oh that you would bless me and enlarge my territory! Let your hand be with me, and keep me from harm so that I will be free from pain." And God granted his request. (2 Chron. 4:9,10)

I often prayed like Jabez. I knew his story was written for our example, and if God answered Jabez's prayer He would answer my prayer, too. And He did, many times. Our territory has been enlarged in many ways. In our business we have increased the capacity and specialization. In my education I earned many degrees, including my doctorate. Socially, I have met renowned people in very high positions, including international speakers, politicians, state senators, professors, doctors, pastors, writers, and actors who became our close friends. In my profession I have been asked to present posters and to speak at professional conferences for primary care providers, nationally and internationally. I was surprised when so much favor flooded my life.

Financially God has blessed us so much. We have had many opportunities to help our parents, sisters, brothers, nephews, nieces, in-laws, friends, and needy people, both in and out of the Church, in the US and abroad. One time we had a list of 60 widows and 20 orphans to provide for. We give to missionaries and churches. I am not writing to boast, but I boast in the Lord because He gives seed to the sower. Bread that is cast upon the water will in due time return a great harvest. He gave us everything, and we have seen the fulfillment of His promises in His Word. For that we give Him *all* the glory. I am just sharing how He answered my bold prayers to enlarge our territory as an example. He will answer your prayers, too. Just decide to follow His prescriptions for blessings when you pray with passion for God to enlarge your territory.

CHAPTER FIFTEEN

Strategic Choices for a Healthy Lifestyle

"... for as he thinks in his heart, so is he."
(Prov. 23:7)

Physically you must choose to follow a healthy diet, exercise regularly, and follow appropriate stress management to prevent disease. Through self-control and discipline you must train your body and reprogram your brain to follow a healthy lifestyle. The Holy Spirit will give you power to make the right decisions and overcome temptation. For example, in fasting and praying, if I decide to drink only liquids for three days I program my brain and in three days I will not touch food. You must have discernment; you must plan ahead and prepare your body, soul, and mind to be preserved. Take action and just do it. If you do nothing, nothing happens. It is the same in health as in business, family life, education and society. You need wisdom to make the right decisions, take the right actions, grow in the knowledge of God, and engage in actions for a healthy lifestyle.

Your actions reflect what decisions you have made, as well as your personality. They reveal what kinds of thoughts are circulating in your brain structures! "For as he thinks in his heart, so is he" (Prov. 23:7). What thoughts you put in your brain and what you feel in your heart, will come out. Thoughts that are critical, judgmental, envious, resentful, jealous, and negative are harmful for your body. Harmful thoughts will negatively affect your brain's pleasure center, causing compulsive eating and other compulsive behaviors to find just a little pleasure. Avoid making decisions when harmful thoughts fill your mind. Make decisions only when you are at peace and your thoughts are in line with Word of God.

To have the gift of self-control and discipline, you need Jesus in your heart. The right basis for a healthy lifestyle comes from a heart and mind filled with knowledge and wisdom from God's Word. Be filled with knowledge, understanding, wisdom and revelation of the Word of God in order to have discernment when deciding how to pursue a healthy lifestyle.

"Spend your time and energy in training yourself for spiritual fitness. Physical exercise has some value, but spiritual exercise is much more important for it promises a reward in both this life and the next. This is true and everyone should accept it." (1 Tim. 4:7-9)

Lifestyle modification for weight loss and stress management is required across the board for preventing diseases. It is well known that unhealthy habits result in atherosclerosis, hypertension, heart disease, fatty liver, fibrosis, cirrhosis, depression, dementia and other diseases. Lifestyle change is preferable to medication. Atherosclerotic diseases are brought on by food high in cholesterol, proteins mainly from animal products, and lack of activity. Drugs such as statins, and other medications, are used in conjunction with healthy diet and regular exercise to prevent heart attack and strokes. But all medications must be combined with lifestyle change for efficient results.

High Cholesterol — Talk to your doctor about treatment for your high cholesterol if you previously had an unhealthy diet and a sedentary lifestyle. You may need to take medication if the benefits outweigh the risks from side effects and adverse reactions. About two thirds of patients with cardiovascular diseases also have metabolic syndrome (obesity, hypertension, diabetes, hypertriglyceridemia, dyslipidemia), which is a preventable syndrome, and reversible to some degree when correct actions are taken.

Hypertension — Uncontrolled hypertension increases the risk for cerebrovascular events known as stroke, as well as damage to the heart leading to cardiac dysfunction, congestive heart failure, pulmonary hypertension and death. Prevention is the key. Your heart will benefit from any exercise, including walking, or when the good parking spots are all taken and you need to park further out and walk more. Instead of getting angry in those situations, think about the benefit. Weight loss is key in reducing risks for metabolic syndrome and its complications and comorbidities. Even a 10% weight reduction can benefit.

Overweight — Losing weight is a big problem. A heavy flow of hormones and neurotransmitters circulate in the body when you lose weight too fast, such as a low calorie intake of 800–900 calories per day. Through prolonged starvation you can develop a fatty liver, that can lead to fibrosis and cirrhosis of the liver. The healthiest way to lose weight is to lose 1–2 pounds a week. You can calculate the calories you need daily, then eat 300–500 calories less per day to prevent weigh gain and lose some weight if you need to. Exercise daily and be active, and you will start to lose weight.

My friend Emy, a cardiologist, stated in her speech at a "Healthy Heart" seminar that overweight people eat three times more than one should normally eat. She also advised her audience to skip some meals during the week, save money, and buy food for the hungry. Another cardiologist stated that nowadays the new way to stay healthy is by "going hungry." It is a new paradigm in the health system to watch what we eat and count the calories. One professor of medicine was teaching his patients that "every crumb counts," so you really need to watch what you put in your mouth if you are overweight. Yet another specialist declared, "Everything that tastes good, you should spit it out," because food that tastes good makes you gain weight.

Sedentary — A sedentary lifestyle is another culprit leading to weight gain, metabolic syndrome and heart disease. With ever newer technologies and the "disuse" syndrome, people become less and less active. The same professor of medicine advised all his patients to keep moving, and not to underestimate any activities.

- getting mail from your mail box
- going back upstairs when you forget something
- intentionally parking further away from the store
- meditating or singing joyfully to create a healthy atmosphere in your brain that will release more healthy neurochemicals

Scientists recognize that most weight loss drugs are not safe, and the side effects cause more harm than good. Even herbal compounds can cause liver and kidney damage. Our built-in free will plays a huge role in our lifestyle choices for a healthy diet and weight loss. Take back your free will and gain control of your body, mind and soul. People are looking for psychological treatments: cognitive behavioral therapy and relapse prevention, behavioral strategies, cognitive strategies, coping with craving, helping us to reflect on the why, what, when, where, and who questions. All of them are beneficial, but when put your trust in God your Creator you will have better results. He wants to lift you up from where you are and bring you where you need to be with your health, if you simply *follow His divine, eternal prescriptions.*

A Healthy Lifestyle Starts in Childhood

"Start children off on the way they should go, and even when they are old they will not turn from it." (Prov. 22:6 NIV)

American public schools talk about "No Child Left Behind", but pediatricians talk about "No child left on his or her behind." Every child must be active to prevent a sedentary life—not sitting in front of TV or constantly staring at the iPod, iPhone, or computer. Children can easily become obese and develop diabetes with complications from a very early age. Fat deposits on the aorta can begin at age two if children are fed a high fat diet, such as French fries and fast foods. Children under stress develop compulsive eating disorders to deal with their emotions—gaining weight and developing metabolic syndrome. Obesity causes obstructive sleep apnea when the tissues around the neck restrict the air flow, compromising the airway and the oxygenation of the brain and other body tissues.

In order to prevent diseases and promote physical and spiritual health, follow the wisdom of God's spiritual prescriptions. In any disease we must first address behavior management before prescribing medication, starting with children. "Start children off on the way they should go, and even when they are old they will not turn from it" (Prov. 22:6).

High levels of stress and unmanaged behavior often lead to depression. Depressed people eat more and gain weight early in life, increasing the risk of developing dementia later on. In 2011 over 16 million Americans had cognitive impairment and neurocognitive disorders.[1] Much work and more study needs to be done in the health field regarding stress management and lifestyle changes.

A simple dietary plan is to divide the food you consume on your plate so that half of your plate is vegetables, one quarter of your plate is healthy high-fiber carbohydrates (fruits, multi-grain bread, whole grains, oatmeal, brown rice or sweet potatoes), and the other one quarter of your plate is healthy protein (fish, eggs, white meat), plus some healthy fats such as nuts, avocado, and olive oil, used sparingly.

There is no better time than now to start adjusting your diet and your activities, and managing your stressors. People everywhere need an awakening to protect against preventable diseases.

CHAPTER SIXTEEN

Awakening Your Heart and Mind

*"The Sovereign LORD has given me his words of wisdom, so
that I know how to comfort the weary. Morning by morning
he wakens me and opens my understanding to his will."
(Isa. 50:4 NLT)*

Awaken Your Heart Through Wisdom

To cope with stress in your life you need to watch out for things that cause fear, worry, anxiety and depression. The Spirit of God can awaken a person's heart through a transformed mind, renewed thoughts for the right perceptions of an unhealthy environment, and a changed character. Your character is encoded in your unique DNA, designed by God, the Super Intelligent Designer. In your DNA lies God's plan for your life, your destiny and purpose on earth. All God's plans for you are in your DNA, encoded from creation. The Bible says incorruptible seed is in you, and thoughts of eternity (Eccles. 3:11). God wrote your destiny before you were born (Ps. 139:16). Activate that touch of eternity in you.

You have precise instructions, inside you since you were in your mother's womb. He called you by name (Isa. 49:1). Read God's Word to learn what God intended you to be. You are created by God's hands and programmed to be who God wants you to be. You just need to let Him open your "understanding to His will" when He wakes you morning by morning (Isa. 50:4 NLT).

The world is trying to reprogram your life with unhealthy thoughts that are toxic for your brain. The customs and attitudes of the world do not follow God's prescriptions. Knowing the Word of God awakens you through wisdom and revelation, to transform you into a person more like God's Son, Jesus Christ. You can reprogram your brain and become who God created you to be from the beginning. You need power, energy from the Holy Spirit, and infilling through prayer. Trust that He who began the good work in you will help you to accomplish it when you follow His prescriptions and instructions. Study His excellent words of wisdom that excel far beyond the science of this world (Phil. 1:6).

The heroes of the Bible were men and women whose spirits were awakened and touched by the Holy Spirit. Daniel and his three compatriots decided not to defile themselves with the food from the king's table. They drew the line and made it known to the people surrounding them (see the book of Daniel). They had an awakening in their spirits, and their appetite was changed. In addition to their healthy physical appetite, they had a "spiritual appetite" in their heart—a hunger for God. We need to train our spiritual appetite, be willing to change our soul's diet and receive nourishment from the Word of God. His prescriptions contain the power, wisdom, revelation and knowledge to change our character and transform our mind and our personality. This is the only way to overcome fear, worry, anxiety and depression and enjoy a healthy life.

CHAPTER SEVENTEEN

God's Word Reprograms Your Brain

"All scripture is God-breathed and is useful for teaching,
rebuking, correcting and training in righteousness."
(2 Tim. 3:16)

"For the Word of God is alive and active.
Sharper than any double-edged sword, it penetrates even
to dividing soul and spirit, joints and marrow; it judges the
thoughts and attitude of the heart." (Heb. 4:12)

Restoring Your Soul

God's prescriptions work for all ages and for all physical, mental and spiritual health conditions. Through the power of the Holy Spirit, the Bible penetrates the deepest part of the soul to preserve it. The Word of God preserved my life under a communist regime, even when the destruction of my soul seemed eminent. The power of the Word of God has often restored my soul, changing my life forever. I was hungry and thirsty for the Word of God, and it fed my mind, bringing confidence in God's power to restore and preserve my life from my enemies. "When your words came, I ate them; they were my joy and my heart's delight, for I bear your Name, LORD God Almighty" (Jer. 15:16).

God's Prescriptions for Neurogenesis

"...but those who hope in the LORD will renew their strength. They
will soar on wings like eagles; they will run and not grow weary, they will
walk and not be faint." (Isa. 40:31)

Scientific research has shown that high levels of stress destroy neurons in the brain.

Enriched environment, exercise and learning for instance, are positive regulators while stress and age are major negative regulators. Stressful life events are not only shown to reduce adult neurogenesis levels but are also discussed to be a key element in the development of various neuropsychiatric disorders such as depression....Additionally, disturbed adult neurogenesis, possibly resulting in a malfunctioning hippocampus, may contribute to the cognitive deficits and reduced hippocampal volumes observed in depressed patients.[1]

Chronic stress leads to impaired cognition and anhedonia (loss of interest in all activities, as a sign of major depression). God's prescriptions for chronic stress enhance neurogenesis, and can help prevent dementia and Alzheimer's disease, thus saving millions of lives. As you wait upon the Lord, meditating on the Word of God and His promises, you promote neurogenesis, creating new neurons. At the end of the 20th century scientists discovered that profound thinking, which I call meditation, causes the brain to create new neurons in our hippocampus.[2] This is the area where cortisol (the stress hormone) destroys neurons continuously during high levels of stress, affecting people's memory and mood. How exciting to know that our brain is programmed to make new neurons during meditation. The Bible says that meditating on the Word of God brings blessings (see Psalm 1).

In our brain we have about 100 billion neurons, but many of them are destroyed by unhealthy actions and behavior, especially when fear, worry and anxiety cause cortisol to increase. Under high levels of stress, many people seek comfort from alcohol, smoking and drugs, killing more neurons. For example, one single serving of alcohol or nicotine will kill over ten thousand neurons. That is why alcohol, tobacco, drug use, gluttony, and sexual immorality are considered sins, because they will destroy the body, which is God's temple.

Now we know that new neurons are developed through healthy behavior and positive emotions such as joy and happiness, and hoping and meditating on God's promises. Isaiah 40:31 stated thousands of years ago, "They that wait upon the LORD shall renew their strength...they shall run and not be weary; and they shall walk and not faint." Waiting upon the LORD is meditating, hoping, and believing His promises. It will even make you younger. Neurogenesis is the natural anti-aging therapy!

Meditation Brings Prosperity and Success

"...keep this Book of the Law always on your lips; meditate on it day and night, so that you may be careful to do everything written in it. Then you will be prosperous and successful." (Josh. 1:8)

God even designed the benefits from meditation. He wants to give us an energized, healthy, prosperous and successful life. Thousands of years later, scientists tell us "...meditation is a complex process involving changes in cognition, memory, and social and emotional control, and causes improvement in various cardiovascular, neurological, autoimmune, and renal pathologies."[3] Meditation is now recognized and used in medicine to treat physical and mental illnesses induced by stress from fear, worry and anxiety. It is documented that meditation causes changes "...in the cerebral cortex, prefrontal area, cingulate gyrus, neurotransmitters, white matter, autonomic nervous system, limbic system, cytokines, endorphins, and hormones."[4]

Meditation prevents neurons from being destroyed by cortisol during high levels of stress. It is interesting that only the hippocampus, where consolidation of memories takes place, has cortisol receptors. Meditation will decrease the stress level and further decrease the level of cortisol. Researchers used PET scans to show that meditation will enhance the hippocampus region by preventing neurons from dying and by forming new neurons for memory and mood. More than 3,500 years ago God told man to meditate day and night on His law and His instructions.

The Best Medicine for Stress

"For the Word of God is alive and active. Sharper than any double-edged sword, it penetrates even to dividing soul and spirit, joints and marrow; it judges the thoughts and attitudes of the heart." (Heb. 4: 12)

The Word of God is alive, active, and able to transform lives. "For the Word of God is alive and active. Sharper than any double-edged sword, it penetrates even to dividing soul and spirit, joints and marrow; it judges the thoughts and attitudes of the heart" (Heb. 4: 12). Just as antioxidants, flavonoids, carotenoids and all the active enzymes from fresh fruits and vegetables are able to detoxify our cells, the Word of God supernaturally performs "surgery in man's spirit and soul", dividing and judging their thoughts and attitudes. God's Word performs spiritual surgery to clean all our filthy thinking. "Nothing is hidden from God's sight" (Heb. 4:13).

The Word gives us directions, even in darkness. Darkness will cocoon you and set limits on your life, but the Word of God goes beyond all limitations, indeed beyond all science. Continue to be washed by the Word of God, meditate day and night, and you will become wiser.

Be Wiser Through the Word

"Oh I love your law. I meditate on it all day long. Your commands are always with me and make me wiser than my enemies." (Ps. 119:97–98)

Meditating on the Word of God gives you wisdom to make good decisions in stressful circumstances. David said, "Oh, I love your law. I meditate on it all day long. Your commands are always with me and make me wiser than my enemies" (Ps. 119:97–98). Wisdom will come when you ask God in prayer for more wisdom. The Word can move you from out of your dark situation, into the light. Are you ready to walk in the light, build a new life and fulfill your God-given destiny?

Treasure the Word of God more than daily food. Value it, crave it, and hunger for it every day. It will give you vision in the dark. Don't let discouragement narrow your vision. Blind Bartimaeus, a roadside beggar, heard the Son of Light and cried out, "Jesus, Son of David, have mercy on me!" (Mark 10:48). The crowd tried to shut him up, but he cried more and more for his healing. Without spiritual vision, without light, people perish. Jesus is the Light of the world. Cry out to Him for spiritual vision.

Under communism we couldn't have Bibles. The communists wanted us to live in darkness, without vision and revelation from the Word of God. Intimidation and unworthiness demoralized people. I had to hide my Bible under my mattress, or in a closet in my college dorm, so I could read the Word when everyone was sleeping. I often feared someone would see me and tell the communist supervisor. During those years I memorized powerful scriptures that gave me wisdom and understanding. Secretly, I was able to read, the New Testament five times during high school. The Word of God transformed my life.

King David meditated on the Word all day long. "Oh, how I love your law! I meditate on it all day long" (Ps. 119:97). Meditating on the Word will bring joy and gladness to your heart. "But let all who take refuge in you be glad; let them ever sing for joy that those who love your name may rejoice in You" (Ps. 5:11). Hope in the promises of God brings encouragement and joy.

The Word Preserves Life

"...to bind up the broken hearted, to proclaim freedom for the captives and release from darkness for the prisoners, to proclaim the year of the LORD's favor and the day of vengeance of our God, to comfort all who mourn." (Isa. 61:1–2)

Hide the Word of God in your heart and memorize it to receive strength. It is such a rich and unimaginable treasure. I have seen people spend three or four hours in prayer, crying to God and reading the Word, who recovered their peace and found comfort.

Good news will always defeat anxiety and depressive thoughts. Jesus was "…anointed to proclaim good news to the poor," and "…to bind up the brokenhearted, to proclaim freedom for the captives and release from darkness for the prisoners, to proclaim the year of the LORD's favor and the day of vengeance of our God, to comfort all who mourn" (Isa. 61:1–2). When you are captive in your dark situation, do not isolate yourself. Seek godly people who bring Good News, who speak words of encouragement and kindness that will bind your emotional wounds and bring you comfort through God's Word.

Acknowledge God everywhere. Nothing is more powerful than the Word of God. Did you know that in Washington D.C., "Praise the Lord" was written on the highest tower in 1884?

The Washington Monument was complete, and it had surpassed the Cologne Cathedral to be the tallest building in the world at that time, at 555 feet, 5.125 inches. Inscribed on the aluminum cap, notable names and dates in the monument's construction are recalled, and on the east face, facing the rising sun, the Latin words Laus Deo, which translate to "Praise be to God."[5]

No one can touch those who praise the Lord. The Word of God preserves America. Where the Word of God is, there is power and connection with the supernatural. In our place of business my husband and I framed pictures with the promises of God in large print, so people can read and find hope in their emotional distress.

Wisdom Through the Word

Everyone is in need of wisdom. The Christian apologist Ravi Zacharias has stated that the leaders of the world are in desperate need of wisdom, and even their cumulative wisdom cannot meet the challenges of this age. The leaders at the highest levels of society need wisdom. God will rescue you from fearful and stressful circumstances when you ask for wisdom without doubting in your heart. Be spiritually aware and willing to live a life of sacrifice, with an appetite for wisdom.

Make a stand for what is noble and God can reveal to you which direction to go. "This is what the LORD says—your Redeemer, the Holy One of Israel: 'I am the LORD your God, who teaches you what is the best for you, who directs you in the way you should go'" (Isa. 48:17 NIV). He will refine your desire and *reveal your dreams* to you through His wisdom. When you are desperate to know God more and to follow His prescriptions for an uncompromised life of victory, He will show you solutions for all the challenges in your life. God wants to transform you, and the entire world, through wisdom from His Word. "If any of you lacks wisdom, you should ask God, who gives generously to all without finding fault, and it will be given to you" (James 1:5).

Wisdom for a Healthy Culture

People are trapped by so many poisonous elements in our modern, toxic culture. Years ago I read about a medical examiner who was dying. He had accidentally contracted HIV through a paper cut, while examining a dead body during an autopsy. The same thing can happen in the spiritual realm, when toxic sins enter your spirit, and then your body, through just a "paper cut" in your spirit. You are sentenced to die from an unnoticed small "paper cut" in your soul, where your spirit lives.

What you allow into your mind will affect your spirit and body. Walk away from bad thoughts and behaviors that can cause irrevocable devastation in your life. Change the way you think, the way you see things, the way you talk, the way you process information. One of my friends, a physician, was diagnosed with cancer years ago. After surgery and all her treatments, she resumed her medical practice. She said she now looks at the patients in her practice completely differently since her tragic experience. She sees "the face of God" in each patient. Her thinking was shaped by her illness. Shape your thinking and change your perceptions according to the Word of God, before tragedy happens.

What kind of "ammunition" will you store in your brain structures to prepare the atmosphere for the spiritual and physical "war" in your soul, spirit and body? Refuse to stay in the danger zone with unhealthy thinking, and do not be afraid to make changes. Do not wait for a diagnosis to change the way you see things. One of my friends, a Nurse Manager for many years in a cardiac unit, lost a very dear friend of hers from an incurable disease at a very young age. That was a devastating loss for my friend. From that experience she decided to renew her mind before any diagnosis might affect her life. She began to pursue a healthier lifestyle.

Ruth's Cultural Wisdom

*"I've been told all about what you have done for your
mother-in-law since the death of your husband—how you left your
father and mother and your homeland and came to live with a people
you did not know before. May the Lord repay you for
what you have done." (Ruth 2:11–12)*

People will notice the Holy Spirit in you through your character. They will know that you have a healthy outlook. Boaz noticed Ruth's character and wisdom and stated, "I've been told all about what you have done for your mother-in-law since the death of your husband—how you left your father and mother and your homeland and came to live with a people you did not know before. May the Lord repay you for what you have done" (Ruth 2:11–12).

People can tell that you have a different personality just by watching you interacting with others and studying your body language. From the Bible account we know that people were watching Ruth, and they noticed her character. She arrived in Bethlehem, widowed, with nothing, to provide for Naomi her mother-in-law and herself. Ruth went into the fields to glean—to pick up the grain left behind by the workers of the day. By law, the Israelites would leave some grain behind for the needy and poor, so they could provide for themselves, like Ruth did.

Ruth wondered why Boaz was so kind toward her, a foreigner. People in Bethlehem knew that Ruth was a loving, kind and compassionate person by her attitude and actions. She gained a reputation that spread, so everyone knew about her. She was faithful and hardworking. These character qualities gave her a reputation that positioned her to fulfill her destiny. God can use you in an amazing way to fulfill your destiny, even through tough times, like Ruth and Naomi. Sometimes people may mock what God is doing in you, but the fear of the Lord leads you, and your godly character will prevail, promoting your spiritual and physical health.

Fear of the Lord is a Treasure

*"The fear of the LORD is the beginning of wisdom; all who follow
His percepts have good understanding." (Ps. 111:10)*

*"Oh that their hearts would be inclined to fear me
and keep all my commands always, so that it might go well with them
and their children forever." (Deut. 5:29)*

The fear of God keeps us close to the Lord and reminds us that nothing is hidden from God. This does not mean we should run away from God. It means we esteem and honor Him as our loving Father. As a teenager I was always trying to please my biological father, to honor his reputation as my father, and make him happy, because he worked hard to make a living for our large family. Our Heavenly Father provided us with spiritual life by giving His only Son to die for our sins. The fear of the Lord causes people to keep His commandments. "The fear of the LORD is the beginning of wisdom; all who follow His precepts have good understanding" (Ps. 111:10). The fear of the Lord will bring favors and benefits to the next generations who keep God's commandments. "Oh, that their hearts would be inclined to fear me and keep all my commands always, so that it might go well with them and their children forever" (Deut. 5:29). This supports the science of epigenetics, through which blessings can be inherited from one generation to the next.

The fear of the Lord is the foundation of wisdom and helps us make the right choice when opportunity comes. Through wisdom a house is built (Prov. 24:3). When I need to make a decision in my business or profession, I ask God for wisdom. I know that on my own I could make a poor decision.

I do not know the future, so I fast and pray for God's wisdom and inspiration through the power of the Holy Spirit. A few years ago I had an impossible situation in my business. It needed Heaven's attention. I called on God with all my strength, even fasting 40 days as Daniel fasted (a partial fast with fruits and vegetables only) for wisdom. I needed wisdom only God could give to make that business decision. The answer came several months later, when I needed it the most.

What was impossible became possible through God's supernatural intervention, activated by obedience. He gives us wisdom and favor with the right people. At that time more than ever, I understood the admonition not to lean on my own understanding. I literally followed the Word, "Trust in the LORD with all your heart and lean not on your own understanding; in all your ways submit to Him and He will make your paths straight" (Prov. 3:5–6).

The fear of the Lord keeps us from sin. Fear of the Lord keeps us and our children from departing from God. Many people think the Lord does not see, but He declared, "I am the LORD of all mankind. Is anything too hard for me?" (Jer. 32:27). Obey Him instantly and fear Him, even if it hurts or you do not see the benefit. Many times in my struggles I had to choose to either fear the Lord and obey, or live my own way, to escape a hard situation. But now, looking back, if I had not obeyed God, where I would be today?

I have no regrets. My heart was completely His and I followed Him with my whole heart. I enjoy my family now, with many blessings, as the result of obeying God in spite of many difficulties. We have great satisfaction from taking care of the elderly with multiple chronic conditions, and dealing with challenging behaviors of marginalized people. The community is our family.

The fear of the Lord changed my life. It will change you, and the world, one person at a time. That is because, "The precepts of the LORD are right, giving joy to the heart. The commands of the LORD are radiant, giving light to the eyes. The fear of the LORD is pure, enduring forever" (Ps. 19:9). People who do not fear God do not endure forever. For example, after 75 years the Communist system in Eastern Europe collapsed because they ignored God completely.[6] Who dreamt of that sudden collapse of communist power in the Soviet Union and surrounding countries after so many years? They did not fear the Lord at all. They were teaching children for decades that there is no God. For decades those children were deprived of blessings, and their futures were destroyed. They lived under the curse. Now the generations after them are completely disoriented and have no knowledge of the Word of God, the Creator of the Universe. They still continue to live under the curse of disobedience.

Communism brought curses upon generations through atheistic teaching and the evolutionists' deception that the Universe was created by chance. If life was formed by chance, there would be no life on earth today, because mutation in human genes, if left to chance, would cause uncontrolled, abnormal cell division and proliferation, leading to cancer and death. Cancer of any kind is an accidental gene mutation with uncontrolled and abnormal division of cells in the body.[7] People who have uncontrolled gene mutations undergo radiation or chemotherapy to eradicate those abnormal cells. To have a healthy body, all cells must function in the perfection created by God, the Supernatural Designer. They must divide according to the divine programming and precise instructions built into our human DNA by the King of the Universe in the beginning, in order for life to exist on this planet.

When the structure of DNA, with a double helix, was discovered in 1953 by Watson, it was the highest accomplishment and a great scientific revolution, proving we have a Creator and life is not by chance. We now know more about DNA and cell function and cannot believe the lie that life appeared on earth spontaneously, by accident. The communists took advantage of the lack of knowledge and lack of scientific proof, and deceived huge masses of people by forcing them through a controlling of dictatorship, depriving them of the blessings of knowing God and the treasure of fearing the Lord.

CHAPTER EIGHTEEN

Favors

" ...these are the ones I look on with favor: those who are humbled and contrite spirit, and who tremble at my Word."
(Isa. 66:2)

You Are God's Favorite

T he Old Testament story of Mephibosheth is relevant for you and me. After King David's friend Jonathan passed away, God moved on David's heart to show kindness to Jonathan's house. Jonathan's son Mephibosheth was brought to David's home because of the covenant with Jonathan. David wanted to restore his best friend's son's joy and his relationship with the royal family without him even knowing. Your Father in Heaven wants to restore the covenant relationship between Himself and His family on earth. Christ wants to restore your relationship with His Royal family by forgiving your sins to bring you joy. Joy is the key to calming and reprogramming your brain. Joy stimulates healthy amounts of neurotransmitters, restoring your memory and mood in your brain's structures

Saul's disobedience and sin brought famine to the land. But Saul's grandson Mephibosheth was protected, because his relationship with the royal family was restored. There is a worldwide famine today—a desperate hunger for relationship restoration. Jesus is our Advocate for relationship restorations. He is waiting for us to decide to come to the King's table. He took away your iniquity and spiritual infirmities. You are covered by the blood of Jesus. That is the kindness of God that leads you to repentance. He took away your sin, with its consequences, so you are called to repent, because "God's kindness is intended to lead you to repentance" (Rom. 2:4). Mephibosheth was the victim of a fall, and King David had never met him because of his disability from the fall. But the King's kindness brought him from anonymity to the king's table.

God, the King of the Universe, made man in His own image. You descend from a Royal family. You carry the image of the King of kings.

You are His child. God cares about you, and His heart is touched by your problems. God wants to raise you up and give you an unending feast at His banquet table. Mephibosheth was elevated from obscurity to the King's table, for life. (2 Sam. 4:4).

Your soul is more precious to God than all the wealth of the world. Let the Holy Spirit guide you, even in the lowest moments of your life. Seek His advice. You are also a victim of a fall, but God wants to put "holy oil" on your wounds. Jesus did the same with the woman caught in adultery. He lifted her up from the calamities of her sins and told her to "go and sin no more." God wants to lift you up from all your circumstances by cleansing away your sin. The blood of Jesus has the power to wash your sins away. You need to obey Him, follow His powerful prescription to "go and sin no more," and have fellowship with the Lord. You will not be a victim anymore; you are the Temple of God, and His favorite.

The Favor of God

In 2006 I was invited to speak to a National Women's Conference in Bucharest, Romania. My husband remained in Portland to manage our business and to be home with our daughter, who was in high school at that time. We were also running the business of one of our friends, who had passed away and left behind her children with many needs. We took on the responsibility of managing her business for one year after she passed away, so her children would have their needs met. During the conference my husband called to say that the live-in caregiver of my friend's business was waiting with her luggage, ready to leave upon my return to Portland. That news struck me so hard I couldn't even talk. My stress level suddenly skyrocketed from that bad news. All I could do was get on my knees and cry out to God with my entire being. If the live-in caregiver left, the business would be lost, and my friend's children would be homeless. My heart was broken for these children who had lost their mom, and now their resources. After that fervent prayer I received a peace deep in my heart, knowing that God would provide.

Three days after I got home from that mission trip, a very nice young lady knocked at the door, desperate for a job. She was well educated, willing to be trained, and ready to take that vacant live-in caregiver position. I knew that was God's favor, and the answer to my prayer in Bucharest for provisions in Portland. We read in the book of Isaiah that " . . . these are the ones I look on with favor: those who are humble and contrite in spirit, and who tremble at my Word" (Isa. 66:2). I had humbled myself and cried out to God, and He demonstrated His divine favor. In order to have favors from God we must follow His standards. God will move in people's hearts to work in our favor when we are under the burden of an increased level of stress from worry.

CHAPTER NINETEEN

Keep a Biblical Attitude

"...see, darkness is over the earth and thick darkness is over the people, but the LORD rises upon you and His glory appears over you. Nations will come to your light."
(Isa. 60:2–3)

You are designed to win, but only when you abandon the world's ways and choose God's way. The world lives in the dark, but God wants His glory to shine on the earth over His people. God's divine prescriptions are for you to win and have an excellent life. Follow His directions, listen to His instructions, and respect His guidelines. This will provide a therapy for your divine restoration from sin—mentally, emotionally, and physically. Do not miss the opportunity. You need power and energy from the Holy Spirit. "The LORD rises upon you and His glory appears over you" (Isa. 60:3). God endowed you on earth with wisdom to live in the light and in health. You have a destiny to fulfill, so be faithful in everything you do, and let your light shine around you. God has an open door for you, but you must have an appropriate attitude and "contend for the faith that was once for all entrusted to God's holy people" (Jude 1:3).

Changing your attitude is necessary for reducing the stress levels in your life and improving your physical and spiritual health. Your attitude should reflect love, honesty, integrity, and unity. Maintain high standards in your life, because darkness covers the earth. Isaiah prophesied thousands of years ago: "See, darkness is over the earth and thick darkness is over the people, but the LORD rises upon you and His glory appears over you. Nations will come to your light" (Isa. 60:2–3). You are called to live with a tender heart, live in the light, and forgive and help others. You must be like Christ for His glory to appear over you.

Power to Change Your Attitude

"Now to Him who is able to do immeasurably more then all we ask or imagine, according to His power that is at work within us" (Eph. 3:20)

Pastor T.D. Jakes, in his book *Reposition Yourself*, challenges us to stop procrastinating or blaming the past. He says we should not embrace the role of a loser, but be the "make-it-happen person." He describes a person who is willing to change their attitude. "There are the people who see what is coming and they make it happen rather than hope it happens or react to what happens."[1] Jakes emphasizes that the power to change your attitude is in you. So we read, "Now to Him who is able to do immeasurably more than all we ask or imagine, according to His power that is at work within us . . ." (Eph. 3:20). God built certain features in us that, if activated by our will and desire to change, will give us divine power to make it happen.

Bad attitudes generate from bad thoughts. Such negative thinking damages our body by releasing abnormal amounts of neurochemicals and hormones, redirecting the blood flow in different parts of the body, resulting in sickness and disease. Worthless secular pleasures that contradict godly standards will enslave you, creating addictions. Addiction is a symptom of spiritual disease, and calls for effective intervention. Pray an emergency prayer to deepen your relationship with God and free you from all bondage. Fasting will improve your self-discipline and help free you from destructive behaviors. You will regain your will power and refocus your attitude. It will impact your thinking and renew your mind. Turn away from useless things, break your addictions, and focus on what matters the most. Time is a precious gift from God, and you need to act now.

An attitude of forgiveness brings healing. Your body delivers natural chemicals for healing, including endorphins (acting as a natural antidepressant) when you change your attitude toward others, forgiving them for offending you or hurting you. Forgiving brings joy. I love this ancient truth: "The joy of the LORD is your strength" (Neh. 8:10). Joy is necessary. It strengthens by releasing healthy amounts of neurotransmitters to restore the body, soul and spirit—beyond science.

You cannot control what other people say, but you can control what you believe and how you react and interact. You cannot control the circumstances and events of life, but you can control how you react in any situation. Your constant meditation on the Living Word of God will increase your faith. Act according to your faith, and your attitude will change. It is a divine exchange. Decide to walk in the light, and receive the rewards of light. You have been chosen by Jesus to bring fruits of joy, peace, kindness, goodness, patience, endurance, self-control, and to walk in the light with a great attitude (1 John 1:7). People will admire your attitude in the light.

Changing Your Mind Changes Your Attitude

"I have set before you, life and death, blessings and curses. Now choose life, so that you and your children may live and that you may love the LORD *your God, listen to His voice and hold fast to Him. For the* LORD *is your life." (Deut. 30:19)*

"...to be made new in the attitude of your minds; and to put on the new self, created to be like God in true righteousness and holiness." (Eph. 4:23)

People get stuck in their human thinking. They spread bad reports of their negative mentality. I had to meditate on this verse many times until it became a part of me: "I can do all things through Christ who strengthens me." Thinking differently today will change your tomorrows. The mind is powerful. God is waiting for you to make choices. Don't let your mind be programmed by worldly things. Take responsibility for your life. We are directed to choose life as we read, "I have set before you life and death, blessings and curses. Now choose life, so that you and your children may live and that you may love the LORD your God, listen to His voice and hold fast to Him. For the LORD is your life" (Deut. 30:19). The Word of God has the power to change your attitude. Watch what you choose in your life and what you are thinking. The Spirit of God renews your thoughts and attitudes. "... to be made new in the attitude of your minds; and to put on the new self, created to be like God in true righteousness and holiness" (Eph. 4: 23).

I allowed the Spirit to renew my thoughts during the communist regime, when the communists declared there was no God. I allowed the Word of God to reprogram my mind, my thinking, my attitude, and my speech, as it is written: "May these words of my mouth and this meditation of my heart be pleasing in your sight, my Rock my Redeemer" (Ps. 19:14). I worked on reprogramming my mind by repeating new thoughts out loud. I would recite verses from the Bible throughout the day. In this way I received new thoughts and new directions. "For out of the overflow of his heart his mouth speaks." I was memorizing verses and poems inspired from stories of Biblical characters who achieved great victories. They are stored in my brain structures, and I can easily activate them and bring them into my conscious mind anytime I want and need them. Those stories are written in the Bible to encourage us and to build our faith in the Almighty God who can do anything, anytime. He has done great things in the past, and He will do more today for you, because He is the same yesterday, today and forever.

God gives us a *new life* through the Holy Spirit. If your heart is overflowing with promises from God's Word, you will share them. People around you will be encouraged, thus their minds can be transformed and reprogrammed. It takes effort and work to change and reprogram your thoughts and help those around you.

I cannot stop thinking about Ruth's attitude. She reprogrammed her thinking to accompany her mother-in-law to Bethlehem, demonstrating a "do-whatever-it-takes" attitude to help Naomi. Through her positive, overcoming attitude Ruth positioned herself for blessings for the rest of her life, and for eternity. Ruth was overwhelmed by the favors God gave her with Boaz. How Ruth cared for Naomi impressed all those around her in Bethlehem. They knew she was a kind, loving, and compassionate woman, and her reputation had spread. Learn God's language and do not be afraid to live it out and speak it out loud. God's language remains unique through the ages. People will notice that your language is different.

Position yourself for the blessings of God through your attitude and character. Ruth's life exhibited admirable qualities. She was hardworking, loving, kind, and faithful. She had gained a reputation for these qualities and for her amazing attitude. Ruth's character remained unchanged, even when the circumstances changed. What do your actions say about your reputation? Remember, a good reputation is something we earn when we live according to our values and beliefs, in line with biblical standards.

Ruth activated the potential that God had placed in her DNA, even though she was a stranger in a foreign country. I love Ruth's story because I was a foreigner on foreign ground, but God was watching over me the entire time, to fulfill His promises in my life. He gave me power to consistently work toward my goals and His plans. Today is the result of yesterday's decisions and actions. Your health problems today are the results of yesterday's bad habits. Learn from your past situation (like the prodigal son) and correct your present to be blessed in the future.

Fruits of Your Attitude

"Stand at the crossroads and look; ask for the ancient paths, ask where the good way is, and walk in it, and you will find rest for your souls." (Jer. 6:16)

"May God Himself, the God of peace, sanctify you through and through. May your whole spirit, soul, and body be kept blameless at the coming of the LORD Jesus Christ." (1 Thess. 5:23)

We have learned that the brain structures (including the thalamus, amygdala, hippocampus, hypothalamus, etc.) are associated with memories, emotions, and processing and storing information. The amygdala is linked to emotions and behaviors relating to fear and pleasure.[2] The Creator gave us a desire for happiness and for socialization, aided by serotonin, endorphin, oxytocin, testosterone and other neurochemicals. For example if the serotonin level is too low for an extended time, fear, depression, eating disorders and other diseases will invade our body, affecting the soul and the spirit. The link between the amygdala, hippocampus, hypothalamus, septal area and prefrontal cortex helps us decide what is right or wrong. The GABA neurotransmitter prevents us from harmful bad behavior and calms down the brain.[3] We are divinely equipped to be able to produce the fruits of the Spirit: joy, love, peace, goodness, kindness, gentleness, patience, faithfulness and self-control. These qualities will create an atmosphere in our brain for healthy amounts of neurotransmitters to store healthy thoughts and emotions. They will affect all your attitudes, everywhere you go.

The entire Bible is a book of restoration and attitude change. From the book of Genesis we know that Jacob met God in a dream. His attitude was changed, his character was transformed completely, and he was then able to look at those around him differently. After your attitude is changed, a Heavenly atmosphere descends on you. In Jacob's situation angels were ascending and descending and changed the atmosphere around him (Gen. 28:16–22). The window of Heaven opens when your attitude is changed through prayer, and your obedience moves the heart of God. When Jacob's heart and attitude changed, his future was changed. Jacob prayed, and after that his heart was transformed. As a foreigner, I had to maintain an attitude of prayer. I vowed to share my blessings with the poor and needy if God would bless me. And He did.

God changes our attitude so we can love the people around us. When you experience the power of the Holy Spirit, you want to share with others right away. When you have an authentic experience with God, people will notice. In the presence of God is joy and rest, as was written thousands of years ago. "My Presence will go with you, and I will give you rest" (Ex. 33:14). To find rest for your soul, choose to walk in a godly way. Change your attitude, to choose the better way when at a crossroads, as we read in the book of Jeremiah. "Stand at the crossroads and look; ask for the ancient paths, ask where the good way is, and walk in it, and you will find rest for your souls" (Jer. 6:16).

If you choose to follow the ways of the world, you open yourself up to experiencing catastrophic things. Only God can keep your whole spirit, soul, and body blameless. "May God Himself, the God of peace, sanctify you through and through. May your whole spirit, soul, and body be kept blameless at the coming of the LORD Jesus Christ" (1 Thess. 5:23). The fruits of the flesh (envy, jealousy, anger, unforgiveness, bitterness, etc.) increase stress levels, and cause the stress hormone cortisol to go up, lowering the T-cell level and compromising your immune system.[4] Prolonged high levels of cortisol due to increased stress levels will cause heart disease, sleep disturbances, depression, and many other complications.

Choose to Have a Different Spirit

*"But because my servant Caleb has a different spirit and follows me
wholeheartedly, I will bring him into the land he went to, and his
descendants will inherit it." (Num. 14:24)*

Repeated actions become habits. Let the Spirit renew your thoughts, "… to be made new in the attitude of your mind" (Eph. 4:23). Many times I have chosen to refuse thoughts of fear and anxiety. Like many successful people, I choose to have a different attitude and a different spirit. God's blueprint is in your spirit. He put His promises in you, but you need to *activate* what God put in you and *decide* to have a different spirit. Develop a spirit of excellence through obedience. A right spirit will give you right attitudes to sustain your relationships in marriage, family, business, and society.

A gentle and quiet spirit is precious in the sight of God. We read in the book of Joshua that Joshua and Caleb received the promises of God because they had a right spirit. Bible characters who followed God's prescriptions disciplined themselves. They are examples for us, so we may consider their character as a model. Discipline can be painful. "No discipline seems pleasant at the time, but painful. Later on, however, it produces a harvest of righteousness and peace for those who have been trained by it" (Heb. 12:11). God chose to give the Promised Land to the sons of Israel, but they had to discipline themselves and faithfully follow God's prescriptions and instructions. God gave us promises for health, family, success, prosperity, etc., but we must follow His advice and recommendations. Choose God's perspective to wake up your spirit.

We learn in the book of Joshua that during Joshua and Caleb's time, the 10 spies missed the true perspective, and lost the blessing. People miss blessings because they lack self-discipline, refuse God's prescriptions, and lose their way. You can develop a right spirit through prayer. Be willing to learn. You are well able to overcome difficulties through an obedient spirit.

Choose a lifestyle of forgiveness, kindness, and faith to prevent adverse effects. Disobedience will separate you from God's promises and from arriving at your God-given destination. We must become the people God wants us to be. God wants people like Caleb. "But because my servant Caleb has a different spirit and follows me wholeheartedly, I will bring him into the land he went to, and his descendants will inherit it" (Num. 14:24).

A different (right) spirit will bring blessings over you and your descendants through the blessings of God, activated by the epigenetics mechanism that facilitates the "good" gene expression for the next generation. You must encourage yourself, even in tough situations. A different spirit was needed in the Promised Land. The other spies had ignorant and contemptuous spirits. You need the right spirit to benefit from God's blessings in your daily life. Cultivate a spirit that follows God's prescriptions and obeys His Word.

You can overcome any circumstances through the power of God. Nothing is impossible for those who believe God's Word and His promises. He promised, "I will never leave you and never forsake you" (Heb. 13:6). He promised to be with us always, if we seek Him and His Presence. If you do not stay in the Presence of God, you will end up in the presence of demons. Leave aside compulsive behavior that you cannot control: cigarettes, alcohol, drugs, lies, cheating, stealing, pornography, adultery and fornication, because these debilitate your life. The enemy tells you it is "only one time," and then again, "only one time." You must say, "*No more.*" Do a "U-Turn" from everything that is ungodly.

Protect your eye gates and your ear gates. TV steals your time. Video games are an addictive stronghold. Addictions start with "one time only," then again, "one time only," and then again, and again, and again. Do not let addictions deplete your body of dopamine. I have seen people crying, trying to get delivered, then experiencing withdrawal symptoms and going back into the same destructive behavior, because they cannot break the bondage of addiction. Those are strongholds that must be broken by choosing to have a different spirit.

Deliverance can be slow, because of the receptors that were developed during the addiction. However, deliverance can be quick when a supernatural intervention from the Spirit of God touches you. Many people cannot feel the touch of God because they are numbed by their addiction. I do not leave room for addictions. The only time I watch TV is when I need to know the news, or watch a Christian channel that builds up my faith. You must pursue knowledge and wisdom to develop a healthy conscious mind, one that is willing to make the right decisions and listen to God's spirit.

Other people will see your changed attitude and your unconditional love for people in distress. They will follow your example when you are transformed according to the Word of God. It takes only one minute to pray the prayer that Jesus taught His disciples to pray, the "Lord's Prayer" (Read Matt. 6:9). Why don't you pray that prayer now? God wants to polish you, and change your attitude and your reputation. You need to become the person God wants you to be. Look at life through your spiritual lenses. Think about what Jesus would do when temptations came. He fasted and prayed and refused to be enticed by the devil's snare.

Communicating Our Attitude

"...the soothing tongue is a tree of life, but a perverse tongue
crushes the spirit" (Prov. 15:4)

Mirroring activity helps people communicate with each other. Science shows us that mirroring, besides being a tool for communication between individuals, also develops knowledge and connections between people. Recent findings in the field of neuroscience have shown the presence of "mirror neurons" in the neural system of both primates and humans. These neurons enable exchanges between people, the development of the psyche, and the inter-subjective processes that are a basic condition for knowledge acquisition from others and for development of relational life.[5] Through the mirror neurons we learn from each other. Who controls your mirror neurons?

> Then those who feared the LORD talked with each other, and the LORD listened and heard. A scroll of remembrance was written in His presence concerning those who feared the LORD and honored His name. "On the day when I act," says the LORD Almighty, "they will be my treasured possession. I will spare them, just as a father has compassion and spares his son who serves him. And you will again see the distinction between the righteous and the wicked, between those who serve God and those who do not." (Mal. 3:16–18)

Communication prevents isolation and further depression and pain. God intentionally created mirror neurons in us with the ability to communicate, develop good relationships and love one another. God gave us the powerful prescription to "love one another" and He gave us the ability to love by using our mirror neurons. That will also reduce our stress level.

Our health flourishes when we communicate with a soothing tongue. Words have the power to either destroy someone's future, or build and transform a life for eternity. "The tongue has the power of life and death"

(Prov. 18:21). What you speak has the power to bring life. God brought all of creation into existence by the power of His Word. He used the Word to create the universe. We who bear God's image have the ability to create through our words. Words can create or destroy. Words have emotions attached to them, based on our perception. As soon as they touch the ears they are processed and stored as a memory in your brain structures, ready to be accessed for healing or destruction. "The soothing tongue is a tree of life, but a perverse tongue crushes the spirit" (Prov. 15:4).

Words arrive as a "breeze" (electrical impulses) in your brain cortex, with the neurons as "a forest of trees containing ten thousand trees per square mile".[6] If those words are kind and pleasant, they will bring fruits of their kind and healing to a bruised soul. But the tongue can also crush the spirit. Harsh and derogatory words spoken to you will crush you: "You are ugly," "You are worthless," or, "You're not so smart." You cannot handle those words. But, if somebody speaks uplifting words, such as: "You look good," "You can do that!" "You are so smart," or, "You are strong," then those words have the power to build you up, shape your outlook, and improve your attitude. Remember to declare the promises of God that bring encouragement, faith, hope and restoration.

There is power in your words. Your words can heal or hurt, regardless of your culture or nationality. Words become thoughts that are stored in your unconscious mind, and they can stay in your unconscious mind your entire life.[7] If unhealthy words caused unhealthy emotions, even those memories can be changed with healthy words (with healthy emotions attached to them) to build new, healthy memories for a healthier future. Mental health specialists deal with people whose episodes of angry outbursts are triggered by unhealthy words spoken to them even 40 or 50 years ago, resulting in unhealthy emotions and hurtful memories. You must select which words you allow to grow in your neurons.

When I was a child, if my Mom gave me an assignment I did everything I could to accomplish the task. One time I heard Mom say to another woman, "She could penetrate even a hard rock if needed, to do what I tell her to do." That comment remains with me today. No matter what is happening and how hard it is, I am determined to complete to my assignments. The Bible says it is important to successfully finish everything we start. Do not give up easily or leave your tasks unfinished.

The book of First Samuel tells us about David and Goliath's epic battle. David saw that Goliath was a giant, but said, "I come against you in the name of the LORD Almighty" (1 Sam. 17:45). He knew God was (and still is) bigger than Goliath. Goliath tried to intimidate David with derogatory words, but David knew that *Jehovah-Jireh* would provide victory, just as He had protected him many times when he fought lions and bears. David knew God as His Rock of Salvation, full of power and victory.

Do not talk against your destiny. In Joshua 6:10–11, "Joshua commanded the army: "Do not give a war cry, do not raise your voice, do not say a word until the day I tell you to shout the shout of victory…Then shout." They followed Joshua's instructions and the impossible became possible because of their obedience. God's promises for victory became real to them. They were commanded not to talk, because the risk and temptation for negative words would bring discouragement and destruction. They could never have been victorious if they had not obeyed and remained silent until the day of victory.

"Do not let any unwholesome talk come out of your mouth, but only what is helpful for building others up according to their needs, that it may benefit those who listen." (Eph. 4:29)

Be conscious about what kinds of words are coming out of your mouth respecting God's prescriptions. "Do not let any unwholesome talk come out of your mouth, but only what is helpful for building others up according to their needs, that it may benefit those who listen" (Eph. 4:29). When you carefully choose your words, you increase people's faith because faith comes by hearing the Word of God. Good words will be deposited in their unconscious mind, and available when needed. Your testimony is a powerful weapon. Your message, your worship, your prayers, and your walk with Jesus can influence those around you. The power of God's prescriptions, His Word, and your testimony about what God has done in your life will change other people's lives.

Sometimes we hear about a good medical specialist, and we highly recommend him or her to our patients. But we all have the Specialist of the Universe giving free prescriptions for life, for us here on earth and for eternity, which I highly recommend. Run to Him and benefit from His presence, wisdom, revelation, healing and restoration.

When Jesus lives through us, others will want to have the same power to change their attitude. Go public with your testimony. "For we are God's handiwork, created in Christ Jesus to do good works, which God prepared in advance for us to do" (Eph. 2:10). Continue to do good to people around you and speak life into other people's lives every chance you get. Be confident that you are who God said you are: a child of God, His Creation, saved by grace. Do not hide your identity. I could have missed my destiny and my calling in life if I had ignored the Word of God.

CHAPTER TWENTY

Thoughts

"...the mind governed by the flesh is death, but the mind governed by the Spirit is life and peace." (Rom. 8:6)

"...we take captive every thought to make it obedient to Christ." (2 Cor. 10:5)

Monitor Your Thoughts Continually

Wholesome thoughts bring life and peace, promote health, and bring glory to God. Refresh your thoughts, your memory, and your heart by meditating on the Word of God and reflecting on its transforming power. Filter your thoughts, selecting only the constructive, healthy ones. God wants you to enjoy a healthy body, soul and mind. He wants to preserve you until the coming of the Lord Jesus Christ. "May my meditation be pleasing to Him, as I rejoice in the LORD" (Ps 104:34). Your thoughts influence your destiny. If your thinking is controlled by the flesh and unwholesome things, it will lead to death from incurable diseases. Let the Holy Spirit control your thoughts, because "The mind governed by the flesh is death, but the mind governed by the Spirit is life and peace" (Rom. 8: 6).

Your thoughts actually do run your life—so be careful what you think. Examine and evaluate your thoughts. You can hide your thoughts from people, but God knows every one of them. When you have better thoughts, your world is better. Thoughts dictate your attitudes and how you walk in daily life. God's thoughts are not like your thoughts. "For My thoughts are not your thoughts, neither are your ways My ways," declares the LORD. "As a result your thoughts dictate your ways. As the Heavens are higher than earth, so are my ways higher than your ways and My thoughts than your thoughts" (Isa. 55:8). Would you like to know God's thoughts? Read His Word and pray for revelation through the power of the Holy Spirit.

Your attitudes and behavior reveal what kind of thoughts you have been focusing on. From your unredeemed heart come evil thoughts: "sexual immorality, theft, murder, adultery, greed, malice, deceit, lewdness, envy..." (Mark 7:21). Those attitudes lead to destruction, and "wrongdoers will be completely destroyed" (Ps. 37:2). You can make every thought obedient to Christ, as written in the scripture, "...we take captive every thought to make it obedient to Christ" (2 Cor. 10:5). Christ's thoughts are pure thoughts.

Pure Thoughts

"Finally, brothers and sisters, whatever is true, whatever is noble, whatever is right, whatever is pure, whatever is lovely, whatever is admirable—if anything is excellent or praiseworthy —think about such things." (Phil. 4:8)

Pure thoughts are the pathway to a right attitude. "Blessed are the pure in heart, for they will see God" (Matt. 5:8). Follow God's prescription from Philippians: "Finally, brothers and sisters, whatever is true, whatever is noble, whatever is right, whatever is pure, whatever is lovely, whatever is admirable—if anything is excellent or praiseworthy—think about such things" (Phil. 4:8). Focus your thoughts on what is honorable, true, pure, lovely and admirable. Think about things that are excellent and worthy of praise. If you put your thoughts on God and His Word, it will be well with you physically and spiritually, because God's perfect peace will flood your mind. "You will keep him in perfect peace whose mind is stayed on you because he trusts in you" (Isa. 26:3).

Rejoice Even in Difficult Times

"...not only so, but we also glory in our sufferings, because we know that suffering produces perseverance; perseverance character, and character, hope, and hope does not put us to shame." (Rom. 5:3)

Choose to rejoice, even in unfavorable situations. "Not only so, but we also glory in our sufferings, because we know that suffering produces perseverance; perseverance, character, and character, hope, and hope does not put us to shame" (Rom. 5:3). God is always working in your life, building your character into who God wants you to be. Character is important. When you go through fiery trials and discouraging situations, God is there with you, to show His glory. His eyes are watching you. "For the eyes of the LORD run throughout the earth to strengthen those whose hearts are fully committed to Him" (2 Chron. 16:9). Our eyes are focused on the trial, but a supernatural intervention will bring joy and accomplishment. Judy Squier, a Speech Pathologist born with no legs and a deformed hand, and mother of three normal girls, wrote in her book *His Majesty in Brokenness*:

Finding God's Masterpiece in your Missing Piece that "our seeming catastrophe can become a blessing in disguise when our last breath gasps, For this I have Jesus! The minute we welcome Jesus on the scene, His Majesty transcends our lowest point so that we "Much Afraids" are seen as pillars of strength, not because we have courage, but because we have Him."[1]

Judy's life was not free of difficulties, but she saw herself strong in her brokenness because she received Jesus in her heart.

Holy Spirit Thinking

"...but the fruit of the Spirit is love, joy, peace, forbearance, kindness, goodness, faithfulness, gentleness and self-control." (Gal. 5:22–23)

Negative, unhealthy thinking, (from lack of knowledge of the Word of God) brings confusion, fear, anxiety, depression, isolation, suicidal thoughts, multiple chronic conditions, complications and premature death. To avoid and prevent all those conditions, you need to clean negativism from your thoughts. Scientists are more interested in studying the effects of optimism on the brain, to develop new interventions and methods to treat depression and anxiety disorder. Have the mind of Christ. Only Jesus can bring maximum hope and optimism. He brought abundant life for those willing to renew their mind. Your thoughts improve when you seek God's thoughts for your life and grow in God's thoughts. "Now I commit you to God and to the Word of His grace, which can build you up" (Acts 20:32). The Word of God is necessary for spiritual growth and healthy thoughts. The Word has the power to build you up and change your thinking by bringing you revelation, knowledge, wisdom and understanding—the mind of Christ. Devour the Word of God to develop positive ways of thinking and an optimistic point of view—beyond science.

The Holy Spirit's presence in your life is shown by the fruits of the Spirit. "But the fruit of the Spirit is love, joy, peace, forbearance, kindness, goodness, faithfulness, gentleness and self-control" (Gal. 5:22–23). Choosing behaviors and thoughts that reflect the fruits of the Spirit can reprogram your mind. If you want your brain to have the right atmosphere for a healthy neurochemical balance and healthy amounts of neurotransmitters (endorphins, serotonin, oxytocin, dopamine, etc.) and to promote healing in your entire body and restore your spirit and soul, then make the fruits of the Spirit your own. The Holy Spirit offers a life full of optimism.

The Holy Spirit wants to live in us, but He can be grieved by our negativism and harmful thoughts. The Spirit gives gifts of wisdom, knowledge, faith, healing, miracles, prophecy, discernment, and speaking in Heavenly languages, according to His will (1 Cor. 12:7–11). Through the power of the Holy Spirit you can speak directly to God. The Holy Spirit will build your faith in Jesus. "But you, dear friends, by building yourself up in your most holy faith and praying in the Holy Spirit…" (Jude 1:20).

When the Holy Spirit comes over you and resides in you, you will change your thinking completely. Fear, worry, anxiety, depression, discouragement are gone—replaced by love, joy, peace, forbearance, kindness, goodness, faithfulness, gentleness and self-control. You need to encounter the power of God through the power of Holy Spirit. "But you will receive power when the Holy Spirit comes on you" (Acts 1:8).

Ruth changed her mind when her father-in-law and her husband both died. She did not allow depression to take over her life. She did not let bitter thoughts and pessimism ruin her life. She made the decision to let the Spirit of God reside in her, to guide and lead her. She cared for Naomi with a changed mind. Ruth was loving, kind and compassionate to her mother-in-law, now an old widow suffering from loneliness.

Ruth, choosing to be possessed by the Spirit of God, positioned herself for future blessings and was admired by people around her, because she had changed her thinking. Instead of going back to her own people—her country, her culture, her old habits—she chose to follow her mother-in-law's God. She was faithful, positive and hardworking, day in and day out. God gave her an amazing reward. The changes she made in her mind changed her future and brought her an eternal reward. She activated the character in her DNA to its maximum potential. She was willing to activate—by God's Spirit—what already existed within her.

Change Your Thinking—Change Your Brain

You can change your brain by changing your thought process. Leading neuroscientists report breakthrough findings of how our brain is wired biologically to be changed by God through healthy thinking. People resist changing thinking. They think they are in control of their life, are independent from God, and can live without responsibilities or consequences. Delaying acceptance of the need for God in our life will sooner or later bring the consequences of disobedience. Denial of a need for divine intervention in our life does not change God one bit, but can prevent us from living a life according to God's will and His divine purpose for creating us. Acceptance that our brief life on earth is temporary may change our perspective. Our attitude might need a makeover, and our brain needs to be reprogrammed to coincide with reality. People need to deal with changes all the time—new cultures, new technologies, new generations, new approaches to manage stress, etc. When you change your thinking you "change your brain".

People feel vulnerable and insecure from all the rapid changes in the world. Acknowledging and admitting that we must adapt our thinking for the changes in technology, and in many other areas of life, does not exonerate us from the responsibility that one day we will leave this planet. We will need to face the Day of Judgment for our life on earth. That is the main reason we need to change our thinking.

Making the change in your mind is crucial. Seek help in the Word of God, and from others who already obey and serve their Divine Creator. From birth to adulthood we must navigate our way through various life stages and changing circumstances that affect our mind. Changes are needed to reshape our thinking and mind. Sometimes we do not like these changes, but we must acknowledge and accept them. God is ready to intervene and help us in our decision to change our thinking. Identifying the need for change, and responding appropriately, is the key to a healthy life.

Listen to God's instructions and guidance; stay connected with all the great giants in faith to preserve your life here on earth, and to secure your place in Heaven, to spend your eternal life with Jesus and His followers. Your miracles are in your thoughts and your faith. When I see people suffering because of bad choices and wrong thinking in the past, such as drugs or alcohol-related dementia, I feel like writing the instructions from the Word of God on the prescription pad. "Urgent: read 10 chapters daily from the Word of God and meditate on it day and night, to preserve your neurons from dying prematurely. Take the Word with prayers and meditation to restore your health. The Word is life for your soul and for your spirit." As a primary care provider, actually I do pray with my patients and encourage them to read the Word of God for their benefit. Medication alone cannot solve all our problems.

Captive Thoughts

The Holy Spirit searches your mind, your thoughts, your emotions. He knows your brokenness. Every thought must be captive and obedient to Christ's teaching (2 Cor. 10:5). We must embrace the mind of Christ (1 Cor. 2) because God has good thoughts for our future (Jer. 29:11). The devil has evil plans for you. He is the one who is looking for ways to steal your joy, kill your passion and enthusiasm for God's promises, and destroy your health by bringing unhealthy thoughts into your mind. Our shortcoming in medicine is that so many people are suffering from anxiety, worry, and depression because of wrong thoughts, poor attitudes, and bad habits. We can reverse those epidemics created by destructive thoughts, replacing them with God's promises that bring healing and restoration. The forces of darkness that bring addiction, sickness and poverty can be overcome with healthy thoughts from the Word of God. Fight the forces of darkness by declaring the promises in God's Word over your life, again and again.

CHAPTER TWENTY-ONE

The Will of God

"... in all things we are more than conquerors through Him
who loved us." (Rom. 8:37)

Accepting the Will of God

Outside the will of God there is never complete success in managing stress. People attend stress management classes, receive pharmacological and non-pharmacological interventions, and try many kinds of therapy classes with different kinds of advice, procedures, and treatments with different medications, but with temporary results. We see relapses all the time. It is an endless battle. Besides all those interventions people need permanent hope—beyond science—to stay strong and firm to overcome stressful situations, especially during a crisis. In order to manage stress you need to have an open mind to the will of God, beyond science, and become the person God created you to be for His glory.

We can see the will of God for mankind in Jeremiah 29:11: "For I know the plans I have for you," declares the LORD, "plans to prosper you and not to harm you, plans to give you hope and a future." The will of God gives hope and a future to a broken heart in a broken world. You need to know God's will for your life and dwell in Him. If you do not know His will you can keep fighting, yet feel that you have lost, because you are on the wrong path. The will of God is built in, inside of you, in your DNA. He has written His will into your physical DNA (Deoxyribonucleic acid). You have the blueprint of God and His language, with all the characteristics that you were created to be. You need to discover His will and learn to know and accept it. His plan may be different than you expect, but His will is the best for you. You know that is God's plan for your life, when you ask something according to His will and He gives you what you ask. Everything that is impossible with men is possible with God. When you pray God's will in faith, you will find solutions for your problems and circumstances.

Being a stable person of faith will bring victory in your life. My husband and I had to believe that God wanted to bring victory in our life. David confessed the same in Psalm 66:17. "I cried out to Him with my mouth; let me tell you what He has done for me." He has done great things for us when we focused our attention on His will. We had to believe and follow His prescription to stay still, until He intervened on our behalf.

You cannot know someone else's thoughts, except through their spoken words and their actions. It is written that the Lord knows your thoughts. "You have searched me, LORD, and You know me. You know when I sit and when I rise; you perceive my thoughts from afar" (Ps. 139:1). People can think lawless and miserable thoughts that contaminate their souls. Dirty, filthy thoughts can enter in your mind through different sources: bad friends with wrong influences, media outlets (internet, magazines, movies), and books that are contrary to God's character. All of those will cause you to feel far from God and in much distress.

Be careful and pay attention to what you hear, what you read, what you see, and what you say, so that you are in God's will. This will reduce the stress in your life. People with unclean thoughts depart from God and end up destroying their future and their family. Those tragedies create ripple effects in their community, city, and nation. Two cities, Sodom and Gomorra, were destroyed completely because of the people's wickedness. (Read Genesis 19.) A good friend's family was destroyed because her husband opened the door to another woman in his life after many years of marriage. Her husband's actions destroyed her life and her children's future. They lived under terrible stress caused by their parents' divorce, which led to anxiety, depression and its consequences. My friend's immune system was compromised and she developed a terminal illness very soon after the shock—caused by a disastrous, unexpected divorce, with overwhelming stress. Jesus gave instructions to His disciples and to us all to watch in prayer, so we do not fall into temptations. In this postmodern era we face multiple temptations, but we can watch vigilantly over our life and stay in God's will.

Many families are destroyed because of a lack of knowledge of the Word of God and His will. They lack faith in God, do not fast and pray, and never know God's will. People lack wisdom from Heaven regarding their families. Where there is peace, joy, and unity there is is victory. Seek peace with your wife or your husband, your children, and everyone around you, giving priority to God's will. It is up to you to live in peace. If you provoke and create pain in somebody's life, start a dialogue and ask for forgiveness to prevent further emotional distress and damage. You must pursue peace and love in any relationship. "And now these three remain: faith, hope and love" (1 Cor. 13:13). These three virtues, faith, hope, love, will last forever. God's will for you is to have faith, hope and love, but love is greatest. When you have love you can live in peace with everyone, because God is love and He loves all His creation.

The will of God is included in all the promises written in the Word of God, which brings Good News for those who believe. Good News brings joy. Physical joy triggers thoughts of happiness that result in healthy amounts of neurotransmitters being released in your body. This repairs the cells affected by thoughts of fear, anxiety, depression, doubt and unbelief. Healthy neurotransmitters will promote a good attitude. Proclaiming the Good News to those around you will cause them to be happy, thus promoting health in their body, and building a healthier community.

I had non-believer colleagues under the communist regime who wanted to spend time secretly talking to me and listening to my testimonies, because they felt that the Good News would bring joy to their heart. People were hungry for the Good News, but it was illegal during the communist regime. The Good News can be mysterious and unexpected.

One day in Romania, I was in the office and the telephone was ringing. A colleague picked up the phone and announced that the call was for me. I was surprised because I did not expect anybody to call me at work at that time. I heard a voice with an accent wanting to talk to me. I asked who she was, and she identified herself and reminded me that she knew me from an all-night underground prayer meeting held at her grandparents' house in 1977. Of course I had to search my memory to find and activate that information from 10 years earlier. I remembered very well that night of prayer and the people who attended. But I was astonished to hear from her after so long, because I had not seen her for 10 years. She told me she had moved to the US because the communists had forced her to leave the country, and now was visiting Romania and wanted to see me. That was such good news and brought so much joy to my heart. A close friend was found! But God had a mysterious plan for me. After our meeting the Lord started to work in my heart, and convinced me that I must leave Romania, too. I was sure that God had a plan for my future, even though everything seemed contradictory to my circumstances at that time.

All the communists started secretly following me, to stop me from pursuing a visa to leave the country. It was very intimidating. They could do anything they wanted to me or my family, to hinder God's plan for my future. My future was not secure in Romania, once I had applied for a visa to leave the country. I had become a problem for them. So, I had to trust God in every situation. I knew my future was in God's hands. Like in Nehemiah 6:9: "…they were all trying to frighten us, thinking, 'Their hands will get too weak for work, and will not be completed.'" But I prayed, "Now strengthen my hands." (Neh. 6:9). This was what happened to me and my husband. They were trying to intimidate us and stop us from planning for our future.

We continued to pursue the exit visa with even greater determination, knowing that they could still stop us from leaving the country. So we continued to pray and believe God for miracles, because the barriers were great. I prayed continuously for strength in that difficult time. If you feel intimidated, or it seems impossible to find a solution for your situation, you must allow God into your life now to strengthen your soul, and declare, "… in all things we are more than conquerors through Him who loved us" (Rom. 8:37).

Did you know that when you are in God's will, you will fulfill your destiny? To find your destiny you must know God's expectations for you. God has a vision for your future, for your destiny. Many people ask, "What am I created for?" "Why I am here on earth?" "Why I was born?" or. "What is the purpose of my existence?" In my profession, and in my business, I spend time at the bedside of many dying patients—people like you and me. They were born, then grew up, and in their childhood and adulthood they often had the same questions about their reason for being on earth. I am sure that God had a plan for each one of their lives, until they arrived in our facility, on their deathbed. God planned a precise destiny for each of us. Life is a mystery, but you need to know what you are here for.

You must discern what is best for your life. As Philippians instructs us, "…you may be able to discern what is best and may be pure and blameless for the day of Christ, filled with the fruit of righteousness that comes through Jesus Christ—to the glory and praise of God" (Phil. 1:9–11). Many people are miserable because they do not know their destiny, or they are apathetic. They are lukewarm and have no passion, living a life that will have discouraging consequences. God wants us to live a life with passion for Him.

God tests us to see if we are hungry to know Him more, and to find out His will for our life. God is working at the level of your desire. If you are hungry and thirsty for more, He will help you achieve more. The spiritual realm is the same as the natural realm. For example, after I arrived in the US, I started cleaning toilets in a nursing home, but my desire was to know more about how to care for the aging population. Slowly I proceeded to take classes, to learn more, and was accepted into different programs for education up to the highest level. In the spiritual realm it is the same. You can have as much of God as you want. Are you thirsty for more of Jesus? When you desire to work more for Him, God will bless you more in everything you do. God gives approval to those who seek His will on earth and who have faith (Matt. 5:45).

Surrender to God

When you surrender to God, the will of God and His presence brings happiness. Turning bitterness into joy will reduce your level of stress. Joy will bring health to your body. He will bless you to impact other people. When we surrendered to His will, He changed our years of bitterness into blessings, so we now can bless others and bring joy into our lives and their lives. Surrender to God in every situation because God wants to give you peace in the storm. He wants to restore your relationships with your loved ones, reconnect you with them, restore your health in body and spirit, refresh your spirit and renew your heart. You may face storms in your life, but you must look to Jesus and pray. Jesus' storm was bigger than ours, and all He did was pray every day early in the morning, or sometimes all night long. Your help comes from the Lord. I have had many storms and tough times, and always when I prayed to the Lord He rescued me (Ps. 91 and Ps. 121).

Remember what God has already done for you. Keep your conscious mind clear before God and man. God is a lover of those who messed up, but wants each person on earth to surrender and live in truth and in righteousness (Acts 24:16). God provided everything for us. Everything comes from Him. Yield your heart to the Lord and you will be blessed by Him. There are consequences if you do not pay attention (Josh. 24:22–24). Many people are not willing to yield to the Lord, and then they must "reap what they sow."

Many people grieve and experience bitterness, because they do not want to surrender to God and repent. Yet true peace is only obtained through yielding and repentance. Selfishness brings bitterness, because you do not get what you want for yourself. You set unrealistic, high expectations, which you are never able to achieve. When you surrender, you will develop a selfless life and a heart of gratitude. Through joy and love you will have a charitable heart that will bring you great rewards. Train yourself to be joyful, even through difficult situations. Get rid of bitterness in your soul with the joy and love of the Lord, Who gives you strength.

True joy in your life happens when you are connected with Jesus' love. Nothing can bring more joy than Jesus the Prince of Peace, the Shining Morning Star, the Sun of Righteousness. There is power in the Name of Jesus. In His name you are able to love people who do not love you back, even people who hurt you. You will be able to forgive them as the Father forgave us, and that will bring healing to your soul and body. Do not blame the Church, or God, or other people for their mistakes. Surrender to God's will and seek God's mercy, grace, and love. When you have a surrendered heart you rejoice with those who rejoice and weep with those who weep.

CHAPTER TWENTY-TWO

Gender Differences

"...that is why a man leaves his father and mother and is united to his wife, and they become one flesh." (Gen. 2:24)

"be fruitful and increase in number, fill the earth and subdue it." (Gen. 1:28)

" ...therefore what God has joined together, let no one separate." (Mark 10:9)

Marriage Is Divine

One major relationship area that can trigger high levels of stress, worry, fear and anxiety is marriage. Marital partners share a physical, emotional and spiritual union, creating an eternal bond together. You desire and expect a safe relationship for life with your spouse, but if one of you gives in to disobedience and unfaithfulness, the marriage bond quickly frazzles and breaks down. What should have been a blessing can become twisted, putting the marriage, and even lives in danger.

God's prescription for marriage establishes wholesome standards for a successful, loving union. Two unique souls become united through intimacy. Sex was created to be a central, holy element in the marriage covenant, yet marriage is not only for having sex. It was God's idea—not man's—that a man and a woman should become one in love, bonding together physically, emotionally, and spiritually for a divine purpose. They need to be as one emotionally and spiritually to be overcomers in spiritual warfare. Husband and wife must be committed to one other. Separation in marriage is not healthy—physically, emotionally or spiritually—because of the overwhelming emotional pain that can result. In cases of divorce, each person experiences the unbearable pain of separation, similar to death. Because man and woman were not designed to bear the pain of divorce, the stress level created by divorce and separation is extremely high, causing real damage to the spirit, soul and body. Divorce is one of the reasons for the "broken heart syndrome".

In marriage relationships, poor communication is the usual culprit leading to divorce, because your words reflect what's inside your heart, mind and soul. Words reveal your internal condition. Words have meaning and power in the spiritual realm. They can bring people closer or bring distance and separation. The power to become closer is in you. You just need to activate it through the power of the Holy Spirit to create the atmosphere in your mind that promotes love, joy, peace and happiness. That is how you strengthen a marriage. One main ingredient in the divine marriage prescription for a lifelong healthy relationship is for both husband and wife to be filled with the Holy Spirit.

Abstinence

*"Flee the evil desires of youth and purse righteousness,
faith, love, and peace, along with those who call on the Lord
out of a pure heart." (2 Tim. 2:22)*

*"...do not be deceived: Neither the sexually immoral nor idolaters
nor adulterers, nor men who have sex with men, nor thieves nor the
greedy nor drunkards nor slanderers nor swindlers
will inherit the kingdom of God." (1 Cor. 6:9–10)*

Medically we know that adultery opens the door to sexually transmitted diseases—chlamydia, gonorrhea, genital herpes, HPV, hepatitis, syphilis, HIV, AIDS, etc. Thus, God gave us prescriptions for how to prevent those diseases: abstinence and self-control. Abstinence before marriage was commanded by God to help people avoid disaster. (Read Genesis 2.) It is one of His instructions for a healthy lifestyle. Marry at the right time with the right person, and stay married for life. God hates divorce (Mal. 2:16). It is important for young men and women to be extremely careful about whom they marry, and to discern the right time. If you are not married yet, look for a godly person, because marriage is for life. When teaching about marriage we must lay out the foundations for future generations. Disastrous ideas pervade the educational system and the media. The constant stream of movies and video games promoting violence, immorality and pornography seems unending. What principles do we want to promote? Do not lose the battle for lack of wisdom.

Due to rapidly changing technologies, our whole culture is constantly changing all around us. We are bombarded with chaotic and conflicting messages on every level. Contrary to God's instructions, worldly attitudes promote countless unhealthy behaviors that lead to chronic physical and mental diseases. Society is becoming sicker and sicker, dying a premature death due to corruption and manmade diseases. In 1 Corinthians 6:9–10 we read "…do not be deceived: Neither the sexually immoral nor idolaters nor adulterers nor men who have sex with men, nor thieves nor the greedy nor drunkards nor slanderers nor swindlers will inherit the kingdom of God" (1 Cor. 6:9–10). None of those have a place in God's Kingdom. That is why Jesus Christ paid for our sins with His blood, and He is calling us to repent and be forgiven of all those sins.

The number of young people having unprotected sex with new partners increased 39% in the U.S., 19% in the U.K. and 111% in France in the past three years, according to a multinational study.[1] Millions are being spent on medical research to discover cures and vaccinations for devastating diseases with minimal results, when simple prevention through abstinence has superior results.

The American CDC reported in 2014 that chlamydia totaled 1,244,180 cases—the highest recorded for any condition.[2] These sexually transmitted diseases are due to sex outside marriage with multiple partners. Even very young children, students in grades 7 to 12, are engaged in destructive behaviors such as gambling, substance abuse, sex, pornography and attempted suicide. "One in four adults–approximately 61.5 million Americans–experiences mental illness in a given year."[3] The costs for their care tremendously increase stress throughout society. When I look at these numbers something screams inside of me, "We must wake up!"

Understanding Our Differences

"So God created mankind in his own image, in the image of God he created them; male and female he created them." (Gen. 1:27 NIV)

To manage stress in marriage you need to understand that God, our Super Intelligent Designer, created men and women differently. No one should doubt that. Physically we have obvious differences in our reproductive systems and their functions. We do not need somebody else to tell us who is a woman or who is a man. There is no confusion in God's creation of a man and a woman. What we cannot see is the hidden physiology in the circulatory system or in the brain. For example, women's arteries are smaller than men's arteries, putting women at higher risk for heart disease, and different circulatory symptoms have different complications. Cardiology studies show differences in women's and men's hearts, and how they are differently affected by stressors.

Because women's arteries are narrower, they carry an increased risk for arteriosclerosis and its complications later in life. Also, in women and men the brain is designed differently and uniquely programmed by God. Male and female brain structures and neurons also have physiological differences.

Our gender differences remain as long as we live. Many women complain about their husband's behavior and make huge efforts to change him after they get married, using manipulation, humiliation, complaints, disrespect, cheating, and flirting with other men or women, jeopardizing their relationship. The same is true for men toward their wives.

Misunderstandings about the differences create further stress. God created men and women with physiological and psychological differences. Not understanding the differences in our brain structures can be extremely stressful for a married couple. The majority of us learn from our mistakes, and only by God's grace are we able to manage the stress in our marriage. Marriage should bring comfort, not worry, fear and anxiety. Looking for comfort from immediate gratification, and entering into marriage primarily for sex, results in bitterness. Not waiting upon the Lord will have repercussions later in life.

My husband and I grew up subscribing to biblical standards about marriage. When our daughter Andreea was in high school, she prepared a list of 35 points and conditions to be met by her future husband. Our daughter knew she would want to get married according to God's instructions and prescriptions and His will for her life. She did not want to "play" marriage. She knew that marriage is for life. I really wondered where she would find a guy to meet all of her 35 conditions! I started praying for a miracle, because these days it would take a miracle to find such a young man with a pure heart. Then God brought Jeff into her life, and each point on her list was checked off quickly. I told myself, "He must be the one." God had prepared the one who was to be her husband for life. She had trusted His promises. "Be still and know that I am God" (Ps. 46:10).

Obedience to the Word of God in marriage is not optional. With God all things are possible when you wait for His divine intervention. God knows everything. You must have faith that He will provide the right person for you. Jesus sees your tears when you cry out to Him for the right one. Do not despair. Prayer and fasting is a key element in this. If we fear God and do His will, He will hear us. Unbelief will only produce fear and cripple your future. Renew your mind and meditate on the Bible's clear instructions about marriage.

We need to enjoy the mystery of God's creation in marriage. Marriage is a lifelong commitment and should be full of love, joy, happiness, peace, and all the fruits of the spirit. The brain's various structures release neurotransmitters in different ways in men and women. Neurotransmitters (serotonin, epinephrine, norepinephrine, oxytocin, serotonin, dopamine, endorphin, and other neurochemicals and hormones) are released in different amounts in each man or woman, based on what kind of thoughts you dwell on. Your thoughts influence your attitude and behavior in your marriage. Dr. Caroline Leaf, in her book *Who Switched Off your Brain-Solving the Mystery of He Said/She Said*, stated, "When the weight of stress and pressure becomes toxic and unhealthy, woman will talk without thinking and man will act without thinking."[4] Male and female thought processes are different and they do affect relationships in marriage.

Read Dr. Caroline Leaf 's book *Who Switched Off your Brain—Solving the Mystery of He Said/She Said* for a clearer scientific picture, and a full understanding—beyond science—of the difference between male and female brain anatomy, physiology and functions. You will gain more insights about gender difference and a different perspective about relationships in marriage.

The Wise Woman

"The wise woman builds her house, but with her own hands the foolish one tears hers down." (Prov. 14:1 NIV)

Oxytocin is the neurotransmitter with a clear assignment to keep the family together. To prevent and avoid divorce in your family, keeping the oxytocin level high, giving you the comfort and assurance of wellbeing in your marriage.[5] The release of oxytocin gives you confidence and comfort in your marriage, so you will not look for the "D" word when things get tough. God is against separation and divorce. Keep love alive in your heart and brain so your relationship in your marriage will last, just as God intended. You are equipped by your Creator for marriage to last your entire life.

To keep her family together and to please God, a woman needs the virtues of the Proverbs 31 woman. (Read Proverbs 31.) By enriching your knowledge and acting more like this woman you will have a life full of victory and success.

We need the word of God in our heart at all times. Study the Bible and memorize the scriptures. This is good not only for spiritual discipline. It can physically create new neurons and restore your emotions and relationships in your marriage. Your brain will produce more healthy neurotransmitters if your attitude is right. Love will never fail because God, the source of love, is infinite. Neuroscientists have discovered that oxytocin is created in the hypothalamus and secreted by the pituitary gland, when triggered by love.[6] Living by the power of the Holy Spirit, you have what lasts forever—love.

Love will cause more joy, peace, goodness, kindness, gentleness, patience, faithfulness, and self-control, and your marriage can be healed. This draws husband and wife together again and again, when you create a healthy atmosphere for the brain to release the right chemicals, as God intended in His intelligent design.

Oxytocin, the "love hormone", facilitates attachment. God's prescription for man is to love his wife. Oxytocin, released when you love, is important for reproduction and survival of the species. It helps develop lifelong bonds for a family to produce offspring in a covenant of marriage. Oxytocin has been important in monogamy since creation.[7] God wrote prescriptions and instructions for marriage between a man and a woman, who were complete strangers in Genesis. "That is why a man leaves his father and mother and is united to his wife, and they become one flesh" (Gen. 2:24). He then gave the command to "...be fruitful and increase in number, fill the earth and subdue it" (Gen. 1:28). Then in Mark 10:9 we read, "Therefore what God has joined together, let no one separate" (Mark 10:9). Oxytocin, released through love, keeps man and woman "glued" together. Since creation—beyond science—what God united, man should not separate. Scientists marvel at the biological mystery of monogamy, enabled through this hormone oxytocin and released through love.[8] Reprogram your brain to love and to increase oxytocin levels through the "power of touch" through hugs, kisses, holding hands, and an intimate relationship.[9] All these expressions will cause the release of oxytocin to improve your relationship with longer, stronger bonds.

Oxytocin also helps bond a mother to her baby. Isaiah wrote (49:15), "Can a woman forget the baby at her breast and have no compassion on the child she has borne?" Oxytocin is released when triggered by love and is involved in nurturing, helping strangers marry for life, and in empathy and compassion. Oxytocin involved in fear and anxiety can be beneficial for an individual's survival. "Flee the evil desires of youth and pursue righteousness, faith, love, and peace, along with those who call on the Lord out of a pure heart" (2 Tim. 2:22).

Oxytocin reduces stress. It helps you forgive others, helps with social skills, and lifts the burden of bitterness from your heart. God's love has been poured out in our hearts. But separated from God, you deprive your body of these amazing resources. Read the 1 Corinthians 13, "Love chapter", which tells us that love never fails. "Now these three remain: faith, hope, and love. But the greatest of these is love" (1 Cor. 13:13). Love will remain forever. Use the "power of touch" to release oxytocin in the brain. This is what touch does for us in our family life. Love is the fruit of the spirit; it is what God desired from the beginning, both for and from His creation. Only through the power of the Holy Spirit, given by Christ Jesus, can we have true love. God is love.

Love

"Let love and faithfulness never leave you; bind them around your neck, write them on the tablet of your heart." (Prov. 3:3)

According to neuroscientists, healthy amounts of neurotransmitters are released in your body through love as endorphin, the natural antidepressant and oxytocin, "the love neurochemical" for nurturing, which together influence your physical health in a positive way. Love will calm your brain. Your anxiety level will decrease, your heart rate will decrease, and your heart can relax, improving circulation, breathing, and the oxygenation of all your cells. It will enhance the immune system's ability to fight infections, viruses, and cancer when you follow this high potency prescription. We read, "Let love and faithfulness never leave you; bind them around your neck, write them on the tablet of your heart" (Prov. 3:3).

Stress can be managed through love. Love is a feeling that will trigger a healthy amount of chemicals to be released in your body, reprogramming your thinking. All is based on love. Jesus gave us the fundamental commandment for the human race: "Love one another" (John 15:9–17). Jesus was driven by love, and everything He did was loving. We must be driven by love too. Love is crucial. We have to live by love. Living without love, we are like a brass cymbal—nothing but noise. If you do not love, you accomplish nothing (1 Cor. 13:1–3). Your influence on the job, at school, and in society is driven by love. We must prove our love. Love is a force, a power, an effort, an exertion, and love has an impact, because God is love. He supernaturally pours His love into our hearts.

Use your imagination. Imagine that God's love from the invisible world "the spiritual realm" hit the threshold of our cerebral cortex transformed in electrical impulses flowing through "the forest of neurons" rushing to the amygdala, casting out all thoughts, emotions and feelings of fear and anxiety. Another neurotransmitter associated with love is Dopamine, with its excitatory function.[10] It is amazing how Jesus gave us instructions about loving one another. He did not explain why, but from creation—beyond science—our heart and brain and spirit were created with the capacity to love. We were created for relationship, and given all the necessary equipment to love. We just need to follow God's prescription. Selfishness is the opposite of love.

Love becomes real when someone touches Jesus, who was consumed with love for us. Love is serving others (Matt. 20:29-34; Gal. 5:13). Jesus served people. In response to His great love you need to be full of holiness, pray for others, and live your life for others. You carry the "living water". Day in and day out you can bring "living water" for the lost. Love-deprived people need our compassion and love.

In our business we have the opportunity to serve homeless people. We know how deprived of love they have been for many years. When they come to our place we show them love through our services, but we also give them hugs and tell them verbally that we love them. We can see joy and happiness in their eyes, from love they had not felt for years. To receive, you must give, and to have harvest, you must sow. These are the signs that point the way to God. God gave His only begotten Son, to leave the glory of Heaven, to be born in the lowest place on earth, and be wrapped in swaddling clothes, lying in a humble manager. He grew in God's wisdom and power, ministered to others, and died on the cross for the entire world. Then He was raised from the dead and ascended to our Heavenly Father to intercede on our behalf, even now, in this moment.

This is how God loved and continues to love us, no matter what. In return we must have a humble spirit. Jesus is now in glory because He humbled Himself on earth. If you want God to give you glory you must humble yourself. We need to be like Christ. He came to break the chain, to cleanse us from our sins, and we must become like Him. Through love you win favors with people and with God. You also promote health and prevent diseases. Through love He will show you His will in everything you do, and He will show you which path to take.

I did not know what to expect when I arrived in the US, but through His love and through fasting and prayer, God showed us what to do every single day. Even though I often felt tired and discouraged, I felt God's love. He gave me strength through His Word, and by the power of the Holy Spirit. I felt His love through His Presence in my lowest moments of loneliness. I kept the Bible open on the table so I could read it each time I had a chance throughout the day, to stay connected with God's love. I memorized the Word of God during my adolescence and adulthood in Romania, and here in the US I recited it to myself to remind me of His promise that He loves me.

You must renew and guard your heart with God's love. Through fasting and praying, we become stronger in the Lord and closer to Him. He promised, "…but those who hope in the LORD will renew their strength. They will soar on wings like eagles; they will run and not grow weary, they will walk and not be faint" (Isa. 40:31). When you hope in the Lord and recognize His love for you, your strength will be renewed.

So hoping in the Lord will give you more energy to function well. It is the hope in His love for you that your brain is programmed to produce healthy neurotransmitters that will increase your energy. I was working two jobs fulltime, with no days off, for almost two years after I arrived in the US. At the same time I studied English daily, late into the night. I was able to run and not grow weary, to work and not be faint, because God's love gave me strength. God will do a new thing in your heart too, if you are sensitive to God's love every day and find your hope for a blessed future.

Focus on the Good News that God loves you, and feed your soul with joy. Always look for Good News in the Word of God that brings joy and excitement to your heart. Beni Johnson stated in her book *The Happy Intercessors*, "When you carry the joy of the Lord with you, all kinds of things happen. Joy brings excitement in the air, and it releases life."[11] Joy comes after you find the Good News. Good News can be unexpected and mysterious, as when God sent Jesus Christ His Son, in the form of a man, to planet Earth. Nothing brings more joy than knowing God loves you.

As young girl under the communist system I was so hungry for God's love, I would wake up at 3:00 or 4:00 a.m. to go to a prayer meeting. We did not have electricity in my village. Our path was lit by the light of the moon in the early morning. My heart was filled with the joy of God's presence. Where God is present, His love is felt. I could sing all day long, working tirelessly, because of His love in my heart. My work was efficient and time passed quickly, even though the work was so hard.

When you love with the love of God, fears will disappear. Love is powerful. God's love gives confidence and encouragement that is fearless. The love of God can change the culture of every nation. People develop their own code of living and call it good, unwilling to recognize the love of God in their life. In the Old Testament it is written in Judges that "… everyone did what was right in their own eyes," not seeking God's advice or recognizing His authority. When people did "what was right in their own eyes" and followed their own fleshly desire with destructive behavior, they put themselves in the position to be destroyed because of their lack of obedience. God always punished disobedience, but He gives blessings beyond imagination to those with a heart after His own heart and to those who surrender to Him through love.

CHAPTER TWENTY-THREE

Meditation and Anti-aging

"May these words of my mouth and this meditation
of my heart be pleasing in your sight, LORD,
my Rock and my Redeemer." (Ps. 19:14)

God Prescribes Meditation

Meditation, a proven anti-aging therapy, produces new neurons in your brain through neurogenesis. New neurons preserve cognition and prevent dementia and Alzheimer's later in life. Turn everything over to God and meditate day and night on His Word, and you will renew your mind. The Queen of England declared in one of her speeches, "Through reflection and meditation we have the power to be renewed."[1]

Spiritual heart disease—sin—brings futility and emptiness. Replace sin in your heart with meditation and the Word of God. "God created mankind upright, but they have gone in search of many schemes" (Eccles. 7:29). We live in a dark world where sin is accepted as normal, and rationalized with the theory of relativism. Those who live in the light are despised or persecuted, as I was under communism. But there is nothing too dark or too dirty to be redeemed by the grace of God. God wants to restore your relationships, renew your spirit, and change your heart. Begin to seek a fresh revelation of Jesus Christ and what He is doing right now in your life, and in the world.

We need fresh spiritual eyes to see who Jesus is, and the Holy Spirit to reveal Jesus to us in our daily life. Jesus is the answer for a broken world, broken nations, broken cities, broken families and broken people. People are drowning in sin, and Jesus is the Rescuer. Where we see Jesus, we see love and grace, and people are transformed by his love and power. We don't need clinical trials to demonstrate the power of Jesus Christ transforming people. The best evidence since Jesus died on that cross over 2,000 years ago has been witnessed over and over. People are healed in the presence of His power. Victory is in Jesus' name. Surrender to God, ask Him to intervene, and let His Spirit rule again.

The world perverts everything: music, science, creativity in the arts, education, economics, technology, sex, and family life. Only God can restore everything back to its original form and give vision, dreams, revelation, and supernatural signs. Our society needs to return to a godly life to receive the provisions of unmerited grace. Grace can transform everyone and everything.

Meditate on God's Word

God is pleased when we humble ourselves. We need to meditate on His precepts so we can hear God's voice when Jesus knocks at the door. "Apart from Me you can do nothing" (John 15:5). When you meditate day and night on God's Word, you hear His voice, because you create an atmosphere in your brain to allow the Holy Spirit to come into your mind and speak to you. Joel Osteen in his daily devotion stated:

> When you constantly focus on external things: distractions, worry, and cares of the world, they become bigger in your mind's eye. But when you focus on what God has given you: peace, freedom, and abundant life, those are the things that you will see manifest in your life. .... Remember, where the Spirit of the Lord is, there is liberty. So focus on Him and focus on freedom!"[2]

"Now the Lord is the Spirit, and where the Spirit of the Lord is, there is freedom" (2 Cor. 3:17 NIV). When you meditate on the work of the Spirit through the Word of God, you grow new neurons in your brain's structure and receive healing, physically and spiritually.

Because our brain structures produce neurotransmitters (like GABA with inhibitory action), we can avoid unsafe actions (protecting us from bad habits and bad consequences). But GABA needs to be activated to calm your brain through meditation. Meditate on the Word of God, because all Scripture is profitable and is inspired by God. Solomon was wiser than everyone else. He wrote about 3,000 proverbs and 1,000 songs.[3] He experienced the power of God's presence, but in spite of his wisdom, he concluded that everything in life is meaningless. (Read the book of Proverbs.) He became pessimistic, departed from the truth, and stopped meditating on God's Word. He could no longer discern the voice of God.

Discerning and being sensitive to the voice of God is the most important thing in life. Solomon, looking for meaning in life, said, "Fear God" (Eccles. 12). Make life count and keep His commandments, meditating on His Word. Solomon talks about how to make life meaningful, with skills that bring success. Solomon is telling us—thousands of years later—to stop and analyze what we are doing. Take time to meditate on the Word of God.

When we do not meditate on the Word of God we can become exhausted. When you lose your passion you work harder, but with little progress, becoming emotionless and spiritually hollow. Authentic meaning is found only in God. Solomon became addicted to things, but he missed out on meeting with God, who had blessed Him. Concentrating on material things, wanting more, and shifting our focus from God only brings depression. Ask yourself what really matters. People sacrifice faith, family, friends, morals, and values for meaningless things, yet reflecting at the end of their life find it meaningless. Then it is too late.

CHAPTER TWENTY-FOUR

Helping Others

*"For we are God's handiwork, created in Christ Jesus to do
good works, which God prepared in advance
for us to do." (Eph. 2:10)*

Be the Answer

Helping others *helps* us manage our stress. Follow Jesus' example: "Because Christ suffered for you, leaving an example, that you should follow in His steps" (1 Peter 2:21), walk as He walked, sacrificing for others. "Whoever claims to live in Him must live as Jesus did" (1 John 2:6). Walk in love, have the heart of a servant, humble yourself and be obedient. "Have the same mindset as Christ Jesus: Who, being in the nature of God, did not consider equality with God something to be used to His own advantage; rather, he made Himself nothing by taking the very nature of a servant, being made in human likeness and being found in appearance as a man, He humbled Himself by becoming obedient to death—even death on the cross" (Phil. 2:5–8). Joanna Weaver, in her book *Having a Mary Heart in a Martha World: Finding Intimacy with God in the Busyness of Life*, stated, "The Lord has gone out of His way to make us His own. Yes, He died and rose again. He sent the Holy Spirit to teach and guide us. He's invested His own life to make us holy, and He'll take what we offer Him and make it into something good. But we're still expected to partner in the process."[1]

Trying to do everything in your own power will bring on stress. Bring your cares and worries to Him. The best prescription, with no expiration date, says, "Come, follow Me" (Matt. 4:19). Find the direction God is leading you, and follow Him. When you are disoriented, discouraged and depressed at a crossroads in life, just remember His instruction—follow Him.

We must also practice servanthood. To see the power of God working in your life you must humble yourself and feed on God's faithfulness. Follow Jesus' example and start helping others. Jesus wants to provide a fresh start for everyone, and through His Spirit *new "spiritual DNA"* is available for all. Find out His purpose for you, and you will have a new passion for this life, and a purpose to prepare for eternal life. Jesus came to give life more abundantly, and eternal life to those who believe in Him. He wants no one to perish. He gave selflessly, and so must we. Help others break free from bondage. You must put your life on the line by helping others. Help somebody who is broken and hurting. God's heart breaks for the needy and the lost. Sacrifice for others, help others, and let your light shine. People will see your light in your good works. You have a treasure in you, given by the Lord Jesus—His seed of love and compassion.

People can be transformed by your acts of kindness, as you help others on your journey to your own destiny. People will admire you and follow your example when you are doing good deeds, and God will be glorified. So many people have a broken spirit, and there is a crying need everywhere for kindness.

Give God the first place in your heart. He rules the Universe, but He will not force His way in your heart. David, when he was devastated by sin, prayed, "Renew the Spirit within me" (Ps. 51:10). With a renewed spirit your heart will break for others. Caring for others is the most wonderful thing. We provide the care but Jesus heals the soul and the body. By helping others we can build a bridge for people who are seeking God.

Serving Others by Grace

"Rejoice with those who rejoice; mourn with those who mourn." (Rom. 12:15)

"Each one of you should use whatever gift you have received to serve others." (1 Pet. 4:10)

"His words burn into me." (Jer. 20:9)

The Mirror Neurons

Joel Osteen, senior pastor of Lakewood Church in Houston, Texas with approximately 30,000 attending every week, stated in his book *Your Best Life Now: 7 Steps to Living at Your Full Potential*, "When God created us, he put His supernatural love in all of our hearts. He's placed in you the potential to have a kind, caring, gentle, loving spirit. You have the ability to emphathize, to feel what other people are feeling. Because you are created in the image of God, you have the moral capacity to experience God's compassion in your heart. But too often, because of our own selfishness, we choose to close our hearts to compassion."[2]

We know that God put mirror neurons in our brain so we can overcome evil through compassion and experience God's goodness and mercy in our life (Rom. 12:21). Also, God made mirror neurons in our brain so we can lay up treasures in Heaven for eternity, through compassion for others and good deeds.[3] Eternity is our true life. After our flesh has died, we will be more alive in Heaven, where God is glorified forever. Mirror neurons in our brain build potential for eternal reward. Jesus had perfect mirror neurons, and great compassion for humanity. He paid the ultimate price, dying on the cross for our sins, so we can have eternal life.

God loves a joyful giver. Overcome worry by finding someone else who needs your compassion. God created our brain with the ability to follow His commandments. He is asking us to clothe ourselves with compassion, because He had compassion (Col. 3:12). He is not asking us to do something too difficult. He knows we have mirror neurons that are activated through the power of God to follow His prescriptions. Pharmacists know how medications are developed to bind with receptors or enzymes in the body to achieve the proposed therapeutic level for a certain condition. God, the Supreme Scientist and Pharmacist gave us the Holy Spirit to activate our mirror neurons to have compassion for needy people, as it is written: "Each one of you should use whatever gift you have received to serve others" (1 Pet. 4:10). Compassion was His ultimate goal. Your mirror neurons will work with the gift that is in you, to serve others with compassion. God will repay, both here on earth and also in Heaven.

We were created for His glory, and we will bring Him glory for eternity. There are benefits beyond this life. Do good deeds and have an honorable character, refreshing others in your community and internationally. Jesus was moved with compassion when He fed the hungry multitudes, healed the sick, delivered the captives from demonic oppression, and raised the dead. Jesus wept at the tomb where Lazarus lay dead, because He mirrored Lazarus' family's brokenness. What can you give when everything comes from Him? Everything is from Him, including our mirror neurons. Consider His goodness and come to Him with a willing attitude.

Through our mirror neurons we are able to feel other people's emotions.[4] If someone laughs, we laugh; if people cry, we cry. The Holy Spirit touches our mirror neurons to show favor, mercy, kindness, and gentleness, and to help us feel the pain of the most vulnerable people. Jesus instructed us to pray for the sick and heal them in His name. He gave us authority to do that, because He knew we have mirror neurons built in us to feel their pain. Because of the mirror neurons in our brain, we are able to feel the pain of those who suffer, and rejoice with those who rejoice, according to

God's prescriptions: "Rejoice with those who rejoice; mourn with those who mourn" (Rom. 12:15). Many times my eyes are filled with tears of sadness and my heart is moved when I see so many needs here in the US (especially at the free clinic, where I volunteer as a PCP). Then I find myself with tears of joy, when I see people recovering from sickness, or when I feel God's Presence in my life. I know that I do not do that by my own power; it is the Holy Spirit who activates my mirror neurons.

We also have the second commandment, to love our neighbors like ourselves. You have the capacity to repair the world around you by helping others (Isa. 58:6–14). The entire Bible is about God's prescriptions for love. He wants us to love one another as He first loved us.

Jesus, our example, poured out His character to the people around Him. His passion for people drove Him to the cross. We must have passion for the human race. Passion in your heart leads you to help others, to pray, to provide emotional support, etc. Beth Moore, in her book *Jesus the One and Only*, wrote, "Your heart means far more to Christ than anything. That your heart is utterly taken with Christ is more important than any amount of service you could render or rules you could keep. If Christ has your heart, He will have your obedience (see John 14:21). God wants to completely captivate your heart and cause it to burn with passion for Him. It is His absolute priority for you according to Mark 12:30; joy and satisfaction will elude you in its absence."[5] Your spiritual passion for Christ will be ignited through prayer and studying the Word of God, the only way for true joy and satisfaction.

When the fire is burning inside you, and when the mirror neurons are activated, all your heart, mind, and soul burn with the desire to help others. Jeremiah said, "His words burn into me" (Jer. 20:9). As a child I grew up in a very poor family. At that time I did not realize I was poor. I saw my family as one of the richest in the village, even though our floor was dirt, we had beds made of wood and straw, and had no electricity or indoor plumbing. Since I was little I always had the desire to share what I had and to help those around me. It seems like my mirror neurons in my brain were activated very early in life! Whenever I heard that a person was in need, I would share what I had. One time as a teenager I felt compassion in my heart so strongly for others that I put my few clothes in a small box and sent it to a needy family who had nothing. I just kept two blouses, two skirts, one pair of shoes, two pair of socks and one scarf, and I sent everything else. I did not buy new ones for a while, because I had enough compared with those who had nothing.

Another time in Bucharest I was visiting a family with 12 children. As I scrutinized the house I saw on the kitchen table a fresh onion, with a few slices of very low quality salami (made of cartilage and fat) for dinner. I realized that that was the single meal for that day for the whole family. That was all, for a family of 14. Deep in my soul, I cried out in prayer to the Lord to help this family. At that time people could not prosper because of the tight controls of the communist dictators. God answered my prayers, and in a few years I received my visa to leave the country. God has blessed us richly, so we are able to help others now, including that family.

Don't ever give up when you pray. God hears your cries and He gives you your heart's desires. Just keep praying. He will either answer your prayers, or He will change the desire of your heart until you pray a different way. The passion of God overwhelms you and changes your thinking, language, attitude, work, and deeds. You cannot keep passion inside. It finds an outlet. "As the deer pants for steams of water, so my soul pants for you, my God" (Ps. 42:1). Passion is a continual desire to pray, to serve with all your heart, to love deeply, to drink from the Word of God's "living water", to give with joy, and "not grow weary in well doing."

Your stress level will decrease when you have that servant's heart (Mark 10:43). Love as the Lord loved us (John 13:34). When you lay down your life for others, God's blessings will explode in your life (John 3:16). True servanthood is to serve not only when it is convenient. Jesus served His disciples and the people around Him to the end. He had a servant's heart to love, even to death on the cross. Do things you are not comfortable with, and you do not feel like doing. Many times I felt like I needed to stop spending my time volunteering in a small clinic for a disadvantaged and marginalized population, but the small voice inside me activated my mirror neurons and did not let me quit. Sometimes there were people who did not have even $5 in their pocket to spend on food or medication.

Jesus loved the community where He lived, and He tells us to love our neighbors as ourselves. Our whole community is our neighbor. Jesus had a passion for His ministry and compassion for the people around Him. His heart was moved with compassion for people's physical and emotional needs, to the point of crying for them. When was the last time you cried for someone who had a great need? Love others as Jesus did.

God has a calling for each person on earth. He is patient for each of us to come to know Him, because He put the thought of eternity in mankind since creation (Eccles. 3:11). God also gives people gifts and talents. Time is the greatest treasure on this planet, but it passes by very fast. We must fulfill our calling for this short life by helping and serving others. We need to live with eternity in our thoughts and be Heavenly minded.

It is not about us, but about those around us (Matt. 5:16). God put us in a community for a reason—to pray for that community, to serve with all our hearts, to spend our resources and energies on those in need and feel their pain. In our business we have opportunities to serve the underserved population, and we discover that many of these people were homeless at some point in their life, or orphans given up for adoption, or abandoned in their childhood, living on the margin—a life full of discouragement. But God brings them into our care facility to spend their last years, months, and days with us, and we treat them like royalty. We do not differentiate between a homeless and a very rich, or a highly educated person with a Ph.D degree. We embrace them, give them hugs, and encourage them so they will feel accepted and loved. One of my old patients said, "You make me smile," when I told him he is special and I love him. He continued, "I did not smile for five years." We understand that this is our calling in life.

We can have compassion for people who live in very stressful situations, and we can help one person at a time. It pleases God when we are clothed with humility, serving others. Your stress level will diminish when you have that approach. "...whoever wants to become great among you must be your servant" (Mark 10:43). Jesus instructed us to "Love one another as I loved you" (John 13:34). When you lay down your life for others, blessings will chase you. "Jesus Christ laid down His life for us. And we ought to lay down our lives for our brothers and sisters" (1 John 3:16). When I'm volunteering I get so busy I don't have time to focus on my problems. I am happy when I can make a difference in someone's life. I prefer to serve, rather than to be in their shoes. I count my blessings when I see so many needs and so much pain in others. God puts us in places to help others, and to tell our story.

God is there when you go through tough situations. Jesus is listening to what we have to say. He answers us in our pain. He weeps with those who are weeping. We are sometimes unemotional toward other people because of our own emotional pain. Sometimes I feel that because of our busy lives, we are dehumanized in our care for others. Jesus wept for Lazarus, and for his family's pain. He wept for the entire city of Jerusalem, and for all the generations on earth until His coming again. What God put in us we must share with others.

As a Primary Care Provider, I realized that I could help people who had fallen into the cracks (lost their jobs and/or their health insurance), and people who could not afford to buy insurance or could not qualify for social programs. Those people were desperate, suffering from many acute and chronic conditions, and without access to the health care system. I always wanted to be a missionary—to help people in need and to tell them about the love of Jesus. It never crossed my mind that I would come to the United States to serve needy minorities—immigrants from around the world have no possible way to pay for their health services. Besides my business (providing care to elderly and frail people with multiple chronic conditions and neurocognitive disorders since 1990) I have accumulated over 3,000 hours volunteering as a general practitioner (Primary Care Provider), taking care of patients in a free health clinic. In my own private practice I serve the most vulnerable population: minorities who have no place to go for care. I choose to, because I was taught at church (Romanian Church, and New Beginnings Christian Center in the Portland area, which we attended since we arrived in the US) that if God blesses us, He does so with a purpose, so we can bless others.

> The King will say to those on His right, "Come, you who are blessed by my Father; take your inheritance, the kingdom prepared for you since the creation of the world. For I was hungry and you gave me something to eat, I was thirsty and you gave me something to drink, I was a stranger and you invited me in, I needed clothes and you clothed me, I was sick and you looked after me, I was in prison and you came to visit me." (Matt. 25:34–36)

Time Well Spent

"Give, and it will be given to you. A good measure, pressed down, shaken together and running over, will be poured into your lap. For with the measure you use, it will be measured to you." (Luke 6:38)

Time well spent is a huge factor in reducing stress. Have you spent time telling others about your hope in Christ? Those who are wise shall shine like the brightness of the firmament, and those who turn many to righteousness will be like the stars forever and ever (Dan. 12:3). That promise from God will bring you much peace and dissipate your frustration from the world's stressors. I heard the other day that the average American spends a total of 15 years, 24/7, watching television during his or her lifetime. Can you imagine 15 years of sitting in front of that box, clicking away their time day and night, seven days a week for 15 years? What a wasted life.

The Bible speaks of many rewards in Heaven, even crowns, for those who have faithfully served the Lord. In fact, I think we will be shocked when the awards are presented in Heaven. Each one of us will be judged based on our deeds on Earth. When you get to Heaven, what will you have to show for your life on this earth? All of your accomplishments will be evaluated when you stand before Christ.

It is not so much a judgment for sin, because all sins if confessed are forgiven by Jesus, but a judgment of how we spent our time. Did you have more passion or excitement for your career, or for a sport, or your possessions, than you had for the things of God? Did you spend your time carelessly, doing nothing for the Kingdom of God? It will all come to nothing: wasted hours, wasted days, wasted years (Matt. 25:31). Do not let anybody distract you or move you from your faithful walk with God. Be faithful in everything you do and your reward will be great. Your crown is waiting for you.

God wants to capture our attention and make a change in our schedule. He wants our heart to break for what breaks His. In Romania, when I was about 17, I traveled 600 km north from Bucharest to see my parents. I had very little money at that time—just enough for food and the trip. I heard about a family with many children (one of them was mentally ill) that lived 6 km from my parents. I walked about six kilometers to their house. Cars in Romanian villages at that time were very rare. I went to give them the little money I had saved from my tiny income. When I arrived at their house the little girl, about six or seven years old, was naked in the middle of the backyard, and her little body was so covered with dirt and mud that it was hard to distinguish even her beautiful, innocent eyes. The mother invited me into their poor house with a dirt floor, and we knelt and prayed with many tears. I left some money for clothes for her little girl. I felt so blessed, and on the way back home I was "flying" those six kilometers, praising God and leaping for joy because I had brought a ray of hope to that mother and her little daughter.

I felt God's hand on me all the way home. Blessings started flowing in my life then, and have continued until today. It was because my heart was broken for that little girl. "Give, and it will be given to you. A good measure, pressed down, shaken together and running over, will be poured into your lap. For with the measure you use, it will be measured to you" (Luke 6:38).

That verse in Luke literally came true in my life. I see now that obeying the Word of God has become my biography. It is not about the "prosperity" mentality. It is God's economy, because God loves a cheerful giver. It is not only about money. If your heart is broken for the needy and suffering, God's heart is broken for you. God's Word doesn't fail. We still continue to give generously to those with a broken heart, or living in poverty, to honor God.

John Bevere stated in His book *Honor's Rewards: How to Attract God's Favor and Blessings*:

> We are to value, esteem, respect and reverence Him above anyone or anything. We dishonor Him if we value anyone or anything above Him. He is the Great King; He is worthy to receive all our respect, not just a portion. To God alone does our honor transcend to worship. Remember the ultimate goal is to honor God.[6]

He Rejoices Over You

"He will take great delight in you; in His love He will no longer rebuke you, but will rejoice over you with singing." (Zeph. 3:17)

To manage stress more effectively, sing and rejoice, because nothing can stop you when you have a happy attitude. Happiness and joy are contagious. People like being around joyful people who smile and laugh, and God instructs us to "...shout and be glad" (Zech. 2:10). Sing and make a melody in your heart to the Lord, "...and walk in the way of love, just as Christ loved us and gave himself up for us as a fragrant offering and sacrifice to God" (Eph. 5:2). Make a decision to glorify God. "May God who gives endurance and encouragement give you the same attitude of mind toward each other that Jesus Christ had" (Rom. 15:5). He is singing and rejoicing over you! "He will take great delight in you; in His love He will no longer rebuke you, but will rejoice over you with singing" (Zeph. 3:17). He is looking for us to rejoice in Him as we follow His supernatural prescriptions.

God has encoded the ability to be joyful and to sing for joy into our DNA. We need revelation to stir the passion of Christ and the joy of the Lord. Everything we do with passion will be remembered in generations to come. Sometimes other people misunderstand our passion. Remember the story in the Bible of the woman who broke the alabaster jar to anoint Jesus' feet with oil? She sacrificed a year's wages because of her passion for the Lord. When you sacrifice, your passion flows freely. We should live out our Christian life with joy—not out of obligation. During the communist era people would ask me why I didn't serve the Lord secretly, so I could still get promotions in the company. I had the degree needed for a managerial position, but I couldn't be promoted because I believed in God. That was against the communist doctrine: "There is no God." But I had so much joy I wasn't able to hide it from people, and for me, God was first, promotion second.

In my heart I always desired to please God, even though I realized that the communists around me despised my Christian beliefs. At the same time, I observed that they liked the fruits of the spirit in my life from the biblical standards I lived by. I was fascinated by that contradictory attitude of the communists toward me. I couldn't have had a Christian's walk without faith in the Lord Jesus Christ. God's Word changed my walk with God, through the power of the Holy Spirit. Since the age of 13, I've had that burning desire to tell others about Jesus and how His powerful Word changes people's lives.

During high school I had communist teenage friends living immoral, adulterous, miserable lifestyles, with no hope for the future. I remember one time during a break I was looking through an open window, feeling the breeze from outside on the 3rd floor, when a fragile young girl who had watched me for a few years approached slowly and asked me with tearful eyes if she could be like me. In her brokenness, she started to pour out her heart. In her desperation, she wanted to find peace for her troubled heart and hope for her future in Bucharest.

The joy of salvation that Jesus has poured into us, we must pour into others' hearts. God loved us so we can love others; He forgave us so we can forgive others; had mercy on us so we can have mercy for others. When you receive Jesus Christ in your heart "He will rejoice over you with singing." There is a supernatural activation of your spiritual DNA. You receive a more tender heart, are able to forgive others, and you become a new creation with a new personality, a new character, a new joy.

Gain by Giving

...the King will say to those on His right, "Come, you who are blessed by my Father; take your inheritance, the kingdom prepared for you since the creation of the world. For I was hungry and you gave me something to eat, I was thirsty and you gave me something to drink, I was a stranger and you invited me in, I needed clothes and you clothed me, I was sick and you looked after me, I was in prison and you came to visit me." (Matt. 25:34–36)

I want to be transparent about our walk with God, and how we dealt with high levels of stress in our own life, by giving. Since arriving in the US, we have always given to ministries, to the poor orphans and widows, and to churches and other charitable organizations. I have worked as a doctor and a nurse practitioner, volunteering as a primary care provider for about 14 years, organizing annual health fairs for those with great needs, and providing free consultations. We help people who cannot afford health insurance and have no financial or material resources to pay for health care. We also have provided treatment to many needy people in the US and abroad. We sent clothes and medications to Romania several times and conducted free consultations there when on mission trips. We have not stopped giving and serving since 1990. That was "bread cast on water," and now that bread is coming back to us in a rich harvest through so many blessings and unmerited favors from God, as His Word promises.

Joel Osteen, pastor of Lakewood Church, many times refers to his mother Dodie Osteen's story. Diagnosed with cancer in 1981, she had just weeks to live. Naturally she should have been on comfort measures and end of life care for her terminal condition, but she chose at that time to declare healing scriptures. She enveloped herself in God's promises for healing. She also started to focus on other people's needs and prayed for their healing. She was healed by God's supernatural power and is alive and well today, many years later. When you serve others your faith will increase. Your love will be contagious, loving unconditionally and serving those around you to become radically generous. You will generously care for others, have more influence in people's lives, and the world will see that you have a different spirit. You gain by giving.

Compassion Changes the Atmosphere

"...and walk in the way of love, just as Christ loved us and gave himself up for us as a fragrant offering and sacrifice to God." (Eph. 5:2)

Caring for lost people is compassion in action. Jesus was moved with compassion each time He met people suffering from physical and spiritual diseases. Emotions are universal; in every culture people are crying and laughing. Everywhere in the world people need food, water, clothes and shelter. Just as physical needs are universal, spiritual needs are universal too. We must share what we have with other people. People need Christ, wherever they live on the planet. We must speak life and words of encouragement to everyone, to change the atmosphere.

Be the voice for the most vulnerable and afflicted people, with compassionate love. The anterior cingulate is stimulated by compassion for others, keeping your brain healthy and active. The parietal lobe keeps you separated from the world and helps you forget your problems when you are in fellowship with God the Father.[7] Prayer puts our focus on others rather than on our self and our own problems, thus reducing our stress.

Compassion changes the atmosphere in the brain—and in real life. Love requires compassion and we can love lost people by praying and fasting for them. Seek the lost and watch for opportunities to help others. Your faith and your prayers will activate the compassion neurons (spindle neurons in the anterior cingulate) used for social skills, to help use your emotions in a positive way.[8]

Jesus came into our world to teach us how to live. When Jesus arrived in a place, the atmosphere there changed. In Nain, He encountered a widow at a funeral service. Moved with compassion by her pain, He raised her son from the dead (Luke 7:11). When Jesus enters your heart, soul and mind, the spiritual atmosphere will change, and healthy amounts of neurotransmitters will be released in your brain. You will demonstrate more fruits of the spirit and respond with more compassion. You will be different. Your thinking and the atmosphere in your brain will change in Jesus' presence. Compassion changes you, and your compassion changes the people in your sphere of influence. All we need is love. Because God is love, we need God. Never confuse love with the lusts of the world.

When you truly love, you are moved into action. When God pours love deep in your soul, it creates a new atmosphere in your brain and changes your heart toward each person you encounter. We know that sexual love is based on surging dopamine levels (the pleasure neurochemical) for a short moment in your brain, and later in your marriage as oxytocin (the love neurotransmitter). That is from God, and it is useful to sustain your marriage. Spiritual love is superior to fleshly love. A spiritually loving person says "No" to worldly things and temporary lusts and has a blessed life with a tender, caring, generous heart. Invest time in spiritual love that creates a place of recovery. Never lose hope (Gal. 6:9).

Start to care authentically for those in need. We are responsible on earth to help somebody in need (Phil. 2:19–21), because it matters to God. God cared for us. He came to earth and walked on the *Via Dolorosa* for all human beings. He shed His blood and gave His life for you and me. Where would all of us be, if Jesus had not died on the cross for us? You know there is chaos in many parts of the world. Those are the regions where we must bring Jesus. Where Jesus is, the atmosphere is changed. Jesus was moved with compassion when He walked on this planet. We need to move into action. Compassion moves us to do something, even if it costs us in comfort, health, and resources.

When my doctor friend was on her deathbed, so much compassion was stirred up in my heart that I gave up my free time and embraced the inconveniences of helping her. I was available to her during the worst time of her life, when she was so vulnerable in her last days, dying of cancer. Compassion will move your heart. Driving home late at night, after long hours of work caring for sick people, then spending time at her house, rivers of tears would flow because of the compassion activated in me by Christ. I did not feel exhausted from those long hours of giving, I was just overwhelmed by emotions from seeing her suffering. The spindle neurons in my anterior cingulate were stretched to the maximum then, and the emotions in my amygdala were used in a positive way.

Value People

"But when you give a banquet, invite the poor, the crippled,
the lame, the blind." (Luke 14:13 NIV)

Value everyone, even those who hurt you. People have values, even if they are different from yours. As a young girl in Bucharest, when everything was under the tight control of the communists, we were not allowed to communicate with people from other nations who came to study there. I remember the first time I met an African student. He visited our church and we became good friends. We visited each other, prayed together, and visited my parents in the northern part of the country where people had never seen a black African person. They were in awe and embraced her fellowship, giving her gifts. It was very risky, but it was amazing because we shared the same Jesus.

Here in the US, I have had close friends from Japan, the Philippines, Ethiopia, Vietnam, Russia, Ukraine and Africa. Three years after I got to the US, I met an international student from Japan named Hiro. She was completely different from me, but when we started to talk we found common things. We spoke different languages and only a little English. We had little money, but loved the same Savior. We were created by the same Father and both followed His culture. That brought us very close. She spent three months in our house for free to save some money for a mission trip that she desired to take. My spindle neurons were activated to develop social relationships and to have compassion for someone in immediate need. The Bible instructs us to love the "strangers" beyond our own personal world. We have the potential, through the spindle neurons in our anterior cingulate, to "take" His prescription, develop social relationships, show compassion, and value people beyond science.

Look at life from Jesus' perspective and your attitude will change. Be open-minded. Open your heart for others of a different color, a different culture, a different nation, or a different profession. That's why we have those spindle neurons in the anterior cingulate of our brain. I worked with minorities, because they are the most vulnerable population. But we all are so much alike in our feelings. We all laugh, we all cry, we all have joy and we all feel pain. We are created by the same Creator and have the same Father and same Savior. We all have feelings. He invites all of us to be like Jesus. Invite the crippled, the lame, the poor, and bless them (Luke 14:12–14). When I started volunteering as a primary care provider I did not know what kind of people I was going to serve. I just wanted to use my knowledge and my profession in the community, and I ended up serving the neediest from around the world. People have left me notes, thanking me for saving their life when they had no access to medical care for their acute or chronic conditions. Reach out, be friendly, and God will honor your sincere efforts.

No Competition

Competition increases our stress. Without Jesus, we were enemies of God, but He showered us with His mercy and grace. Putting on the mind of Christ will reduce your stress level, and you can stop comparing yourself with others. The stress of competition dissolves when your mirror neurons (for compassion) are activated. Instead of struggling to please everyone, simply humble yourself, desire to please God, and have the attitude which was in Christ Jesus. Humble yourself and he will exalt you. Knowing Jesus and being more like Him will free you from desiring competition and all its stress. He is pleased when you say, "I want to be like Jesus." He likes that attitude. God is transforming people's lives and changing destinies. The potential is in you to change yourself, if you choose to do so.

CHAPTER TWENTY-FIVE

Prayer Reduces Stress

Meditation through prayer is the best way to cope with stress. It is well documented in scientific literature that prayer has a healthy impact on the brain. Prayer enhances your ability to perform and solve problems. It reduces stress, decreases anxiety, prevents panic attacks, depression and bad behavior, corrects unhealthy emotions, reduces pain, lowers blood pressure, promotes rapid healing, and prevents infection. Prayer promotes good behavior and wise choices. Prayer promotes a healthier lifestyle, triggering a positive attitude that leads to physical and emotional health.

Meditation through prayer will calm an overactive brain and positively stimulates its structure. Neuroscientists have discovered that the frontal lobe can shrink with aging, causing Alzheimer's disease, but prayer stimulates the frontal lobe and prevents shrinking![1] Prayer is an anti-aging exercise that causes new neurons to develop when you meditate in prayer. Through prayer you activate the mirror neurons and develop compassion for others, which positively affects the anterior singulate, the brain area responsible for compassion and empathy.

Prayer reduces activity in the parietal lobe, causing you to forget about your own problems and focus on other people's needs. The parietal lobe helps you separate from worldly things and forget your problems. Prayer activates the compassion center in your anterior cingulate area, suppressing worry about your own emotional and physical pain.

Scientific Benefits of Prayer and Meditation

Prayer significantly increased pain tolerance in 202 patients with chronic pain. Scientists have proven that prayer and meditation help patients cope better with pain and stressful situations, and they can be included in pain management as coping mechanisms to manage stress from chronic diseases.[2] Scientists have proven that God's instructions and promises work in people's life. Prayer and meditation will create an atmosphere in your brain to create new neurons through neurogenesis, improve your cognition, positively affect your decision-making ability, slow the aging process and increase your quality of life.

Frequent Prayer and Your Health

"Pray without ceasing" is what God tells us. Another study demonstrated that patients who prayed more often, forgave more, and those who attended church services handled stress better by excreting less cortisol and lowering blood pressure.[3] Low cortisol also will preserve the function of the immune system, prevent diabetes, and prevent certain infections and cancer.

Prayer is important for children, too. Children and teenagers need prayer to cope with stress and their struggles with peer pressure. One study found that prayer influenced children positively in their health and social connections.[4] Children's behavior is affected by all the abnormal neurotransmitters and hormones released in the body during adolescence, causing more emotional and physical pain and more behavior problems. Prayer will calm the overactive brain, reduce anxiety, lower the cortisol level and promote healthy growth in children.

Prayer and Chronic Illness

Prayer works even for people who are dying from incurable diseases. "Long survival was also significantly related to both frequency of prayer (positively) and judgmental attitude (negatively)," and patients with AIDS who prayed experienced "less distress, more hope, social support, healthier behaviors, helping others, and lower cortisol levels.[5] It has been demonstrated through recent studies that people have better physical and psychological health when their mindfulness is at a higher level. These people experience fewer episodes of mood disorder and cope better with stress. But many people become vulnerable and experience the consequences of stress when their mindfulness decreases. A high level of mindfulness is obtained through constantly studying the Word of God. Doing what it tells us to do promotes psychological and physical health.[6] In addition, meditation has neurological benefits like a medical treatment and affects the cingulate cortex that regulates mood.[7]

Scientists agree that meditation is powerful in regulating the release of neurotransmitters and their receptors in the body. Beyond science, the Book of Joshua admonishes: "…keep this Book of the Law always on your lips; meditate on it day and night, so that you may be careful to do everything written in it. Then you will be prosperous and successful" (Josh. 1:8). Illness and disease cannot make you prosperous and successful. Physical and spiritual health will give satisfaction to your body and soul and they are necessary for a prosperous and successful life.

The Bible says, "...the tree is planted by streams of water, which yields its fruits in season and whose leaf does not wither—whatever they do prospers" (Ps. 1:3). Meditate on the Word of God. When the Word is stored in your brain it "waters" your thoughts in the neurons, yielding the "fruit" of healthy actions. Healthy thinking will become a normal part of your being (your "spiritual" DNA), producing good fruit and helping you prosper in your body, mind and spirit. Your dendrites in your neurons, the nerve cells you use for thinking and cognition, have the configuration of a tree where thoughts flow. If those neurons have the "living water" of the Word of God, your soul, body and mind will prosper in health, your body will be healthy, your emotions and relationship with family, friends, and society will be healthy, and you will prosper. Our Lord delights when His servants prosper in health, family relationships, and friendships in the church and community. "May those who delight in My vindication shout for joy and gladness; may they always say, 'The LORD be exalted, who delights in the well-being of His servant.'" (Ps. 35:27).

The Atmosphere for Neurogenesis

It is well demonstrated in scientific literature that meditation creates an atmosphere for neurogenesis in the brain, the new neurons improve memory and diminish the chances for neurocognitive disorder and Alzheimer's diseases. It also slows down the aging process. Meditation is a strong part of your lifelong anti-aging formula. With such great benefits from meditation, people would be wise to follow God's prescriptions.

Thinking beyond your circumstances requires creativity and meditation that creates new neurons. The great Psalmist David never knew about neurogenesis, but he was inspired by the Holy Spirit of God to write about a renewal of our mind when we hunger for the Word of God and meditate on His precepts.

All God's prescriptions have positive outcomes, according to the promises written in the Word of God. All instructions found in God's Rx lead to positive results: "Whatever is true, whatever is noble, whatever is right, whatever is pure, whatever is lovely whatever is admirable—if anything is excellent or praiseworthy" (Phil. 4:8). God put purpose in everything for your good, even though sometimes you may see only the opposite.

When memorized Scriptures pop into your conscious mind your life will be changed. There is a still, small voice—the Holy Spirit—Who speaks to our conscience and transforms our life if we obey. The Word of God is God's breath. He breathes life into every cell of your body, reprogramming your "spiritual" DNA. You receive Christ's "spiritual DNA" when you invite Him to come into your heart through His Holy Spirit. You need to "feed" your mind with the Bible. Read the Bible to nourish your spiritual soul, and as you eat spiritual food you nourish your spiritual DNA. Your spiritual DNA makes the person you are, spiritually, with the personality needed to fulfill your destiny.

Let the Word of God occupy your mind and heart and take control over your feelings, thoughts and emotions. Life is in the Word of God. God wants the Word to live in us, so we can live in truth, love and peace and have a healthy body, soul and mind.

Prayer…Beyond Science

"The LORD is my portion; therefore I will wait for Him.
The LORD is good to those whose hope is in Him,
to the one who seeks Him." (Lam. 3:23–25)

Dr. Helming explains, "Prayer serves as a connection to God but secondly, prayer bonds human beings to human beings. Surely a sense of oneness with humanity and oneness with the Divine were essential aspects of the lived experience of healing through prayer."[8] Medical and health care providers also recognize that there is good evidence supporting the physical and spiritual benefits from prayer.

Dr. David Levy, MD, an Award-Winning Neurosurgeon, in his book *Gray Matter: A Neurosurgeon Discovers the Power of Prayer…One Patient at a Time* stated:

> As I have addressed patients' spirituality and made prayer a regular part of my patient interactions, the response has been impressive. I have seen lives brought to a level of spiritual, emotional, and physical health that my patients had never enjoyed before. In the process, I have learned two important thing; that there is a limit to what I can do as highly trained and experienced surgeon and that there is no limit to what God can do to touch a person emotionally and spiritually, not just physically.[9]

When we pray without ceasing we can expect supernatural results. Praying in the Holy Spirit brings supernatural results. The Holy Spirit intercedes for our needs and knows the answers to our prayers.

A new chapter in your life starts with prayer. Jesus prayed with a loud voice—crying out. He prayed earnestly. Jesus wrestled with God for His future, especially in the Garden of Gethsemane before giving His life for the sin of the world. Prayer becomes powerful when we wrestle with God, and then say, "Thy will be done." Many Bible characters wrestled with God, saying, "…until You bless me." They knew God's will was to bless them. God had something good for them, and He has something good for you. In fact, everything you have comes from God. Through prayer you can rekindle your passion for His presence and for His blessings.

When you are passionate for God, all things become new (2 Cor. 5:17). To follow God's will and stay on the right path to your goal, you must have a vision. A new passion will bring a new destiny and a life transformed. Transformation, new vision, and revelation for new things come through fervent prayer. When you pray, hearts are transformed, lives change, cities are blessed, and nations are revived. Do not give up in prayer (2 Cor. 4).

Since arriving in the US in 1990, I focused on the possibilities of open doors, yet knowing that nothing happens without prayer. I faced all the challenges of a different culture, but because of Jesus I found out that in Christ there is the same culture—Heaven's culture—and it is global. Having passion, praying and standing in the gap for the needs of others, and seeing opportunities to serve will transform you and those around you. For all your generous prayer, passion, love, caring, emotional support, experience, training, and devotion, the reward will be in Heaven. The three Wise Men sacrificed their time, energy, and material possessions, to come worship the King of kings and the Lord of lords when Jesus was born on earth. They came to worship. Worship is the most important part of your prayers.

I cannot wait to see what God will do in my future. For the past two years I have been prompted by the Holy Spirit to pray for about an hour almost every morning. I know from my past that perseverance brings victory, and I am forceful in my prayers through the power of Holy Spirit. The assertive woman who had the issue of bleeding for twelve years reached out boldly, touched Jesus' garment as He walked by, and laid hands on her destiny. (Read Luke 8:43–48.) Step into the future forcefully and boldly with a brand new perspective for a safe and healthy future. God can do anything. Ask Him to do something supernatural, something beyond your own power.

To enter into the spiritual realm where the supernatural is normal, you need forceful prayer to break through the enemy's strongholds. Charles Stanley is a Bible teacher and the senior pastor of a 12,000 member church in Atlanta. In his book *Handle with Prayer: Unwrap the Source Of God's Strength for Living* he stated, "Our responsibility as Christians is to tear down these strongholds through Spirit-filled prayers. How? There is only one weapon—the sword of the Spirit. We must fight these lies with God's Word. We must fight specific lies with specific truths."[10]

You need God's power to know that God is with you when you pray. God gives you power to do things that you cannot do by yourself. He gives you everything you need when you access Him through the power of prayer. God will accomplish in us what He called us to do, more than you can ask or imagine. So everything you have, your talents, your profession, your expertise, your wisdom, your power to invent, to create, to innovate, your network, and your relationships are gifts from God. Step into His presence and access God's power for a new mind and a new thinking process. It is God's idea to bless you through prayer.

How was I able to overcome so many things in my life without compromising my faith? It was only through prayer. God has promises for you and your life. Finding God's way for your life takes discipline in prayer. It is like when a physician prescribes exercises for his patients that fit his or her condition. You start exercising to promote your health and prevent diseases in your body, including your mind. He gives you directions about what kinds of food to eat, with the right nutrients for health. But the benefits from following the Great Physician's prescriptions to pray without ceasing and walking in God's way are eternal.

God wants to restore your physical and spiritual health through a life of prayer. His mercy is new every morning, restoring your future. "Because of the LORD's great love we are not consumed, for his compassions never fail. They are new every morning; great is your faithfulness. I say to myself, "The LORD is my portion; therefore I will wait for Him. The LORD is good to those whose hope is in Him, to the one who seeks Him" (Lam. 3:23–25). He wants to bless you when you hope in Him and wait for Him. Waiting for Him is an active process; do not let anything disrupt your connection with God. I have received showers of blessings through fasting and prayer. Try a new experience. Fasting and praying makes us strong spiritually. Faith and confidence in God's promises will bring joy and peace, and the love inside you will increase when you believe, trust and continue to pray.

Prayer for His Glory

*"Not to us, LORD, not to us, but to your name be the glory,
because of your love and faithfulness." (Ps. 115:1 NIV)*

David's fame spread far and wide when God used him to destroy the enemy, because he did everything for the glory of the LORD. (Read the book of Psalms.) David was constantly connected with Jehovah *Elohim* the King of the Universe, giving Him glory in his prayers. Nothing just happens or is an accident or a coincidence. We should never take the glory for what we have received from God. The glory belongs to God. The highest calling in this world is to be like Jesus Christ, who prayed without ceasing and served others tirelessly. The Holy Spirit will give you the power to accomplish what you cannot do in your own abilities. To build and to heal your house, you must care for others, spend your life for your family, and pour out your life for others. Then it will be well with you for God's glory.

CHAPTER TWENTY-SIX

Giving Thanks

"Rejoice always; pray without ceasing; in everything give thanks; for this is God's will for you in Christ Jesus." (Thess. 5:16–18)

Manage Stress by Giving Thanks

"Enter His gates with thanksgiving, and His courts with praise." (Ps. 100:4)

Trusting God and His promises will create in us an attitude of thanksgiving. God promised, "You have all sufficiency of all things" (2 Cor. 9:7). God will supply all your needs (Phil. 4:19) through prayer, if you believe (Mark 11:24). When discouraging thoughts flood your mind, claim the verse, "I can do all things through Him who gives me strength" (Phil. 4:13). In 2010 I was invited to speak at the Women's Conference for mothers of children with disabilities in Iasi, Romania. I was asked to encourage them and teach them ways to manage stress in their life. You might have stress, but imagine having three disabled children who will never be able to walk, speak or function normally in society for the rest of their lives. Those parents are devastated. They feel like they are always carrying a dying person on their shoulder. The motto of the conference was, "I can do all things through Christ who gives me strength" (Phil. 4:13).

So many tears were flowing at that conference. I had to stay strong, even though inside I felt like crying the whole time. I had nothing to offer them but an abundance of tears of compassion, flowing down my face, and they were crying more, mirroring my compassion for them! I felt like the least qualified person to speak at that conference, because I could give them nothing. But the Word of God and His promises were sufficient. They were encouraged because the Word of God has the power to comfort anyone through the power of the Holy Spirit. As it is written, "No Word that comes from the mouth of God is missing the power," and, "There is glory in infirmities" (2 Cor. 12:9). Out of your painful situations and brokenness a great destiny is possible.

Like these children's parents you may be asking why God allowed these children to be born with disabilities. I asked the same question myself. The answer was that God wants to get our attention to remind us that life is short. We are not our own, and He wants to shine through our disabilities and brokenness. We need to stop, reflect, be thankful, and show love to those around us so God can receive the glory. All life is in God's hands. These children have their destiny too—to awaken the rest of us to live with eternity in mind and to be thankful for our life. We are more than conquerors in Jesus (Rom. 8:37).

God answers your prayers so the Father will be glorified in the Son (John 14:13). He is ready to give us all things when we ask according to His will (Rom. 8:32). Your iniquities are forgiven and all your diseases are healed (Ps. 103:2–4). So nothing is held against you to hinder your prayer when you live in obedience. He who redeemed your life from destruction offers mercy and lovingkindness. A thankful heart will calm an overreacting mind.

Gratitude

"He who offers a sacrifice of thanksgiving honors Me; and to him who orders his way aright I shall show the salvation of God." (Ps. 50:23)

Giving thanks to God with a grateful heart brings you peace, but many things can block our gratitude. The greatest quality of the human soul is thankfulness. This should be our basic Christian attitude. On one of my visits to Romania, the small voice inside me started insisting, "Bring thanksgiving as a sacrifice, because everything you asked God has done for you, and He will continue to give to you more than you ask. I did not need to hear that inner voice twice. Right away I began a 21-day Daniel Fast. (The "Daniel Fast" is a 21-day partial fast, eating fruits and vegetables only, to give the Lord thanks for everything He has done in our lives.) By offering praise and giving thanks in everything, we glorify God. This is the will of God (1 Thess. 5:18).

All our prayers should incorporate thanksgiving. Priscilla Shirer, in her book The Armor of God, stated that "gratitude to God for Who He is and what He's already done should thread throughout every prayer, because ultimately His Name and His fame are the only reasons any of this matters."[1] Give thanks and praise to the Lord at all times. Shall we not accept adversity as we accept blessings? You must praise God no matter what you are going through, to release the blessings of God in your life.

What about when everything goes wrong? God ultimately programs everything in our life, according to his will. Paul's "thorn in the flesh" strengthened his character. Jesus' crucifixion brought the joy of salvation and an eternal inheritance to the entire world. God develops endurance in us for the long run. He develops and strengthens our character. God plans events behind the scene to strengthen us. We put our hope in Him, not only here on earth but for eternity.

Keep looking ahead to what God has for you. Paul learned to be content with every circumstance in life. The key to a peaceful life without stress is thankfulness in every situation. This will keep all your brain neurochemicals in balance, as we know from Philippians. "Be anxious for nothing, but in everything by prayer and supplication with thanksgiving let your requests be made known to God. And the peace of God, which surpasses all comprehension, shall guard your hearts and your minds in Christ Jesus" (Phil. 4:6–7).

When you start to feel anxious, recognize the anxiety as a call to prayer to calm your overreacting brain. Beginning your prayer with thanksgiving will link your spirit to the peace of God, guarding and keeping you in Christ. Prayer is likened to incense in scripture, and thanksgiving is the ingredient that makes your prayer a "sweet savor" to the Lord. You have so much to thank the Lord for that you could keep on thanking Him forever, and it wouldn't be long enough. The Bible's strongest prescription to prevent anxiety is "Rejoice always; pray without ceasing; in everything give thanks; for this is God's will for you in Christ Jesus" (Thess. 5:16–18). Giving thanks reminds us of good things and brings joy to our heart and soul. Neuroscientists have found that rejoicing causes the right atmosphere in the brain to release a healthy amount of natural anti-anxiety and antidepressant neurotransmitters (endorphins, serotonin, oxytocin and dopamine,) which will heal the cells damaged by stress.

Give Thanks

"He who offers a sacrifice of thanksgiving honors Me; and to him who orders his way aright I shall show the salvation of God." (Ps. 50:23)

The Word of God says, "In everything give thanks." You must believe that "God causes all things to work together for good for those who love God, to those who are called according to His purpose" (Rom. 8:28). It's not easy to give thanks for all things, but if you do, you benefit from walking in faith, pleasing God, and showing Him that you trust Him.

Be thankful every day. Sing and rejoice! Nothing can stop you when you have a happy attitude. Happiness and joy are contagious. People enjoy being around joyful people who smile and laugh. The book of Zechariah says,

"Shout and be glad" (Zach. 2:10). Sing and make melody in your heart to the Lord "… and walk in the way of love, just as Christ loved us and gave himself up for us as a fragrant offering and sacrifice to God" (Eph. 5:2).

Glorify God with your mind and your voice. "May God who gives endurance and encouragement give you the same attitude of mind toward each other that Jesus Christ had" (Rom. 15:5). Our joy encourages people around us. "He who offers a sacrifice of thanksgiving honors Me; and to him who orders his way aright I shall show the salvation of God" (Ps. 50:23).

Joyful thanksgiving can also save you from panic attacks, which come from our spiritual enemy. The first generation of Israel that left Egypt died in the wilderness without attaining their Promised Land. Their "grumbling and complaining" brought diseases among them. Grumblers and complainers will spend their lives in unhappiness and die anxious and depressed, because complaining brings bitterness, not joy. God wants us to walk in all the promises in His Word, but it takes faith, a contented spirit, and patience to inherit the promises (Heb. 6:12). So let us turn our complaining into thankfulness. It improves our physical and emotional health, and the people around us benefit from our gratitude through mirror neurons, mirroring our attitude.

One blind resident in our memory care often said, "I had such a good life and the Lord has been so good to me." He died peacefully at 92 years old, never being bed bound or suffering, not even one single day. His grateful heart ushered him into the presence of the Lord.

God's Presence in Thanksgiving

"Let us come before His presence with thanksgiving…" (Ps. 95:2)

Thanksgiving brings us into the presence of the Lord. "Let us come before His presence with thanksgiving" (Ps. 95:2). "Enter His gates with thanksgiving and His courts with praise" (Ps. 100:4). In these verses, we see that to enter His presence we must come with thanksgiving. Start your day by telling the Lord how thankful you are, and you can enter into His presence first thing in the morning. By keeping a thankful heart all day, you can abide in His presence. This is the happiest and most successful way to live. Neuroscientists talk about the importance of counting our blessings to maintain a peaceful mind, normal blood pressure, and normal blood sugar. It even improves the immune system, helping to prevent infections, even from the common cold.

You have God's favor when you live in an atmosphere of thanksgiving. This is God's will for you. Thanksgiving has the power to transform your thinking and your mind. The plans of the enemy will be stopped when you give thanks. You need insights from God. All my insights, inspiration and discernment come when I spend time in prayer with thanksgiving.

Always I start my prayers with thanksgiving, and I start to feel God's presence when I meditate on the amazing things God has done in my life. Confusion, anxiety, and worry disappear in His presence. I receive clarity and discernment in making decisions. In a world of uncertainty, insecurity, and confusion, we need clarity to hear from God. We need His presence in this postmodern era more than ever. He gives us wisdom, revelation, inspiration and guidance through the power of the Holy Spirit when we spend time to give Him thanks.

Thanksgiving has the power to cast out fear, worry, anxiety, and depression and to calm the brain. Thankfulness can change any situation. Your feelings, signs and symptoms will change too. Your mind's eyes will open and start to understand the purpose of your life. You will become eternity oriented and live with eternity in mind. Everything changes around you when you decide to have a life full of thanksgiving.

Sacrifice of Praise

"Through Jesus, therefore, let us continually offer to God a sacrifice of praise—the fruit of lips that openly profess his name." (Heb. 13:15 NIV)

Have an attitude of gratitude, and offer the sacrifice of praise with your lips. The Lord's prayer starts by praising the Father for who He is. We magnify His Name because His is the kingdom, the power, and the glory forever and ever (Matt. 6:9). Praise Him for everything He has done for you, even when things do not go your way; it is a sacrifice of praise. I often like to fast, just to bring Him a sacrifice of praise and thanksgiving. God inhales our praises and then breathes His Holy Spirit over us in our worship time with His healing power. Extend your hands in thanksgiving. Raise up your hands with excitement, praise Him confidently with songs, and bless His Mighty Name, declaring the wonders of God. Sing in the spirit spontaneously. The Holy Spirit is prompting us to praise our Father in our Heavenly language.

God gives us wisdom to discern His voice from the voice of the enemy. When you shout praises to God, the enemy gets confused. The walls of Jericho fell down when Israel's army shouted, as the Lord commanded (Josh. 6:20). The enemy got confused. Praise brings us victory in our life at a specific time. When you praise Him continually and bring a sacrifice of praise, you build confidence in the power of the Lord. Then your fear will be gone and faith will increase, creating an optimistic atmosphere in the brain for a healthy amount of neurochemicals. The stress level will go down and healing and restoration will come. Cortisol levels decrease and serotonin levels increase to a healthy amount when you are joyful, and your depression and anxiety will be healed. Praising God occupies your mind with positive thoughts and connects your mind and spirit with Heaven's power.

Follow God's prescription, giving thanks in all things, through all things. You are in control of your feelings. Be determined to have faith in the Word of God and you will be successful. Sing praises and give thanks to the Lord, for His love endures forever. Just a few months ago I took care of a dying resident who was blind her entire life, but she was a strong believer. I spent time at her bedside during the dying process, and I whispered many times into her ear, "His love endures forever, His love endures forever." She knew exactly what I was talking about and what that meant. Her smiling face glowed, looking up toward Heaven. Her spiritual battles were won through praising and singing worship songs throughout the day in her room, until her soul left her body, escorted by angels into the arms of Jesus.

In times of stress and worry, praise the Lord and affirm deep in your heart that "He is your hiding place" (Ps. 32:7). God wants people to praise Him all the time. He gave instructions throughout His Word not to forget the Lord's kindness and benefits. Everything you have is from Him, the Creator of the Universe. Do not forget, He is the One who gives you breath in your lungs as well as everlasting life. We were created for His glory.

Praise Through the Trials

"But I will sing of your strength, in the morning; I will sing of your love;
for you are my fortress, my refuge in times of trouble." (Ps. 59:16 NIV)

Paul and Silas praised the King of the Universe when they were chained in a prison. They were praising in the midnight hour, and God listened from Heaven. Then the earth shook and the chains fell from Paul and Silas' feet. (Acts 16: 16-40). God is shaking things on earth on your behalf when you praise His mighty name. In the book of Jonah we read that Jonah was in the fish's belly for three days. When he started to praise the Lord, there in the deep sea, in the belly of that big fish, God heard him and delivered him. (Read Jonah 2) Praise Him through your trials. You cannot wait until the battle is over. God likes your new song, a new hymn of praise in trials (Psalm 40). I have done this often when I am going through trials. I have praised God in my loneliness, even though many times my heart was filled with emotional pain and my soul was crying. I read all the Psalms in the Bible, and I praised Him, and He gave me victory so many times. With praises in our mouth, we overcome our struggles and spiritual battles victoriously. The "real estate" in our brain is filled with contentment, bringing peace, joy and happiness, because God's glory changes our thinking forever. Jesus praised God with His life on earth and in His humility received glory from the Father.

Through praise and thanksgiving God will open closed doors for you, because He holds the keys. It is reassuring to know that God opens doors for you that nobody can close. Likewise, it is He who closes doors. God has opened many giant doors for me and my family since I was a little girl in a poor village. I could write another book about that. Gloria Copeland, in her book *Blessed Beyond Measure: Experience the Extraordinary Goodness of God*, emphasized the importance of thanksgiving during prayer. She stated,

> Fill your mouth with thanksgiving. Jesus said in Mark 11:24 "to believe that you received it when you pray." What do you do when you receive something? You say "Thank you!" The appropriate and powerful thing you do after you pray is to be thankful. Maintain a thankful attitude all the time, and it will go a long way in undergirding faith and patience.[2]

CHAPTER TWENTY-SEVEN

Lifestyle Change

"This day I call the Heavens and earth as witnesses against you that I have set before you life and death, blessings and curses. Now choose life, so that you and your children may live." (Deut. 30:19)

Manage Stress through Lifestyle

Whether or not we follow God's high potency prescriptions really becomes a "life or death" situation. To obey God—or not— becomes a critical lifestyle choice with eternal consequences. "This day I call the Heavens and earth as witnesses against you that I have set before you life and death, blessings and curses. Now choose life, so that you and your children may live" (Deut 30:19). A.V. Rzheshevsky asserted:

Negative factors, such as the "magnificent" five that include alcoholism, smoking, unhealthy food, lack of movement, and negative emotions, accompany a person almost from birth and trigger powerful internal biochemical reactions leading to disastrous consequences. Those new deleterious reactions force the organism to mobilize all of its internal reserves to neutralize, at least temporarily, the destructive effects of these negative factors. As a result of this continuous struggle for survival, body parts degenerate, starting from connective tissue protein molecules to entire newly formed organs (such as adipose tissue). Today we can state with certainty that the reason for the majority of widespread pathologies causing premature aging and death, such as atherosclerosis and arterial hypertension, is exactly those external negative factors that a person voluntary introduces into their life. However, the margin of safety that Nature enclosed in the human body is really amazing, allowing light-minded and self-destructive people to live up to 60 years and longer. It is quite possible that the lifespan will increase up to 100 years and more if a person stops destroying himself/herself with negative emotions and bad habits, including unhealthy food and overeating. This article examines the possible interconnection between unhealthy overeating and the theory of programmed aging and phenoptosis."[1]

God will enable us to live a longer, better quality life with our family and children under His blessings—if we follow His prescriptions that reach far beyond science.

People dislike change, because they are comfortable with their old ways. They do not want to get out of their comfort zone or alter their lifestyle. Perhaps for many years your lifestyle has led you into a rut, and you cannot seem to make changes. The failures in your life have given you an identity that threatens your future, and you are losing control of your life and feeling hopeless. Hopelessness keeps you from reaching your maximum potential and fulfilling your purpose and destiny.

By understanding the disease process in the human body, you know you can reverse many diseases with lifestyle changes. Most diseases are due to bad habits and an unhealthy lifestyle. For example, atherosclerosis (coronary artery disease), myocardial infarction, cerebrovascular accidents, congestive heart failure, diabetes, cancer, obesity, and high cholesterol—all are caused by high levels of stress. Thus, complications of stress are responsible for all physical and spiritual pain and premature deaths in the world.

While studying for my doctorate at Oregon Health & Science University, I found that "The most widely recognized of the metabolic risk factors are atherogenic dyslipidemia, elevated blood pressure, and elevated plasma glucose.[2] In addition:

> The metabolic syndrome (MSDR) also is recognized as the major risk factor for cerebrovascular (CVA), chronic kidney disease, and the complications from those chronic conditions. Patients with MSDR also are susceptible to other conditions as polycystic ovary syndrome, fatty liver, cholesterol gallstones, asthma, sleep disturbances, and some forms of cancer. The atherogenic dyslipidemia consists of elevations of serum total apolipoprotein B (apoB), triglycerides, small particles in low density lipoprotein (LDL) and low levels of high density lipoproteins (HDL). An elevated glucose can be in the range of impaired fasting glucose (IFG), which is called pre-diabetes, or at the level of diabetes. Other risk factors are advancing age, physical inactivity, hormonal imbalance, endocrine dysfunction, smoking, high levels of stress, alcohol intake, and genetic or ethnic predisposition. Operationally, the risk factors that exacerbate the MSDR are elevated blood pressure > 130/80, elevated glucose > 110 mg/dl, increased serum triglyceride > 150 mg/dl, reduced HDL cholesterol (HDL-C < 40 mg/dl), elevations of plasminogen activator inhibitor-1 and fibrinogen, and a pro-inflammatory state.[3]

Patients with MSDR need treatments to control blood sugar, blood pressure, and cholesterol. They also need coaching in lifestyle changes to stop smoking, follow a healthy diet, get regular exercise, and anti-platelet therapy.

They need an eye exam, dental care, foot care, and stress management. Patients with MSDR need regular follow-up visits for their conditions: regular physical exams, counseling on medication use, educational classes, and referrals to a nutritionist, ophthalmologist, podiatrist, and dentist.

Identification and modification of lifestyle risk factors associated with the syndrome is important for its effective prevention and for reducing the risks of CVD in this population. The beneficial effect of lifestyle intervention on the metabolic syndrome components provides important evidence of the value of this approach to those with blood pressure, weight, and lipid disturbances in general.[4] Although most lifestyle change interventions were found effective in achieving short-term adherence, the evidence is limited regarding specific strategies that are most helpful for the long-term maintenance of lifestyle changes.[5] The evidence, however, is limited and it lacks the respective attention to specific behavioral or motivational factors in helping patients to adhere to the multifaceted lifestyle changes.[6]

Motivation to change one's lifestyle is the key to improving physical and spiritual health. Take to heart God's divine prescription, given to motivate us to choose life and blessings, in Deut. 30:19: "This day I call the Heavens and earth as witnesses against you that I have set before you life and death, blessings and curses. Now choose life, so that you and your children may live."

Bad behavior, stress from fear and worries, and unhealthy diet negatively alter the gene expression through epigenetic mechanism. All these increase the risk for physical diseases such as heart disease, diabetes, obesity and stroke, and emotional diseases including anxiety, depression, and dementia later in life. Science has discovered that second and third generations can be affected by those diseases. The Bible calls them generational curses that can be broken through new good habits. Our DNA contains the genetic code, the blueprint in our cells for protein synthesis necessary for life, which is influenced by our lifestyle. For example, healthy foods—fish, whole grains, green vegetables and citrus fruits—are rich in methyl and will suppress (through methylation) those bad genes that are pre-programmed to trigger chronic diseases. Hydration is extremely important for mood regulation and cognition. It is recommended to drink 1,500–2,000 mls during the day. (Avoid drinking after 5:00 PM so you do not need to wake up at night to void, and interrupt your sleep).

Sleep with the Lord at Your Side

"When you lie down, you will not be afraid; when you lie down, your sleep will be sweet. Have no fear of sudden disaster or of the ruin that overtakes the wicked, for the LORD will be at your side and will keep your foot from being snared." (Prov. 3:25–26)

"In peace I will lie down and sleep, for you alone, Lord, make me dwell in safety." (Ps. 4:8 NIV)

Sleep is the most important factor for healthy brain regulation. Excessive amounts of adrenalin, norepinephrine, and anxiety keep the brain very busy and awake, causing sleep disturbances and leading to insomnia. The deep sleep phase is affected by excess cortisol due to high level of stress, making people very tired. Their energy is low, they cannot concentrate, and their emotions are fragile, leading to depression. Major depression and extremely severe and prolonged stress will further increase cortisol. Excess cortisol is toxic for the brain and further impairs emotional regulation, damaging the brain and shrinking the hippocampus area.

To sleep well you must avoid caffeine (drink < 500 gm in the morning), alcohol, tranquilizers, narcotics and even prescription drugs for sleep. Even over the counter Melatonin can cause depression if taken in excess of 0.5 mg at bedtime. Exercise regularly (at least two hours before bedtime) and keep calm, with no TV or computer use before bedtime (follow instructions for sleep hygiene).

To sleep in peace is a divine order. Do not go to bed angry. Anger causes stress, disrupting the neurotransmitter balance in the brain. This will create sleep disturbances. Thomas Unbehaun's group, using an electroencephalogram in their study, concluded:

> Specific sleep stages are defined which occur in a distinctive order during the night. Sleep regulation means mechanisms to induce wakefulness and sleep as well as the alternative occurrence of REM and non-REM sleep. In this regulation a specialized neuronal brain network is involved, including the ascending reticular activating system (ARAS), the Raphe nuclei, Locus coeruleus, ventrolateral praeoptic nucleus, tuberomammilare nucleus, the laterodorsal and pedunculopontine tegmental nuclei. Several neurotransmitters like acetylcholine, norepinephrine, serotonine, dopamine, GABA. histamine, orexine and adenosine are mediating the interaction between these brain centers. Reciprocal inhibition and circadian rhythms are two regulating principles within this network. Conclusion: Any external influence upon this interaction of neurotransmitters could induce sleep changes and may be the mechanism by which several substances induce or disturb sleep.[7]

God's prescription—beyond science—is "...in your anger, do not sin. Do not let the sun go down while you are still angry, do not give the devil a foothold" (Eph. 4:26). We are programmed to sleep 7–9 hours a night. We read in Isaiah, "He wakes me morning by morning" (Isa. 50:4). The neurotransmitter adenosine builds up daily to just the right level to allow us to fall asleep after a day of work or a day of rest, then we can sleep through the night, be rested, and wake up in the morning. Adenosine is a neuromodulator with an inhibitory mechanism in the central nervous system that suppresses arousal, promoting sleeping at night. When the adenosine level is raised, dopamine is low and blood pressure is naturally lowered. People who sleep less, or more, can develop depression due to the unhealthy amounts of several neurotransmitters, including serotonin, acetylcholine, norepinephrine, dopamine, orexine histamine, GABA and adenosine. We can correct or prevent insomnia through good sleep hygiene, including physical activity during the day, limiting liquids before bedtime, avoiding naps, and meditation and prayer to reduce fear and anxiety, thus calming the overactive brain.

The Word of God tells us we must sleep in peace, because He promised to watch over us. Worry, anxiety and stress will keep us awake and activate genes that lead to depression. Sleep is an amazing phenomenon. The cells enter into a sleeping phase, and the whole body is refreshed and restored upon waking up. The brain performs right where it left off just before falling asleep. The brain at night regulates our sleep time through different phases, including (as I call it) a "natural anesthesia" phase that reduces blood pressure, constricts our bronchioles, and then wakes us up without a post anesthesia rehabilitation phase, and without side effects. Then the brain commands the liver to produce new glucose, increasing the blood sugar level automatically through glycogenesis for the right amount of energy to get out of bed in the morning.

We wake up refreshed and renewed with energy, ready to start the tasks where we left them. Everything is programmed to accomplish our normal daily routine of rest at night and work during the day. At the unconscious level, through apoptosis during the night, our body is cleansed from damaged cells and eliminates the cells that are programmed to die, not causing inflammation or cell proliferation, and keeping our body in homeostasis. The brain is sculpted by this process of neural apoptosis during embryonic development. This astonishing process renews our strength every morning.

Renewing Our Spirit and Body

*"Because of the LORD's great love we are not consumed, for His
compassions never fail. They are new every morning;
great is your faithfulness." (Lam. 3:22–23)*

The process of apoptosis as a built-in feature programmed in our DNA is
an astonishing example of how God cares for us and what our body does at
the unconscious level to keep us alive, even after all our destructive behaviors
and bad choices. God renews our strength every single day by His Spirit, and
through apoptosis. Apoptosis is

> …a genetically determined process of cell self-destruction that is marked
> by the fragmentation of nuclear DNA, is activated either by the presence
> of a stimulus or by the removal of a stimulus or suppressing agent, is a
> normal physiological process eliminating DNA-damaged, superfluous,
> or unwanted cells (as immune cells targeted against the self in the
> development of self-tolerance or larval cells in amphibians undergoing
> metamorphosis), and when halted (as by genetic mutation) may result in
> uncontrolled cell growth and tumor formation—called also *programmed
> cell death.*"[8]

Defeating the Disuse Syndrome

*"The Lord God took the man and put him in the garden of Eden to
work it and keep it." (Gen. 2:15)*

*"All hard work brings profit, but mere talk leads
only to poverty." (Prov. 14:23)*

Advanced technology opened the door for the "disuse syndrome". This
inactive, sedentary lifestyle kills millions. Advanced technology in developed
countries has displaced much of the traditional workforce, yet physical labor
is a healthy activity that we need. "The Lord God took the man and put
him in the Garden of Eden to work it and keep it" (Gen. 2:15). Scientists
continue to discover physiological benefits of an active lifestyle, proving the
benefits of following God's plan. There are many physiological rewards for
our obedience to the Word of God, even for the active lifestyle. I tell all my
patients that it is extremely important to be active, even if they live in luxury
and do not need to work.

For example, during physical activity the chemical neurotrophin is
released, helping to repair the brain. Physical activity increases blood and
lymph flow to all organs, including the lungs and heart, to clean them from
the buildup of toxins. Benefits from physical activity are multi-faceted and

are mentioned in the Word of God. God tells us to be active always. "All hard work brings profit, but mere talk leads only to poverty" (Prov. 14:23). He also says, "The one who is unwilling to work, shall not eat" (2 Thess. 3:10–12). It is ethical to work to obtain our food and not be a burden on others or on the government. In the health field, scientists have found that a lack of physical activity results in calories deposited as fats. Moreover, toxins from inside the body and from the environment will be deposited in the fatty tissue.

I started to work at about six years old, helping my parents with farming. I would wake up early and do whatever needed to be done: take care of the animals, work in the garden or the field, or inside the house cooking, cleaning inside and outside, and even painting the walls of the house. I knitted my own clothes and did many other things. At the same time I attended school fulltime through the 8th grade in my home village, then moved to Bucharest 600 kilometers away to attend a vocational school and high school, to be able to support myself. After two years of school, before I was even 17, I got a full-time job and continued school as a fulltime student to finish high school. Then I attended the Academy of Economic Sciences in Bucharest. I have never stopped working.

When I arrived in the US, even though I was a professional Economist, I began by cleaning toilets and making beds in a nursing home because I did not speak English. I washed and painted the walls of my friends' houses, and helped the elderly as a nursing aid. How many healthy young people, full of energy, are now on welfare, without work! This is so detrimental for their health and for society as a whole. We must take on responsibilities in life to live more abundantly. Jesus died on the cross to give us life more abundantly. He did everything for us. We must just enter in to fulfill what was done for us at Calvary. You can rise up from your situation, pray, and change your thoughts, attitudes and habits. God can bless you with many blessings you never dreamed of, if you change your attitude and follow God's Word.

One Bible story tells about a weak, disabled man lying on a mat. Jesus told that person to take up his mat and walk. And the sick person obeyed, and got up and was healed. (Read Matthew 9.) God is asking us to take action, move, get up and have an active life that will benefit our health, as well as others in our community and society as a whole. Jesus will help us but we need to obey, change our attitude, and keep moving.

One day my daughter heard me praying on my knees, asking God to protect me from the spirit of laziness. She started to laugh, asking me, "Protect you from what?" Then I explained to her that many people struggle all their life with the spirit of laziness. She then understood and followed my example, studying hard at school, working hard at home, and volunteering at a very young age. She still continues to work hard for her family and at her job, where she has huge responsibilities as a Doctor of Pharmacy and clinic manager at The Anticoagulation Clinic—and volunteering at church.

Elizabeth George, in *A Woman After God's Own Heart*, advises the reader:

> Keep moving—Remember the principle of momentum: A body at rest (human or otherwise) tends to remain at rest, and a body in motion tends to remain in motion. Use this law of physics to your advantage. Tell yourself, "Just one more thing …just five more minutes." Keep moving and you can cross one more thing off your to do list![9]

Taking Action

Many people, by their own choices, fall prey to diseases that will kill them, either suddenly or slowly. The way you choose to live, what you eat, how much you exercise, how you manage your level of stress, and other habits such as drinking, sleeping, using drugs, having pre-marriage sex, adultery, smoking, and your choice of friends will determine who you become in the future. Take responsibility for your health to prevent disability and premature disease, suffering, physical and emotional pain, stress and premature death of the body, soul and spirit. For example, it is a fact that by lowering your low density lipoprotein (LDL) bad cholesterol to less than 100 mg/dl, and your blood pressure to less the 120/80 mg/dl, and quitting smoking, you will reduce your risk of heart attack before age 65 by more than 80 percent. You must take action today to reduce the risk for heart attack or stroke. You can see the difference even after 4–8 weeks of dietary changes.

The "Daniel Fast" works extremely well, since you eat only fresh fruits, vegetables and legumes. In one year I was able to follow the Daniel Fast six times, which helped me and my husband to lower our total cholesterol, low density Lipoprotein (bad cholesterol), and triglycerides by half, and also to raise the high density Lipoprotein (good cholesterol). We lost about 8–12 pounds each time we fasted. Besides lowering all the numbers, we also received answers to our prayers, reduced our worry and stress, and improved our immune system. We were able to exercise more and became more efficient in our jobs, providing care for the elderly and others, became more relaxed and calm, and our quality of life increased.

In the clinic I see many patients suffering from metabolic syndrome, and I teach them (besides the medication as needed) to also try the "Daniel Fast" for better results. Those who follow my instructions usually see benefits.

After adjusting their lifestyle, many of my patients using several medications for their medical conditions were able to decrease their number of meds.

Diabetes, hypertension and hypercholesterolemia and their complications can be prevented with lifestyle changes as discussed earlier. Statistics shows that four out of ten Americans are dying from heart attacks, due to an unhealthy lifestyle. About 90 million are pre-diabetic, and if not addressed, they will become diabetics, with all the complications. Studies show that coronary artery diseases result from a diet high in sugar, fat and cholesterol, high levels of stress, and lack of exercise.[10]

These diseases are on our plates every single day when we eat sugary, fatty foods, high in cholesterol, with extra calories. Studies show that patients on a very strict vegetarian diet actually widened their arteries, and the heart muscle received increased oxygenation. Heart disease even reversed itself with a healthy diet and lifestyle changes. We must go beyond the American Heart Association's recommended diet.[11] A healthy diet rich in fibers (fresh fruits and vegetables, legumes, and whole grains) prevents many diseases and their complications. Beyond science, the Bible has been teaching that for thousands of years. For example, Daniel's fast (Dan. 1:8–14) was written in the Bible thousands of years ago—a diet low in cholesterol, and high in fiber and antioxidants needed to detoxify the cells to prevent cancer.

To reverse heart disease, it is recommended to reduce the LDL-bad cholesterol levels in your blood to 100mg/dl, lose weight, drop your blood pressure to 120/80 mmHg, stop smoking, reduce stress, stop drinking alcohol and other destructive habits. You can achieve that goal by reducing fats in your diet, reducing simple carbohydrates, substituting with healthy foods (fresh vegetables, legumes, fresh fruits, whole grains as complex carbohydrates, etc.), and exercising regularly. Even walking 60 minutes a day has great benefit. Eliminate sweets, reduce salt, resist temptations, and cook at home. Your food can be your medicine. How much extra it costs us to buy unhealthy food from the store, and then go see the doctor and buy the prescribed treatment for the diseases caused by our unhealthy food choices!

Check your blood pressure. Hypertension is the silent killer, because the body compensates slowly and you don't experience symptoms until a stroke or sudden heart attack. One in three Americans has hypertension, but does not know it. The body compensates until the heart becomes very weak, developing congestive heart failure and cardiac insufficiency. The higher the blood pressure the greater the risk for heart disease. Salty food consumed daily is the number one cause of high blood pressure. When we eat too much salt, our electrolyte balance is affected, also leading to heart disease.

Excess weight causes the heart to work harder to administer nutrients to the body, and blood pressure goes up. It's like attaching a big truck to a small engine, expecting it to work normally. Too much fat and cholesterol in our diet causes stenosis in the arteries, blocking them and causing a heart attack or stroke. Lack of exercise, high stress, smoking, alcohol and estrogen affects your heart condition. Obesity will impair blood circulation, affecting your thinking process and leading to dementia.

Drugs will not cure hypertension; they can only control it. They cannot prevent arteriosclerosis or heart attack. Only lifestyle changes can quickly reverse hypertension without drugs. When you reduce salt in your diet and lose weight, your blood pressure will drop without medication. Reducing weight sometimes is the only needed treatment. If you take medication and make a major change in your lifestyle, your blood pressure will improve. But *do not stop* taking medication or heart pills without consulting your doctor, even if your blood pressure is lowered by changes you made. The damage to your heart was done a long time ago. You may need both medication and lifestyle change, but remember that medication alone will not cure your diseases. Talk to your doctor about any changes.

You must read the labels of the food you buy to avoid diseases. Cerebral vascular accidents (strokes) occur due to atherosclerosis. Plaques in the blood vessels cause the occlusions or thrombosis. During the occlusion process the plaque that is formed can be dislodged, or a clot can form, blocking the small arteries that supply blood to the brain. Then the artery can break and cause a hemorrhage in the brain—a stroke. High blood pressure will cause the arteries to break when forcing blood through the small, stiffened arteries, causing them to rupture. Hemorrhage cuts off oxygen to that portion of the brain, and it dies, causing paralysis. Stroke can be severe, or fatal. High blood pressure, high cholesterol, high triglycerides, elevated sugar, uncontrolled diabetes, sedentary lifestyle, obesity, high level of stress and smoking are all serious risk factors for cerebrovascular accidents or stroke.

Stroke, like heart attacks, can be prevented through lifestyle changes to decrease blood pressure and promote healthy arteries. Check your blood pressure regularly, do not smoke, lose weight, reduce your salt intake, exercise regularly, eat a very low fat diet, increase fruits and vegetables to 4 or 5 servings a day, increase fiber, and manage stress; then you will enjoy a good, healthy life. It is God's will for you to have a healthy body, soul, and spirit. Read your Bible every day to find God's prescriptions for a healthy spiritual heart that will support your emotional and physical health.

Americans consume tons of aspirin. Aspirin will help with atrial fibrillation, *but ask your primary care provider if aspirin is OK for you.* I recommend aspirin (81 mg) for patients with a history of diabetes, or myocardial infarction or stroke for secondary prevention. Thickened arteries can open again when you start a diet very low in fat and higher in fiber. You also can develop collateral circulation when you exercise regularly. Even walking for 30–60 minutes a day will make a huge difference in the circulation of blood to your heart, and your whole body will improve.

A Mediterranean diet contains anti-inflammatory nutrients because of its emphasis on healthy foods such as fruits, vegetables, whole grains, legumes, flaxseeds, omega-3 fatty acids, and nuts, as well as spices like chili, black pepper, cumin, ginger and sage. They may reduce the risk for heart diseases, depression and dementia. Stress management will also keep your neurotransmitters at a healthy level to protect your heart. You need to be serious about a healthy lifestyle before damage is done.

During exercise, the brain produces the natural antidepressant, the "feel good" hormone endorphin, making you feel well and think clearly. Work on reaching a healthy body weight. Monitor your risks for diabetes, check your blood sugar regularly if you suffer from diabetes already, and consume less than 200 mg/dl cholesterol per day. Eating more fruits and vegetables and food rich in Omega-3 (salmon, nuts, mackerel) increases circulation of blood in the brain and prevents not only heart disease but Alzheimer's. If you change the conditions of your blood vessels you can prevent dementia. Avoid fatty meats, butter and creams, high synthetic sugar or simple carbohydrate products such as starches. All of them are artery-clogging foods. Keep your blood pressure under control, as it is the number one risk factor for stroke.

If you experience tightness in your chest, chest pain, shortness of breath upon exertion with activities, fast heartbeat, indigestion, nausea and unusual stomach pain, drooping face, weakness in one arm or leg, or difficultly in speaking, call 911 and go to the emergency room immediately.

Change your bad habits today. Throw away saltshakers, salty snacks, and fast foods. You need to do a U-Turn in your life to prevent disaster. No matter how old you are, or your health history, you can add quality years to your life by starting today to make changes in your lifestyle. You will be healthier, have more energy, and be more efficient in everything you do. Your thinking process will improve with all the healthy neurotransmitters in your body, making you look younger. Lifestyle change is the least expensive anti-aging treatment.

You are in control of your life through the power of your thinking process. You can make changes using your will power and your gift of free choice. If you have a chronic disease such as diabetes, high blood pressure, asthma, arthritis, depression, bladder incontinence, immunodeficiency disease or other conditions, keep your follow-up visits with your provider and act upon your lifestyle changes (even losing two pounds can make a difference in improving your health condition) as described above. You can improve your health and decrease the stress level in your life. Attend a nutrition class and talk to your health care provider about all the changes you need to make in your lifestyle, and adjust your treatment accordingly.

Many cancers develop as a consequence of unhealthy habits and the environment. Approximately 80 percent of cancers can be prevented though improved lifestyle.[12] For example, cancer of the lungs, lips, mouth, tongue, throat, esophagus and bladder can be prevented. Colon cancer in men and women, prostate cancer in men, and breast cancer in women are related to overeating, overweight, too many fats, and a low level of melatonin causing lack of sleep. The following are risks factors for cancer; tobacco, red meat, junk food, inactivity, overeating, alcohol, and high levels of stress. Changing those risk factors and not smoking, not drinking alcohol, and following a Mediterranean diet very low in fats and high in fibers can reduce your cancer risk. A diet low in fat and cholesterol reduces the risk of heart disease, stroke, diabetes, and cancer. Fasting was prescribed by God in ancient times, and it is still His prescription for us today—beyond science—to maintain our well-being, stay in balance, and get closer to God for better physical and spiritual health.

CHAPTER TWENTY-EIGHT

Prayer and Fasting

Prayer Changes the Atmosphere

Prayer transitions your spirit, passing beyond the threshold of the natural world into God's supernatural sphere. Bondages can be broken and attitudes can be changed through prayer when you surrender and let Christ live in you. Prayer changes the atmosphere, even when you are tempted to have a bad attitude, and keeps you away from temptation. When you pray you turn 180 degrees from your filthy thoughts and destructive habits. You cannot pray sincerely and then resume a bad habit.

I remember my first prayer in public. I was in 5th grade and my uncle asked me to pray aloud at the prayer meeting. That launched me into a life of prayer. I also remember that as a child I longed to get closer to God, to know Jesus more and to receive the power of the Holy Spirit. I sought out prayer meetings and spent time in prayer, but I knew I needed to do something more. Then I heard teaching about fasting, and I knew in my heart that I needed to fast in order to get closer to God. I began a life of prayer and fasting very early on, and God honored that. I have seen His protection and His favors on my life.

I could have been arrested many times in communist Romania for speaking publically about my faith in God. The police threatened and investigated me a few times, making me give an account for my Christian walk and my values and beliefs. I was scared because the communist police in Romania at that time were very mean, rude and rough. One time as a teenager, when I went to a prayer meeting at my grandmother's house with some relatives and friends, a policeman took us from my grandmother's house and forced us to walk 5 kilometers through the snow to the police station for a day-long investigation. It was winter, and very cold, and we had nothing to eat or drink that day. They threatened us, then let us go back home—under police supervision. Through all of those trials God's eyes were upon me, and I felt His divine protection everywhere I went. Prayer and fasting brings spiritual breakthrough and divine intervention.

Prayer—the Anti-Aging Exercise

Exercise prayer and faith for a victorious life, for "without faith it is impossible to please God" (Heb. 11:6). If you do not have faith, Jesus says He cannot hear your voice. Faith in the body of Christ is a spiritual gift. You can know God more through prayer. On Mount Sinai Moses asked God, "Who are You?" and JEHOVAH showed a glimpse of His glory to Moses. He will do just the same for you when you ask with a sincere heart and are desperate for His presence. He is the Great I AM, today and forever, as He was for Moses more than 3,500 years ago.

You must be willing to know Him to receive a greater revelation, because whoever has more knowledge will be given more knowledge about Him (Matt.13:12). We are blessed to have eyes to see and ears to hear. In our facility many of our residents are blind or hard of hearing, and it is heartbreaking to see them live with such devastating disabilities. We must accommodate the surroundings for them to meet their needs. In order to rearrange our vision, Christ is willing to rearrange our surroundings. He took Peter, John and James to the mountain to see the glorious transfiguration of Christ. Ask God to let you see who He truly is, and to recognize Christ.

We know very little about prayer. When I was a teenager in Bucharest, a Christian woman whom I considered as a mentor in prayer would pray one hour every day. She prayed for many people by name, then for churches, for communities, for cities, for nations, for presidents, leaders in government, senators, politicians, judges, teachers, doctors, nurses, lawyers, business people, and more. She had a notebook, just like a student, listing all the countries around the world, and she interceded for each one of them by name every morning. I am sure that her prayers, and those of many others, contributed to the entire communist system collapsing in the surrounding countries only a few years after her prolonged times of intercession.

The disciples asked Jesus, "Lord teach us how to pray" (Matt. 6:9). Prayer will change your relationship with God. God never will change, but we will. God's ways are still higher (Isa. 55:8–9). God wants to train us to pray, even though we do not see results. We must practice prayer.

When I examined my very first patient I was a bit unsure how to start the exam. Even though I felt confidence in my knowledge (after more than 10 years of medical education), I was trembling at first, because any beginning is stressful. But after a while I became an expert. With prayer it is similar.

You become more confident spiritually by spending more time with God in prayer. You will know Him better, and you will learn to discern His distinct voice. I wanted to hear God, to know Him and learn how to hear Him speaking to me. I needed to know Jesus. Dr. Heidi Baker, PhD, stated in her book *Birthing the Miraculous: The Power of Personal Encounters with God to Change Your Life and the World*, "Without Him our efforts produce nothing spectacular, no matter how much we strive. The one thing we can do is respond to the Father's Words over our lives. We can position our hearts in humility and hunger. Hunger always delights the heart of God."[1]

Spend time with Him to know Him. Engage in a personal relationship with your Heavenly Father. Choose to meet with God in prayer (Ps 51:1). Expect God to meet you in that place of humility, dedication and surrender. Our Father God is a consuming fire. He is holy. Establish a priority in your prayers that His will should be done on Earth, as it is in Heaven. When you delight in the Lord, He will give you your heart's desire (Ps. 37). If you abide in Jesus, you may ask whatever you wish and He will give it to you. It is for God's glory that your prayers will be fruitful (John 15:7–8). Surrender to *His agenda* and pray for His will to be done in your life, and develop a day-by-day mentality in prayer. Prayer calms your brain, reduces worry and fear, increases peace, and keeps you healthy on a daily basis.

On the other hand, fear causes death. Your fearful thoughts, worries and anxieties actually damage your body. Dr. David Stoop, PhD, in his book *You Are What You Think*, says, "The key to breaking the paralyzing cycle of worry and anxiety is to find something solid in which we trust. For me, the only thing worth trusting for the future is God Himself. Jesus points out the obvious choice we have to make when it comes to solving the patterns of worry and anxiety."[2] When you trust God and pray, your faith will increase and your fear, anxiety, and depression will resolve. Jesus prayed in the Garden of Gethsemane one night before His death on the cross, and the fear of death was gone. Death was defeated forever, bringing eternal life for all those who believe in Him. When fear is defeated, anxiety and depression will have no place.

It is well documented in scientific literature that depression or feelings of depression, *once resolved*, will lead to lower blood pressure, decreased pain, and a more positive outlook on life. Lack of fear, anxiety, and depression will give us a longer, healthier, and happier life. Prayer impacts your brain, enhances your ability to solve problems, and prevents mental decline or Alzheimer's. Neuroscientists have proven that prayer also decreases stress and negative emotions, stroke risk, heart attack events, neurocognitive disorders and panic attacks. It enhances your ability to think clearly and function well, increases lifespan, and increases physical and emotional health over all.

The promises of God are positive affirmations that lead us to a positive attitude. Strengthen your brain through the power of prayer and claim God's promises. What is going on in your brain affects your physical body. Thoughts of faith affect your mental and physical being in a positive way. When you do not pray, fear settles in and degrades your mental condition. The frontal lobe can shrink with aging, causing mental decline and Alzheimer's disease, but prayer stimulates the frontal lobe, preventing shrinking. Prayer is an anti-aging exercise.

Pray without Ceasing

"Rejoice always; pray without ceasing; in everything give thanks; for this is God's will for you in Christ Jesus." (1 Thess. 5:16–18)

Prayer connects us with God at a deeper level, and fasting requires even more self-discipline. We need to disconnect from the world in order to get closer to God. Jesus prayed often, and He asked the disciples to pray. God created in us the ability to pray continually, and He is asking us for unceasing prayer. So how is that possible? Dr. Larry Dossey, MD, in his book *Healing Words: The Power of Prayer and the Practice of Medicine*, remarked, "A state of prayerfulness has infiltrated not just the conscious mind but the unconscious as well, including sleep and dream."[3] We learned the activities in the unconscious mind are taking place 24/7, without ceasing. If you have a prayer life and meditate day and night on the Word of God, your unconscious mind is in the mode to pray without ceasing. The disciples, who traveled and lived alongside Jesus, who prayed throughout the night, tasted the power of prayer. They gave us instructions through the power of the Holy Spirit to pray without ceasing.

When the Holy Spirit is in us we cannot stop praying, because He is praying in us without ceasing when we are awake or asleep. The devil will try to interrupt your prayers, because he knows the power of prayer. The devil wants to steal your peace, bringing unexpected disturbances. Everything around you becomes dark when you lose your peace. You see things from the world's perspective and negative thoughts flood your mind. Anger can build up and sour your spirit, releasing unhealthy amounts of neurochemicals, with unpleasant symptoms, killing neurons and modifying the brain's structure.

How much better it is for us to seek God's face and His presence. When you pray and enter into the presence of God, great joy will flood your soul.

You have had an audience with the CEO of the Universe! When you pray, the Presence of God brings you peace, even in the middle of a "storm". God uses storms to wake us up, to seek His presence. No one can sleep through a disastrous storm, and serious action is immediately required. Prayer is hard work. Sometimes you must pray for the strength to pray. When you go through difficult times, whether in physical or emotional pain, or discouragement, you can receive peace deep in your heart when you pray. God's ways are beyond our understanding, but if you pray and choose not to worry, you will receive the peace that only God can give through Jesus Christ, the peace that passes all understanding.

When I was in 7th and 8th grade, if I did not like a person's character, my mind would be full of anxiety, anger, selfishness, and unhappiness. Even though I lived in a Christian family I still struggled with wrong thoughts. I kept trying to get closer to God, memorizing His Word and meditating day and night. Then, when I had my amazing encounter with God, my thought life was transformed.

Our insight is changed only through the power of the Holy Spirit, by the washing of the Word of God and unceasing prayer. Invite the presence of God into your life and pray for God's mercy and power. Believe that He hears your prayer for your specific needs. Change and shape the world around you through the power of prayer and fasting. We can overcome all circumstances through prayer, the power that changes things. Through prayer and fasting we can expect something out of the ordinary. God will give you power; but you need to know what to do with that power from Heaven (Acts 1:8). God instructs us in the Bible how to receive the Holy Spirit through prayer and fasting. Step out in faith, and God can do miracles.

The Lord Fights for You

"The LORD shall fight for you, and ye shall hold your peace." (Ex. 14:14)

As a young child I believed that God could do anything, so I prayed. I remember that during the communist regime a few of my friends and I frequently attended all night prayer meetings, crying out to God for a clean heart so we could fight the enemy of our souls. Now I wonder what would have happened to us if we had not prayed. Where would we be today? God listens to your prayers—just ask. He answered Joshua's prayer, when he was distressed at the enemies' attack (Josh. 10), and the sun and the moon stopped miraculously for about one day until they had won the battle.

It is easy to get discouraged during the battle, but God is fighting your battle for you when you pray. People in the Bible (Nehemiah, King Asa,

King David, Apostle Paul, and others) prayed often, even all night long, when they were surrounded by enemies. The most powerful people on earth were people who prayed. They overcame fear. Whom should we fear? Fear paralyzes us—but it is not from God. The devil wants to reduce us to silence, but the power that created the world is in us. In the beginning, the Spirit of God moved over the chaotic Universe and organized our world. He can create order in your life, too, as He has done many times in mine.

Through prayer we activate the promises of God. To illustrate, I prayed the prayer of Jabez (2 Chron. 4:10) every single day for a few months, asking God to enlarge my territories. He did, and He continues to work in our life. Heaven is open for business, and the angels are waiting to be released on your behalf—sent through by prayers—to fight the battle for you. They are waiting to receive the assignment from the Father, at your request.

Pray a Big Prayer

"If you can?" said Jesus. "Everything is possible for one who believes."
(Mark 9:23 NIV)

Pray a big, bold prayer when you are stressed. Cry out to God from the depths of your heart, and He will have compassion on you. When I arrived in the US without my daughter or husband, the only thing I knew to do in my troubles was to pray a big prayer. Leaving Romania in 1990, I woke up early in the morning to catch the train to Bucharest. My two-year-old Andreea was still sleeping in my mother-in-law's house and I knew I would not see her again soon. Needless to say, like any mother I wanted to be there for her every moment—to watch her waking up every morning, playing, learning new things, and then tucking her into bed at the end of the day. I had her sleep with me until she was one year old. I wanted to hear her breath, to feel every move she made. But that morning I left, I knew it would be a long time until we were reunited and I could once again enjoy her childhood. I did not have a clue then about God's plans for our future life. But He gave me strength that morning to kiss her goodbye, not knowing I wouldn't see her for a few years. I needed to pray a big prayer.

During those years I had so many struggles. Negative thoughts would bring me to the point of panic. My body suffered all kinds of signs and symptoms from anxiety and depression. These biological responses to my thoughts of fear and worry caused neurotransmitters to be released in unhealthy amounts. The devil whispered so many lies in my ears, bringing all kinds of accusations and threats on my life. But I kept praying the promises of God over myself and my family, every single day. I kept on believing and declaring, "If God is for us who can be against us" (Rom. 8:31). I believed His promise: "I will never leave you nor forsake you" (Heb. 13:6). I believed that the God who took care of my needs and my future during the communist era would continue caring for my family.

I remember when I left my parents' house and went to Bucharest for vocational school. I was a stranger in the city, 14 years of age, with no family around me. I felt lonely and threatened by the corrupt communist society, but I prayed, "Lord, help me have a clean heart; help me know You more." I was living in a dormitory, and we were not allowed to have any religious material. But I had the New Testament with me, hidden under some books and clothes in my closet, or sometimes under the mattress when I read late at night.

I had the Word of God in my heart, but I needed to learn more. I also found time during breaks at school to pray in the bathroom. Everywhere I went I first located the bathroom because I needed a place to hide and pray. My number one priority as a teenager was to learn the Word of God, and to pray. God helped me so much in school that I became one of the best students. The adults around me noticed that my behavior and character were different from the other boys and girls. They could trust me with anything.

The Lord answers prayers (Ps. 138). He has answered so many of my prayers and He will answer yours. Through prayer and the power of the Word of God you can push the limits of your life. Believe God for big things. I have pushed the limits in my life since I was young, through prayer and fasting. Nowadays I am still harvesting the fruits of all the fasting and praying in my early years. God has worked miracles in my life. He knows everything about your life, so do not give up in prayer. Pray until something happens. There is no expiration date on God's promises or on His prescriptions for your health and prosperity.

Glorify His Name

"Answer me, LORD, answer me, so these people will know
that you, LORD, are God, and that you are turning
their hearts back again." (1 King 18:37 NIV)

God allows things to happen in your life to get your attention. You can pray and He will answer your prayer, so you will know that He is God and He will receive the glory. The world can be changed through your prayer. Remember the prayer of Elijah: "Answer me, LORD, answer me, so these people will know that you, LORD, are God, and that you are turning their hearts back again" (1 Kings 18:37 NIV). God answered his prayer so all the

Israelites would know that He was and is God, and always will be. Prayer changes things in your life and people around you will know that God is in control of all things. Through prayer you can accomplish things of eternal significance for God's glory.

God Hears Impossible Prayers

"...so do not fear, for I am with you; do not be dismayed, for I am your God. I will strengthen you and help you; I will uphold you with my righteous right hand." (Isa. 41:10)

God will take the broken pieces of your heart and make everything new. Break up with the past because He makes all things new in your life. I have heard testimonies and seen people facing all kinds of catastrophes:

- lost jobs
- broken relationships
- business failures
- natural disasters
- health problems
- addictions
- criminal behavior, etc.

But when they started to obey the Word of God, their life began to change. Through divine restoration, things started to turn around in their favor, to a life of victory in Jesus Christ, the Savior of the world.

I was one of those people. I am a living testimony of God's work. When we see lives being transformed we do not need more scientific evidence or proofs. Just get on your knees, lift your hands and cry out to God. Repent first, and ask for forgiveness to be reconciled with God. Lee Strobel, in his book *The Case for Christ: A Journalist's Personal Investigation of the Evidence for Jesus*, explains, "Jesus has done for us on the cross what we couldn't do for ourselves: he has paid the death penalty that we deserve for our rebellion and wrong doing so we can become reconciled with God."[4] Your prayer can be, "Lord I cannot sustain myself. I need strength from You." Wicked ways only bring destruction, and people perish. Do not forsake your family or church, but serve them with a pure heart because Jesus paid the death penalty for you.

God gives us reassurance when we pray big prayers. "So do not fear, for I am with you; do not be dismayed, for I am your God. I will strengthen you and help you; I will uphold you with my righteous right hand" (Isa. 41:10).

He has continued to uphold our family with His right hand and fulfilled our dreams. Do not be afraid and do not fear, but be bold and bring your big prayers to God. He honors bold prayers. "Let us therefore come boldly to the throne of grace that we may obtain mercy and find grace to help in time of need" (Heb. 4:16 NIV). Let the word of God occupy your mind, and ask the Holy Spirit to fill you, so your impossible prayers are heard. "'If you can?'" said Jesus. "Everything is possible for one who believes" (Mark 9:23 NIV).

Do Not Give Up

Pray until something happens. There is no expiration date on God's promises, so do not listen to people who speak discouraging, negative things into your life. Keep your prayer line open at all times. If other people share their doubts, and negativity and unbelief enter your heart, your brain will perceive that as a threat, raising your stress level and producing physiological symptoms (a biological response to those stressors) and causing more distress.

Pray out loud, because life and death is in the power of your tongue. Our faith will be built on our words. Faith comes by hearing. If you hear negative words, your faith becomes negative, producing fear. When you speak positive words and pray God's promises out loud, you will build your inner faith and develop a constructive attitude. God loves people with great faith and is pleased with their faithfulness. We know that without faith it is impossible to please God.

We live in a world with so much chaos, violence, war, catastrophic weather events, earthquakes, famines, nuclear breakdown, political crises, terrorists, occupiers, and accelerating sexual perversion. Whole nations are scared and overstressed. In the middle of all these situations there is hope in Jesus Christ. He is the answer to every stress in life. Jesus, Ruler of the kings of the earth, is the King of kings, Judge, Redeemer, Savior, Healer, Intercessor, and Counselor. He is the Head of the Church. He functions as the greatest Prophet and Priest. He has power and authority over the world, dispatching angels to earth to help those who please Him. Your attitude toward God must be right at all times.

Jesus governs the affairs of the earth and is in control over the entire world. Satan has no autonomy or authority on this planet. God shakes the earth to destroy the work of the devil when you pray. Have discernment and take refuge in Him through constant prayer. He is the Ruler of the kings of the earth. "…and from Jesus Christ, who is the faithful witness, the firstborn from the dead, and the ruler of the kings of the earth" (Rev. 1:5 NIV). The earth is in His care. Worship the Lord.

Manage Stress Through Fasting

Fasting is also recommended for recovering your health and preventing diseases, physically and spiritually. Dr. Don Colbert, MD in his book *Toxic Relief, Revised and Expanded: Restore Health and Energy Through Fasting and Detoxification*, stated, "I believe that many diseases are a direct result of excessive buildup of these toxins."[5] He gives us a list of diseases that "... are often directly linked to a buildup of toxins: food and environmental allergies, asthma, headaches, fatigue, fibromyalgia,, chronic pain, eczema, chronic acne and other skin conditions, insomnia, depression, irritable bowel syndrome, decreased sex drive, menstrual period, abdominal bloating, belching, gas, memory loss, chronic diarrhea, Crohn's disease, ulcerative colitis, atherosclerosis, hypertension, obesity, constipation, angina, multiple sclerosis, coronary artery disease, cancer, mental illness, diabetes."[6]

Fasting is recommended for a healthy lifestyle. However, any time you plan to fast without food or water for more than 24 hours and you are on medications for any of those diseases, you must consult your primary care provider first. A partial fast is the most beneficial for your body, especially if you are taking medication for different conditions. But fasting should be for a spiritual benefit, even though the side effect of a partial fast will benefit your health by eating only fresh fruits, vegetables and legumes in moderation for 21 days at a time. I call it "Daniel Fasting" because it is mentioned in the Bible, in the book of Daniel chapter 10. I also recommend reading Dr. Don Colbert's book *Toxic Relief* for more details about detoxification through fasting, as well as restoring your physical and spiritual health and your energy, and preventing physical and spiritual diseases.

God, wanting us to be healthy, gave us prescriptions to stay healthy and prevent diseases (3 John 1:2). While earning my Masters and Doctoral degrees at Oregon Health & Science University I was fascinated with classes about health promotion and disease prevention. That was the catalyst to motivate me to write this book. God gave us instructions long ago on how to stay healthy and how to regain our health again if we become ill. The Bible gives directions from God about what to eat, what to wear, how to behave, how to stay calm in the storm, trust Him and obey His instructions, in order to improve our health and prevent diseases. Those instructions are in our DNA. But our disobedience will lead us to unhealthy behaviors, destroying our God-given DNA. Many times we try to do things by ourselves and fail, because we do not rely on God's instructions. Deceptions in the world blind people's eyes so they cannot see God's intentions for our health.

Your lifestyle can have a deeper meaning when you fast (Isa. 58:3). Do not focus on food but on your dependence on God. In order to get results do not do as you please (Isa. 58:8, 9). Let a new chapter in your life begin. Fasting brings deliverance from selfishness. According to the Word of God, in order to break the spirit of heaviness related to depression, oppression, condemnation, worry and fear, one must fast and pray, and help others. Jentezen Franklin, a popular conference speaker and pastor, stated in His book *Fasting: Opening the Door to a Deeper, more Intimate, more Powerful Relationship with God*, that "Americans use drinking, smoking, drugs, medications, overeating and other harmful behaviors to try to lift the spirit of heaviness."[7] He goes on to say, "Instead of looking for more stuff to put into our body to ease the pain, we should fast and seek the God who gives us a garment of praise for the spirit of heaviness that afflicts so many"[8]

According to Dr. Horne, studies showed that "...decades of routine fasting was associated with a lower risk of diabetes and coronary artery disease. This led us to think that fasting is most impactful for reducing the risk of diabetes and related metabolic problems....The fat cells themselves are a major contributor to insulin resistance, which can lead to diabetes.... Because fasting may help to eliminate and break down fat cells, insulin resistance may be frustrated by fasting."[9] Newswise reports: "Fasting reduces cholesterol levels in pre-diabetic people over an extended period of time, new research finds."[10]

The first time I fasted was for two days (48 hours) without food and water, was when I was 16 years old, before I received the power of the Holy Spirit. I did not understand much about fasting, but I felt the physical and the spiritual benefits right away, even though I was hungry and thirsty and felt discomfort during the fast from the detoxifying process. After fasting physically I felt lighter, able to run better, move faster, and think clearer. Meditation on the Word of God amplified all those benefits.

By following God's prescriptions for a healthy life I was able to concentrate more on spiritual things and focus more on my attitude and behavior. I started to have more compassion for people around me and was able to focus more on good things and to discern right from wrong. Then I realized that fasting could bring more positive results, so I read the Bible more about fasting and developed a lifestyle of prayer and fasting.

One time in Bucharest I was in a Max, a common transportation vehicle, with a group of believers from our Church. I heard some older women whispering to each other about a missionary in Africa who visited Romania and told about a revival going on there. They said people in Africa were fasting three days and nights without food or water for a spiritual breakthrough, to break the bondage and yoke of witchcraft in that region. I was stunned to hear people could fast that long. I read the book of Esther and found out that Esther, and all the Jews at that time, also fasted three days and nights with no food or water, and God took note of their sacrifices and gave them a miraculous victory over their enemy. After reading the Book of Esther many times I began to understand the power of fasting for three days and three nights.

I started to consider the possibility of fasting three days and nights to see God's hand work in my life, to obtain victory in my own spiritual battles. I thought it would be impossible for me to fast that long. I prayed and asked God to help me, and He did. After that I fasted many times like Esther, and God intervened to show Himself strong on my behalf. He opened many closed doors that needed to be opened for me, and closed many doors that the devil would open to try to deceive me and lead me into temptations and destruction.

Fasting for Spiritual Health

Fasting will help you solve problems and remove limits that hinder God's plan and blessings in your life. We have been blessed in our life because of a lifestyle of fasting and praying. We still continue to fast and pray, both in the good times, and any time we have a problem, and the burden is removed. Ezra 8:23 tells us that when the Jews wanted to rebuild the walls for their old city, the enemy of Israel opposed the progress for restoration and renewal. But when they "fasted and besought their God," He heard and gave Ezra directions and victory (Ezra 8:23). God brings revival and harvest during stressful times through fasting and prayer.

Prayer and fasting will bring us from darkness to light and restore our emotions. Following God's prescriptions develops a heart that is clean, humble, joyful, thankful, kind, trusting, open, forgiving, confident, pure, wise, sincere, sensitive, happy, undivided, tender, whole, fervent and secure. You can have that kind of heart through consistent prayer and fasting. "Above all else, guard your heart, for everything you do flows from it" (Prov. 4:23 NIV). There must be a hunger for change. During the time of the prophet Samuel people fasted one whole day (1 Sam. 7:6) and confessed their sins. They confessed to sinning against the Lord, found forgiveness, and their lives were spared.

Your fasting can also influence others positively and change their future, bringing them blessings. "Thy righteousness shall go before thee" (Isa. 58:8). As a young girl I had the opportunity to lead to Christ a few atheist girls who were able to understand my righteousness in Christ. Their lives were completely changed, and the lives of their extended families and close friends. Through fasting "the glory of the Lord will be your reward" (Isa. 58:8).

In 1992–1993, during my studies at Multnomah Bible College in Portland, I heard a radio announcement about a catastrophic earthquake that was coming to Portland. At that time my family was still in Romania. Fear overcame me, my heart started racing, and I became very anxious—almost panicking. I knew what an earthquake at such a high magnitude could do, from my experience in the 1977 Bucharest earthquake. My knees started shaking, epinephrine rushed through my body, anxiety grabbed me, and I could not eat or sleep. As my stress increased so did my depression. So I decided to fast the "Esther's Fast" as described in Esther 4:16: "Go,…and fast ye for me and neither eat nor drink three days, night or day: I also and my maidens will fast likewise; and so I will go in unto the king, which is not according to the law, and if I perish, I perish." But she obtained favor in the king's eyes and he held out to Esther the golden scepter.

It was really hard to fast at that time, because I was providing care by myself to four elderly residents with multiple chronic conditions, 24 hours a day in my house. I had to cook for them three daily meals and snacks for good nutrition; I had to give them showers and provide personal hygiene; transfer them in and out of their bed, chair, and toilet all by myself; and do all the laundry and housekeeping. I was tempted to give up fasting, but when I thought about a possible catastrophic earthquake, and that I might not see my family again, I humbled myself to seek God's face with all my heart. I cried out to God and called upon His name to intervene and prevent that catastrophic event. I re-read the book of Esther and was strengthened in my spirit, believing God for a divine intervention for our city. Who knows if those three days and nights of fasting did not prevent that catastrophic earthquake in Portland? I'm sure many other Christians also fasted and prayed about that. Another example is the Biblical city of Nineveh. When the whole city repented, fasted and prayed for three days and three nights, their city was spared by the mighty hand of God. Do not underestimate the power of fasting when everything is going well—and even more in terrible circumstances.

When Daniel fasted he did not want to defile himself with the king's meat nor with his wine (Dan. 1:8). Daniel and his friends, who ate only fruits and vegetables, appeared healthier than those who ate meat and drank wine at the king's table. Isaiah 58:8 says, "…thy health shall spring forth" when you fast.

If you have a medical or mental condition, you must consult your doctor before you fast. I guarantee you will have only benefits from a healthy fasting diet of fresh fruits, legumes and vegetables. I have always been very healthy all my life and worked very hard. I've never been to the emergency room. I am still very healthy and strong to this day. Through fasting, God has helped me make many crucial decisions in stressful times.

After Paul met the Lord on the road to Damascus, he did not eat or drink for three days and three nights. His entire life changed in a moment. He made the decision to follow Christ, even though he had been extremely zealous in persecuting Christians. The will of God had grabbed hold of his life, and he became the greatest evangelist of all the ages (Acts 9:9). If you are worried about your future and do not know which direction to go, start fasting. "…then your light shall break forth as morning" (Isa. 58:8). For me the light came when my husband won an unexpected visa lottery—a miracle from God—so we all received green cards and became American citizens. After a six-year struggle our deliverance came from above.

Through fasting you can help others who are going through stressful situations. During your fast you can put aside food for hungry people and "…deal thy bread to the hungry" (Isa. 58:7). When you share your food with the hungry during your fast, God will make you prosperous and bless you miraculously. In 1 Kings 17:16 "…the barrel of meal wasted not neither did the cruse of the oil," as the Lord promised to the widow and her son who were preparing to die from famine. She prepared the food for the hungry man of God from the last resources they had. They gave away their last meal and received, in turn, bountiful provision for their life and prosperity.

You can start with fasting two or three days a week, or with no food or water for 24–72 hours, or try three–four days with liquids only, or 21–40 days of the "Daniel Fast" with fruits, vegetables and legumes. Overall, begin to use more whole grains and cereals, many fresh fruits, and fresh vegetables and legumes. Green vegetables contain as much calcium as milk; yellow vegetables contain vitamin A; use nuts sparingly; and use beans, soy products, quinoa, and peas for protein. You can have a protein drink during this time of fasting. Your muscles need protein to function. Eat foods rich in Vitamin D (about 800–1,000 mg) to modulate your cell growth and reduce inflammation, improve your immune system and neuromuscular function. You do need to consult with your doctor before you start any diet, or fast, or other changes in your life. You must do your blood tests as appropriate; even test your vitamin D-3 level. I must emphasize that vitamin deficiencies are unhealthy, but excessive amounts of vitamins cause toxicity that can be harmful too.

It is well known that antioxidants found in fresh fruits and fresh vegetables neutralize free radicals, which cause cancer. But before you start any extended period of fasting (more than three days fasting), talk with your doctor or nurse practitioner to make sure all your labs are within normal limits. Your medications may need adjustment during this time. Many patients have the perception that if they have a condition such as diabetes, high blood pressure or high cholesterol and are treated with medication they are not supposed to fast. I tell my patients that it was the overeating and unhealthy diet that actually caused almost all heart disease and diabetes in the first place. The body uses the necessary amount of energy from the calories we ingest, and the rest of the extra calories will be deposited in the fatty tissues, increasing the circulation demands for maintenance and the deposit of toxins in the fatty tissues.

For example, when we eat too much sugar, the pancreas must produce more insulin. Sometimes we "shock" the pancreas with all the deserts rich in sugar, and then the cells from the pancreas will be damaged by those extra demands and soon will die. Then there will be no insulin available to carry the sugar particles, causing damage at the macro and microscopic levels in all the organs, including nerves, cells, eyes, kidneys, and blood vessels. Fasting actually will improve your condition at the micro and macroscopic level, and your lifestyle change can help you reduce the number of meds you take. But you need close monitoring by your provider to change your medication, whether you fast or not.

Because of multiple chronic conditions, or increased responsibilities in life that are above one's ability to perform, many people feel stressed, and they get depressed. You can treat your situational or major depression with medication and counseling. But a spiritual lifestyle change, and reducing your stress, is needed to get help combat your depression. You are the person who needs to initiate looking for help.

Increased health care costs increase the financial burden on everyone. Researchers say that reducing the rates of diabetes and high blood pressure by 5% would save $9 billion a year in health care costs. The study estimated $24.7 billion would be saved over time by a corresponding reduction in health problems related to those diseases.[11] How about 50% or 100%? We must revolutionize people around us by teaching them to change their lifestyle, not only eating right and exercising regularly, but we must teach people around us about healthy habits and behavior. For example, teach teenagers about abstinence from drugs, alcohol, gambling, smoking, and sex until they get married, etc.

We must focus on healthy behaviors and then lead by example, teaching and influencing our younger generation so the devil will not steal and destroy our children. If we are ignorant, it will cost us our future: our children, their children and the generations after them through the epigenetic mechanism discussed earlier. It is our responsibility to educate the future generation. By having compassion for people who live in stressful situations, we can help one person at a time. God's way is the best way for a healthy lifestyle. To be successful and able to overcome the challenges in the world, change your spiritual nutrients. Feed on the Word of God by radical obedience and discipline, and God will give you wisdom and strength to change your habits and your lifestyle.

CHAPTER TWENTY-NINE

Reassurance and Redirection

*"As for you, if you redirect your heart and lift up your
hands to Him in prayer..." (Job 11:13 HCSB)*

People Are Lost Without Direction

*P*eople whose lifestyle runs contrary to the Word of God put themselves in very dangerous situations. I see ignorance in my practice all the time. I give instructions to patients for lifestyle changes, and they ignore them completely. One time I instructed a patient with a serious heart condition to follow up with me for her treatment, and with her cardiologist for further cardiac investigations and interventions, to prevent a fatal event. She ignored my clinical advice, did not follow my strict instructions, and a few weeks later she collapsed on the street. She was taken to the ER and resuscitated there for several minutes, then spent weeks in intensive care and in the hospital, at great cost.

People can end up in terrible situations by ignoring God's instruction. Having no direction in life, their careless behavior often results in tragic consequences. We are known by our character, personality and lifestyle. The Bible warns about the falling away before the coming of Christ. "Don't let anyone deceive you in any way, for that day will not come until the rebellion occurs and the man of lawlessness is revealed, the man doomed to destruction" (2 Thess. 2:3). Only the Holy Spirit can draw us back to Jesus.

People who depart from faith and truth are on a path to death. "Whoever strays from the path of prudence comes to rest in the company of the dead" (Prov. 21:16). People need to know about Jesus so their life may be written in Heaven's Book of Life. If their name is not in the Book of Life, they will be cast into the lake of fire (Rev 20:15). Many people's names will be missing from the Book of Life, due their ignorance of God's prescriptions (Rev. 3:3).

CHAPTER THIRTY

Relationships

Neuroscientists have studied in depth how mirror neurons in people's social life can affect a healthy lifestyle. The mirror neurons in our brain enable our social relationships and allow for healing to take place. Our brain, in fact, is reshaped through the mirror neurons according to the power of our relationships. Louis Cozolino concluded:

> Our understanding of mirror neurons and their significance to human relationships has continued to expand and deepen. A great deal of neural overlap has been discovered in brain activation when we are thinking about others and ourselves. This raises many questions, including how we come to know others and whether the notion of an "individual self" is anything more than an evolutionary strategy to support our interconnection. We are just beginning to see the larger implications of all neurological processes—how the architecture of the brain can help us to better understand individuals and our relationships."[1]

Manage Stress Through Healthy Connections

God honors connections, and high on His list is friendship. God's plan includes relationships between people, for we are not meant to do life alone (Acts 5:2). Jesus' disciples were involved in preaching publicly, as well as going from house to house. When our plans go wrong and we need advice, we must seek the right connections and study God's Word for direction. When I was going through my "valley", I read the Psalms every day and prayed and fasted, seeking God's direction for my future and for the right connections and friendships.

Our spiritual vision and our social connections need constant adjustments and corrections. When we lose our way in life, we need a higher wisdom than our own (Prov. 15:22). We must encourage one another to find the right direction and the solution for our disorientation. (Heb. 10:25). In my work with people disoriented by neurocognitive disorders, I find myself reorienting and redirecting all the time—not only my patients and residents, but even their families who are directly affected by the struggles of their loved ones. I must remind them all the time to seek connections and stay connected with support groups. Church networks and loyal friends provide strong connections and healthy relationships to prevent depression, fear and anxiety, because we need each other.

Scientists have recently discovered that support groups are effective in rehabilitation from drugs, tobacco and alcohol abuse. But we know the Word of God—beyond science—instructs us not to neglect the saints' gatherings. We are to encourage each other with the promises of God, singing psalms and songs, and lifting each other up (Col. 3:8–17). Christians grow stronger when supporting each other and caring for each other's needs. It is the empathy in the mirror neurons, enabling us to feel others people's pain and taking action to help. We are created to have healthy connections and to help each other.

God's Word is the ultimate prescription for healing relationships. Nothing is more effective. Jesus was the Word in the beginning, and the Word became flesh (John 1:1). "He sent out His Word and healed them; He rescued them from the grave" (Ps. 107:20). He came to revive us and restore our relationship with the Father in Heaven, as well as our relationships with one another. Even when people hate each other and their relationship is broken, Jesus has the power to redeem and restore. The cross is the place where we learn what love and surrender mean. God promises in His Word that He will never forsake us in our emotional and physical distress. His Word promises that He is with us, and will bless us with complete physical and spiritual restoration in our time of trouble. The Word of God, the same power that raised Jesus from the dead, lives in us. Through the power of prayer, He can heal and transform our relationships. My whole life has been changed by the power of the Word, transforming my perspective on life and for eternity. We must embrace and appropriate God's unmerited grace and favor, activate our mirror neurons, and consolidate healthy, positive emotions in our limbic system. When all our brain structures align with the miraculous Word of God, we receive physical and spiritual healing in our connections and relationships.

Everyone has a God-given capacity to see the unseen world through faith, and to understand and access God's Kingdom principles. Memory has a huge impact on our daily life. What we remember from the Word (deposited in our brain structures) determines and directs how we live. Caring for people with dementia and Alzheimer's disease, we observe this every day. Neuroscientists know that to maintain a healthy brain we must socialize and stay connected with friends. Stress is lower when we have support from family and friends through healthy relationships. Communication with healthy people exercises the brain and helps keeps our memory healthy.

Say "No" to Destructive Behaviors

It is a mystery how God uses natural inhibitory neurochemicals and neurotransmitters in our physical body to protect us from destructive behaviors, such as GABA that works automatically in our subconscious when we approach a potentially harmful situation (touching a hot stove or electric socket). When we activate our spirituality through fasting and prayer, we create the atmosphere in our brain for more discipline to prevent us from wrong behavior. Fasting, according to Isaiah 58:6. can "loose the bands of wickedness" that stress our life. That means we can be delivered from the power of sin and the strongholds on our life through *the power of saying "No"* to lying, lust, doubt, laziness, discouragement, covetousness, addictions, envy, inconsistency, anger, discontentment, resentment, impulsiveness, judgment, harshness, self-indulgence, hypocrisy, pride, apathy, and more. You can have the power to overcome any addiction through prayer and fasting. You will live victoriously when you say "No" to destructive behaviors.

Jesus said, "This kind goes not out but by prayer and fasting" (Matt. 17:21). I have been invited to many parties where my colleagues were indulging in harmful behaviors, but I had the strength to say "No" because I had spent time in prayer and fasting. Who knows where I would be today if I had not said "No" to those harmful invitations. The seed of sin and misbehavior is planted in everyone because of Adam and Eve's fall. Will you produce bad fruit, destroying your entire future and your eternity? Or will you overcome your sin nature? Read the Word of God, plant a new seed, and powerful spiritual thoughts that bring good fruit will remain forever. With fasting and prayer you reprogram what I call your "spiritual GABA" in your brain to say "No" to destructive behaviors.

Manage Stress with Passionate Worship

"Praise ye the LORD. I will praise the LORD with my whole heart, in the assembly of the upright, and in the congregation." (Ps. 111:1 KJV)

We are asked in Matthew 6:33 to seek first the Kingdom of God. He must be our ultimate passion. The best example is the woman in the New Testament who broke an alabaster jar to anoint Jesus' feet with oil. She sacrificed something precious to worship Christ with passion. Jesus in His passion for us left His glory in Heaven and chose to come to earth to humble Himself and die on the cross. God loved us so we can love others; He forgave us so we can forgive others; He had mercy on us so we can show mercy to others. His love was perfect.

When you meet Jesus face to face in worship your life is changed. You become a new person and leave behind all the old things that kept you from experiencing a glimpse of Heaven. You enter God's kingdom through passionate worship. That gives you authority over your stressors in life. Leif Hetland, president and founder of Global Mission Awareness, stated in his book *Seeing Through Heaven's Eyes: A Worldview That Will Transform Your Life*:

> Those who have the keys to the castle of a king, for example, can access any part of it, from the front door to the back door, from the pantry to the treasury. Those who have been given "the keys of the kingdom of Heaven" have access to the castle of the King of kings, which is another way of saying that they have the power and authority of Heaven over things in the spiritual realm."[2]

In passionate worship the Kingdom of God fills your heart and you overcome fear, loneliness, rejection, intimidation, shame, loneliness, addiction, perversion, dysfunction, emptiness—everything that brings high levels of stress and a chemical imbalance in your brain. The prodigal son had to radically change his thinking and return to His father's house, when all his resources were gone and the fear of destruction crippled his soul. Thoughts that ruined his life changed to thoughts of a bright future when he returned to his father's house (Luke 15:11–32). Worldly thoughts can ruin your life, but passionate worship will restore hope for your life and for eternity. Connect with God's treasure in worship and "Set your minds on things above, not on earthly things" (Col. 3:2).

CHAPTER THIRTY-ONE

Our Hope Is in Heaven

"Then I saw a new Heaven and a new earth, for the first
Heaven and the first earth had passed away, and there was
no longer any sea." (Rev. 21:1)

"He will wipe every tear from their eyes, there will be no
more death or mourning or crying or pain, for the old order
of things has passed away." (Rev. 21:4)

*D*eath is the most undemocratic thing on earth, and it raises the stress level in our lives without preference. We all leave this planet sooner or later. We can't choose when we come into the world, and we can't decide when we leave it. The Word of God informs us about Heaven, and we had better believe what the Word of God says about life after death. God's Word has the power to transform us into a new creation, and to give us a relationship with God, our Super Intelligent Designer, while we are here on earth. He designed our physical body to function as a whole, and to progress from birth to death, living with purpose and a hope for Heaven in our hearts and minds.

From the day we are born, millions of our cells die daily through the process of apoptosis, ridding the body of unnecessary toxic materials and debris. When the body dies, the soul is freed from its earthly shell to live forever in eternity. Over and over again I have seen the pain and suffering of people with multi-organ failure at the end of life. All their systems shut down, and their soul leaves the body in their last breath.

Internal Thoughts Are Eternal

"My son, pay attention to what I say; turn your ear to my words. Do not
let them out of your sight; keep them within your heart; for they are life
to those who find them and health to one's whole body." (Prov. 4:20–23)

Live with eternity in mind, because your life is in God's hands. The Bible says, "My son, pay attention to what I say; turn your ear to my words. Do not let them out of your sight; keep them within your heart; for they are life to those who find them and health to one's whole body" (Prov. 4:20–3). Listen to His Word, the wellspring of life. Words can bring healing to your heart, body, soul, and mind. You are not what people around you say you are. You are a child of God, with a purpose on earth and a destiny in Heaven. Even facing death, you can have peace and hope with God. (Read Psalm 23.) When we walk with God there is no fear of death.

A close friend had Parkinson's disease and knew that he was slowly dying, day by day. He said, "I know I am dying, but whom shall I fear when I have served a Mighty God my entire life? Now I will go and meet Him." He spoke with so much confidence and with a smile on his face. He had lived his entire life with purpose and hope for eternity, under communist persecution in Romania. The Word says that whether we live or die, we are the Lord's. He loves us in all circumstances.

Fear has no room when His love fills your heart and mind. Feel the love of our Father. Jesus said, "Who loves Me will be loved by my Father and I too will love them and show myself to them" (John 14: 21). Even though the devil puts his seed of fear in people's minds to frighten them, the love of God casts out fear. "Do not be afraid" is the most quoted instruction in the Bible.

He Fights for You Even in Death

"When you pass through the waters, I will be with you; and when you
pass through the rivers, they will not sweep over you.
When you walk through the fire, you will not be burned;
the flame will not set you ablaze." (Isa. 43:2)

"The LORD your God, who is going before you,
will fight for you." (Deut.1:30)

As God promised in Isaiah 43:2, "…when you pass through the waters, I will be with you; and when you pass through the rivers, they will not sweep over you. When you walk through the fire, you will not be burned; the flame will not set you ablaze" (Isa. 43:2). He is fighting for you. "The LORD your God, who is going before you, will fight for you" (Deut.1:30) and will show Himself strong on your behalf if your heart is entirely His. "For the eyes of the LORD range throughout the earth to strengthen those whose hearts are fully committed to Him" (2 Chr. 16: 9). Turn away from foolish things and do not believe the deceiving lies of satan. This entire world loses the battle at the end. Nobody leaves earth alive. Only in Jesus is eternal victory.

Jesus said that He has gone to prepare a place for us in Heaven. Our true citizenship is not of this earth. In His time, Jesus will come again to take all of us to Heaven. Have hope in God, and He will bless you. You have the anchor of your soul in the hope of Jesus the High Priest, " so that what you hope for may be fully realized" (Heb. 6:11). First Thessalonians 4:16–17 states, "…for the LORD Himself will come down from Heaven, with a loud command, with the voice of the archangel with the trumpet call of God, and the dead in Christ will rise first. After that, we who are still alive and are left will be caught up together with them in the clouds to meet the LORD in the air. And so we will be with the LORD forever." This is our hope and purpose, and we must encourage each other with this truth.

The Lord is sovereign, and the Universe proclaims and declares His majesty and glory. He created you, and He will call you to Heaven when He decides. Our hope is anchored in His promises. The righteous, even in death, have hope (Prov. 14:32). For Christians, dying is gain. Those who die in Christ have hope in death, because they will rest from their work after this life on earth is done. Life and death are real, as we see with our own eyes, but Heaven is real, too. You do not know what day your life will end and the Lord will call you to Heaven. You must be ready at any time. We read in the book of Luke 12 about the wealthy man who neglected the real purpose of life and lost his soul at the end. The purpose for our life here on earth is to prepare us for eternity.

Where Your Heart Is, There Is Your Treasure

"Do not store up for yourselves treasures on earth, where moths and vermin destroy, and where thieves break in and steal, but store up for yourselves treasures in Heaven, where moths and vermin do not destroy, and where thieves do not break in and steal. For where your treasure is, there your heart will be also." (Matt. 6:19)

Jesus' purpose on Earth was to provide salvation and eternal life in Heaven, through His death on the cross and His triumphal resurrection. Jesus, the author of social transformation, carried all of humankind's sorrow, grief and mourning. Jesus Christ indeed fulfilled His purpose. We are His treasure. After His departure from earth, His followers began serving others, developing Christian communities and charitable services, such as hospitals and organizations with biblical names that are relevant to this day: Good Samaritan, Emanuel, Providence, Adventist, St. Mary, Mt. Sinai, etc. Christians through the ages have followed God's Rx to care for others with compassion, dignity, love, and respect. Even today this is what medical and nursing schools teach practitioners and health care providers. Jesus Christ changed the world entirely. He started a new culture on earth, showing us how to live life with purpose.

These days we live in the "Christian era" that began when Christ was born about 2,000 years ago. Time on most countries' calendars is divided into "Before Christ" (BC) and "After Christ" (AD). We have traveled in Europe, visiting all the ancient ruins and cathedrals, and the guides always refer to the "Before Christ" and "After Christ" eras when talking about what was built there. But Jesus' Kingdom is forever, and has no end (Luke 1:32–33). Jesus' philosophy even inspired kings to apply Kingdom principles. He was without sin, but He still befriended tax collectors and sinners to bring them into His Kingdom. Wisdom and knowledge are gained only when you love God with your entire heart, mind and soul. Jesus valued training and education, and we need to prepare our mind to focus on the eternal treasure in Heaven.

We were created with built-in desires to be like Jesus. People pray in Jesus' Name in their desperation. Jesus was and is the most recognized Person on Earth. He is the center of the Universe. He is the light of the world and the Hope for mankind, giving us a life with purpose. The Bible tells us that we are citizens of Heaven, and we must treasure that which cannot be destroyed. "Do not store up for yourselves treasures on earth, where moths and vermin destroy, and where thieves break in and steal, but store up for yourselves treasures in Heaven, where moths and vermin do not destroy, and where thieves do not break in and steal. For where your treasure is, there your heart will be also" (Matt. 6:19).

Not Afraid to Die

"Rid yourselves of all such things as these: anger, rage, malice, slander, and filthy language from your lips, and be renewed in knowledge and put to death…sexual immorality, impurity, lust, evil desire and greed." (Col. 3:8)

It is time to seek knowledge and wisdom from God and follow Jesus' principles for Kingdom living. Love God and seek wisdom and understanding through the Word of God. We have no excuse for not seeking wisdom from Him, for we must eventually give account for ignoring God's prescriptions in His Word. "For since the creation of the world God's invisible qualities—His eternal power and divine nature—have been clearly seen, being understood from what has been made, so that people are without excuse" (Rom. 1:20).

We have no excuse for not knowing God, because we can see His creation. The Universe declares His Majesty. All mankind is created in the image of God and reflects His image. Those who knew Jesus and His power were not afraid of dying. Only our guilt of not living according to the Word of God causes us to fear death. We must follow His instructions to "Rid yourselves of all such things as these: anger, rage, malice, slander, and filthy language from your lips," and be "renewed in knowledge," and "put to death...sexual immorality, impurity, lust, evil desire and greed" (Col. 3:8). All of these cause us to fear death, and they will bring down the wrath of God.

Everything on earth must be done from Heaven's perspective. Live your life to affect eternity, and invest in the invisible spiritual world by ministering with a heart that is where your treasure is. Living according to God's instructions and prescriptions for life will reduce your stress from fears, including guilt and fear of death. Power is released in your life when you respond to the Word of God that is working in you, transforming your thinking and life. God wants to deliver you from the fear of death. "...so that by His death he might break the power of him who holds the power of death—that is, the devil—and free those who, all their lives, were held in slavery by their fear of death" (Heb. 2: 14–15).

Joy in Death

"But we are looking forward to the new Heavens
and new earth..." (2 Pet. 3:13)

As a teenager I always looked for wholesome, trustworthy relationships, longing to belong to a group that I could trust. While searching for that perfect group I felt lonely and insecure—even hurt by colleagues and friends who did not understand my longing for an unpolluted spiritual environment. One night as I went to bed feeling sad and disappointed, the Holy Spirit touched me and I felt my soul and spirit lifting from my body, into the spiritual realm. I was immersed in "a sea of multitudes of souls" in perfect unity, peace, and unspeakable joy. I saw my earthly body lying down as if numb. I did not want to leave that indescribable moment of great joy and perfect peace in my soul and spirit. I even recognized some of the spiritual heroes of earlier eras, who served God reverently on earth. It was only a glimpse, but that was enough for me to have an impression of the atmosphere in Heaven.

Jesus Christ set people free from the fear of death. "Because through Christ Jesus, the law of the Spirit, who gives life, has set you free from the law of sin and death" (Rom. 8: 2). Set your mind on the Spirit's desires, because the mind set on the flesh is death. The Spirit of God can deliver you from the fear of death. Even thinking about the dying process can be joyful. Your life is like a moment to God; each of us is but a breath (Ps. 39:5). We have an obligation to prepare for our life after death. People get very busy and do not spend enough time to know God more. God shakes us to wake us up and get our attention. We are not on this planet forever. God loves this generation and wants us to put our trust in Him.

We must be filled with overflowing joy. Jesus said, "I have told you this so that my joy may be in you and that your joy may be complete" (John 15:11). The devil can make you bitter when you think about how someone you loved has died. Some people turn to drugs to numb their emotional pain after a close friend dies. We must be realistic about life passing by quickly. Second Peter 3:13 states clearly, "But we are looking forward to the new Heavens and new Earth." He has promised us a new world filled with God's righteousness. When you close your eyes in this life, you open them in another life. Entrust your life into God's hands. Be reassured in every moment that, "If God is for us, who can be against us?" (Rom. 8:31).

Jesus went to the cross to give us eternal life. Even when you are threatened by disease, violence, or painful emotions, you must be determined to finish the race well. There is pressure to give up and not finish the race. Press on, despite all circumstances. God will respond to you when you seek Him. Your Creator will provide the strength and resources you need to physically and spiritually fulfill your destiny and prepare for Heaven.

He who created you will give you joy. God knows the effect of joy in our spirit, soul and body. "Rejoice in the Lord always. I will say it again: Rejoice!" (Phil. 4:4). Our great commission on this earthly journey is to be filled with the knowledge of the Word of God and lead other people to Jesus, which produces great joy in Heaven. You will feel His joy and goodness. God's glory is God's goodness; you are made to be profoundly affected by God's presence. During our journey to Heaven, He is pruning us to be more effective. God called us to continue to pour out what we have received, so that at the end of our life our joy will be complete.

The apostle Paul considered death as something to be gained. He said, "I am torn between the two: I desire to depart and be with Christ, which is better by far" (Phil. 1:23 NIV). When your days are finished your physical body will die, because your days are numbered. If you have lived according to the Word of God, then when your days are finished, you will move into your eternal home in Heaven with the Lord.

Heaven as described in the book of Revelation is real, and one day you will step right onto the streets of gold. There is a glorious, shining city with mansions, streets of gold, rivers of living water, trees with healing leaves, and animals that harm no one. Many books have been written about Heaven based on people's near death experiences—even by medical providers such as cardiologists and neurosurgeons, based on their own experiences.

You and I are all going to die. Even kings die sooner or later. One hundred years from now none of us will be here. It is important that we finish well. John stated in Revelation 14:13, "…I heard a voice from Heaven saying unto me, 'Write, Blessed are the dead which die in the Lord from henceforth: Yea', saith the Spirit, 'that they may rest from their labors; and their works do follow them'" (Rev. 14:13 KJV). All your deeds will follow you.

The reward in Heaven is great. Rejoice, for we are going to Heaven when our temporary "visa" on this planet expires. There will be eternal peace. There will be a glorious day when we will meet all our loved ones. When our life on earth finishes, we will be raised from death on the resurrection day. "Brothers and sisters, we do not want you to be uninformed about those who sleep in death, so that you do not grieve like the rest of mankind, who have no hope" (1 Thess. 4:13). In Heaven you will meet all those who died in the Lord—your close relatives and friends. Live with hope in eternal life, in resurrection. Jesus was the first resurrected One who ascended to Heaven.

There will be a day when all of us will see God and give an account for our life. Check yourself. Are you ready for the day when you're called to Heaven, your eternal home? Dr. Randy Alcorn, founder and director of Eternal Perspective Ministries, in his book *Heaven* emphasized:

> Home as a term for Heaven isn't simply a metaphor. It describes an actual, physical place—a place promised and built by our bridegroom; a place we'll share with loved ones; a place of fond familiarity and comfort and refuge; a place of marvelous smells and tastes, fine food, and great conversations; a place of contemplation and interaction and expressing the gifts and passions that God has given us. It'll be a place of unprecedented freedom and adventure.[1]

Persevere according to the Word of God that releases you from stress and from worrying about death. He is calling you to live at peace with Him. Your stress will be less, your entire physical body will relax, and the signs and symptoms of fear will diminish or disappear completely. If your life ended today, where would you go? God longs for you to go to Heaven and live with Him. Paul lived a life filled with the Holy Spirit. He knew that for him it was better to go to Heaven to be with Lord, but for others on earth, it was better for him to remain here, to keep preaching about eternal life through Jesus Christ. You have not yet finished your assignment that you were called to do on earth.

Live for Christ while you can, and when you leave, Heaven will gain. Over the last 26 years of providing end-of-life care in our facility, I have often seen people dying. I could fill a whole amphitheater with the people who have passed on in our foster homes and our memory care facility. I sense their fear of death and their struggle in the last days or hours of their life. I whisper in their ears when they are on their deathbed: "Do not be afraid to go. The Lord is sending His angel to usher you home to Heaven in His presence." Then I pray for them so the angel will come to take their soul to Heaven when they are ready. I continue to pray for forgiveness for each dying person. The atmosphere changes each time I pray where a person is dying.

Once at a funeral service where I was invited to speak, I told the congregation how I talk to these special people when they are dying, and how I pray for them at their bedside, in addition to the medical and health care we provide. We play music and worship songs throughout the day for their physical and spiritual comfort. You can feel the presence of God in the room. At the end of that service, one lady said to me, "I know where I will go to die when my life is almost finished—Tabor Crest" (the name of our business). Natural death demands courage, but death is part of your destiny and your life story.

The Bible is about dying to self and becoming alive in Christ Jesus. When you live with eternity in mind, you will live forever. It is written,

> Brothers and sisters, we do not want you to be uninformed about those who sleep in death, so that you do not grieve like the rest of the mankind, who have no hope. For we believe that Jesus died and rose again and so we believe that God will bring with Jesus those who have fallen in sleep in Him. According to the Lord's word, we tell you that we who are still alive, who are left until the coming of the Lord, will certainly not precede those who have fallen asleep. For the Lord Himself will come down from Heaven, with a loud command, with the voice of the archangel and with the trumpet call of God, and the dead in Christ will rise first. After that we who are still alive and are left will be caught up together with them to meet the Lord in the air. So we will be with the LORD forever. Therefore encourage one another with these words. (1 Thess. 4:13–18)

What a fascinating, joyful promise! God, knowing we would be afraid of death, wrote this to encourage us. We will be with the Lord forever, even though we must face the pain of separation from death. We are also instructed to encourage those around us. I hope you are encouraged by this clear message about life after death.

If the Spirit who raised Christ from the dead lives in you, then you are not afraid to die, for in Genesis 26:24 God promised that He is with you.

"That night the Lord appeared to him and said, 'I am the God of your father Abraham. Do not be afraid, for I am with you; I will bless you.'" God is with you in all seasons of your life. Trust His promises and do not despair in your tribulations. We learn in the Word of God that all the Bible characters faced death with courage—Esther, Daniel, Shadrac, Meshac, Abednego, Joseph, and many prophets—as well as many Christians thrugh the centuries. All the apostles took courage when threatened with death. Their Lord, whom they loved and served with a pure heart, was with them. Take courage. God promised all of us, "I am with You." His presence is with you. Appreciate the presence of God and enjoy His presence in your life.

Manage Stress with Courage

Can you imagine living without fear, weakness or vulnerability? Strive for a noble character. Esther had a noble character in the face of an enemy and made a stand for what was right, for herself and her nation. She did everything in her power to save their lives and stated, "If I perish, I perish" (Esth. 4:16). The enemy is threatening you over and over again with the thing you fear the most. You may have many ifs in your mind right now, like all of us; what if my child, if my husband, if my business, if my job, if my church, if my parents, if my friends, if my nation, if my world?…What if…? In all situations God wants us to trust Him. Courage comes when our heart is convinced we are loved. Love casts out fear, when you take courage. God loved us so much that He gave His only Son to come to earth and die for us in humiliation, hanging on the cross. There is no greater love on the face of the earth than the Father's and the Son's. His pleasure is to give you the Kingdom, to invite you to live with Him in eternity after your physical body dies. Live with no fear of death.

He will create a new Heaven and a new Earth. "See, I will create new Heavens and a new earth. The former things will not be remembered, nor will they come to mind. But be glad and rejoice forever in what I will create, for I will create Jerusalem to be a delight and its people a joy. I will rejoice over Jerusalem and take delight in my people; the sound of weeping and of crying will be heard in it no more" (Isa. 65:17–19). God's prescription for us is to rejoice in Him when our life is finished.

God did not give us a spirit of fear. My father, before he died, gave instructions for my oldest brother to read Psalm 91 at his funeral service, so everyone attending would know not to fear death. We just need to position ourselves under the shadow of the wings of Jehovah *El Elyon*, the Most High God, where there is no fear.

Going to Heaven

Insecurity and uncertainty about your last days on earth, and where you will spend eternity, will cause more fear. If you prepare now, the fear of death will disappear. You do not need to go through stress and emotional pain because of the fear of death. Recently at the gym I met a young Christian mother with three children, and in our discussion she said, "I cannot wait to get to Heaven." I considered this with a professional ear and mind, and clearly that was not a suicidal thought—it was genuine happiness, knowing where her journey on earth will end and where she is heading. She was so excited about God. As my silent evaluation continued, I realized that she loves her children and is reading books on how to raise children and how to be the wife God wants her to be. She wants to help her husband reach his full potential and fulfill his destiny here on this planet.

When you know where you will spend eternity, you will be at peace. You will desire to see your future real estate in Heaven, even though you committed to earthly assignments and obligations. You can persevere and live according to the Word of God, while waiting to meet your Creator. God promised eternal life to all who obey Him and follow His prescriptions beyond science—His commandments, instructions and directions. God is calling you to live at peace with Him during your short time on earth. He wants you to serve Him. Nobody will avoid seeing death. King David asked the Lord to tell him when the end of his life would be, so he could count his days on earth. David lived with eternity in mind. God's answer was that life is extremely short, like a vapor, and one day we will go to Heaven.

Trust the Lord and have confidence that He cares for you. I have had to remind myself over and over again: "The Lord is my Helper; I will not be afraid. What can mere mortals do to me?" (Heb. 13:6), and, "Jesus Christ is the same yesterday and today and forever" (Heb. 13:8). We look forward to Heaven because our current location is not an enduring city (Heb. 13:12, 14).

Preparing for the Last Move

Although most people look at death as a tragedy, it is meant to be a move to your eternal home in Heaven, to live forever with your Lord. We have had to move many times, both in Romania and here in the US. Maybe you have moved a lot, too. Each time we had to make huge preparations for moving day. It was stressful getting everything ready on the day.

Our last move will be when we leave this earth, but for that day we must make a major spiritual preparation. We all have real estate waiting for us in Heaven, promised by Jesus Christ and prepared by Him for those who follow

His teaching. It is important that you and I finish as more than conquerors. All the saints in the Bible kept eternity in mind and followed God's plans for preparation. That will indeed be a glorious, peaceful day. No spirit of fear, and no more stress. Heaven is a "Stress Free Zone".

Hope in Eternity

"For the Spirit God gave us does not make us timid, but gives us power, love and self-discipline." (2 Tim. 1:7)

Many are anxious and frustrated at the thought of facing death. Proverbs 12:25 states: "Anxiety weighs down the heart but a kind word cheers it up." Emotionally you are affected by fearful thoughts. Proverbs 14:10 explains, "Each heart knows its bitterness, and no one else can share its joy." But God has not given you a spirit of fear, according to 2 Timothy 1:7. "For the Spirit God gave us does not make us timid, but gives us power, love and self-discipline." We will feel the pain of a temporary separation—no one can avoid that. But in God we have hope that in eternity we will be together again with our loved ones. Paul Manwaring, Registered General and Psychiatric Nurse, former Prisoner Manager in England, and Global Legacy Overseer, in his book *What on Earth is Glory? A Practical Approach to a Glory-filled Life* stated:

> …we are all called to an eternal journey that will take us from glory to glory and ultimately to the great cloud of witnesses, where we will watch as those who follow us continue and complete the work of revealing the fullness of God's glory on earth, culminating the most glorious wedding and family reunion, which will last for eternity."[4]

Your Days Are Numbered

"Your eyes saw my unformed body; all the days ordained for me were written in your book before one of them came to be." (Ps. 139:16)

As the psalmist said, your days are numbered. "Your eyes saw my unformed body; all the days ordained for me were written in your book before one of them came to be" (Ps. 139:16). Before you were born, your life on earth and your destiny was written by God. Before you were born you were in God's thoughts. That eternal thought of God materialized when it crossed the threshold of your parents' emotions, and oxytocin rushed through their brains. Their physical bodies united, releasing a half-cell from your mother and another half from your father to form an amazing, new little baby human in just over nine months—you! Learn more about that by reading about embryology. It is fascinating. Your life starts and ends with

God. He knows your destiny. Check yourself. Are you ready for that day when you are called back home to Heaven?

The Reality of Heaven

You were born because you are important. You must stay here until the Lord decides for you to go. Paul said, "If I live, I want to lift up the name of Jesus Christ." We must stay here to lift up the name of Jesus Christ so more souls will be saved for eternity. Your death is controlled by the power of the Holy Spirit. He decides your time to go. You do not need to worry about the timing. Your days are numbered and must be fulfilled, until the angel is sent to escort you to the throne room of God. Live for Jesus Christ now, here on earth. Rely on God's promises and He will wipe every tear from your eyes. There will be no more death, or sorrow, or crying or pain (Rev. 21:4). All these things will be gone forever. Our citizenship is not here. Heaven is real, as described in the Book of Revelation. Have faith, and hope in God. He will bless you and give you victory, even in death.

Thinking About Heaven

Fear of death, and the unknowns of life after death, can trigger anxiety. That fear created the cliché: "Death is the mother of all religions." People do become more spiritual when they approach the end of life. Medication will not take away the fear of death. In uncertain situations and unpleasant circumstances you must have faith in God and experience His transforming power. Faith comes from hearing, and hearing by the Word of God (Mark 11: 23). The Word becomes alive in your heart, and when you live accordingly it becomes your biography. You are not the same anymore when you have faith. The righteous live by faith.

I have had to live by faith all my life. I couldn't live without faith. When doubt and unbelief tried to come in, I cried out to God to increase my faith, and he did. We know that without faith it is impossible to please God (Heb. 11:6). Unbelief puts fear in your heart, with all its unhealthy symptoms. Have faith, resist the devil, and he will flee from you. Through faith you defeat the devil because "your faith might not rest on human wisdom, but on God's power" (1 Cor. 2:5).

Heaven's Culture

"He has made everything beautiful in its time.
He has also set eternity in the human heart; yet no one can fathom
what God has done from beginning to end." (Eccles. 3:11)

You and I were born with eternity (Heavenly citizenship and Heaven's culture) in our DNA. I had to change my citizenship after I moved to the US. In order to get my US citizenship I had to learn everything about America's history and learn the laws. I also had to adopt American culture to be able to function here. I did that with much joy and gladness, knowing all the benefits and advantages I would have to live on American soil as an American citizen. Spiritually, our citizenship is in another, supernatural realm, with a Heavenly culture based on God's character. We need to follow Heaven's laws to get our Heavenly citizenship. We also must adopt Heaven's culture to live in God's Kingdom. God puts desires in our heart that cannot be satisfied here on earth. This is because we must desire things from above and seek the supernatural, eternal kingdom of God.

Thousands of years ago it was written, "He has made everything beautiful in its time. He has also set eternity in the human heart; yet no one can fathom what God has done from beginning to end" (Eccles. 3:11). We know that earth is not our home. You and I are here with a temporary visa. When our earthly visa expires, we must move to our eternal home, where our permanent citizenship is. It is very easy for me to go on a mission trip to Romania or Europe, where I have been before. I have a picture already in my mind about those places. But it is very hard to go places where I have never been. It is difficult to yield to something unseen. I have a picture in my mind of those places based on others' descriptions, but I am sure the idea I have in my mind is far from reality. We are afraid of the unknown, so we need God's supernatural power to overcome that fear.

On the Way to Heaven

When the first Europeans landed in North America, hundreds of years ago, they did not know what the United States would be like in a few hundred years. America exists because long ago people from Europe desired to come at any cost. They were motivated to start over in a different land. When I left Romania in 1990, I came with hopes and expectations, yet not knowing exactly what my future would hold. You must live with hope, desire, expectation and motivation to move on to your Heavenly home when your life here is over. Whatever happens in the natural happens in the spiritual. Thinking about Heaven, we do not know how we will get there, but God has promised us a new Heaven and a new earth, with streets of gold. We must live with expectations. What we believe, we receive.

We are on the way to Heaven during our entire life. We are on the way to the promises of God. Walk like a person who belongs in Heaven, a member of a royal priesthood, part of God's family, created in His image. In our Heavenly Kingdom there are no graves. The devil will never enter there. Heaven is prepared for those who have accepted Heaven's identity through the blood of the Lamb. We travel around the world and we see people who desire to go abroad; they desire a new land. There is power in desire. Our desire must be driven by our thought of eternity in our DNA, to go to the land prepared for us by Jesus. Do not lose your focus. Those who believe in Jesus will overcome the world. Delight yourself in the Lord and He will give you the desires of your heart. It all begins with a desire in your heart. You can overcome huge mountains if you have the desire.

Character for Heaven

"For physical training is of some value,
but godliness has value for all things, holding promise
for both the present life and the life to come." (1 Tim. 4:8 NIV)

The only thing you take to Heaven is your character. Do not waste your time on earth with unnecessary things. Train yourself to develop a godly character. You must work hard and do what is right according to the highest standards, and God will build your character. Eternal issues are the most important things in life. Training for godliness is important (1 Tim. 4:8). All training is good, but training for eternity is the most beneficial.

People get distracted, wasting their eternal God-given gifts. A hurting generation needs godly training and character to heal the broken souls. People deceive themselves with temporary pleasures. One day they will be on their deathbed, asking the tough question: "Where will I spend eternity?" He promised we would walk on streets of gold, but first we must live intentionally to obtain godly character. You are in the right place to obtain God's promises right now, if you are willing to invest in and develop your Heavenly character.

Death Is the Beginning of Your True Life

"Jesus said to her, "I AM the resurrection and the life.
The one who believes in Me will live, even though they die;
and whoever lives by believing in Me will never die.
Do you believe this?" (John 11:25–26)

Dying looks like the end, but it is just the beginning of an eternal new life. All of us will die sooner or later. Kings, presidents, politicians, business people, intellectuals, actors, rich and poor—all will die at the end of their life. The time will come for all of us to go to our eternal home. There will be a weeping for those who are not ready. You must surrender to God's plan. When you surrender, your stress will decrease because you have put your trust in God's promises. Jesus answers our questions about life after death. "Jesus said to her, "I AM the resurrection and the life. The one who believes in Me will live, even though they die; and whoever lives by believing in Me will never die. Do you believe this?" (John 11:25–26).

God gave us His prescription to treat fear: "So do not fear, for I am with you; do not be dismayed, for I am your God. I will strengthen you and help you; I will uphold you with my righteous right hand" (Isa. 41:10). That prescription can be used in any situation, even on our deathbed. Jesus' love opens our spiritual eyes, and we realize earth is not our home; we are just passing through to a new Heaven and a new earth. The aging process is a downsizing process, preparing for our exit from this world to our eternal home.

People stress themselves when they hear that a family member or close friend is dying. I see people dying all the time, and I see the stress that family members and friends experience. One day each one of us will leave this earth. People need to be ready. We cannot move on to a new earth and new Heaven with an old body. We will enter the throne room of God with a new body. If we come boldly to Him in faith, Christ will make us perfect and He will do it according to His pleasure. Death is necessary; it is not a punishment. Our soul will join our spirit, and we will leave the body behind. We need to make sure our soul and spirit are ready.

No Short Cuts

Jesus said, "Look I am coming soon!
My reward is with Me, and I will give to each person
according to what they have done." (Rev. 22:12)

People want to know their calling and purpose on earth. God doesn't want anyone to die eternally. God wants us to see His kingdom come, His will to be done on earth as in Heaven, as described in the Lord's Prayer. We need the gift of the Holy Spirit to see the manifestation of the Kingdom of God on earth. The Holy Spirit works to positively encourage people. People need to seek wisdom from God, find life, and get His favor. "For those who find me find life and receive favors from the Lord" (Prov. 8:35). Wait on God and see what He wants to say. Take time with the Holy Spirit. There is no substitute for time with God. In medicine, if a practitioner uses short cuts, the outcome can be severe, even resulting in unexpected death. We must spend real, sincere time with God. The heart and nature of God is of a Father with a true love. We cannot be what He is, but we can have what He has—His love, wisdom, inspiration, and anointing.

We need to honor those people who can teach us how to get into God's presence. Observe where the presence of God is resting and go there. When I hear about God showing His power at a saints gathering, my husband and I go there, even though we have to drive one or more days or go on an airplane. I like to read the Word of God, memorize verses, and read inspirational books. God's motivation for each human being is love. His love motivated Him to send Jesus to die on the cross for the world's sins.

Allow God to change your "spiritual DNA" and character through His love, as you get ready for Heaven. Jesus is building His Church for Himself from Heavenly-minded people. He is ready to come and get us soon. Jesus said, "Look I am coming soon! My reward is with Me, and I will give to each person according to what they have done" (Rev. 22:12). We must accept our Heavenly citizenship, walk in the right path, and live in a Heavenly culture.

Dangerous Zone

Refuse to stay frustrated because of failures in your life. Do not allow frustration and anxiety to consume you. A sense of insecurity and uncertainty from careless living will devastate you. God will always use somebody to help you up. Train your senses to notice when God sends somebody into your life to help you. Your senses are trained to discern right from wrong. Get up and move away from dangerous situations. I was afraid of the unknown in Bucharest, and later in the US, but God brought many people into my life who shared good advice. I had to choose those people with godly advice and avoid dangerous ideas.

You must be willing to pay the price to fulfill your destiny. Your efforts, hardships and personal sacrifice will give you a story that motivates others. The story of your life and your testimony, with all the difficulties you are going through, must be written so others will be encouraged. Jesus wrote His story with His own blood, with the power to transform the world. Have faith like a little child, receive Jesus, and worship Him in prayer and in truth. Trust and obey God. Guard your heart with all diligence and your stress levels will decrease.

Eternal Reward

"If we live, we live for the Lord; if we die,
we die for the Lord. So, whether we live or die,
we belong to the LORD." (Rom. 14:8)

We were born needing to belong to our Super Intelligent Designer. To belong to the Lord is an eternal prescription. Many of us at some point in life pass through a valley of discouragement, or get depressed about bad news, or bad things happen to us, or disabilities and infirmities happen with no apparent reason. Your struggle is God's instrument to convince you, to discipline you, and to catch your attention to prepare you for Heaven.

God uses human instruments to prepare us for eternal life. My friend Dr. Lea stated that nothing could catch her attention for Heaven "except getting cancer." Only a diagnosis of cancer motivated her to come to Christ and get saved. God knows exactly what will move you to seek salvation. In the middle of suffering, it is hard to see eternal victory. You may see your life as ruined, but God gives you a crown that will last forever. He has more in Heaven for each one of us. You just need your spiritual eyes to be opened and to trust in His powerful hands, because He holds your soul in His everlasting love. Only in Heaven will we find out why God allowed so much suffering in our life. Each one of us has questions for Heaven. Save your questions for that time.

If you are not sure if you are saved, and not sure where you will spend your eternity, do not wait for that incurable diagnosis to force you to come to the Lord. You can lift your hands toward Heaven right now and say from the bottom of your heart:

> "Father God in Heaven, I sinned against you. I recognize and confess all my sins, since I was born until today. Please forgive all my sins and wash them away with the precious blood of the Lamb. I bring all my sins to the cross. Cleanse me with the precious holy blood that was shed by the Lamb of God, Your Son, Jesus Christ. Come into my heart through the power of the Holy Spirit and be my personal Lord and Savior. Transform my life. Today I want to start a new life with you, Jesus Christ, who died on the cross for my sins, was resurrected on the third day and ascended to Heaven, and Who is sitting at the right hand of God, the Father, the Creator of the Universe, to intercede for me, my family and the entire world. Thank You. In Jesus' Name I pray."

That powerful prayer will change your spiritual DNA and make you a new creation in Christ Jesus. You will receive unspeakable joy and peace— and no stress!

I pray that our Heavenly Father will seal your decision to live for eternity from this moment on. I pray that God will give you a pure faith, courage, boldness and authority over worldly temptations. Your pain and suffering are not without purpose. Your faith is more "precious than gold" and will bring you honor and glory when Jesus Christ comes. Keep your faith and look at all your circumstances with Heavenly eyes. All the stories in the Bible are examples of great people who trusted God, believed in eternal life, and overcame worldly temptation.

God Is Not Finished with You

*"It was good for me to be afflicted so that I might
learn your decrees. The law of your mouth is more precious
to me than thousands of pieces of silver and gold." (Ps. 119:71–72)*

God wants you to be victorious, even when you feel that your heart is broken into pieces. God puts all the small pieces from your broken heart together to fulfill His plan in you for eternity. He has not finished with you yet. "If we live, we live for the Lord; if we die, we die for the Lord. So, whether we live or die, we belong to the LORD" (Rom. 14:8). Many times discouragement, pain, suffering, and brokenness overwhelm our heart and we don't see anything good from our disaster. But in eternity you will see that this suffering was a precious opportunity to turn your attention to the Word of God, for the salvation of your soul.

The Psalmist said, "It was good for me to be afflicted so that I might learn your decrees. The law of your mouth is more precious to me than thousands of pieces of silver and gold" (Ps. 119:71–72). God knows what is best for you, more than you know. Sometimes even catastrophic events are allowed to wake us up.

Death Is Part of Your Destiny

*"But if Christ is in you, then even though your body is subject to death
because of sin, the Spirit gives life because of righteousness. And if the
Spirit of him who raised Jesus from the dead is living in you, he who
raised Christ from the dead will also give life to your mortal bodies
because of his Spirit who lives in you." (Rom. 8:10, 11)*

If you believe the Word of God you are already dead to sin, and you need not fear death anymore because Christ lives in you by faith. "I have been crucified with Christ and I no longer live, but Christ lives in me. The life I now live in the body, I live by faith in the Son of God, who loved me and gave himself for me." (Gal. 2:20). We are redeemed and have a house in Heaven. "And God raised us up with Christ and seated us with him in the Heavenly realms in Christ Jesus" (Eph. 2:6). "Now this is eternal life: that they know you, the only true God, and Jesus Christ, whom you have sent" (John 17:3). Thinking of eternity gives you courage, and death demands courage. Death is part of life.

But if Christ is in you, then even though your body is subject to death because of sin, the Spirit gives life because of righteousness. And if the Spirit of him who raised Jesus from the dead is living in you, He who raised Christ from the dead will also give life to your mortal bodies because of His Spirit who lives in you." (Rom. 8:10, 11)

Take courage, because the Lord will not abandon you. You are the work of His hands. He is with you every moment. "The Lord will vindicate me; your love, Lord, endures forever—do not abandon the works of your hands." (Ps. 138:8)

... in all these things we are more than conquerors through Him who loved us. For I am convinced that neither death nor life, neither angels nor demons, neither the present nor the future, nor any powers, neither height nor depth, nor anything else in all creation, will be able to separate us from the love of God that is in Christ Jesus our Lord. (Rom. 8:31, 37–39 NIV)

That reassurance allows us to live life without fear, weakness or vulnerability.

Full of Courage

There are many examples of courageous people in the Bible. One that amazed me was the story of Esther. Esther was full of courage and determined that nothing could be against her when she decided to go into the "king's presence to beg for mercy," despite all the rules and regulations of that time. The King's rules were unbearable for his close family, and the queen herself said, as we read in the book of Esther,

All the king's officials and the people of the royal provinces know that for any man or woman who approaches the king in the inner court without being summoned the king has but one law: that they be put to death unless the king extends the gold scepter to them and spares their lives. But thirty days have passed since I was called to go to the king." (Esth. 4:11)

Even though she knew that the probability she would die was very high, she was willing to take the chance after three days and three nights of fasting for the Jewish nation, with no food or drink.

Go, gather together all the Jews that are present in Shushan, and fast ye for me, and neither eat nor drink three days, night or day: I also and my maidens will fast likewise; and so will I go in unto the king, which is not according to the law: and if I perish, I perish." (Esth. 4:16 KJV)

She was determined to stand in the gap for her people selflessly, and thus fulfilled her destiny to save a nation from annihilation. Her courage preserved the lineage of the coming Messiah to bring salvation and eternal life to the entire world. We are called away from self-preservation to be courageous, determined to fulfill our calling. You can make choices; you can decide not to look back. The power of choice has an impact on your destiny and where you will spend your eternity. You are fully responsible to God for your life.

You are called to be courageous. "Be strong and courageous. Do not be afraid or terrified because of them, for the LORD your God goes with you; He will never leave you nor forsake you" (Deut. 31:6 NIV). You are one decision away from starting a new chapter. You can be brave. Your narrative and your spiritual resumé can be changed. Become a courageous person, overcoming your old thoughts through a divine exchange, choosing thoughts that can change your life now and for eternity. Nobody is an obstacle to your destiny but yourself. God has no intention of leaving you this way. One brave decision can turn your path toward a healthy body, soul and spirit. Bravely follow God's supernatural prescriptions to manage stress from the worry, fear, anxiety and depression that can kill you. *Do not be afraid. Fear not.*

Conclusion

We are now convinced by science that our emotions influence our thinking process, which dictates our lifestyle as well as the amount and quality of the neurotransmitters and neurochemicals released in our body. Thus, our emotions, thoughts and lifestyle keep changing the structures of our brain. Science has demonstrated that we can rewire our brain by renewing our mind and our thoughts and emotions through a process called "neuroplasticity". Dr. Jeffrey Barsch stated in his book *Praying for the Brain: Rewiring the Brain Through Prayer*:

> We now know that the brain has the ability to reorganize itself by forming new neural connections throughout life. The brain is not limited by age or by past learning, rather it adjusts to new situations and new environments in life. The more stimulation the brain receives the more likely it is to be vibrant and ready for life. Our life experiences rewire us. It will be very exciting to have our brains rewired by the Lord through brain exercises and prayer."[1]

He emphasized throughout this book that "brain rewiring" can be achieved by renewing our mind, as written in Romans 12:2.

With a mind renewed (one of the powerful supernatural prescriptions in the Word of God) through meditation on God's promises—prayer, fasting, compassion, gratitude, worshiping and rejoicing in the Lord—we receive the supernatural solution—beyond science—to manage stress from fear, worry, anxiety and depression. Lucinda Bassett, the Founder of the Midwest Center for Stress and Anxiety, Inc., in her book *From Panic to Power: Proven Techniques to Calm Your Anxiety, Conquer your Fears, and Put You in Control of Your Life*, stated,

> Prayer can give you the opportunity to clarify what is bothering you, to put it into perspective, and to know that somebody else is sharing the burden. Prayer is God's gift to us and when we know how to use it most effectively, it can offer us great rewards. A wise person once said when you pray, look for specific answers.[2]

However, scientists have also discovered that our brain's structures are hardwired to be resistant to changes, thus preserving a consistent personality.

But worries of all kinds, as well as our belief system, dictate our emotions and contribute to the development of our character and personality. Dr. Brian King, PhD, neuroscientist and comedian, in his speech "The Habits of Happy People" cited Corrie Ten Boom's statement: "Worry does not empty tomorrow of its sorrow. It empties today of its strength."[3]

Worry creates fear, distress, anxiety, panic attacks and depression. It greatly reduces our potential years of healthy life. We have read that "… the joy of the Lord is our strength." Through joy and happiness we can reduce the damage that high levels of stress have caused to our brain and our physical body. Joy, happiness and gratitude will reduce fear, anxiety and depression by calming an overactive brain through healthy amounts of neurochemicals released as a result. Happiness has recently become the focus of new scientific research. We know that—beyond science—"merry heart" is the best medicine.

Body, soul and spirit form our personality on earth. A spiritually transformed mind plays a huge role in promoting health in our physical body and soul. Body, soul and spirit cannot be separated and must be preserved entirely until the coming of Jesus Christ. Bill Johnson, in his book *The Power that Changes the World: Creating Eternal Impact in the Here and Now*, stated:

> There is also a great hunger among us to see the medical community thrive with excellence, while its workers maintain the heart of a servant. It would be a dream come true if we find out that this great part of every community had discovered the connection between spirit, soul and body. Part of that dream would be seeing them provide health care to the whole person through divine wisdom.[4]

By following God's supernatural prescription, depositing God's promises into your conscious and unconscious mind, and meditating on His Word day and night, you can reprogram your brain. Through protein synthesis and neurogenesis its capacity will increase, creating new, stronger neurons for a healthier life, physically and spiritually, both here on earth and in Heaven forever.

Endnotes

Introduction

1. Joseph Goldberg, "The Effects of Stress on Your Body," Stress Management Health Center. http://www.webmd.com/balance/stress-management/effects-of-stress-on-your-body. (March 1, 2015)

2. Ibid. (March 3, 2015)

3. Carl Sagan, "Words of Wisdom." Carl Sagan on Science and Technology. Big Think Editors. http://bigthink.com/words-of-wisdom/carl-sagan-on-science-and-technology. (June 1, 2015)

4. Mary Blaszko Helming, "Healing Through Prayer: A Qualitative Study." Holistic Nursing Practice 25, no. 1 (2011): 33–44.

5. Chetty, S., Friedman, A. R., Taravosh-Lahn, K., Kirby, E. D., Mirescu, C., Guo, F., Krupik, D., Nicholas, A., Geraghty, A. C., Krishnamurthy, A., Tsai, M. K., Covarrubias, D., Wong, A. T., Francis, D. D., Sapolsky, R. M., Palmer, T. D., Pleasure, D., and Kaufer, D., "Stress and glucocorticoids promote oligodendrogenesis in the adult hippocampus," Molecular Psychiatry 19, (2014), 1275–1283

PART I

Chapter 1

1. Billy Graham, The Journey: *How To Live By Faith In An Uncertain World.* (Nashville, Tennessee; W Publishing Group, 2006), 63.

2. Shaneen Clarke, *Dare To Be Great: Forget Your Past! Live Your Dream.* (Charlotte, NC: Lifebridge Books, 2009), 69.

3. Nick Hall, PhD, "Understanding Stress and Immunity." 2013, p. 6, 7 http://ce.nurse.com/course/60089/understanding-stress-and-immunity/. (February 2, 2013)

4. Jim Folk, Marilyn Folk, 2016. "Anxiety Symptoms" (including Anxiety Attacks, Disorder, and Panic Signs and Symptoms). http://www.anxietycentre.com/anxiety-symptoms/chest-pain-anxiety.shtml. (April 27, 2016)

5. Homeostasis. Human Physiology/Print Version — Wikibooks, 2015. https://en.wikibooks.org/wiki/Human_Physiology/Print_Version. (April 28, 2016)

6. Katie Gallant . "The Lymphatic and Immune Systems." 2015. https://quizlet.com/73298649/info. (April 28, 2016)

7. Stahl, S., Briley, M., "Understanding pain in depression," Human Psychopharmacology: Clinical and Experimental. 19, (2008): 9–13.

8. Jeanie Lerche Davis. 2000. "Patient, Heal Thyself", WebMD Health News 2000. http://www.webmd.com/balance/news/20000907/patient-heal-thyself. (May 2, 2016)

Chapter Two

1. Action potential. From Wikipedia, the free encyclopedia. https://en.wikipedia.org/ wiki/Action_potential. (April 29, 2016)

2. Purves D., Augustine, G. J., Fitzpatrick D., et al., editors. Sunderland (MA): Sinauer Associates; 2001. "Neurotransmitters" Neuroscience. 2nd edition.http://www.ncbi. nlm.nih.gov/books/NBK10795/ (April 29, 2016)

3. Schikorski, T., and Stevens, C. F., 2001. "Morphological correlates of functionally defined synaptic vesicle populations." Nature Neuroscience 4: 391–39

4. "The Limbic System—Boundless" https://www.boundless.com/...function.../the-limbic-system-154-12689/ (April 29, 2016)

5. Brain & Nervous System. http://homepage.psy.utexas.edu/homepage/class/Psy301/ Salinas/04Brain&NervousSystem.htm. (April 30, 2016)

6. Amygdala — Wikipedia, the free encyclopedia. https://en.wikipedia.org/wiki/ Amygdala#cite_ref-18. (April 30, 2016)
Frontiers in Human Neuroscience 2012; 6: 80.

7. Deborah E. Hannula and Anthony J. Greene (2012). "The hippocampus reevaluated in unconscious learning and memory: at a tipping point?" http://www.ncbi.nlm.nih. gov/pmc/articles/PMC3324888/ (April 30, 2016)

8. Human Physiology/The Nervous System, Wikibooks, open books https:// en.wikibooks.org/wiki/Human_Physiology/The_Nervous_System. (April 30, 2016)

9. "The Autonomic Nervous System—Thinking Through the Body" www.thinkbody.co.uk/papers/autonomic-nervous-system.htm. (April 30, 2016)

10. Caroline Leaf. *Switch On Your Brain: The Key to Peak Happiness, Thinking, and Health.* (Grand Rapids, Michigan: Baker Books, 2013), p. 125.

11. Ohno, M., Ohno, N., Kefalides, N.A., "Studies on human laminin and laminin-collagen complexes." Connective Tissue Research. 25(3–4) (1991):251–63.

12. Robert Goldman, M.D., Ph.D., D.O., FAASP Ronald Klatz, M.D., D.O. Joseph C. Maroon, M.D., Nicholas DiNubile, M.D. Anti-Aging Tip of the Day. Worldhealth. net Anti-Aging News http://www.worldhealth.net/anti-aging-tips/ (May 1, 2016)

13. Human Physiology/Homeostasis https://en.wikibooks.org/wiki/Human.../ Homeostasis. (May 1, 2016)

14. David H. P. Streeten, "The Autonomic Nervous System" - NDRF. www.ndrf.org/ ans.html. (May 1, 2016)

15. George P Chrousos, "Organization and Integration of the Endocrine System" — NCBI Sleep Med Clin. 2007 June; 2(2): 125—145. www.ncbi.nlm.nih.gov/ (May 1, 2016)

16. "Neuroscience: Science of the Brain. An Introduction for Young Students." British Neuroscience Association European Dana Alliance for the Brain. p. 5 http://www.uni-heidelberg.de/md/izn/teaching/neuroscience/img/neuroscience-of-the-brain-english.pdf. (May 1, 2016)

17. Caroline Leaf, *Who Switched Off My Brain?: Controlling Toxic Thoughts and Emotions.* (Southlake, TX: Improv, Ltd. 2009), p. 52.

18. "Neuroscience: Science of the Brain. An Introduction for Young Students." British Neuroscience Association European Dana Alliance for the Brain p. 35–36.

http://www.uni-heidelberg.de/md/izn/teaching/neuroscience/img/neuroscience-of-the-brain-english.pdf. (May 1, 2016)

19. Brian Luke Seaward, 2006. ☒Health & Fitness. "Managing Stress: Principles and Strategies for Health and Wellbeing." https://books.google.com/books?isbn=0763735329. (May 1, 2016)

20. Don P. Demyers. 2015. "Human Physiology" https://en.wikibooks.org/wiki/Human.../Print_Version. (May 1, 2016)

21. Robert Sapolsky, 1996. "New studies of human brains show stress may shrink neurons" (8/96) news.stanford.edu/pr/96/960814shrnkgbrain.html. (May 1, 2016)

22. Jenkins, F. J., Van Houten, B., Bovbjerg, D. H., "Effects on DNA damage and/or repair processes as biological mechanisms linking psychological stress to cancer risk," Journal of Applied Biobehavioral Research 19 no.1. (2014): 3–23.

23. Debbie I. Craig, 2003. "Brain-Compatible Learning: Principles and Applications in Athletic Training." Journal of Athletic Training. 2003 Oct-Dec; 38(4): 342–349. www.ncbi.nlm.nih.gov/ (May 1, 2016)

24. Wesson, K., "Do We Really Use Only 10% of Our Brain?" Science Master. (2003) http://sciencemaster.com/articles/49-do-we-really-use-only-10-of-our-brain. (March 1, 2015)

25. Susan Perry, 2011. "Neurotransmitters: How Brain Cells Use Chemicals to Communicate." Society for Neuroscience. http://www.brainfacts.org/brain-basics/cell-communication/articles/2011/neurotransmitters-how-brain-cells-use-chemicals-to-communicate/ (May 1, 2016)

26. U.S. Department of Justice Drug Enforcement Administration Demand Reduction Section. "The Dangers and Consequences of Marijuana Abuse." DEA 2014 http://www.dea.gov/docs/dangers-consequences-marijuana-abuse.pdf (May 1, 2016)

27. Neurotransmitters—Anatomy & Physiology. 2013 https://en.wikivet.net/Neurotransmitters_-_Anatomy_%26_Physiology. (May 4, 2016)

28. "Clinical Application: Acetylcholine and Alzheimer's Disease." https://web.williams.edu/imput/synapse/pages/IA5.html. (May 1, 2016)

29. Deane Alban, 2012. "Balance Your Neurotransmitters to Take Control of Your Life" www.bebrainfit.com/balance-neurotransmitters/ (May 1, 2016)

30. "Neuroaddiction—The Chemical Carousel." www.dirkhanson.org/neuroaddiction.html. (May 1, 2016)

31. Gardner, Eliot L., 2013. "Brain reward pathway: Topics by Science.gov." www.science.gov/topicpages/b/brain+reward+pathway.html. (May 1, 2016)

32. Rajita Sinha. "Chronic Stress, Drug Use, and Vulnerability to Addiction." Ann. NY Acad Sci. 2008 Oct; 1141: 105–130.

33. Colette Bouchez. "Serotonin and Depression: 9 Questions and Answers." Web MD 2011. www.webmd.com/depression/features/serotonin. (May 1, 2016)

34. Opioids | Pain Community Centre www.paincommunitycentre.org/article/opioids. (May 1, 2016)

35. David M. Lovinger, PhD. "Communication Networks in the Brain." NIAAA Publications. http://pubs.niaaa.nih.gov/publications/arh313/196-214.htm. (May 1, 2016)

36. Adam Hadhazy, 2010 "Think Twice: How the Gut's 'Second Brain' Influences Mood and Well-Being." Scientific American http://www.scientificamerican.com/article/gut-second-brain/ (May 1, 2016)

Chapter Three

1. Vincent E. Giuliano, "Anti-aging firewalls—the science and technology of longevity." 2014. www.vincegiuliano.name/Antiagingfirewalls.htm. (May 1, 2016)

2. Jeffrey Grant, *Creation: Remarkable Evidence of God's Design.* (Colorado Springs: Waterbrook Press, 2003), 154.

3. Frederic Martini, *The Fundamentals of Anatomy and Physiology* 4th ed. (Prentice Hall, 1998), 68.

4. Jeffrey Grant, *Creation: Remarkable Evidence of God's Design.* (Colorado Springs: Waterbrook Press, 2003), 154.

5. "Cancer Cell Development" — Canadian Cancer Society http://www.cancer.ca/en/cancer-information/cancer-101/what-is-cancer/cancer-cell-development/?region=qc. (May 1, 2016)

6. NIMH "Brain Basics." http://www.nimh.nih.gov/health/educational-resources/brain-basics/brain-basics.shtml. (May 1, 2016)

7. Suvrathan, A., Rao, R. P., Chattarji, S., Tandon, P. N., Tripathi, R. C., Srinivasan, N., "Effects of stress on cognitive versus emotional function, cells, circuits and behavior," Expanding horizons of the mind sciences, 141–157 (2013): 495.

8. Action potential. Wikipedia, The Free Encyclopedia https://en.wikipedia.org/wiki/Actionpotential. (May 20, 2016)

9. Luke Mastin, "Neurons & Synapses" 2010. http://www.human-memory.net/brain_neurons.html. (May 1, 2016)

10. Patrick Toalson, R.Ph., Saeeduddin Ahmed, MD., Thomas Hardy, MD., PhD., and Gary Kabinoff, M.D. "The Metabolic Syndrome in Patients with Severe Mental Illnesses" Journal of Clinical Psychiatry. 2004; 6(4): 152–158. http://www.ncbi.nlm.nih.gov/pmc/articles/PMC514841/. (May 1, 2016)

11. Val Willingham, 2010. "Diabetes or prediabetes predicted for half of Americans by 2020." http://thechart.blogs.cnn.com/2010/11/23/diabetes-or-prediabetes-predicted-for-half-of-americans-by-2020/ (May 1, 2016)

PART II

Chapter Four

1. Cheryl D. Conrad, "Chronic Stress-Induced Hippocampal Vulnerability: The Glucocorticoid Vulnerability Hypothesis" Rev. Neurosci. 2008; 19(6): 395–411 http://www.ncbi.nlm.nih.gov/pmc/articles/PMC2746750/ (May 1, 2016)

2. Holz, N. E., Buchmann, A. F., Boecker, R., Blomeyer, D., Baumeister, S., Wolf, I., Rietschel, M., Witt, S. H., Plichta, M. M., Meyer-Lindenberg, A., Banaschewski, T., Brandeis, D., Laucht, M., "Role of fkbp5 in emotion processing: Results on amygdala activity, connectivity and volume," Brain Structure & Function. (2014).

3. Adriana Feder, Eric J. Nestler, and Dennis S. Charney. "Psychobiology and molecular genetics of resilience" Nature Reviews Neuroscience 2009 Jun; 10(6): 446–457. http://www.ncbi.nlm.nih.gov/pmc/articles/PMC2833107/ (May 2, 2016)

4. Elise Lebeau, PhD., "A Review of the Biological, Psychological and Spiritual Basis of the Empath Experience." https://www.eliselebeau.com/a-review-of-the-biological-psychological-and-spiritual-basis-of-the-empath-experience. (May 2, 2016)

5. Jane Anderson, MD, FCP. "The Teenage Brain: Under Construction." American College of Pediatricians. 2011. http://www.acpeds.org/the-college-speaks/position-statements/parenting-issues/the-teenage-brain-under-construction. (May 2, 2016)

6. Daniel J. Siegel, MD, "An Interpersonal Neurobiology Approach to Psychotherapy: Awareness, Mirror Neurons, and Neural Plasticity in the Development of Well-Being." http://www.ithou.org/node/2730. (May 2, 2016)

7. Liz Szabo, "Number of Americans taking antidepressants doubles." 2009 http://usatoday30.usatoday.com/news/health/2009-08-03-antidepressants_N.htm. (May 2, 2016)

8. Laurence Steinberg. "A Social Neuroscience Perspective on Adolescent Risk-Taking." Dev Rev. 2008 Mar; 28(1): 78–106. http://www.ncbi.nlm.nih.gov/pmc/articles/PMC2396566/. (May 2, 2016)

9. "Human Physiology/The gastrointestinal system." https://en.wikibooks.org/wiki/Human_Physiology/The_gastrointestinal_system. (May 2, 2016)

10. Ray J. Dolan and Peter Dayan. "Goals and Habits in the Brain Neuron." 2013 Oct 16; 80(2): 312–325. http://www.ncbi.nlm.nih.gov/pmc/articles/PMC3807793/ Accessed May 2, 2016

11. George F. Koob and Nora D. Volkow, "Neurocircuitry of Addiction." Neuropsychopharmacology. 2010 Jan; 35(1): 217–238. http://www.ncbi.nlm.nih.gov/pmc/articles/PMC2805560/ (May 2, 2016)

12. Shazia Veqar Siddiqui, Ushri Chatterjee, Devvarta Kumar, Aleem Siddiqui, and Nishant Goyal. "Neuropsychology of prefrontal cortex." Indian Journal of Psychiatry. 2008 Jul-Sep; 50(3): 202–208. http://www.ncbi.nlm.nih.gov/pmc/articles/PMC2738354/ (May 2 , 2016)

13. Heather S. Anderson, MD; Chief Editor: Jasvinder Chawla, MD, MBA. "Mild Cognitive Impairment." 2016 http://emedicine.medscape.com/article/1136393-overview. (May 2, 2016)

14. "Meet brain waves: Alpha, Beta, Theta, Delta and Gamma." https://www.pinterest.com/pin/89368373832147237/ (May 1, 2016)

15. Omar N. Bradley, "US General Omar Nelson Bradley Quotes." http://quotes.lifehack.org/omar-n-bradley/i-learned-that-good-judgment-comes-from/ (May 1, 2016)

16. J. P. Bounhoure, "Takotsubo or Stress Cardiomyopathy" Cardiovasc Psychiatry Neurol. 2012; 2012: 637672. Published online 2012 http://www.ncbi.nlm.nih.gov/pmc/articles/PMC3465868/ (May 2, 2016)

Chapter Five

1. "Total Number of Retail Prescription Drugs Filled at Pharmacies." http://kff.org/other/state-indicator/total-retail-rx-drugs/ (May 3, 2016)

2. Garry Small, "Using Brain Power to Fight Pain", Mind Health Report, March 2014, 6.

3. Peter R. Breggin. "Psychiatric drug-induced Chronic Brain Impairment (CBI): Implications for longterm treatment with psychiatric medication." International Journal of Risk & Safety in Medicine 23 (2011) 193–200. www.breggin.com/index.php?option=com...gid. (May 3, 2016)

4. "Harnessing the human body's natural analgesic for pain relief." http://www. enzolifesciences.com/science-center/technotes/2012/may/harnessing-the-human-bodys-natural-analgesic-for-pain-relief/ (May 11, 2015)

5. "What Are Endorphins?" http://altered-states.net/barry/newsletter260/ (May 11, 2015)

6. Millecamps, M., Centeno, M. V., Berra, H. H., Rudick, C. N., Lavarello, S., Tkatch, T., Apkarian, A. V., "D-cycloserine reduces neuropathic pain behavior through limbic NMDA-mediated circuitry." Pain. 2007;132:108–123. http://www.ncbi.nlm. nih.gov/pmc/articles/PMC3224847/ (May 3, 2016)

7. Beth Moore, *JESUS the One and Only*. (Nashville Tennessee: Boardman & Holman Publishers 2002), 166.

8. Asmir Gračanin, Lauren M. Bylsma, and Ad J. J. M. Vingerhoets. "Is crying a self-soothing behavior?" Front Psychol. 2014; 5: 502 http://www.ncbi.nlm.nih.gov/pmc/articles/PMC4035568/ (May 3, 2016)

9. Billy Graham, *The Journey: How To Live By Faith In An Uncertain World*. (Nashville Tenessee: W Publishing Group, 2006), 35.

10. Larry Huch, *Free at Last: Removing the Past from Your Future* (Pennsylvania: Whitaker House, 2004), 159.

11. Claudio Lavin, Camilo Melis, Ezequiel Mikulan, Carlos Gelormini, David Huepe, and Agustin Ibañez. "The anterior cingulate cortex: an integrative hub for human socially-driven interactions" Front Neurosci. 2013; 7: 64. http://www.ncbi.nlm.nih. gov/pmc/articles/PMC3647221/ (May 3, 2016)

12. Michael J. Owren, PhD *Handbook of emotions – Scholars at Harvard* – Harvard University 2008 The Guilford Press A Division of Guilford Publications, Inc. 72 Spring Street, New York, NY 10012. www.guilford.com http://scholar.harvard.edu/files/schacterlab/files/handbook-of-emotions.pdf?m=1441732584. (May 3, 2016

13. Elena Rascol-Rady, *Flight To Freedom: God's Faithfulness in Communist Romania*. (San Bernandino, CA: Amazon Company, 2015), 5.89.

14. John Hagee, *In Defense of Israel: The Bible Mandate For Supporting the Jewish State*. (Lake Mary, FL: Front Line, 2007), 17.

PART THREE

Chapter Six

1. Randy L. Buckner. "Memory and Executive Function in Aging and AD: Multiple Factors that Cause Decline and Reserve Factors that Compensate." Neuron, Vol. 44, 195–208, September 30, 2004, Cell Press Review. http://www.cogsci.msu.edu/DSS/2004-2005/Buckner/RLB%20neuron2004.pdf. (May 3, 2016)

2. "Epigenetics and Inheritance", http://learn.genetics.utah.edu/content/epigenetics/inheritance/. (May 3, 2016)

3. Edith Heard and Robert A. Martienssen. "Transgenerational Epigenetic Inheritance: myths and mechanisms." Cell. 2014 Mar 27; 157(1): 95–109. http://www.ncbi.nlm.nih.gov/pmc/articles/PMC4020004/ (May 3, 2016)

4. T. D. Jakes, *Reposition Yourself: Living Life Without Limits*. (New York, NY: TRIA BOOK, A Division of Simon & Schuster, Inc. 2007), 102–103.

5. Riya R. Kanherkar, Naina Bhatia-Dey, and Antonei B. Csoka "Epigenetics across the human lifespan" Front Cell Dev Biol. 2014; 2: 49. http://www.ncbi.nlm.nih.gov/pmc/articles/PMC4207041/ (May 3, 2016)

6. "What is Epigenetics? Epigenetics: Fundamentals." www.whatisepigenetics.com/fundamentals/ (June 1, 2015)

7. J. Bartell, MA, Behavior Modification, Self-Improvement. 2012. https://jbartellnews.wordpress.com/tag/behavior-modification/page/2/ (May 3, 2016)

8. Results from the 2013 NSDUH: Summary of National Findings - samhsa http://www.samhsa.gov/data/sites/default/files/NSDUHresultsPDFWHTML2013/Web/NSDUHresults2013.htm. (May 3, 2016)

9. Eric J. Nestler, M.D., Ph.D., "The Neurobiology of Cocaine Addiction." Sci Pract Perspect. 2005 Dec; 3(1): 4–10. http://www.ncbi.nlm.nih.gov/pmc/articles/PMC2851032/ (May 3, 2016)

Chapter Seven

1. Daniel Weiss, 2013 "Youth are exposed to pornography, worldwide Harms of pornography, Making wise choices, Protect your keep, Sex trafficking" http://www.brushfiresfoundation.org/youth-are-exposed-to-pornography-worldwide/ (May 3, 2016)

2. Arun Abey, Andrew Ford, 2009. "How Much is Enough?" Business & Economics. https://books.google.com/books?isbn=1929774834. (May 3, 2016)

3. Larry Huch, *Free at Last: Removing the Past from your Future*. (Pennsylvania: Whitaker House, 2004)

Chapter Eight

1. William B. Strean, PhD, "Laughter Prescription" Canadian Family Physician. 2009 Oct; 55(10): 965–967. http://www.ncbi.nlm.nih.gov/pmc/articles/PMC2762283/ (May 3, 2016)

2. "Neuroplasticity" — Wikipedia, the Free Encyclopedia https://en.wikipedia.org/wiki/Neuroplasticity. (May 4, 2016)

3. "God and the Quantum World" | Set Free Seminars. http://setfreeseminars.com/science/god-and-the-quantum-world/ (May 4, 2016)

4. Chris, H., "Twelve Ways Jesus Changed the World" 2016. http://christnow.com/12-ways-jesus-changed-the-world/ (May 4, 2016)

5. "Gamma-Aminobutyric acid" — Wikipedia, the free encyclopedia. https://en.wikipedia.org/wiki/Gamma-Aminobutyric_acid. (May 4, 2016)

6. *Bible*, The (FAQ's: the Bible) — TheWordOut.Net http://www.thewordout.net/pages/page.asp?page_id=56513. (May 4, 2016)

7. "Respectfully Quoted: A Dictionary of Quotations." 1989. http://www.bartleby.com/73/1211.html. (May 4, 2016)

8. Wendy McDougal, "Macrophages: Definition, Function & Types." http://study.com/academy/lesson/macrophages-definition-function-types.html. (May 6, 2016)

9. "Necrotizing soft tissue infection." https://www.nlm.nih.gov/medlineplus/ency/article/001443.htm. (May 4, 2016)

10. Rakesh K. Pai, MD, George Philippides, MD, "Electrical System of the Heart." http://www.emedicinehealth.com/electrical_system_of_the_heart-health/article_em.htm. (May 4, 2016)

Chapter Nine

1. "The Heart-Brain Connection" https://www.heartmath.org/programs/emwave-self-regulation-technology-theoretical-basis/ (May 4, 2016)

2. Everett L. Worthington, Jr., "The New Science of Forgiveness." 2004 http://greatergood.berkeley.edu/article/item/the_new_science_of_forgiveness. (May 4, 2016)

3. Phil Mason, Quantum Glory: *The Science of Heaven Invading Earth.* (Maricopa: XPpublishing, 2010), 288.

4. Ibid.

5. Ibid.

6. Benny Hinn, *Good Morning Holy Spirit.* (Nashville Tenessee: Tomas Nelson Publisher, 2004), 12.

7. Jim Rose, "Neuroscience and the Mind of Christ: A Reaction to The Huffington Post", 2013. http://www.covenanteyes.com/2013/01/10/neuroscience-and-the-mind-of-christ/ (May 5, 2016)

8. Saul McLeod, "Unconscious Mind" | Simply Psychology. 2009 http://www.simplypsychology.org/unconscious-mind.html. (May 5, 2016)

9. Richard J. Joseph, BS, Miguel Alonso-Alonso, MD, M. Phil, Dale S. Bond, PhD, Alvaro Pascual-Leone, MD, PhD, and George L. Blackburn, MD, PhD, "The Neurocognitive Connection between Physical Activity and Eating Behavior", Obes, Rev. 2011 Oct; 12 (10): 800–812. http://www.ncbi.nlm.nih.gov/pmc/articles/PMC3535467/ (May 5, 2016)

10. Pain management — Wikipedia, the free encyclopedia. https://en.wikipedia.org/wiki/Pain_management. (May 5, 2016)

11. http://www.washingtonpost.com/sf/brand-connect/wp/enterprise/these-researchers-are-looking-for-317-billion-inside-americans-brains/ (May 5, 2016)

12. Joyce Meyer. *Power Thoughts: 12 Strategies to Win The Battle of the Mind.* (New York, NY: Faith Words, Hachtte Book Group, 2010), 116–117.

Chapter Eleven

1. "How many egg cells (ova) are produced in a normal and healthy female?" 2013. http://answers.webmd.com/answers/2018881/how-many-egg-cells-ova-are-produced-in-a-normal-and-healthy-female. (May 5, 2016)

Chapter Twelve

1. Jentezen Franklin, *Right People, Right Place, Right Plan: Discerning the Voice of God.* (New Kensington, PA: Withtaker, 2007), 75.

2. Tiz Huch, *No Limits No Boundaries: Praying Dynamic Change Into Your Life, Family, & Finances.* (New Kensington, Pennsylvania: Whitaker House. 2009), 64.

Chapter Thirteen

1. Michael Mercandetti and Joseph A Molnar, "Wound Healing and Repair", Medscape. http://emedicine.medscape.com/article/1298129-overview (September 1, 2015)

2. Norine Dworkin-McDaniel, "Touching makes you healthier." 2011 http://www.cnn.com/2011/HEALTH/01/05/touching.makes.you.healthier.health/ (May 5, 2016)

3. Pastor Robert Hurst. "Wisdom Calls" 2013. https://hurstrobert.wordpress.com/2013/05/ (May 5, 2016)

4. Abraham Lincoln, "The National Fast"; Proclamation by the President of the United States. The New York Times. Published: April 30, 1863. http://www.nytimes.

com/1863/04/20/news/the-national-fast-proclamation-by-the-president-of-the-united-states.html. (Mar 11, 2015)

Chapter Fifteen

1. Cognitive Impairment: A Call for Action, Now! The number of people living with cognitive impairment in the United States is equal to twice the population of new York City. 2011. http://www.cdc.gov/aging/pdf/cognitive_impairment/cogimp_poilicy_final.pdf. (May 5, 2016)

Chapter Seventeen

1. Margherita Lee, Andreas Reif, Angelika Schmitt, Philip Cowen, Trevor Sharp, Jennifer Lau, "Major depression: A role for hippocampal neurogenesis?" Behavioral neurobiology of depression and its treatment. (2013): 153–179.

2. Dr. Caroline Leaf, Scientific FAQs. General Questions Regarding Science. "God the Creator." http://drleaf.com/about/scientific-faqs/ (May 5, 2016)

3. Jindal, Vishal, Gupta, Sorab, Das, Ritwik, "Molecular mechanisms of meditation," Molecular Neurobiology. Vol. 48 (3), Dec 2013, pp. 808–811.

4. Ibid.

5. Washington Monument. District of Columbia. History and culture. http://www.nps.gov/wamo/learn/historyculture/index.htm (March 16, 2015)

6. Anna, M., The University of Kansas. http://acienciala.faculty.ku.edu/hist557/lect20.htm. (May 6, 2016)

7. Geoffrey M. Cooper, "The Development and Causes of Cancer. The Cell: A Molecular Approach." 2nd edition. 2000. http://www.ncbi.nlm.nih.gov/books/NBK9963/ (May 5, 2016)

Chapter Nineteen

1. T. D. Jakes, *Reposition Yourself: Living Life Without Limits.* (New York, NY: Atria Books, A Division of Simon & Schuster, Inc., 2007), 102–103.

2. Amygdala — Science Daily. Wikipedia, the free encyclopedia https://www.sciencedaily.com/terms/amygdala.htm. (May 6, 2016)

3. "Learn How Neurotransmitters Chemically Generate." The Neuro Link – Neurotransmitters. http://www.iwr.com/becalmd/transmitter.html. (May 6, 2016)

4. "Stress Weakens the Immune System." American Psychological Association, 2006 http://www.apa.org/research/action/immune.aspx. (May 3, 2016)

5. Brunori, Luisa [Ed]; Pines, Malcolm [Ed]. "The other side of the coin: The psychological implications of microcredit," Social brain and social group: How mirroring connects people. (2013): 47–64.

6. Brad Harrub, PhD., "The Human Nervous System: Evidence of Intelligent Design." Apologetics Press. http://www.apologeticspress.org/APContent.aspx?category=249&article=1581. (May 6, 2016)

7. Unconscious cognition. Wikipedia, the free encyclopedia. 2015 https://en.wikipedia.org/wiki/Unconscious_cognition. (May 6, 2016)

Chapter Twenty

1. Judy Squier. *His Majesty in Brokenness: Finding God's Masterpiece in Your Missing Piece.* (Self-Published by Judy Squier, 2010), 104.

Chapter Twenty-Two

1. Matt Cantor, "Around the Globe, More Youths Having Unsafe Sex." http://www.newser.com/story/129532/around-the-globe-more-youths-having-unsafe-sex.html. (September 5, 2014)

2. CDC Grand Rounds: "Chlamydia Prevention: Challenges and Strategies for Reducing Disease Burden and Sequelae," Morbidity and Mortality Weekly Report (MMWR). http://www.cdc.gov/mmwr/preview/mmwrhtml/mm6012a2.htm. (August 15, 2014)

3. Ken Duckworth, MD, "Mental Illness FACTS AND NUMBERS". National Alliance on Mental Illness.2013. http://www2.nami.org/fatsheets/mentalillness_factsheet.pdf

4. Caroline Leaf, *Who Switched Off Your Brain?: Solving The Mistery of He Said/She Said.* (Southlake, TX: Inprov, Ltd., 2011), 141.

5. Marie Ellis, "Oxytocin: the monogamy hormone?" 2013. http://www.medicalnewstoday.com/articles/269365.php. (May 6, 2016)

6. Markus MacGill, "Oxytocin: What is it and what does it do?" 2015 http://www.medicalnewstoday.com/articles/275795.php. (May 6, 2016)

7. Luciana Gravotta, "Be Mine Forever: Oxytocin May Help Build Long-Lasting Love." Scientific American. 2013. http://www.scientificamerican.com/article/be-mine-forever-oxytocin/ (May 6, 2016)

8. Ibid.

9. C. Sue Carter. "Neuroendocrine perspectives on social attachment and love." 1998 The International Society of Psychoneuroendocrinology. Volume 23, Issue 8, Pages 779–818

10. Neurotransmitters—Anatomy & Physiology. 2013. https://en.wilivet.net/Neurotransmitters_-_Anatomy_%26_Physiology. (May 6, 2016)

11. Beni Johnson, *The Happy Intercessor.* (Shippensburg PA: Destiny Image Publishers, Inc., 2009), 131.

Chapter Twenty-Three

1. "10 Insightful Things the Queen Has Said About Her Relationship With God." 2016. http://africanleadership.co.uk/blog/?p=8235. (May 6, 2016)

2. Joel Osteen, "Today's Word with Joel & Victoria," https://us-mg6.mail.yahoo.com/neo/launch?.rand=ftsf2uodsg75o. (November 19, 2015)

3. Bible Hub. 1 King 4:32. http://biblehub.com/1_kings/4-32.htm. (March17, 2015)

Chapter Twenty-Four

1. Joanna Weaver, *Having a Mary Heart in a Martha World: Finding Intimacy with God in the Busyness of Life.* (Colorado Springs: Waterbrook Press, 2000), 197.

2. Joel Osteen, *Your Best Life Now: 7 Steps to Living at Your Full Potential.* (New York, NY: Warner Faith, 2004), 241.

3. "Empathy" — Wikipedia, the free encyclopedia. https://en.wikipedia.org/wiki/Empathy. (May 6, 2016)

4. Lea Winerman, "The mind's mirror. A new type of neuron—called a mirror neuron—could help explain how we learn through mimicry and why we empathize with others." 2005 American Psychological Association, Vol 36, No.9. http://www.apa.org/monitor/oct05/mirror.aspx. (May 6, 2016)

5. Beth Moore, *JESUS the One and Only*. (Nashville Tennessee: Boardman & Holman Publishers 2002), 328.

6. John Bevere, *Honor's Rewards: How to Attract God's Favor and Blessing*. (New York, NY: Faith Words, 2007), 209.

7. "Does Prayer Work?" — Facebook https://www.facebook.com/notes/wardina.../does.../409296912467743. (May 6, 2016)

8. "Spindle neuron" — Wikipedia, the free encyclopedia https://en.wikipedia.org/wiki/Spindle_neuron. (May 6, 2016)

Chapter Twenty-Five

1. Dr. Andrew Newberg, "Strengthen Your Brain Through The Power of Prayer" The Mind Health Report http://fgbt.org/Health-Tips/strengthen-your-brain-through-the-power-of-prayer.html. (May 6, 2016)

2. Dezutter, J., Wachholtz, A., Corveleyn, J., "Prayer and pain: the mediating role of positive re-appraisal," Journal of Behavioral Medicine. 34(6):542–9, 2011 Dec.

3. Tartaro, J., Luecken, L. J., Gunn, H. E.,"Exploring heart and soul: effects of religiosity/spirituality and gender on blood pressure and cortisol stress responses," Journal of Health Psychology. 10(6):753-66, 2005 Nov.

4. Rew, L., Wong, Y. J., Sternglanz, R. W., "The relationship between prayer, health behaviors, and protective resources in school-age children," Issues in Comprehensive Pediatric Nursing 27(4):245–55, 2004 Oct-Dec.

5. Ironson, G., Solomon, G. F., Balbin, E. G., O'Cleirigh, C., George, A., Kumar, M., Larson, D., Woods, T. E. "The Ironson-Woods Spirituality/Religiousness Index is associated with long survival, health behaviors, less distress, and low cortisol in people with HIV/AIDS," Annals of Behavioral Medicine 24(1):34–48, 2002.

6. Ciesla, J. A., Reilly, L. C., Dickson, K. S., Emanuel, A. S., Updegraff, J. A., "Dispositional mindfulness moderates the effects of stress among adolescents: rumination as a mediator," Journal of Clinical Child & Adolescent Psychology. 41(6):760–70, 2012.

7. Xue, S., Tang, Y. Y., Posner, M. I.. "Short-term meditation increases network efficiency of the anterior cingulate cortex," Neuroreport. 2011 Aug 24;22(12):570–574. http://www.ncbi.nlm.nih.gov/pubmed/21691234. (September 1, 2015)

8. Mary Blaszko Helming, "Healing Through Prayer: A Qualitative Study," Holistic Nursing Practice. 25 (1): (2011): 33–44.

9. David Levy, MD, *Gray Matter: A Neurosurgeon Discovers the Power of Prayer . . . One Patient at a Time*. Tyndale House Publisher, Inc. Carol Stream, Illinois. 2011, p. 11.

10. Charles Stanley, *Handle with Prayer: Unwrap the Source of God's Strength for Living* (Colorado Spring CO:SP Publications, INC, 1982), 118.

Chapter Twenty-Six

1. Priscilla Shirer, *The Armor of God*. (Nashville, TN: LifeWay Press, 2015), 192.

2. Gloria Copeland, *Blessed Beyond Measure: Experience the Extraordinary Goodness of God*. (Tulsa Oklahoma: Harrison House, 2004), 185.

Chapter Twenty-Seven

1. Rzheshevsky, A. V., "Fatal 'triad': lipotoxicity, oxidative stress, and phenoptosis," Biochemistry-Russia. 78(9):991–1000, 2013 September.

2. Grundy, S. M., Cleeman, J. I., Daniels, S. R., Donato, K. A., Eckel, R. H., Franklin, B. A., Gordon, D. J., Krauss, R. M., Savage, P. J., Smith, S. C. Jr., Spertus, J.A., Costa, F., American Heart Association, National Heart, Lung, Blood Institute. "Diagnosis and management of the metabolic syndrome: An American Heart Association/ National Heart, Lung, and Blood Institute Scientific Statement," Circulation. 112: (2005), 2735–2752.

3. Grundy, S. M., "A changing paradigm for prevention of cardiovascular disease: emergence of the metabolic syndrome as a multiplex risk factor," European Heart Journal. 10: (2008): B16–B23.

4. Orchard, T. J., Temprosa, M., Goldberg, R., Haffner, S., Ratner, R., Marcovina, S., Fowler, S. "The effect of metformin and intensive lifestyle intervention on the metabolic syndrome: The Diabetes Prevention Program Randomized Trial," Annals of Internal Medicine. 142(8): (2005), 611–9.

5. Fappa, E., Yannakoulia, M., Pitsavos, C., Skoumas, I., Valourdou, S., Stefanadis, C. "Lifestyle intervention in the management of metabolic syndrome: could we improve adherence issues?," Nutrition. 24(3): (2008):286–91.

6. Rodica Malos, "Doctor of Nursing Practice portfolio of Rodica Malos" http:// digitalcommons.ohsu.edu/etd/480/ (February 1, 2014)

7. Unbehaun, Thomas; Jahne, Andreas; Riemann, Dieter, Sucht: Zeitschrift fur Wissenschaft und Praxis. "The relationship between addiction and sleep: Basic information on sleep regulation." Vol.59 (1), Feb. 2013, pp. 17–23.

8. Definition of apoptosis. Dictionary: apoptosis, Merriam-Webster. www.merriam-webster.com/dictionary/apoptosis. Merriam Webster. (March 29, 2015)

9. Elizabeth George, *A Woman After God's Own Heart*. (Eugene, Oregon: Harvest House Publisher, 1997), 182.

10. "Coronary Heart Disease Risk Factors." National Institutes of Health. 2015 https://www.nhlbi.nih.gov/health/health-topics/topics/hd/atrisk. (May 6, 2016)

11. Hans Diehl, Aileen Ludington. "Dynamic Health." Health & Fitness 2003. Page 33. https://books.google.com/books?isbn=1591852315. (May 6, 2016)

12. Preetha Anand, Ajaikumar B. Kunnumakara, Chitra Sundaram, Kuzhuvelil B. Harikumar, Sheeja T. Tharakan, Oiki S. Lai, Bokyung Sung, and Bharat B. Aggarwal, "Cancer is a Preventable Disease that Requires Major Lifestyle Changes." Pharmaceutical Research. 2008 September; 25(9): 2097–2116.

Chapter Twenty-Eight

1. Heidi Baker, *Birthing the Miraculous: The Power of Personal Encounters with God to Change Your Life and the World*. (Lake Mary, FL:Carisma House, 2014), 108.

2. David Stoop, *You Are What you Think*. (Grand Rapids, MI: Revell, 1982), 136.

3. Larry Dossey, *Healing Words: The Power of Prayer and The Practice of Medicine*. (New York, NY Harpers Collins Publishers. 1993), p.70.

4. Lee Strobel, *The Case for Christ: A Journalist's Personal Investigation of the Evidence for Jesus*. (Grand Rapid, MI: Zondervan, 1998), 268.

5. Dr. Don Colbert, *Toxic Relief, Revised and Expanded: Restore Health and Energy Through Fasting and Detoxification*. (Lake Mary, Florida: Siloam Charisma Media/ Charisma House Book Group, 2012), 147.

6. Op. cit., 149.

7. Jentezen Franklin, Fasting: Opening the Door to a Deeper, More Intimate, More Powerful Relationship with God. (Lake Mary Florida: Charisma House a Strang Company, 2008), 135.

8. Jentezen Franklin, *Fasting: Opening the Door to a Deeper, More Intimate, More Powerful Relationship with God*. (Lake Mary Florida:Charisma House a Strang Company, 2008), 136.

9. Benjamin Horne, http://www.eurekalert.org/pub_releases/2011-04/imc-sfr033111.php (April 3, 2011)

10. Newswise. "Fasting." http://www.newswise.com/articles/fasting-reduces-cholesterol-levels-in-prediabetic-people-over-extended-period-of-time-new-research-finds. (June 16, 2014)

11. Barbara A. Ormond, PhD, Brenda C. Spillman, PhD, Timothy A. Waidmann, PhD, Kyle J. Caswell, PhD, and Bogdan Tereshchenko, "Potential National and State Medical Care Savings From Primary Disease Prevention", American Journal of Public Health. 2011 January; 101(1): 157–164. http://www.ncbi.nlm.nih.gov/pmc/articles/PMC3000727/ (September, 2015)

Chapter Thirty

1. Louis Cozolino, "The neuroscience of human relationships: Attachment and the developing social brain (2nd ed.)." (2014), 632.

2. Leif Hetland, *Seeing Through Heaven's Eyes: A Worldview That Will Transform Your Life*. (Shippensburg, PA: Destiy Image Publisher, 2011), 192.

Chapter Thirty-One

1. Randy Alcorn, *Heaven* (Carol Stream, IL: Tyndale House Publishers, Inc., 2004), 457.

2. Paul Manwaring, *What on Earth is Glory?: A Practical Approach to a Glory-filled Life*. (Shippensburg, PA, Destiny Image Publisher, Inc., 2011) 222–223.

Conclusion

1. Jeffrey Barsch, *Praying for the Brain: Rewiring the Brain Through Prayer*. (Ventura, Ca: Beneath His Wings Publishing Company, 2013), 56.

2. Lucinda Bassett, *From Panic to Power: Proven Techniques to Calm Your Anxiety, Conquer Your Fears, and Put You in Control of Your Life*. (New York, NY: Harper Resource, 2001), 246.

3. Brian King, "The Habits of Happy People: A Seminar for Health Professionals," Institute for Brain Potential. (Portland, OR, October 23, 2015).

4. Bill Johnson, *The Power that Changes the World: Creating Eternal Impact in the Here and Now*. (Bloomington, Minnesota: Chosen Book, 2015), 14.